Fumbling Toward Divinity
The Adoption Scriptures

FUMBLING TOWARD DIVINITY
THE ADOPTION SCRIPTURES

To Elijah,
Take care of your blessings
With Love

CRAIG HICKMAN

Craig J Hickman
July 4, 2005

Annabessacook Farm
MAINE
2005

THIS IS AN APPALOOSA BOOK
PUBLISHED BY ANNABESSACOOK FARM

Copyright ©2005 by Craig Hickman

All rights reserved under International and Pan-American Copyright Conventions.
Published in the United States by Annabessacook Farm.

www.hometown.aol.com/abcfarmbooks

ISBN 0-9762462-0-1

This is not fiction. All the characters are real, the events, lived.
Some of the characters names have been changed to protect their privacy.

Much of the history and descriptions of Harvard University buildings contained herein is
summarized from text on the University websites.

The presentation of child's play in the chapter entitled *Church* is a riff on the description of a
similar game in the poem *Beginners* from
Bethlehem in Broad Daylight by Mark Doty (David R. Godine, 1991).

Journey from *Deep Talk* by Thomas Grimes (Parfait de Cocoa Press, 1995).
Reprinted with permission.

*Mothers, The Virtuoso, Lost, Deliverance, Broken Eardrums, Maestro, If You Please,
Shoptalk, Field Trip,* and *Little Black Girls* previously appeared in
Rituals: Poetry & Prose (Parfait de Cocoa Press, 1994).

The Wedding Song is a riff on the description of a similar ritual between Sethe and her
daughters in *Beloved* by Tony Morrison (Alfred A. Knopf, 1987).

Set in Goudy Old Style
Printed and bound by McNaughton & Gunn,
Saline, Michigan
Designed by the author

Manufactured in the United States of America

First Edition
February 2005

For my husband

To my mothers

To my fathers

For my entire family

"With an adoptee, the family tree can be very interesting. The branches can represent the adoptive family's ancestry and the roots can represent the birth family's ancestry."

–Laura Moskowitz

To my foster family, the trunk of my tree, wherever you are, thank you for keeping me safe and sound through the middle passage.

THE NAMES AND ORDER OF THE BOOKS OF THE BOOK

ROOTS

THE REVELATION OF CRAIG 3	BELOVED 61
THE RESURRECTION TABLE 9	COMMENCEMENT 71
THE DEED 19	MARRIAGE 78
THE TREE ACCORDING TO JAMES III 24	THE QUEEN ELIZABETH VERSION . . . 85
VIATICUS 40	VERITAS 89
THEIR EYES WERE WATCHING GOD 53	EVA NAOMI'S ROOM 101
NO SLEEP BLUES 56	SECRETLY, THAT SUMMER 108

BRANCHES

MEET ME IN MILWAUKEE 115	ROOSEVELT 160
PARADISE 122	CHURCH 165
COMMON UNITY .137	A MOTHER'S PRAYER 171
GRACE 139	HAZELLE 176
UP AT THE NET 149	MARY JUANITA .180
SARAH AND JOSEPH 152	

LEAVES

SHADOW 189	WHITE CHRISTMAS 232
LOVE: A LETTER 197	WEEKEND IN MAINE 234
THE FEAST OF FAMILIES 201	PILGRIMAGE 237
ANOTHER COUNTRY 214	MERCURY IN RETROGRADE 248
STOLEN MARBLES 220	GO TELL IT ON THE MOUNTAIN 253
NATALIS 224	THE BENEDICTION 257

LIGHT

YOUR MOTHER 265	THE CHOSEN ONES 299
SORORITAS 269	THICKER THAN BLOOD 308
WHITE LIES 282	SWEET HOME 315
REFLECTIONS 290	THE WEDDING 319

APPENDICES

THE DOCUMENTS OF HIS GENESIS 325	THE BOOK OF SONGS 359
THE LAMENTATIONS OF CRAIG 351	

Book I

ROOTS

A man without knowledge of himself and his heritage is like a tree without roots.

—Dick Gregory

Just as a tree without roots is dead, a people without history or cultural roots also becomes a dead people.

—Malcolm X

THE REVELATION OF CRAIG THE ADOPTED

I revealed myself to those who did
not ask for me;
I was found by those who did not seek
me
To a nation that did not call on my
name,
I said, 'Here am I, here am I.'...

—ISAIAH 65:1

1 The first time he sees her face, the first time he looks into her eyes, the first time he feels her arms around him and his around her, his water will break, and he will wail three decades and three years of tears.
And time will stand still.

2 And it came to pass on the twenty-seventh day of April in the nineteen hundred and sixty-ninth year that Craig Von Hickman went permanently to the home of Hazelle and Mary Juanita Hickman on Thirteenth Street in Milwaukee, Wisconsin. He was sixteen months of age.
He grew up fast. Way too fast according to Mary Juanita.
In elementary and high school, although many suspected it, and Craig did very little to hide it, no one really knew the truth about him, about him and the boys, about him and Juneau Park, about him and his savior Seldon called Roy.
Oh yes, many knew that he was adopted. That was no secret. And yes, anyone could see he was black. That was no secret either. But no one knew that other truth about him, not his girlfriends, not his would-be girlfriends, not his wannabe girlfriends.
Only his dear friend Joseph the Swimmer knew the truth. Or, perhaps, they all knew the truth, but only Joseph accepted it. Whatever the case, Joseph was the only person to whom he actually told the truth. And though Joseph knew the name Mary and Hazelle had given Craig, Joseph called him Craig van den Landenberg, a name with a bit of Dutch in it.

4 / Fumbling Toward Divinity

3 On April 16, 1993, Craig's alter ego and stage persona was born. And he called her April Marie Lynette Jones, but he didn't know why, and she was a hairdresser who worked in J's His and Hers Salon, but he didn't know why, and she appeared wise, and seemed to give great advice, and talked about how everyone else could fix their lives, but she had some deep, mysterious, unspoken pain inside her. And he didn't know what it was all about, and he didn't ask her, and she didn't tell him.

4 On April 16, 1996, he went to see the film SECRETS AND LIES at the Kendall Square Theater in Cambridge, Massachusetts. When he saw how the black woman in the movie sought and found her birth mother, a white woman, he could hardly stay seated. Could hardly contain the rumblings and tremors and trembling within, signifying a great internal quake. He knew his earth was about to open for all those around to see, and for this, he was not ready.

When the film ended, Craig left the theater and went home. There he allowed a bit of earth to break, but not too much, for he was not ready.

For the next two weeks, he would lie on the floor of his apartment, in the fetal position, unable to function—yearning, longing, waiting, hoping for the day when *his* eyes would be opened.

"You will seek me and find me when you seek me with all your heart," God had said, and so he did. His beloved friends and roommates, Darlin the Musician and Gail the Writer, picked him up off the floor and held him.

And so it was that they began walking with him on his journey toward the light.

5 On January 11, 1997, the Documents of His Genesis came from the Children's Services Society of Wisconsin, the agency that handled his adoption. The Documents provided his medical and social history, but any information that would identify or could be used to trace his people was blacked out, stricken from the record with what must have been a thick, black magic marker.

The next day, Craig met again Jacobus called Job on the Internet while he was looking for colleges in Huntsville, Alabama (the striker of record slipped up and left that location uncovered), the place where the Documents said she had attended college.

Eight years had passed since he first met Job and he knew then, as he knew now, that this was the man with whom he would spend the rest of his life.

A photograph, which he had found that very morning, of Seldon called Roy sat atop the computer looking down on him, bearing witness to this Internet reunion.

Seldon called Roy was his savior. A savior rarer than the name Seldon was given but never called. Craig had misplaced the photograph five years prior and had not seen it since. But almost out of nowhere, it appeared. When Craig moved his desk in order to retrieve his favorite pen, which had fallen behind it, Roy's photograph was right there, face up, lodged between the heating pipe cover and the white brick wall.

And so the photograph of his savior also bore witness to him finding Oakwood College on the Internet. Oakwood College. The only religious-affiliated college in Huntsville, Alabama. Affiliated not with the Latter Day Saints, as the Documents of His Genesis erroneously indicated, but with the Seventh Day Adventists, who base their religion on the Three Angels Message from Revelation 14:6-13. Besides, Craig knew no black Mormons, several black Adventists, and the Documents of His Genesis identified his people as Negro.

Oakwood College. This must be where I was conceived, thought Craig. And so, along with Gail the Writer and Darlin the Musician, he poured through the Documents of His Genesis looking for any sign that might tell them who she was and where he could find her.

The social history was typed. Craig realized that they could count how many letters and spaces were behind the black streaks simply by comparing their length to the lines above or below. Sometimes the marks left tiny bits of letters discernable to their six eyes.

When they finally calculated that her first name was eight letters, beginning with the letter *j*, an *i*, or a *t* and ending with an *r*, and that her last name was five letters ending with an *e*, the first thing they thought was Jennifer White. The second thing they thought was Jennifer was right, but White was not. That would have been too easy. Much too easy.

And so they dismissed White as quickly as they thought it up in the beginning and Craig retreated to a place with no light.

6 On February 13, 1997, SECRETS AND LIES was nominated for an Academy Award™ for Best Picture, as were the actresses who played the seeker and the sought in their respective categories. Job asked Craig if they could see the film together, and he replied, "I don't know if I will ever be able to see that movie again." Certainly if I never find her, he completed the thought to himself.

On October 28, 1997, Job took Craig to see Lloyd Sheldon the Revelator at Black Star Enterprises in Harvard Square in Cambridge, Massachusetts. To Lloyd Sheldon, Craig revealed his date of birth. He revealed nothing else.

Among other things, the Revelator, who kept his eyes closed, revealed to Craig, speaking while writing:

> *Your psychic number is 8; your life number is 7. You have lived 100 years in 30!!*
>
> *You are most complex! Very few people understand you.*
>
> *There is distance from your father; your natural father is far away from you. He has strong features and you look just like him.*
>
> *There is some connection to the family in Maryland / Washington D.C. / North Carolina / Virginia / <u>Georgia.</u>*
>
> *You'll go to France, Holland, Belgium?? Germany in nearly 2 weeks, 10 days to 2 weeks. Be sure to take a camera on <u>your</u> trip.*
>
> *You have been searching long and hard for information. This has taken a lot of time. It is very important, tracing family. One ancestor is bi-cultural—*African American and Caribbean.*
>
> *You are not looking in the right places. If you really want to know—look. Your name was different. Birth certificates were changed.*
>
> *There is a Great Book inside of you that you have yet to write. It comes after you find what you are looking for.*
>
> *You have manuscripts that will be considered. If you are wise, you will collapse two into one!*
>
> **You will be reunited with your origins inside of four <u>years</u>. You must do the <u>research!!</u> Yourself. <u>In person.</u>*

Lloyd Sheldon spoke and wrote many other things on the three pieces of wide-ruled paper he folded like a letter and put in a gray number 10 envelope. On the face of it, he wrote the date and handed it to Craig. On their way home, Craig read its contents to Job. He wouldn't read it again until October 25, 2001. While compiling primary material for the big project he was about to undertake, Craig found the envelope stuck like a bookmark in the black journal he thought he'd lost years before.

7 On Craig's thirty-third birthday, December 8, 2000, Job made more than a mess of things.

And so Craig told Job that this would be the very last birthday he would ever allow a mess to be made of, his birthdays being already so empty.

In the first three months of the following year, Craig lost himself in his work; he became short-tempered and ornery; he separated emotionally from

Job. For more than forty nights, he could not sleep.

His boss, Octavio, had a baby boy, his firstborn son, and everyone in his office was able to hold the newborn, except Craig.

And he saw himself in this firstborn, held by the newborn's mother, and his chest was heavy with pain.

And so she appeared in his daydreams, for he could not sleep at night, her face shrouded with hair.

He could not see her face, which was shrouded with hair, and his chest was heavy with pain.

And somewhere in the midst of this, Job took three weeks off from work, completed and defended his dissertation at Brandeis University in Waltham, Massachusetts. Thus, after an eight-year journey to receive his Doctor of Philosophy, he would graduate the Sunday following Mother's Day.

And somewhere in the midst of all of this, the 1967 Yearbook came from Oakwood College Archives.

And the yearbook revealed that he and Darlin and Gail had been right in the beginning: she was, indeed, a White girl. Jennifer White. So he was a White, too. Joseph B. White. And his uncle was a White, III. James E. White III. All J's. His and hers.

And there, near the back of the book, in the college directory, it was—the permanent address where Jennifer lived when he was conceived: 3232 North Sixteenth Street on Milwaukee's north side, just around the corner from the first home he lived as a Hickman on Thirteenth Street.

He used the address listed to search for James White, III on the Internet. It took a month, but all he could find was the telephone number of an England Martanna White, who lived on Ella Lane in Dalton, Georgia, and had been married to a James E. White.

This James E. White, born October 25, 1924, had died August 24, 1998, and had apparently lived within the past ten years at the same address on Sixteenth Street.

Was England of Ella Lane in Dalton, Georgia his grandmother? The woman who had orchestrated, according to the Documents of His Genesis, the entire drama unfolding therein?

The real estate archives in the Milwaukee County's Register of Deeds could tell him.

8 On April 1, 2001, Craig shared the Documents with his beloved friend and next-door neighbor, Joseph the Leo. And Craig said, "I must find her. Will I ever find her? I just have to. I wanna know things that only she can tell me. Do you think she's thought of me all these years?"

And Joseph replied, "You have sisters. And she has told your sisters about you."

"How do you know *that?*"

"Because I just do. You have sisters. You have three sisters and she told them about you. And yes, Joseph, you'll find her."

Craig could hardly contain the earthquake. So he ran home to Job, who he had been separated from emotionally for three months, and he fell on their bed, and more water came.

And Job, saying nothing, held him, and Craig broke wide open and cried a river. When it dried up, Job asked, "What is it that you need from me? What can I do?"

"You need to take another week off from work. We need to go to Milwaukee. And we need to drive."

And so it was that, without hesitation, Jacobus called Job, a man of hesitation, simply replied, "Okay."

They knew the time was near.

THE RESURRECTION TABLE

1 On April 11, 2001, Craig and Job loaded up their black Jeep Grand Cherokee and pulled away from their house on Ridge Street in Roslindale, a hilly neighborhood in the southwestern part of Boston, Massachusetts. They began the thousand-mile journey to Milwaukee in search of the house on Sixteenth Street and where it might lead them. They decided to traverse Pennsylvania on interstate 80, intending to return to Boston through upstate New York a week or so later.

Somewhere in Pennsylvania, Craig looked at his husband and felt a surge inside, a surge he had not felt in a long, long time. Somewhere in Pennsylvania, his love began to breathe again, breathe again, so full was he with the ease of coming back to love again, so satisfied they had finally returned to Paradise. Somewhere in Pennsylvania, fulfillment lulled him into a slumber where all he could dream about was how they had gotten to Paradise in the first place.

When Craig woke up, they were already in Chicago. Craig drove the rest of the journey, while Job took his turn at sleep in the stretched-out-flat passenger seat. They arrived in Milwaukee late Saturday morning and tired as a mule, Craig drove by Sharon Seventh-Day Adventist Church on Teutonia Avenue on Milwaukee's north side. Services had just ended and Craig wondered if any of the people, clad in white and pastel Easter raiment posing in front of the church, were his relatives.

"C'mon, honey. Let's just get to the hotel. I need to stretch all the way out," said Job, awakened by the slow tempo of the car as they passed the church.

"I'm so tired I could fall out, but I wanna drive by the house first. It's only a few blocks from here. After that, I promise, we'll go to the hotel. It's a quick dash downtown on the highway." Craig drove about half a mile up Teutonia Avenue, turned right onto Burleigh Street and left onto Sixteenth. Almost at the end of the block on the right side of the street sat 3232, the house with white siding and green trim.

"It looks like your parents' house, Craig," said Job as they pulled up. Craig stopped in the middle of the street. "It's smaller because it's a single-family, but it's just like your house. Same color and everything. The only thing missing are the pine trees."

"Surreal." Craig looked in the rearview mirror and saw no car coming behind them. "Take a picture."

Job retrieved the Canon from the camera bag, rolled down the window, and snapped two photographs. Craig tried to imagine the family that had lived behind the front door thirty-three years before, but nothing came into view. He sighed and pulled away as Job put the camera back in its case.

Craig drove downtown where they checked into the Hotel Wisconsin, one of the city's oldest. It was the same hotel where Craig once met a man whose number was written neatly on the stall of a bathroom in the Grand Avenue Mall, which stretched for three blocks right across the street.

2 "When was the last time we all had Easter dinner together, Craig?" asked Gina.

Craig searched the annals of his memory while scanning the red walls of the kitchen alcove where his family gathered. "Nineteen eighty-six," he finally said. "My last year of high school.

"Has it been that long?" asked Mary.

"At least that long. I never came home for Easter during college and I haven't been home for Easter since. When did you paint these walls red?"

"Last year around this time." Gina eyed the macaroni and cheese. "I hired this guy, a friend of Bernadine's, to do it. You like it?"

"I love red walls. Somehow, I didn't think Mama would go for it though."

"Oh, so you don't think your mother has any taste?"

"Why even go there?"

"Here's to an Easter reunion." Job interrupted the inevitable mother-son banter, raising his wine glass for a toast.

"Gina, get me some water, please. I forgot my glass up front." Gina went to the living room to get Mary's glass and freshened it with tap water before sitting back down. They all raised their drinks.

"Here ye, here ye," announced Hazelle, Pabst Blue Ribbon in hand, "I'd like to thank The Almighty for bringing my sons—both of my sons—safely to the table and making this an extra special Easter. I couldn't have asked for anything better."

They toasted and drank from their cups.

"Craig, bless the food." Mary reached for Craig.

They all held hands and bowed their heads.

"Dear Lord, we thank you for this food we're about to receive. Continue to bless the hands that prepared the meal and nourish us with love. We also want to thank you for this coming together of family on the occasion of your resurrection. May we all experience our own rebirths in the here and now. Amen."

"Wait a minute," blurted Hazelle before they raised their heads and let go their hands. "Lord, we also want you to guide our son on his search for his birth mother. Help him find the answers to all of his questions. Now, let's eat."

"Amen," rang the chorus of their voices.

"Job, why don't you carve the ham." Mary opened a moist towelette and wiped her hands.

While Job carved the brown-sugar-and-maple-glazed ham, Gina heaped the macaroni and cheese Craig had baked onto her plate and passed it around the table. "Save some macaroni for the rest of us Gina, you old greedy thing, you."

Hazelle laughed. "You know she can't get enough of her brother's cooking, Mary."

"It might be another fifteen years till I have some more of it," said Gina, digging her fork deep in the pile, "so I'm taking my fill now. Yall don't have enough, too bad. Every tub stands on its own bottom."

Mary's turnip greens, Hazelle's hot-water cornbread, and Gina's creamed pearl onions made it round the table.

After Job carved the ham and served a few slices to each of them, he sat down, pulled his chair up to the table, and said, "*Eet smakelijk.*"

"Ate who?" said Hazelle. Gina cackled.

"*Eet smakelijk.* Say it, Daddy," encouraged Job.

"Uh uh. I can't say that."

"Yes you can. Craig, what's it sound like in English?"

"Daddy, think of a smock and licking your lips." Craig spoke deliberately. "Smock-a-lick."

"Ate smock-a-lick," repeated Hazelle.

"That's it." Job laughed and led Craig and Gina in applause.

"Well, I say," was all Mary could say.

"What's it mean, son?"

"It means eat with taste, Daddy. In Holland, we say it before every meal. The French say, '*Bon appetite,*' and we say, '*Eet smakelijk.*' Americans don't say anything."

"I don't know about Americans, but we pray before we eat, honey," said Mary. "We pray."

There was a stretch of silence—not silence, really, but the peace-filled quiet of people eating good, good food.

"Mama, how was church this morning?"

"It was beautiful. Just beautiful. We didn't go to sunrise service like we usually do, but I helped the ladies out first thing this morning serving Easter breakfast. Your father had to sing at the eight-o'clock and ten-thirty services. I went to the eight-o'clock service and came on home and took me a nap. Jeffrey Watkins' kids are getting so big. I told him you were home. He hopes to see you before you go back. How long you gonna be here, anyway?"

"Not sure."

"Are you gonna go and see Roosevelt's grave while you're here?"

"I don't know."

"You remember Mister Washington, don't you, Craig? He used to sit in front of us every Sunday. Well, he passed, God bless his soul. Had cancer. Zachary's mother asked about you too. Zachary got married overseas; he's in the military now. And Dante"—Craig sat up straight; Mary continued—"I haven't seen him in a long time. I see his brothers Marcellus and Tyreese every now and then, but since they go to Zebaoth, they don't come to Siloah too much. But Dante came today. He looked real good too. Much better than the last time I saw him."

Even after twenty-five years, the simple mention of Dante's name forced blood between Craig's legs. "Did he ask about me?"

"No, son, but I told him you were here. Oh, and Millicent, Millicent Avery from your class, son, remember when you had a crush on her? Well, Millicent had a heart attack, yes she did. She's got two kids, one eleven and one eight, and according to Missus Avery, it was the oldest one who called the ambulance to go to his house when she didn't pick him up from school. Can you believe that? He must've had a feeling. Or maybe Millicent seemed sick before he went to school. Isn't it just beautiful that a young boy would be levelheaded enough to call the ambulance in that situation? The Lord works in mysterious ways, I say to you, yes He does. We had a prayer for her today at church. Her mother said she needs to lose a lotta weight. And we had prayer for Jerry Baker too. Wasn't he also in your class, son?"

"He was a grade ahead of me, Mama."

"Well, he has diabetes *and* HIV. I don't know if he's married or what. He's been on dialysis over at St. Joseph's Hospital, so we said a prayer for him too. But church was beautiful, son, it sure was. Pastor Westendorf gave one of his better sermons and the regular choir sounded good. Even the gospel choir had it together this morning, and I'm telling you, when they first started a couple years back I wished they'd never got up there and sang. They sounded like dying birds, I'm telling *you*." Mary threw back her head and mimicked the sound of dying birds. She cracked herself up. "You know I can't carry a tune and I sounded better than they did." They all laughed. "But they're much better now, son, you oughtta hear'm sometime."

"Craig, guess who was in town a few weeks ago?" Gina overlapped Mary's last out-loud thought.

"I haven't the slightest."

"Halle Berry."

"Yeah, that Eric brings her around to see his mother sometimes," said Mary. "She looks just like Gina."

"Eric Benét?" asked Job, his tone hued with disbelief.

"Eric Jordan." Mary punched the word *Jordan*.

"Yes, honey," Craig replied while Mary went on:

"I know him as Eric Jordan. I don't know where he got that highfalutin-tootin Benét from. His mother lives right over here not too far from Rufus King where his cousins, Eurieal and Persephone, went to high school with Craig."

"You don't remember," Craig continued, looking at Job, "when I told you that Gina went out with him on and off for several years before he got his big break?"

"Now I do. I did like his first album, though." Job spooned glaze over his ham.

"Me too. That is, until I read the liner notes and saw that he didn't thank Gina for one single thing." Craig looked at his sister. "Nearly every song on that album was about you, girl. And not only that, you practically funded his life here in Milwaukee while he was a struggling to get noticed. I remember when you played his demo tape for me. I know you helped pay for that—I wouldn't be surprised if you bankrolled the whole thing—even though you never said so. You totally believed in him, said you knew he would make it. And he did. And what thanks do you get for supporting him? Nada. He better hope and pray I don't run into him anytime soon."

"That's how your sister's always been." Mary was exasperated. "Generous to a fault. Puts herself on the line, does so much for so many of these Negroes and when all is said and done, she doesn't have anything to show for it. Now she's wasting her time on that Maurice from the Seventy-Sixers basketball team. I don't know *what* I'm gonna do with my daughter. I do miss Eric's little girl, though, that precious Asia. Reminds me of Gina when she was little. Asia's like a granddaughter to me. I sure wish I could see her again."

"Anyway." Gina rolled her eyes repeatedly during Mary's speech. "Eric wanted me to meet Halle Berry again. I think it was their first time back here since they got married. Eric first wanted me to meet her when I was modeling for Wilhelmina in New York, talking some nonsense about wanting my approval before they got married. Ha."

"Well, did you meet her?" asked Craig.

"No, honey. Uh uh. I first turned him down in New York when I told him I couldn't care less who he married, and I turned him down again. I told him he didn't really want me to meet her anyhow. If I did, I'd tell her what she could expect from him. But she'll find out soon enough. That's probably why she married him in secret. That was the only way she could do it. She must not've wanted anybody discouraging her, telling her what a player he was. She had to sense it, somehow, in some way."

"Umph, umph, umph. Well, I say," was all Mary could say.

"That's an understatement. Seem to me like he's trying to prove something to himself running around screwing every woman who'll have him."

"Craig, what are you trying to say?"

"I'm not trying to say anything, girl. I told you before what I thought about him. If there's *any* truth to what I sensed about him the first time I met him standing in this very kitchen, let's just say Eric wouldn't be the first man, or the last, who tried to overcompensate with women for—"

"Now looky here," Hazelle chimed in, his words splashes of cold water on their faces, "yall gone sit round the dinner table on this beautiful day gossipin bout people who ain't even worth the breath you wastin on'm?"

"Quiet, Hazelle. Hush your mouth. Ain't nobody talking to you. You make me wanna put down my religion."

"Long as you pick it back up. And I don't have to hush my mouth. I'm sitting in *my* kitchen at *my* table with *my* family, and I'll say what I want."

"Job, don't you pay your father-in-law, don't you pay Hazelle no mind. He's only showing out because you're here. *Humph*. Who does he think I am, sitting over here with wide eyes and more desire? Guess he thinks I'm chopped liver. *Humph*. *His* kitchen, *his* table, *his* family."

"Ma, I learned my lesson when I came to his defense the last time I was here." Job laughed. "I'm keeping my mouth shut."

"Good idea, son. Good idea. That's why I always call you the peacemaker. Be married long as we have, you make it that far, you see what I'm talkin about. Old silly thing. Always gotta open his mouth when nobody's talking to him. It'll be fifty-five years this June twenty-third. I was ninety-eight pounds soaking wet when I married that man all those years ago. You make it this far, you hear me, Job? Then you come and tell me I don't know what I'm talkin about." She caught her breath and took a drink of water.

"How's your mother doing?"

"She's been doing much better since after she broke her hip last year. She still complains a lot, but she's getting around much better. She's planning to come to my graduation next month."

"That's beautiful, son, just beautiful. I send her a card now and then. I sure hope she gets'm. I don't know if I put enough postage on'm or not."

"I'm sure she gets'm. She probably forgets to tell me when we talk." Job paused for a moment and then looked across the table. "Gina, do you have any commercials coming out or are we gonna see you in any more music videos soon?"

"Not anytime soon. Lemme be positive, Job: not *yet*. I'm heading down to Chicago later this week to audition for a Tampax commercial. My agency also got me an audition for an Ice Cube video. We'll see what happens."

"Why did you come back here from New York? Does Wilhelmina still represent you?"

"Technically, they do, but they also know I'm not there right now, so they're not actively looking for work for me." Gina swallowed whatever she was chewing and wiped her mouth. "You know, Job, New York is no joke. I probably had one really good year there, you know what I mean, when I had the gigs to bring in enough cash flow to make it worth my while. Let's face it, at five foot nine, I'm not tall enough to do runway, and as big as Wilhelmina is, they just couldn't get me enough print work on a consistent basis to justify my staying there. Besides, the industry is starting to get to me. I came home to take a break, reflect on my life, and reassess my options. I think I might wanna get into styling, which would allow me to be creative. I might even start designing jewelry."

"What is styling?"

"If you open up a LAND'S END catalog, for instance, you might see the models posing in a log cabin setting. The stylist creates that habitat for the photographer to work with."

"Kind of like a movie set designer," said Craig, "but for print advertising photo shoots."

"Exactly. Stylists can also put together a model's entire look, right down to the most minute accessory, for a photo shoot. Craig keeps telling me I need to do something creative, and I'm beginning to think he's right."

"Gina can draw. She used to draw the most amazing portraits and illustrations just sitting up at the kitchen table doodling on a piece of paper. Her work was easily as good as anything I've ever seen on the cover of the NEW YORKER."

"Your father can draw a pretty good picture, too," said Mary.

"Craig wasn't bad either," said Gina. "He used to paint beautiful watercolors."

"I know," said Job, "we have a couple of the ones he painted way back in the seventh-grade hanging in our living room."

Craig swallowed his last bite of macaroni and cheese and looked at his father. "So, Daddy, have you planted your garden yet?"

"Not yet, son. It's been colder this spring than it usually is, so I haven't gotten everything I want in the ground yet. I planted some collards and some peas, but that's about the size of it. I don't wanna rush it. Frost'll fall and ruin the seedlings. Then I'll have to start all over. The soil is ready to go, though. Gervis came over with his Rototiller a few weeks ago. In due time, I'll plant me some cucumbers, mustards, turnips, corn, radishes, some green onions, tomatoes, string beans, and watermelon. This year, I'm gonna try potatoes. Mister Fate said to just plant them whole, about a foot into the ground. He had a good little crop right across the street last fall."

"So, Job, tell me, how was the drive?"

"Long. Your brother slept most of the way. We decided to stay at the Hotel Wisconsin downtown because we didn't wanna be so far away at the hotel you found for us."

"I didn't know exactly what you guys wanted. Brookfield is a hike, but it was the best rate I could find on such short notice. I never even thought about the Hotel Wisconsin. I thought it was kind of seedy myself."

"I'll say. Kind of creepy, too. The room numbers don't seem to go in any order so you get lost trying to find your room when you get of the elevator. And speaking of the elevator. That thing must be a-hundred-years-old. It has one of those grated gates that slide like a flat accordion behind the door. And it creaks and shakes as it moves so slowly, you don't think you're ever gonna get to your floor. I swear it's a death trap. Even though we're staying on the seventh floor, we take the stairs. The décor is Depression era, and the place is surely depressed. The mirrors hang crooked on the walls, and some of the room numbers dangle from the doors or have simply fallen off. It's like a hotel in a horror movie. But it's cheap and the sheets are clean, so, there you have it."

"The Hotel Wisconsin. Isn't that where Teddy Roosevelt was shot?" asked Mary.

"I think it was." Hazelle pushed his plate away and went to the refrigerator to get another beer.

"Actually, he was shot by an anarchist at point-blank range in front of the Hotel Gilpatrick, which is now the Hyatt, right across the street," said Craig. "The Hotel Wisconsin can claim that it happened in front of it, and I guess, technically, it did, since it happened across the street."

"Roosevelt was holding a copy of a really thick speech he was about to give and that stopped the bullet from killing him," said Mary.

"I didn't know that. That must've been one mighty long speech. I'll have to re-read the article about Roosevelt when we go back tonight and see if that's in there. There's a lot of great history about Milwaukee hanging on the walls of the lobby in framed newspaper clippings and old original photographs. Mama—Daddy, you too, I'm sure—would love some of the stuff they have. We've already spent a good amount of time reading it all. Seems like we spent most of last night down there. It's all really interesting. Gina, can you pass me the mac and cheese?"

"Please." Mary frowned.

"*Please.*" Craig laughed. "You didn't give me a chance, Mama." Gina handed the Pyrex to Mary who handed it to Craig. He scooped a small portion onto his plate.

"You had a chance. Lord have mercy, you act like you ain't been raised right." Mary finished her last bite and pushed her plate away from her. "Now, tell me, son, what are you gonna do while you're here? How exactly are you gonna go about finding your birth mother?"

"Did you drive by the house yet?" asked Gina. "Soon as you called me and gave me the address, Bern and I drove right over there."

"Looks a lot like this house," said Job.

"Sure does and I almost went and knocked on the front door." Gina couldn't contain her excitement. "I don't know what I would've said if somebody answered. Bern had to talk some sense into me, keep me in the car."

"We're gonna try and locate as much information as we can, Mama. Tomorrow we'll go to the public library to look up newspaper archives for obituaries and wedding announcements, try to find out what Jennifer's last name might be, since it's probably not White anymore. We might go to vital records to see if we can get any information there but we'll definitely go to the courthouse to the Register of Deeds to find out exactly who owned the house on Sixteenth Street in the late sixties. John, that guy, if you remember, who was renting a room from us and who moved to California the day before we left, suggested that we buy a video camera to bring with us on this trip. We've always wanted a video camera anyway so we took his advice. We're gonna document whatever we can of the search while we're here and see what happens. I have a really good feeling about it, though. A *really* good feeling. Best one I've had in the five years that I've been searching."

The family was quiet for the rest of the meal. Everyone was too full for even the tiniest piece of Hazelle's blackberry cobbler. Mary wasn't supposed to eat any anyhow.

Mary retired to the couch up front and watched television. Gina read in her room and talked to her friend, Persephone, on the phone. Job and Craig cleaned up the kitchen and joined Hazelle in his basement barroom for a drink and some B.B. King before taking a plate of cobbler and returning to the hotel.

Morning couldn't come soon enough. Craig knew he wasn't going to sleep. But at least he could "rest his eyes," as Mary was wont to say when caught napping on the couch in front of whatever religious program she was trying to watch. In a tornado of thoughts, Craig rested his eyes with Job spooned at his back, snoring in his ear.

At least one of them could sleep.

THE DEED

1 The Milwaukee Public Library, with its ornate columns, stands majestically on Wisconsin Avenue in downtown Milwaukee. Listed on the National Register of Historic Places, it recalls the greatest libraries of the world. Built in 1898 for all of seven hundred and eighty thousand dollars, the one-block-long limestone monument mixes French and Italian renaissance styles commonly known as Neo-renaissance.

Inside, Job and Craig navigate its wide, sky-lit hallways and expansive rooms until they locate the rows and rows of flat drawers full of boxes and boxes of the nation's archived newspapers. Craig searches through volumes of the Milwaukee Journal and the Milwaukee Sentinel, looking for the obituary of James E. White where he hopes the full names of his children will be listed. Job searches through editions from 1970 to 1985 hoping to find a Jennifer White in the marriage announcements. After two hours of loading up, scrolling through, and unloading countless cartridges of film, they find nothing, pack their notes, and move on to the courthouse.

The Milwaukee County Courthouse stands just behind the Milwaukee Public Library on Ninth Street. Its architecture nearly eclipses the restrained beauty of the library in grandiosity and scale. Like the library, the courthouse's architectural design resulted from a nationwide competition. Faced with Bedford limestone, the courthouse features columns on all sides, stone owls, lioness' heads, and inscriptions, all of which reminded Craig of the renditions of the pre-ruin Parthenon he'd seen in books from his high-school Latin class. The courthouse was completed in 1932 for eight-and-a-half-million dollars and in 1976, it was designated a National Landmark.

Craig and Job walk through the dark bronze anodized revolving door and follow the signs for the Register of Deeds, located on the lower level.

"I would like to know where I can find historical property records for this address," Craig says to the woman with the dark-brown bob behind the help desk.

"Is the property in Milwaukee County?"

"Yes."

"Then the first thing you're gonna need to do is go back upstairs to the treasurer's office and get the legal description of the property. Once you have that, come back to me and I will show you where you can find what you're looking for."

"Thank you," says Craig, turning away. He turns back to the woman. "By the way, what is your name?"

"Ann. I'm the only one here today."

Job walks around through the stacks of casebound books while Craig goes to the county treasurer's office to get the legal description. When he returns, Craig rings the help-desk bell. Ann comes over and tells him how to proceed. "How far back are you looking?"

"I need to get information from the sixties, maybe the fifties."

"All records before ninety-six are on microfiche. Follow me." She leads Craig over to a row of computers. "Here you'll follow the instructions on the screen. Type in the legal property description. You will get a number. That number includes the book number and page number of the documents you want." She leads Craig into the stacks where Job still looks around. "Over here, find the number of the book. Go to the page with your property description. You'll see a column with volume numbers and a column with film numbers. Each time the property changed hands, or there was some event at the property, a foreclosure perhaps, there's an entry in the register. Select the ones you want and then come over here," she leads Craig back to the help desk, "fill out these cards and give them to me. I'll bring you the microfiche, which you take over to the viewers just opposite the computers. Do you know how to use the viewers?"

"I'm sure I can figure it out."

"Well, let me know if I can be of any help. Good luck."

Job has come out of the stacks. "Did you hear any of that, honey?"

"Some of it. What do you need me to do?"

"Nothing, I don't think. I guess I'll just go ahead and get started."

Within half an hour, Craig is sorting through microfiche on one of the viewers. Ann has given him the deeds from 1950 to 1992. During that time the property changed hands only three times.

The third time was the charm.

For there, on the third transaction, are the instructions, the text a constellation set against the midnight-blue sky of film, able to be seen as the light filters into its spaces from the bulb behind the screen. The stars say that after the sale of the house in 1992, Iretha Starr-Johnson, the new owner, whose tiny signature is almost indiscernible, was to send all loan payments to the address at Ella Lane in Dalton, Georgia. James E. White, Jr. and England White, the sellers, also signed the deed.

"Job, come here." Job rushes right over when he sees Craig's face, transfixed by the heavens. "Look."

"Wow. There they are."

There they are, or what Craig can see of them, smell of them, feel of them through their signatures. James' signature is entirely legible, executed with perfect penmanship, the neatest signature of any man, except perhaps his own father's, that Craig has ever seen. It is the signature of an artist. England's signature, also entirely legible, nonetheless, seems marred by restraint, as though her hand could not flow freely through the strokes as it created them. It is the signature of a person under perpetual duress. For what seems to Craig like hours, he stares at these signatures—dissecting, rearranging, tracing them—as though they are the DNA on which his genetic code is signed.

"I'm gonna take a picture." And so Job does.

Now they know it without any doubt. Craig rifles through his briefcase, finds the Internet printout for the deceased James E. White and studies it; the woman in Dalton Georgia is, indeed, his grandmother. He holds her telephone number in his hands.

Sitting in the bowels of a building that will, without a doubt, someday be considered a classic, Craig holds another whole world in his hands.

2 Craig wrestled with his angels. He knew there were other ways to locate Jennifer, avenues that didn't require him talking to the woman in Dalton, Georgia. But those paths were more complicated, more time-consuming, more frustrating.

Later that evening, alone in the kitchen, Craig pondered these things. Hazelle had just closed the swing door between the kitchen and the living room. Hazelle knew that his son needed a brief and quiet separation from the family sitting on the other side.

Alone in the kitchen, Craig told himself to keep it simple. You can do this. Relax. Take a deep breath. If she won't give you the information you need, you will be in the exact same place you are now and you can try another route.

And so it was that on Monday, April 16, 2001, at 5:25 p.m., Central Daylight Time, alone in the kitchen, he called the woman in Dalton, Georgia.

His heart begins to palpitate. She answers the phone on the second ring.

"Hello, ma'am. My name is Melvin Dixon, a friend of James from Oakwood College. I promised to keep in touch with him after I left Oakwood, but I'm afraid I haven't done so. It's been twenty years since we last spoke, and I've no idea where he is. I hope you can help."

"When were you at Oakwood College?"

While talking, Craig tries to visualize the woman who possesses the smoky voice he hears on the other end of the phone. How weary she sounds. He already knows that England is virtually the same age as Mary, but England sounds twenty years older than his mother.

It is hard to visualize this woman with that voice. This woman who has put darkness in places where there ought to be light.

Craig thinks about the Documents of His Genesis and his heart palpitates faster. He thinks about the Documents of His Genesis and he remembers how he and his friends Gail the Writer and Darlin the Musician tried to visualize this woman in the living room of their apartment back in 1997. How Darlin sat down and played gospel riffs on the piano. How Gail mimed donning a big hat and sat down on the couch, testifying from the congregation. How Craig aged his face and his voice, preaching the wages of sin is death to the falling-out-in-the-aisle, caught-up-in-the-Holy-Spirit woman in the congregation. He thinks about the Documents of His Genesis and he remembers that, within five minutes of reading them, he came to hate this woman.

And now, four years later, over the phone, he is listening to a hated woman whose voice sounds so weary, so full of woe, it nearly breaks his heart to hear it. He wants to tell her who he really is, how he really feels about her, but he suspects his search will end right here, right now, if he reveals himself, even devoid his hate, to her. With another lie, he answers her question instead.

"Um, I was at Oakwood for just two years, sixty-seven and sixty-eight."

"Then you must know my daughter Jennifer?"

And his chest is heavy with pain.

He takes a moment before he can continue. Job peeks through the swing door, sees the telephone at Craig's ear, and quickly disappears back to the other side.

A single moment contains the then, the now, and the hereafter. As though a bottle shatters and time begins to spill everywhere at once. As you sense time spreading uncontrollably around you, you exist with an awareness unmatched by anything you've ever known. You might want to run around, frantically, gathering it up, pouring it back, sealing it away. But it's too late. Or too early. Time will do what time has done when time does it. If you are wise, you allow it.

"I knew James had a younger sister," he answered at last, "and I'm sure I must have met her once or twice, but, no, I didn't really know her."

"Where are you calling from?"

"Boston."

"And how did you get my number?"

"From the Internet."

"The Internet? I don't think so. This number wouldn't be listed on the Internet. Not this number."

"Well, it was."

"And where are you calling from again?"

"Boston." He hears the sound of pages rustling in the background. "I have twelve numbers for a James White and this one is the eighth on the list."

"This was the eighth number you called?"

"Yes, the eighth number."

"The eighth number on your list?"

"Yes. The eighth."

"And how many numbers are on your list?"

"Eleven."

"I see. The James White that lived here was my husband, who is now deceased."

"I know. I'm sorry for your loss, ma'am."

"How would you know about my husband?"

"From the Internet. Same place I got your number."

"I see. What did you say your name was again, young man?"

"Essex Hemphill."

For another spilling moment, England says nothing. Craig still hears the rustling. "Here it is. Here is James' telephone number." He writes it down as she reads it. "You can call him directly. He's out in California. I hope everything is okay."

"It will be. Thank you for your help, ma'am. And God bless you."

"God bless you, too."

THE TREE ACCORDING TO JAMES III

1 Armed with the ten digits that possessed the potential to bring in all sorts of light, Craig thought his heart would jump right out of its container. With the two-hour time difference between Milwaukee and California, he decided to wait a few hours before making the call.

Meantime, Mary mother of Craig came to him while he sat rocking in the chair that once belonged to his never-met grandfather, the rocking chair his Granny Alma had given them, the chair that had become his father's favorite place to rest while awake. Mary stood in front of the television, blocking whatever insignificance flashed on the screen. She turned to her son, looked him in the eyes, cocked her head subtly to the right, but not so subtly that he didn't notice. "Are you *sure* you're ready for this?"

"The only thing I'm sure of is that I'm gonna call that number. There's no turning back now, Mama. What's the worse that could happen? That I'll find her and she'll slam the door shut in my face? At least I will have seen her face, Mama. If nothing else, I will have seen it. I wanna see it, Mama. I wanna look her in the eye." He paused, found his mother's eyes. "I'm as ready as I'm ever gonna be."

She focused her eyes intently on his. Satisfied that what she saw there was real. "Then when are you gonna call Uncle James?"

For the next few hours, every five minutes it seemed, one of them—his mother, his father, his husband—asked if he'd called the man in California yet.

Three times he tried; three times the voicemail greeting greeted him. He left no messages.

"I will try again when we get back to the hotel."

✍

At 8:50 p.m., Craig phones James while Job goes to the hotel concession area to get ice. This time, a man answers.

"Is this James White?"

"Yes."

"Let me jump to the point. My name is Craig Hickman, but I was born Joseph Bernard White."

"Joseph White?"

"Yes."

"And could you say that middle name again?"

"Bernard."

"Hold on one second."

Job returns with a bucket of ice, pours himself a drink, and turns on the video camera.

"Joseph White. Madison, Wisconsin?"

Craig hears a rattling sound in the background. "Yes."

"December nineteen sixty-nine?"

"Nineteen sixty-seven."

There is a pause.

"Boy, have I been wanting to talk to you. Man, do I have a lot to say to you. There's so much that I wanna tell you."

"There's so much I wanna know."

"My whole life has been all about you, man. Just today, I finally finished a book and took a video I watched last week back to the video store. You know what they were called? The book was called THE BOURNE IDENTITY and the movie, A STRANGER AMONG US." James laughs and continues:

"You are African, Jewish, Irish, German, Cherokee, African, and Geechie. You are a direct descendant of William Penn. Now your great grandmother, Madree Penn, was one of the founders of the Delta Sigma Theta Sorority, a nationally known black sorority. You've heard of them, I'm sure. I have to find her obituary and read it to you. She was quite a woman. Somewhere in here, I have my father's and grandfather's, too."

While James looks for obituaries, Craig grabs his briefcase-cum-shoulder bag and retrieves a pen and the journal where he keeps most of his research notes.

"Now your great grandfather, Madree's husband, although they got divorced—actually, she divorced him, which hardly any women did at that time—your great grandfather was one of the first black physicians in the United States. He lived in St. Louis with Madree before their divorce when she then moved to Cleveland. He lived in Mt. Vernon, New York, where he took up with a young mistress before he returned to St. Louis, which is where he died. Now Madree, which means mother in Spanish, went to Howard University in Washington, D.C. I wish I could remember where my grandparents met, but I can't. Now my father, your grandfather, worked in his mother's print shop in St. Louis when he was young. Now your Aunt Grace, his sister—matter of fact, I just talked to her today, she just had eye surgery—lives in Cleveland and her son James Otis Ware, who changed his name to Oloye, is like you. You would wanna meet him. I hope you get a chance to meet him. Aunt Grace is gonna die when I tell her about you. Her son Oloye is a genealogist and has done a lot of research on both sides of his family, but mainly his father's father's side and his mother's mother's side, that's how we know Madree is descended from the William Penn who founded Pennsylvania. He lives in Cleveland, too. He traced his father's side of the family all the way back some thirteen hundred years to Nigeria and the Yoruba people.

"Now the Geechie in you, that comes from my grandfather's side of the family. He was from Edenton, North Carolina, near an island off the coast where the Geechie still live and speak their own language. Gullah, I think it's called. They are direct descendants of African tribes from Sierra Leone. Now they were brought over to work the rice plantations along the coast of the Carolinas down through to northern Georgia. Now one of your great great, or is it great great great, I'm not sure—actually, it's not great at all, but maybe your third or fourth or fifth—but you have a cousin named George Henry White who was a North Carolina U.S. Congressman during Reconstruction, the first black in the House of Representatives in the nation. Supposedly we still have a relative in that area, just outside of Edenton. Her name is Mignon Jenkins. Mignon Jenkins, I'm pretty sure that's it. Yes. Mignon Jenkins. My travels haven't taken me there yet, but I hope to visit her someday to see where we all came from.

"Now the Cherokee—I consider the Cherokee Nation the Jews of the Indians—the Cherokee also comes from my father's side. Your great grandfather's mother was half Cherokee from Tennessee.

"Now the Jewish comes from my mother's side of the family. Now my mother, your grandmother, was from the other side of the tracks and, in fact, my father's parents thought he married beneath him. Her people are from Mississippi. Her grandmother Mary was married to a man of African descent, however, she was pregnant before she got married by a Jewish man who was passing through. His name was Howard Rosenberg. My mother doesn't know for sure, but she thinks he was from Russia. The Irish and German also come from her side. Her mother Rosie, who was the daughter of Mary and Howard, was married to Herman Turner and his mother was part German, part Irish."

Craig struggles to keep the phone between his shoulder and ear while writing as quickly as he can.

James speaks fast and doesn't seem ready to stop anytime soon. His words are silken threads spun into a beautiful web. Craig is all caught up. "Every major event in my life it seems had something to do with you. By the time I get off this phone, I hope to show you how. We were both rejected from the family. But it was harder for me because I was rejected from the family but still *in* the family, whereas you were rejected from the family *outside* of the family. I don't know if it was harder for me, but it was different, and the same. You understand what I'm trying to say?"

"I think so."

"Now I'm ill. I'm on disability. I'm ill now. I was diagnosed with bipolar disorder in nineteen eighty-two and had to sell my practice and go on disability. I have nothing but time on my hands now and so I'm on a quest for God and the truth. I do a lot of reading and I love religion. I'm on the quest for God and the truth. My religion is family. I study all religions in the quest for truth. I'm a Jew. I'm more Jewish than a real Jew"—he laughed—"I'm James Eathel White, so my initials actually spell Jew. How many Jewish people you know can say that? That's how I sign my name. J. E. W. My Jewishness defines me more than anything else. I'm a Jew.

"I'm here to try and make unity out of diversity. My religion is family. Now, religion is supposed to teach love, its ultimate theme and purpose, but this mission has been subjugated by institutional madness and dogma. Family is about love. Religion is about love, or it's supposed to be about love. If a religion isn't about love, it's not about anything. That's why I had to get out of the Adventist church. Nothing but a bunch of hypocrites who believe everything Ellen G. White wrote and prophesied, and she was known to suffer from temporal lobe epileptic delusions based on a head trauma she endured as a little girl in Maine. I was in Maine once.

"Nobody in my family understands me. Nobody wants to understand me. Now my mother, your grandmother, probably understands me the most, but she likes to act like she doesn't. I'm into numbers, the meaning and significance of numbers. I have a whole theory about life that can be distilled right down to numbers. My mother is into numbers, too, but she tries not to let anybody but me know because Adventists don't really believe in numbers. And that's crazy because the Bible is full of numerology.

"Did you know? Craig. Craig, right? Now did you know that you were supposed to contact me first? You were supposed to contact me first. You were supposed to find me first. You know that, don't you? You were supposed to find me before you found anyone else."

"Why's that?"

"That's because I wanted to take you myself. I wanted you. I stood in the back of the court that day when my mother and sister were getting rid of you, and I said, 'I'll take him.' But since I was just getting ready to go to medical school, my mother wouldn't hear of it. I'll take him. That's right. I'll take him. But you know you were supposed to find me first."

"There *was* something about the look in your eyes in your sixty-seven yearbook picture that I connected with." Craig moves from the old maroon chair to the matted carpet on the floor. "I could only imagine that you might have been blamed for your sister being pregnant, seeing as though you were her big brother and all, and just the two of you were down in Huntsville at Oakwood at the time."

"Now you see, I had gotten a girl pregnant myself and could not marry her. After I got her pregnant, she left Oakwood. I never found out whatever happened to the girl or the child. I always thought Jennifer told my mother about this because she thought I told her about you."

"Did Jennifer ever wonder about me?"

"Now you have to remember, Craig, that we didn't see eye-to-eye on so many things, especially after I left the church. In fact, the last time I saw my sister, I don't know exactly how long ago it was now, but the last time I saw your mother I tried to share with her something that I thought was important, something that I had recently discovered in Jewish texts, and she didn't wanna hear it. We don't talk too much about too many important things."

"So you don't know if she ever wondered about me."

"She might have thought about you, she might have wondered about you, but she never talked about it. Not to me, anyway. I doubt to anybody. I would imagine by now that she at least told her daughters about you. I'd be surprised if she hadn't done that. I know why she named you Joseph, though. I know why she named you Joseph."

"Why?"

"Yeah, I know why she named you Joseph. I don't know where she got Bernard from. But she named you Joseph after the Old Testament Joseph. After the Joseph in the Old Testament."

"Did she tell you that?"

"No. And she didn't have to. I know why she did it. She named you Joseph because that was her way making sure that you would come back to her. You know the story of Joseph from the Bible?"

"Yes."

"Well then you know he was reunited with Israel and his family before Israel died. That's why she did it. So you would come back to her before she died. You came back in order to heal the family. Adventists think they're Jews, you know. Counterfeit. I call Adventists counterfeit Jews. My mother calls them that, too. But if Adventists and Latter-Day Saints and Jehovah's

Witnesses could come together, if we could take the best parts of their tenets and their beliefs and reconcile them with one another, then we could really do some damage. Then we could heal the world. We're all Jewish, you know, all of us, descendants of Adam. You know that don't you?"

"Where is Jennifer now?"

"Georgia. She lives with Tanzania, my favorite niece. You have three sisters, Tanzania and the twins Rwanda and Burundi. You might not believe it, but Jennifer is actually a good mother. She did everything for those girls. She got a lot of help from my mother and me when the girls were little, but she's a good mother. She's divorced from Ahmad, the girls' father. He used to be Laurence, but he changed his name to Ahmad. I don't know what was going on between them, but one day she called me up from Las Vegas and told me to come get her. Said she was gonna kill him. When I got there, you wouldn't have thought anything was going on between them. Jennifer was calm. I don't know what the problem was, but she called me and I went to get her. I brought her to Loma Linda, California. Your sister Tanzania was born at Loma Linda Seventh-Day Adventist Hospital where I first practiced after I got my medical degree. I did my residency there, too. Your Uncle Josh, my brother Joshua, also got his medical degree there. Now he's a pediatrician with two sons, Joshua Junior, who we call Little Josh, and Christian. They all live in Georgia, in Dalton, Georgia. My mother lives there, too."

"All of their names came up as possible residents of the house on Ella Lane."

"Now your grandfather, he died—"

"August twenty-fourth nineteen ninety-eight."

"—How'd you know that?"

"From an Internet site where you can search for people. For a nominal fee, you can basically run a background check on somebody."

"I gotta see that. But he died in nineteen ninety-eight just a few days after my birthday. Now my mother is lonely. She doesn't talk to anybody really but me. In fact, I just had a long conversation with her earlier tonight. She's a member of the FBI. You know what that means? Fat Black and Independent: the FBI. Her and a few churchwomen from Sharon Church back in Milwaukee came up with that. And she's still Fat Black and Independent." He laughs—cackles, actually—in a shrill outburst that makes Craig pull the phone away from his ear. "By the way, how did you find me?"

"I got your number from your mother. I told her I was a long-lost friend of yours from Oakwood College."

He cackles again. "Boy, you're too much, boy. That's the only way you could've found me. I'm not listed anywhere anymore. My wife is listed but I'm not. I haven't been in any phone books in ten years myself. Now how did you find my mother?"

"On the same Internet print out. I had looked up your father by using the address on Sixteenth Street in Milwaukee, which was listed in the back of the nineteen-sixty-seven Oakwood College yearbook. It also listed Ella Lane as one of his possible addresses, and all the people who lived in that house. It even has the neighbors and any phone numbers listed for any of them. Your mother's number was right there."

"I'd like to see that. You got all that information from the Internet?"

"I did."

"Do you know who your father is?"

"I've narrowed it down to either Edward Cartwright or Frank East. Both of them were athletes, as my adoption papers say, and they were the two I looked the most like. Edward Cartwright is the only one in the whole yearbook that has ears that look anything like mine."

James cackles.

"You thought your father was Edward Cartwright? Well, it's Frank East. Frank East is your father. But Frank, Edward, and I hung tight in college. We called ourselves the Yick-Yacks. We all played flag football together."

"Because I didn't know for sure, I've only done preliminary research on Edward Cartwright and Frank East. It turns out that Frank East is back in Dania, Florida, where my adoption papers said he was originally from."

"You have at least one brother. Now Frank was a ladies' man. Had more girlfriends than Casanova. He got a girl named Verita pregnant at Oakwood same time as my sister. Now Verita was a pretty, *pretty* girl. Smart, too. I wanted her for myself, but she wouldn't give me the time of day. She and Frank dated on and off for a few years."

"Did she know about Jennifer?"

"She would've been a fool not to. Verita left Oakwood before Jennifer did. She and Frank got married and moved to Dayton, Ohio. I can't remember when his son was born, but it had to be about the same time you were. His name is Butch. Actually, it's Frank Junior, but they call him Butch."

"That's what my father calls my mother sometimes. Where did you say Jennifer was again?"

"She's in Atlanta with Tanzania. She works for Kirby in sales. She's done well for herself with Kirby. She worked for a photographer in Denver. She's also sold Tupperware. She's lived all over. Denver, Colorado; Tuscon, Arizona; Loma Linda; Lincoln, Nebraska; Huntsville; Milwaukee. She lived in the house on Sixteenth Street after my parents moved to an apartment out near Brown Deer. Matter of fact, the girls went to school right there at Sharon Academy. The church was called Sharon Seventh-Day Adventist church and your sisters went to school at Sharon Academy. My mother taught at that school. Before they sold the house and moved to Dalton to live in the house that Josh built. After we were all out of the house, she went to school and got her degree from the University of Wisconsin at Milwaukee. Your mother moved down to Huntsville when the twins were old enough to go to Oakwood Academy. Where did you go to college? You went to college didn't you? With our genes you had to go to college."

"I went to Harvard."

"That's the oldest college in the country isn't it?"

"Sure is. Founded in sixteen thirty-six."

"You know what happened in nineteen forty-eight, the year between my sister and me? Israel became a nation. I was born in forty-seven, your mother in forty-nine, so forty-eight is between us. Now when we first started talking do you remember how I said sixty-nine? That I thought you were born in sixty-nine? Do you remember that I said sixty-nine instead of sixty-seven? Now I'll tell you why. Sixty-nine was the year my wife Sonja's son, Jason, was born. He was murdered a few years ago, and Sonja's never gotten over it. But her brother, Sonja's brother, was like a father to him. So even though Jason was the nephew, he was more like a son to Sonja's brother. That's how I see you. You're my nephew, but you're more like a son. I didn't have any sons myself. My first wife Brenda and I had two daughters. You wanna know what I named them?"

"What?"

"You wanna know what I named them? I name them Trisha Denise and Tamara Diane. What are their initials? T.D. Both of them. T.D. Touchdown! I didn't have any boys, but I got me two touchdowns anyway." He cackles. "Trisha is a teacher in Riverside, just like her mother, my ex-wife Brenda. Tamara is studying for her masters in mathematics. She's like me, she likes numbers.

"Brenda and I were born on the exact same day. My first wife, my daughters' mother, and I were born on the exact dame day. August the eighteenth. Leos. Both of us. And she could be quite the lioness, let me tell you. She doesn't have too much to do with me anymore because of how I treated her after my breakdown when I had my first episodes.

"Let me get your information. I'm gonna come to Boston to visit you as soon as I can. I've been to the east coast. I was in Portland, Maine, back in ninety-seven, ninety-eight. Always wanted to go to Boston. See all of Harvard. See all that history. Now I got a nephew-son telling me he went there. Well, I wanna see it. Sonja works for the airlines, for US Airways, so I get to travel for free wherever I need to. Let me get your address."

Craig gives him his address, phone number, and email address.

"Now how long are you gonna be in Milwaukee? Maybe I should just come there. I've got some things to do here, some appointments and whatnot, but maybe... Let me work at rearranging a few things. You know, I have all this stuff I can bring to show you. Like this here—I found the obituaries of your grandfather, and both your great grandparents on my father's side. Just in case I don't come, I got some things I gotta take care of first, let me read them to you. Hold on while I get my glasses."

Craig plugs his cell phone charger in the wall outlet because the battery is beeping.

"Okay. Now here is your grandfather, who you say you found on the Internet.

"James Eathel White, Jr. was born October twenty-fifth, nineteen twenty-two, in St. Louis, Missouri. He was the second child of Dr. James E. White, and Madree Penn White. He and his sister, Grace, had a happy childhood.

"James received his formal education in the St. Louis Public School System. He attended Stowe Teacher's College for two years and then pursued a graphic arts degree at Lincoln University in Jefferson City, Missouri. In nineteen forty-five, he began his long career as a linotypist, printer, and compositor, beginning in his mother's print shop, the Triangle Press.

"James met England Turner in March of nineteen forty-five. They were married on December seventh, nineteen forty-six in St. Louis, Missouri. God blessed their union with three children, James Eathel III, Jennifer Minnie, and Joshua Herman.

"It was James' desire that his children receive a Christian education. In nineteen fifty-one, James heard the preaching of the Three Angels Messages of Revelation Fourteen. He accepted God's call and was baptized into the Berea Seventh-Day Adventist Church. He was so excited, he now knew God in a new and enthralling way.

"Now, he could be assured his children would share in his experience by the fulfillment of his dream in having them educated in the worldwide educational system of the Seventh-Day Adventists.

"James served in many church offices: First Elder, Leader of the Missionary Men, Pathfinder Director, Leader of the Master Guide Club, a member of the Deacon Board, MV and JMV Sponsor, and Sabbath School Teacher. He enjoyed most the offices where he worked with young people.

"James retired from Western Builder Publishing Company in Wauwatosa, Wisconsin, in nineteen eighty-seven.

"He and England moved to Dalton, Georgia, in nineteen ninety. Here he continued to live by his life's motto: To help young people know God. He did all he could to be a blessing to all he met on this life's highway.

"He especially cherished being actively involved in building homes for Habitat for Humanity, Inc. It was in this setting that he died on Monday, August twenty-fourth, nineteen ninety-eight." He takes a breath.

"Now, here's your great grandfather's obituary: The civic and social community of the City of St. Louis, Missouri, mourns the loss of Dr. James Eathel White, Sr., a dynamic leader of human rights, and a great humanitarian and a champion of the people.

"Dr. White, one of the earliest pioneers in the struggle for human dignity and the seventh child of Samuel Edward Lee White and Louisianna Elizabeth White was born July twenty-fifth, eighteen eighty-seven in Edenton, North Carolina.

"He confessed Christ at an early age and continued his services to God as a Sunday School teacher, superintendent of Sunday School, Chairman of Trustee Board and Chairman of Deacon Board wherever he resided. His final membership was at Antioch Baptist Church in St. Louis.

"His quest for education led him to graduate with honors from Roanoke Institute in Elizabeth City, North Carolina. His medical career began with pre-medical training at Howard University in Washington, D.C., and the conferring of the Doctor of Medicine degree in nineteen fifteen from Leonard Medical School, Shaw University in Raleigh, North Carolina. He did post-graduate study in gynecology at Long Island Medical College in Brooklyn with further study at Meharry Medical College in Nashville, Tennessee, and the School of Medicine, University of Pennsylvania in Philadelphia. Here he later served as head of the hematology department.

"Dr. White served his country from nineteen eighteen to nineteen as sergeant in the Nineteenth Medical Infirmary, Sixty-Fifth Pioneer Infantry, Camp Funston, Kansas. He is the cousin of the first black U.S. Congressman from North Carolina, George Henry White, who served from eighteen ninety-seven to nineteen hundred one. He was the first black man to serve in Congress during the post-Reconstruction period. Standing as a monument to the family is the town of Whitesboro, New Jersey, a town George White founded in nineteen hundred one.

"Dr. White moved to St. Louis in nineteen twenty with his bride Madree Penn, national founder of the Delta Sigma Theta Sorority, to work in the office of the City Coroner. A recipient of numerous awards and citations, Mayor Kiel's commendations to Dr. White for his outstanding service during the influenza epidemic in nineteen twenty and the Red Cross award for his service in public health in nineteen fifty are only a few of his honors.

"During his residence in St. Louis he was president of the Mound City Forum and a member of the National Medical Association. Several of his medical papers appeared in the National Medical Journal. Dr. White was among those who were responsible for the establishment and building of Homer G. Phillips Hospital. After the death of H.G. Phillips, he became chairman of the hospital committee. He realized a need for medical service for black people, a need for trained black nurses, and a need for a medical center where black doctors could train, practice, and provide medical care for people who were victims of discrimination.

"Working with the NAACP, the Urban League, serving as a consultant on racial problems for Mayor Bernard Dickman and encouraging outstanding, young, potential, black leaders to choose St. Louis as their home was also his quest.

"Dr. James White was a charter member of the Upsilon Chapter Omega Phi Psi Fraternity and was considered the father of the chapter. He was also instrumental in establishing an Omega Chapter in Memphis, Tennessee.

"His cultural interests involved working with the culture committee of Mrs. Annie Malone, who sponsored outstanding artists at famous Poro College. As a member of the Odeon Theatre committee, he played an active role in the presentation of famous blacks to the St. Louis community.

"Dr. White served on the staff at People's Hospital, St. Mary's Infirmary, Homer G. Phillips' Hospital of St. Louis. He also served on the staff at King's County Hospital, Brooklyn, New York, Long Island Medical College Hospital, Long Island, New York and Pennsylvania University Hospital of Philadelphia.

"He counted among his personal friends: A.S.A. Spalding, E.S. Herndon, Ernest Cooper, Dr. Julian, Dr. Charles Drew, A. Phillip Randolph, William E.B. DuBois, Roland Hayes, Paul Robeson, Carl F. Murphy, Joseph E. Mitchell, Sterling Brown, Langston Hughes, W.C. Handy, James Weldon Johnson, Rosamon Johnson, Marian Anderson, Paul Laurence Dunbar, Carter G. Woodson, Alain Locke, Dr. Charles H. Wesley, Roy Wilkins, Lester Granger, Mary McLeod Bethune, Mary Church Terrell, E. Coleman, George Washington Carver, Congressman Adam Clayton Powell, General Benjamin O. Davis, Sr., Dr. Middleton Lambrant, President Franklin D. Roosevelt, Satchel Paige, Dr. Samuel Sheppard, Jr., James E. Cook, Robert Hayman, Sr., and other noteworthy individuals.

"Dr. White's interest in civil rights was first indicated by his leadership in founding the Carondelet Colored Protection League in nineteen twenty-four, and later by his work with the National Association for the Advancement of Colored People, the Urban League and other similar organizations.

"Leaving St. Louis in nineteen thirty-six, he lived for twenty years in Mount Vernon, New York, and Philadelphia before returning here in nineteen fifty-six to resume partial practice and to serve as a school physician.

"Up until the time he was stricken with a heart attack, only five days after his eighty-fourth birthday, he was engaged in limited practice at an office located in his residence, Forty-Eight Thirty-Five Anderson Avenue.

"Now here is Madree's. Her obituary begins with a poem that she wrote that goes like this: Behind me stretches an array of days, dark days filled with bitterness, bright days too short for gladness, gray days gloomed with melancholy, another year of life draws to its close. What is written is written. Neither regret nor tears can wipe away the pride of joy or foolishness of it. Yet the future lures, hope ever beckons on, faith gives her strength to fading fingers that they may write upon the new page. Life offers purer words, kinder thoughts, better deeds.

"Then the obituary reads: She walked with kings and never lost the common touch. Mrs. Madree Penn White, one of the earliest pioneers in the struggle for human dignity, was born November twenty-first, eighteen ninety-one, in Atkinson, Kansas, of John Penn and Mattie Gordon Penn.

"Her quest for education led her to graduate with honors from elementary school through college. She majored in classical languages, aspiring toward understanding wisdom and a full life. She was a nineteen fourteen graduate of Howard University, Washington, D.C., earning an A.B. degree, magna cum laude, school of Liberal Arts.

"She won the distinction of being the first woman elected associate editor of the Howard University Alumni Journal. In conjunction with twenty-one other young coeds, she founded the Delta Sigma Theta Sorority, January nineteen thirteen. At the same time, she gave first evidence of her militancy in the field of women's suffrage and human rights. She enjoyed the honor of being the only Negro woman who, with Carrie Nation, in nineteen thirteen, was granted an audience with President Harding and later, Woodrow Wilson and John F. Kennedy. A national figure in journalism, she was recognized as an author of papers, short stories, poems, an editor and publisher.

"She engaged in business and financial endeavors as vice president of an insurance company, oil company president, investment administrator, public relations and advertising.

"So there you go. Those are their obituaries."

"I guess I come from some serious people. I haven't met any presidents, but my life has led me down many of the same roads as Madree's, from classical languages, to writing and publishing, from founding an organization in college to working in finance, public relations and advertising. It didn't say when she died. When did she die?"

"January thirty-first, nineteen sixty-seven. Same year you were born. Now let's see, you were born December the eighth. Now I'm an obstetrician-gynecologist so I can figure these things out. You would've been conceived in mid-February, and Madree died January thirty—hey, man, you believe in reincarnation?"

"Of course."

"My mother does, too. Not supposed to, though, because Adventists don't believe in reincarnation. The only spirit they believe in is holy. But my mother believes she's the reincarnation of Ellen G. White, who founded the

Adventist church. My mother was born exactly one hundred years after Ellen G. White and both of them married men named James, and both of them bore first sons named James. She wouldn't tell you if *you* asked her, but that's what she believes, all right. Now, Sonja, my wife, Sonja, might be a relative of Ellen G. White."

"Interesting. When I saw on my adoption papers that my great grandmother was a college graduate, I first thought of Howard University. It never crossed my mind that she would've founded the Deltas."

"Madree was too much for any man or any woman. My mother and her were at war."

"What did they fight about?"

"Religion. Especially after my mother converted to Adventism. You know my father didn't convert for nearly two years. His obituary is wrong. My mother converted in fifty-one, but my father didn't convert until fifty-three, partly because his mother spoke so fervently against it. But her and my mother would go at it. She told my mother the Bible was full of shit and only a blind fool could believe that all of it was divinely inspired."

"Goodness gracious."

"Told my mother she was gonna ruin her children if she forced the way she believed on them. I must've been around seven or eight when they fought the most. Now Madree knew classical Latin and Greek, she knew Hebrew, studied Sanskrit, and if you asked her, she would tell you she was around when Aramaic was spoken"—he cackles—"I'm telling you, man, Madree was no joke. She claims to have read the Bible in its entirety in Hebrew and Greek and would go toe-to-toe with my mother quoting scriptures. She could tell my mother about scripture that didn't even make it into the King James Version and long passages that had been translated to mean nothing near what the original text stated. Nobody could win an argument with her, certainly not about the Bible, but really, not about *anything*. She dropped dead of a heart attack while she was on the radio."

"Did she have a radio show, too?"

"No, but she'd called into some political radio show and she was arguing down some racist who thought the civil rights movement was the work of the devil."

"I wish I could've met her. Surely a woman on a quest for wisdom and a full life, a woman who'd read the Bible in its original languages would have found *some* value on its pages."

"Madree didn't turn a blind eye or a deaf ear to the Bible's wisdom, no. But she thought it was at least as full of shit as it was wisdom, if not more so."

"I really wish I could've met her."

"What do you say I try to get there tomorrow or the next day? You gonna be there that long?"

"I certainly can be."

"Okay. I gotta check on a few things. If nothing else, I'll get your mother's number from my mother. She's gonna wonder why I'm calling her trying to get Jennifer's number, but I'll work it out. You said you just talked to her today yourself to get my number, right?"

"Right."

He cackles, this time much longer than the times before.

"Well, I'll call you back after I talk to her. And let me see if I can work out the details of a trip to Milwaukee."

"You mean—wait a minute—you mean you really might try to come to Milwaukee this week?"

"I'll see what I can do and let you know. I'd like to meet your parents, too."

After their goodbyes, they hang up.

Craig exhales. He throws himself backwards on the bed like he is falling off a diving board into a deep pool.

"Honey, something fell off of your face. Something, I don't know, something brittle. But while you were talking to him, whatever it was just crumbled and fell right off your face," Job turns off the video camera. "The last time I saw you look like this was the day we got married. You are so beautiful." Straddling Craig on the bed, Job leans, slowly, over Craig and kisses him on his dewy forehead, on his tear-streaked cheeks, on his trembling lips. They embrace.

"I am that man," says Craig. "That man is I."

2   On August 18, 2001, at 4:52 p.m., James was the last passenger at Mitchell International Airport, gate D51, to deplane US Airways Flight 509 from Pittsburgh. Craig and his cousin, Bernadine (his mother's older sister's daughter), waited on tiptoe while Job stood nearby, pointing the video camera at the gate. Wearing a blue tie, a black leather jacket, black dress pants, and black pointed-toe loafers, James walked toward Craig. His head, close-cropped and balding, was egg-shaped, just like Craig's. His breathing seemed labored. Like a robot's, his bifocaled eyes darted side to side, up and down, deciphering, processing every visual stimulus in his surroundings. Craig recalled the image of James in the 1967 Oakwood College yearbook. Thirty-three years had little mercy on the man who walked right up to Craig and said, "Christian." They hugged. "That's the first thing I thought when I first saw you standing at the end of the corridor. You look like Christian. That's my brother's son. You look like Christian."

Craig introduced him to Bernadine and Job. On the way to the baggage claim, James asked, almost in a whisper, "Who is Job?"

"My partner."

"What kind of business?"

"The business of life."

"Oh. I see."

"I'm glad that you see."

James collected his gray Samsonite suitcase and they left the airport and drove to the Hotel Wisconsin.

✍

"Seven eighteen," said James, looking at the number on the door of his room. "Seven eighteen: that's my brother, Josh. His birthday is July eighteenth."

"Job's is the sixteenth," said Craig.

When they got inside, Uncle James opened one of his carry-on bags and took out a book of baby names, obituaries, photographs, yearbooks, and other family memorabilia, including James the Physician's original business card, which pre-dated zip codes.

"Wow," said Bernadine. "How did you keep that card in such good condition. And how did you find it so fast. You musta collected some pictures, found the card and said 'I'm ready to go.'"

James cackled. "You can keep that."

"Are you kidding me?" Craig stared at the card.

"Will you look at that." Job stood over Craig's shoulder, zooming in on the card with the video camera.

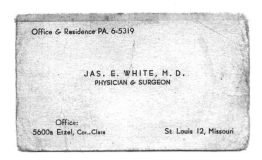

In the "Ocadian," the Oakwood Academy (high school) newsletter, Craig saw pictures of Frank East that looked identical to pictures of himself as a youngster at Rufus King High. The newsletter also included Frank's birthday and middle name. Now Craig could find him too.

"Here is a picture of your grandparents at their fiftieth wedding anniversary," James handed Craig two photographs, "and them again when they were first married in forty-six. December seventh, Pearl Harbor Day."

"Oh, my word, that's the day between my mother's and my birthday." Craig studied the first one. "Bernadine, come take a look at this." Bernadine rose from the bed, came near, and looked. Craig pointed to the image of England. "Doesn't she look like Grandma Magnolia?"

"Mercy." Bernadine eyed the image with raised eyebrows. "She *does* look like Grandma Maggie."

"Who's she?" James looked at Bernadine.

"She's our grandmother, my mother's mother and Aunt Mary's mother. She passed two years ago now I think it was."

"And look on the picture when they got married." Craig passed the picture to Bernadine. "My grandfather looks like my father, same hairstyle and everything. My parents were married in forty-six, too. June twenty-third."

"That's my oldest sister's wedding anniversary as well," said Job.

"That's my wife's birthday." James cackled.

"My, my, my," was all Bernadine could say.

They talked about more coincidences between all their families, which, by now, didn't seem to be coincidences at all. Their families were closely woven textiles whose lattices—metaphysical, ineffable, undeniably real—astounded the mind.

The Weavers' work was of the highest artistic expression. "Let's take all this stuff with us and go see my parents. They're simply gonna die."

VIATICUS

1 Yesterday, when Craig told him James was coming, Hazelle the Father went downstairs to his basement sanctuary and turned on his stereo. Here thousands of vinyl LP's climbed the walls on the pecan-stained shelves he'd built. Here he lost himself in jazz. Here was the foxhole where he ducked from the verbal missiles his wife fired at him without surcease. He split open a Pabst and poured himself a shot of Courvoisier.

Yesterday, when Craig told her James was coming, Gina exclaimed, "This is wonderful! Look at your face. All this weight is gone. Ooh, child, I've only seen you look this way two or three times in your whole life,"—she laughed and touched his face, smoothing away a tear with her thumb—"and you better be thanking your boss for releasing you, for freeing you up. Take it as a blessing because if you were working, you wouldn't be here, you wouldn't have that face. Look at you! God don't like ugly. Octavian, or whatever his name is, will be taken care of later. But this here is a good thing,"—she laughed and threw up her arms—"*too* good. I'm so excited I just don't know what to do. I have to go down to Chicago tomorrow for a modeling gig, but I'll be back to meet him as soon as I can."

Yesterday, when he told her James was coming, Mary mother of Craig fought back tears and said repeatedly just how beautiful and just so excited and just how happy she was from the outright thrill of it all. Sitting on a stool in Hazelle's basement den where she'd followed her husband and son, she also said, "Now you have to help your sister find her people. Maybe when Gina finds her people, she'll calm down." She scratched her scalp, her voice wistful. "I sure hope she finds her people while my eyes are still open." When he was a child, Craig had seen his mother beat the living daylights out of his sister. Seen his mother beat the living stew out of her, too. Just because his sister had missed her curfew. "Anybody turn up pregnant round here, they're on their own," Mary would shout. "I'm too old to be raising any more babies. If you can't keep your legs closed, you better use some protection. Don't you bring no babies to me, talking about, 'Mama, I'm sorry, it was an accident.' Uh uh. Accident, my behind. I don't wanna hear it." By now, she would be pacing the floor or straightening out the magazines or knickknacks on a table. "Better use some precautions, or keep your legs closed like you're supposed to anyway till you get married." Nobody in the house was foolish enough to believe Gina would keep her legs closed that long so she must have used some mighty reliable protection. She brought home no babies. Sometimes Craig wondered if Mary would have been happier with a grandbaby than she was with Gina's running. When they were teenagers, no, actually, when they were young children, Gina started running—from boy to boy, man to man, job to job, interest to interest. She had more talent in her little finger than most could claim their whole body held. Problem was she couldn't figure out how or where or on what to use it. Mary wanted her to use it, for Christ's sake, and stop flying here, flying there, wasting all her energy on some old *mess*. No matter how far she went, Gina would always find her way back to the nest. Between stretches in Chicago, Atlanta, New York, Philadelphia, Portland (Oregon), and Stockholm, Gina would settle down in her bedroom in the back of the house on Twenty-Ninth Street. She'd say that she had to keep an eye on Daddy. That "nobody's getting any younger round here and you know Moms is really flipping out because, quiet as it's kept, without me around, Moms don't really have nobody to talk to." Whether this was truth or one of the ways Gina self-justified her pit stops, Mary didn't mind her daughter's homecomings. Gina was always welcome, her room always ready. Mary wanted the best for her daughter—a good husband on the outside, a good calm on the inside (if not both, at least one)—and she thought finding her people would give Gina the best chance to have the best. That's why, just yesterday, Mary told her son to help her daughter find her people.

Now, Mary was looking through the front-door blinds when her son's Jeep pulled up to the curb out front and he and one of *his* people—the one he just found two days ago, the one who flew in from Murrieta, California a few hours ago—got out and walked toward the door. Hazelle stood in the living room behind her. Mary's niece and Bernadine's younger sister, Miki, sat on the couch. Mary opened the door and yelled, "Come on in here, you long lost relative of mine," beckoning him with her right hand. James climbed the porch stairs, cackling.

When her son and her long-lost relative came inside, Mary couldn't stop telling everybody how excited she was. The Hickman family introduced themselves to the man who shared their son's genes. They all sat down and James showed Mary, Hazelle, and Miki everything he'd brought. Mary looked, but did she see? Did she? "Naw. Uh-uh. No, she don't." James' mother didn't look anything like Grandma Maggie. "Not to me you don't. You look like me." Craig didn't look anything like his birth mother. "He most certainly does not." Hazelle didn't look *anything* like James' father. Nobody contradicted Mary. For who could try and force her to see that what she held most dear was part of something else? Something someone else could claim? Nobody, that's who.

Gina didn't get back from her gig in Chicago in time, so she would have to wait till tomorrow to meet the man who flew to Milwaukee on no notice to see the boy he said his whole life had been about, even though he'd forgotten to make that completely clear to Craig on the phone when they first talked. Meantime, Mary and Hazelle, Craig and Job, and Miki and Bernadine, who had arrived after picking up Chinese food on the way over from the hotel, ate and drank and laughed and reminisced and inquired and listened. Listened to the long lost relative tell (and re-tell) the family history compiled in the photographs spread across the table. To the philosophies catalogued in his mind. The memories sprung forth from his heart. On this here night, all of them went to bed. Full.

2 The next day, Job slept in. Craig and his uncle got up early (neither of them could sleep much) and drove around Milwaukee. They discussed numerology, astrology, metaphysics, psychic phenomena, the book of Isaiah, the two (and very different) genealogies of Jesus Christ in the gospels of Matthew and Luke, their marriages, their parents' best qualities and biggest mistakes, the Harlem Renaissance, the Jewish calendar, modern-day prophets, Karen Armstrong's HISTORY OF GOD, Neale Donald Walsch's CONVERSATIONS WITH GOD, Deepak Chopra, Toni Morrison, James Baldwin, Zora Neale Hurston, the grave consequences of the media's insidious terrorism, homosexuality in the church, the Defense of Marriage Act, Hollywood and the decline of American cinema, the problems of the electoral college, the unprecedented and shocking machinations of the Supreme Court in BUSH V. GORE, the inevitability of another war in Iraq, and the foolishness of the new president. "Believe you me," said Craig while driving through one of Milwaukee's many well-groomed neighborhoods with green, green lawns, "when George W stood up there with his swashbuckling accent and told the public with a sly little smirk and a glint in his eye, 'In my first year as president, I can guarantee America's gonna see some things it's never seen before,' I took it as a threat *and* a promise. I don't know what he and his puppeteers got up their sleeves, but I can guarantee

it'll be ugly. Real ugly." They visited the White's house on Sixteenth Street where James' family lived when Craig was born, the houses where the Hickmans lived on Thirteenth and Twenty-Fourth Streets, Siloah Lutheran Evangelical Church and School where Craig attended elementary school, James' father's print shop, and the church formerly called St. Philip's where Craig was baptized. They walked through abandoned lots and talked about whose young souls were saved between the walls that once stood there.

Intent on introducing Craig to his Jewishness, James asked Craig to drive him all the way out to Brown Deer to the Temple Menorah Synagogue where James had visited thirteen years ago and made friends with the Rabbi. Craig obliged and drove the twenty miles to one of Milwaukee's northern suburbs. On the way, he told his uncle how his family, when he was growing up, brought in the year with a kosher meal. When Uncle James informed him that the meal probably wasn't kosher since he couldn't imagine it was prepared in a kosher kitchen, Craig conceded. Nonetheless, at the end of every year, Hazelle brought home a few bags of groceries from the small deli and kosher food store across town. Craig told James about the slab of corned beef Hazelle simmered all day in his own blend of spices till it was tender enough to cut with a fork. About the sauerkraut his father boiled and the matzo ball soup, to which he added Cajun filé powder and thickened with a roux, making it more of a gumbo than the soup he called it. About Mary's fried potato and beef knishes, built from scratch. About her outstanding pastry, made from the cream cheese and flour dough she'd prepared the night before and baked on New Year's Eve. She swore by the extra cinnamon and a dash of nutmeg, sneaking in a few dried cranberries to go with the raisins and orange marmalade filling—all of which made hers a far cry from the batches the nice old Jewish lady from down the street gave to Mary's family during the holidays when she was a child. The Hickman family enjoyed Rugalah Mary at the end of every New-Year's-Eve-"kosher" dinner Craig could remember. Weren't all those meals, asserted Craig, over all those years enough to qualify Craig as Jewish? Absolutely not, Uncle James told him, but maybe so. They laughed then.

✍

When they walked into the synagogue, posters and children's drawings of the Purim festival on the hallway walls reminded Craig of his first professional theatrical role when he played Mordecai the Jew in a biblical burlesque comedy called PURE POLYESTHER. A gentle, soft-spoken woman who introduced herself as Minnette showed them around. At the gift shop, Uncle James bought a Tanakh and a Jewish prayer book for Craig. When Minnette told them that the Rabbi wouldn't be back until the evening

Ma'avri, they decided to come back later.

Before they got in the car, James asked Craig to look closely at the front of it. "Now do you see here how the grate in front of this Jeep Grand Cherokee has seven sections? That comes from the seven-pointed star that symbolizes the Cherokee Nation. Each point represents the seven original clans of the Cherokee and also the seven characters that make up the word in the Cherokee language that means nation. Remember when I told you that I believed that the Cherokee were the Jews of the American Indians? Well, you may have noticed that the original menorah also has seven branches. The Jews, like the Cherokee, are a nation and the menorah symbolizes the nation of Israel, which shall be a light unto the nations according to Isaiah forty-two, six." He opened the passenger door. "Coming to the synagogue here reminds me: I wanna go to America's Black Holocaust Museum."

✍

I HAD TO LIE TO SURVIVE.

Stenciled in white letters against a black plaque, the confession was one of the many testimonies of slaves, runaway slaves, and freed slaves, one of the many captions hanging near black-and-white photographs and renderings throughout the museum. Here, in a place where he'd never been until his brand new uncle wanted to come, Craig learned that throughout the slave era, Texas, not Virginia, as he once thought, had the largest population of slaves. He also learned that in Marion, Indiana, in August of 1930, a sixteen-year-old black boy, falsely accused of participating in the murder of a white man, had survived a mob beating and attempted lynching. The black boy's name was James Cameron and fifty-eight years later he founded the very museum in which Craig now stood discovering things he didn't know. Craig stared in front of him at the enlarged newsprint paste-up that told him these things and asked himself, If a man could survive a lynching, couldn't a man survive, also, a crucifixion?

In the museum gift shop, Craig picked up a copy of MOTHER'S LOVE: IN PRAISE OF AFRICAN AMERICAN MOTHERS, a pocket-sized gift book full of quotes about motherhood by famous black women—mothers, some of them; daughters, all. Moved by what the women said, Craig bought two of the books: one for his mother, and one for *her*. That is, if she would have him. She would have him, wouldn't she? Why wouldn't she? It's not likely she could still be ashamed after all these years. Could she?

The time was near.

3 "Look at your short nail beds," exclaimed Gina, taking James' right hand and pulling his fingers close to her eyes. The jovial waiter had just taken their order. "*Un*-believable. Craig has the exact same ones. I used to be like, Damn, Craig, where are your fingernails? He has these cute short little nails with shallow beds. Just like yours. Craig, show'm to him." Craig handed her his left hand and she raised it to James' eyes. James lowered his glasses. "Look at that."

James looked. "He's got the Turner syndrome, too."

"What's that?" Gina gave her brother back his hand.

"That pushed-out jaw and severe under bite some of us get from my mother."

"Yes, yes! Craig wore braces for three years and a retainer for five more, and look at him. Jaw pushed out further than it was before they strapped his teeth in all that hardware." Now Gina was cackling. Her face a cartoon.

"Orthodontists can't do a damn thing about the Turner syndrome." They all laughed then. "Josh is the only one of the three of us—my sister and brother and I—who didn't get it. Josh looks more like my father did. Craig's sisters, Burundi and Tanzania, have it too. Rwanda doesn't really look like anybody on our side."

"This is what I wanna know: how did Jennifer go from naming him Joseph to naming her daughters Rwanda, Burundi, and Tanzania?"

James cackled. The waiter served their drinks.

"She must really like exotic names." Bernadine poured sugar into her iced tea.

"I don't know what my sister was thinking, to tell you the truth."

Gina, along with Bernadine and Job, had joined her brother and his uncle at the museum earlier. Now they were waiting for the waiter to serve them their lunch in Elsa's, one of Gina's favorite restaurants on the east side. While they waited, Gina couldn't stop staring at James. At his hands, his gestures, his face. Gina looked at James, then at Craig, then back at James. Her laughter burst forth like trumpet sound when she saw from where Craig's under bite and chin point came. His tiny ears and egg-shaped head. The timbre of his voice. "*This* is what I've lived for." Her delight was deep as desire. "The day when I would see someone who looked like—and I mean *really* looked like—me or my brother. Being adopted, we never saw that, you know what I mean? This is a beautiful thing, I'm telling you, child. A beautiful *thing*."

Over lunch, James caught Gina up on everything she'd missed. He also told her of their plan to drive down to Atlanta before the sun got up the next morning. "You're just gonna show up without calling first?" Gina's face, wiped clean of expression, could have been a bread plate. "I don't know about all of that. What if she's not there?"

"Oh, she'll be there. My sister doesn't go anywhere on the Sabbath. After sundown she'll be home listening to gospel music and studying the Adventist Sabbath school lesson."

"Craig, how do you feel about that?" Gina furrowed her brow.

"Uncle James says it's the way to do it. He knows her better than we do, so I'll take him at his word. If he thinks a face-to-face meeting without preparation will be best, I'm prepared for the consequences."

"Better hope she don't have a heart attack," said Bernadine, laughing.

"My sister won't have a heart attack. Now she might have an attack of the heart, but it won't be a coronary." James cackled.

✍

After lunch, the three men went back for the Ma'avri at Temple Menorah. There, they donned yarmulkes and participated in the service from the back row. After the hour-long service, James told Rabbi Isaac his nephew's story. On the inside front cover of the Tanakh that James bought for Craig, the rabbi wrote:

MAY G-D BLESS YOU AS HE BLESSED THE BIBLICAL JOSEPH

✍

Craig was already ready to start the journey to Georgia, but they returned to his parents' house as planned. Craig gave Mary the book of quotes he bought for her at America's Black Holocaust Museum. Mary had gathered up more pictures of Craig's childhood from her archives. She insisted Jennifer have them, so Craig and Job went back out to Kinko's to make color copies. When they returned, James was downstairs talking to Gina and Hazelle. "Go downstairs and get one of your spelling bee trophies out of the display case," said Mary. "I've had you for thirty-three years and she has nothing. Give her one of your trophies. Get some of your blue ribbons and gold medals from track, too." Craig did what she told him. While he was downstairs, he told James it was time to go. They came upstairs.

While Craig was packing the pictures and ribbons and medals, Mary said, "And here, son, take this." She handed Craig the small book of motherhood quotes he'd just given her. "I think she should have this, too."

"No, Mama. That's yours. You keep it. I bought another one for her."

They said their farewells. Job stopped videotaping long enough to hug Gina, Mary, and Hazelle. Craig hugged his parents and his sister and started to walk out the door. Before James followed, he turned to his nephew's parents. "I've always believed that it's best for a child to be raised by at least one biological parent. But that's only in optimum circumstances. It's not always possible for this to be the case, as it wasn't here. I wanna say to you that Craig couldn't have been in better hands. I can see that. I'm honored to have met you both." He hugged them.

Hazelle gave thanks. Mary kept her tears from coming. She watched her son put the bag that held her memories of her "little angel" in the car. She watched her son like he was going off to college, or to war, or to someplace so far away he might not ever come back.

"Craig," cried Mary, drawing out his name, "come on back here and give me another hug." When he got back to the porch, she stretched out her arms like a cross and buried her face in his bosom. She held on. She turned her head to one side and leaned hard against him. She held *on*. He smoothed back the silver-gray hair from her face and kissed her on the forehead.

"Mama, everything's gonna be all right. Mama. I promise. It's okay. Mama. It'll all be okay. Mama. I'll call you soon as we get there."

4 On Friday, April 20, 2001 at 4:55 a.m., the three men began the eight-hundred-mile drive to 1902 Greenhouse Drive in Roswell, Georgia. About forty minutes into the trip, just before they crossed into Illinois, curtains and curtains of thick, thick rain came crashing down. Craig could hardly see in front of him as the pewter torrents slammed against the windshield. Was this an omen? If so, what might it portend? "Honey, maybe you should pull over."

Craig thought to take Job's advice, but blinding weather was not going to keep him from moving closer to what he had been waiting his whole life to see. It would be different if he were hungry or had to relieve his bladder. In the absence of both, Craig couldn't bring himself to stop moving forward, visibility be damned. "Don't worry. I'll manage."

In the middle of the storm, which lasted through Indianapolis, Craig's cell phone rang. It was James' wife calling to tell them what James had known from the start: Jennifer was in Roswell. Sonja had booked herself a flight to Atlanta where she would arrive at 9:30 a.m. Saturday morning. Then, she called Jennifer and told her that she and James were taking a last-minute trip to the Bahamas and wouldn't it be nice if they stopped in Atlanta for a visit on the way. Jennifer agreed to pick them up at the airport the next morning. Now, Craig knew it too: Jennifer was in Roswell.

The time was near.

The three men ate breakfast in Indiana, lunch in Kentucky, and other than snacking occasionally on the Crunch'n Munch, Tostitos, Goldfish, Oreos, Chessmen, and Lorna Doones they bought along the way, not one of them had an appetite for dinner. Somewhere in Tennessee, anxiety crept up on Craig like a wraith. As much as he wanted to drive the whole way, Craig ceded the wheel to Job. Craig stretched out in the backseat and wished for a master switch to turn off all the potential scenarios that looped nonstop in the frenzy inside his head. Somewhere in Tennessee, something else was sneaking up on James. His back-and-forth need for Copenhagen chewing tobacco (to raise the lows) and Budweiser (to steady the highs) increased as the distance to Roswell decreased. Somewhere in Tennessee, a snag tore through Job's nerves. He fumbled in his pocket till he felt his lighter, dug it out and lit a Kamel Red from the pack he'd thrown on the dashboard when he took the wheel. "So, Uncle James, how do you think Jennifer is gonna react to Craig being gay?"

"Well, Job, I'll tell you, I might've had a problem with it myself twenty years ago. It was about that time when I became good friends with Darius, a guy that used to work for me in Denver. He died of AIDS in eighty-four. I helped him when he got pretty sick there toward the end. My sister will have a problem with it because of the Bible, but I'm sure she'll be happy to see him. She isn't gonna close the door in his face, I can tell you that much. My brother's wife, Crystal, has a brother who's gay. H.L. Meeks is his name. When my father died, H.L. brought his partner to the funeral. They were together the whole time, sat next to each other throughout the service and everything. It was no big deal. He was just *there*. Nobody turned up their noses, at least not that I saw. H.L.'s partner is white, too. I can't remember his name, but he's white, too."

"Ha! You hear that, Craig? We won't be the first. The family already has an interracial gay couple."

"You look closely enough, there's at least one fag or dyke in every family tree. An uncle and his *friend* show up for every family holiday and reunion, and to the delight of all the grown folk, he keeps the crumb-snatching nieces and nephews, who consider him their absolute favorite uncle, in check." They laughed. "Uncle James, have you all ever had a family reunion?"

"Other than funerals and weddings, I'd have to say no. My father's funeral in ninety-eight was the last time the entire family, in-laws included, got together. My father's funeral was a huge event. Your Uncle Josh has the whole thing on videotape. Seemed like the whole state of Georgia attended. It was quite an affair."

"In Zaire, after everyone wailed and purged whatever they had to about the person who'd died, every funeral became a celebration for the entire village, full of dancing and smoking dope and eating. The family of the deceased had to put out. And I mean put *out*. Slaughter their chickens and goats; empty all the fish from their ponds to feed the hungry partygoers. The celebration could go on for seven days." Job rolled down the window. The curling smoke he blew up disappeared like a stray thought.

"You don't stop that smoking and I'll be planning your funeral soon."

"Sonja doesn't let me smoke. I'm the boss; she's the decision maker. So she decided I couldn't smoke." James cracked himself up. "But anyway." He caught his breath. "Now there's a place I hope to get to before I die. Africa. I still feel more connected to my Jewishness than I do to my African heritage, but I'd love to visit northern and western Africa. Zaire—they call it something else now—is in central Africa, right?"

"Correct. In ninety-seven, I believe it was, Zaire became the Democratic Republic of Congo. It's very close to the equator. Actually, part of Zaire is on the equator. Some of the most beautiful and biggest palm trees in the world grow there. Almost everything I ate in Zaire was cooked in palm oil."

"If you had to sum up your experience from the entire—what was it, three years?—the entire time you treated kids there, how would you do it?"

"I don't know. It was such a great experience. To see some of these little children who couldn't walk get out of their casts and walk for the first time, and knowing I had something to do with it—if I saw nothing else the whole time I was there, I would've left Zaire completely fulfilled. I could do without the bats and the termites and the rats and the garden snakes and the tons of ants. We had to set the legs of our dining table in little cans filled with petroleum so the ants wouldn't crawl up on the table. Oh, and I'll never forget the time when there wasn't a roll of toilet paper to be found anywhere for weeks. I used the cover of a TIME magazine with a picture of Ronald Reagan on it to wipe my ass." They all laughed. "The heat was almost oppressive. Coming from Holland, where it rains or is overcast most of the time, I wasn't used to such intense heat. But I felt so free. I loved Tshiluba, the language of one of the tribes there. And then there was the driving. Going anywhere outside of Kinshasha was a long day's journey into night. There were almost no paved roads. Some of the dirt roads would be flooded by rivers or rain, and you'd have to go *way* out of your way to get somewhere. One of my most memorable trips was my first trip to Mweka. I even wrote about it and sent the story to Holland where the regional newspaper in my town published it."

"What happened?" James adjusted himself in his seat, turning his torso toward the driver. Several times, Craig had heard the story Job was about to tell; every single time, Craig loved it. This time would be no exception, even though Job would tell it almost verbatim, as he had all the other times. Craig remained alert from the backseat.

"We had tried for months to get one of the Catholic missions interested in supporting our work and to accommodate us in evaluating and treating children with polio and clubfeet. Mweka lies in the northern part of the West-Kasai province of Zaire. It's a pretty good-sized city, the regional capital, and the political seat of the King of the Bakuba, who was the political chief of that region. His actual palace and royal seat was situated in Mushenge, several miles north of Mweka. Mweka is situated about a hundred and sixty miles northwest of Kananga, which is where I lived. There were no straight roads to Mweka. You had to drive a semicircle either by the northeastern route through Demba and Kakenge or the northwestern route through Katombe and Luebo. We'd heard that the western route had been recently repaired so we decided to take that route, even though it was a few more miles. We loaded the Land Rover with what we needed: iron bars, wood, old tires, leather and tools, the basics to make a brace for a paralyzed child, and ten containers with *mazut*—that's the diesel fuel—to make the trip. Needless to say, there are no gas stations outside of Kinshasa, the capital. My friend, Roberta, a Peace Corps volunteer who was getting it on with another Dutchman named Evert, had never been to the north so she wanted to join me and Musangelayi, the brace maker, on the trip. The trip went fantastically smooth. I was sure that I was gonna set a record, the highest average speed during a trip, which was, up till then, somewhere between fifteen and twenty miles per hour. I hit areas where I felt I was flying at thirty-five miles an hour. Lots of chickens and goats had to hit their best stride to avoid being a part of that evening's supper. But, as usual in Zaire, nothing good lasted too long. About five hours into the trip, one of the tires blew. No problem; we had a spare. After an hour we continued our journey, only to be surprised when another tire blew. The spare was gone, no village in sight. Only about two hours from Mweka, we waited for the next vehicle to come down the road. Some people in an old beat-up truck made it our way and Roberta went with them to Mweka to get the nuns and another spare tire. Roberta had complained about having a terribly sore boil on her butt. In Zaire, having a boil was as common as having an itch. Unfortunately for her, the seat in the old truck had little covering left and she had to sit for two hours on the exposed springs. Four hours later, the nuns arrived with a spare and we finally made it to Mweka three hours after that. A hundred and sixty miles in thirteen hours wasn't gonna win any records, that's for sure.

"After all of that, our stay in Mweka turned out to be rather uneventful. The nuns weren't as organized as they could've been and we didn't see too many children. The trip back was fantastic. The first hundred and forty-five miles were behind us in six hours, and I was closing in on new record. But, once again, the car had other plans. A strong smell of burning rubber came from under the hood and the temperature gauge went into the red. I stopped the car, lifted the hood, and besides the smell, I didn't notice anything unusual. I got back in the car and kept driving. The smell got worse, it was awful, and the car was truly overheating. I stopped, got out, lifted the hood again and saw this mangled piece of rubber near some wheels. Just the other day, I had learned that that piece of rubber was the fan belt, and wouldn't you know, I had an extra one. But I had no clue how to put it on. I tried hard to stretch the belt over the three metal wheels, but to no avail. Next, I put the new fan belt on the rather hot motor block to soften it and after many tries I got it on. If only I had known that all I had to do was loosen one of the wheels and just slip it on. Ha! All proud and happy, I started the car again and we were back on our way only to smell the same rubber-burning smell five minutes and one mile later. The fan belt was now in shreds and we didn't have another one. Now what? We had some leather in the back of the car, made a loop out of it and tried it on. It lasted less than a minute. We needed elastic, I guessed. I thought of our underwear. That was the only thing in the car that was elastic. So, I took mine off, cut the elastic out and put it where the fan belt used to be. That lasted four minutes. Since we hadn't planned to stay more than one night, I didn't have any more underwear. Roberta was wearing this cute piece of lingerie that Evert had given her. She said, 'I'm not giving up my drawers, Job.' I said, 'Too bad, because yes you are.' She did, and less than a mile later, the car began to overheat again. We had ten containers in the back of the car that held the diesel fuel, which, by now, had all been put into the tank. As fate would have it, we were close to a river and we filled all the containers with water. We doused the motor to cool it off, waited, drove a mile, doused it again, got a lovely steam bath, waited, drove a mile, and so forth. The last fifteen miles took us almost ten hours. So even though the roads were perfect and the conditions were ripe for setting a record, the car had a mind of its own."

"I always say, you plan your course, God laughs." James laughed like God. "But that story just goes to prove one of my philosophies, and that philosophy is this: the solution always, without fail, precedes the problem. Whenever you are faced with a problem, you've already been given the solution. It might not be readily apparent, but it's there."

"Well, it was quite the adventure, and other than the second spare tire, I guess we had what we needed to solve the problem." Job lit another cigarette. "How're you doing back there, honey?"

"Are we there yet?" Craig mimicked the voice of a little boy.

They laughed.

"Job, are you from a religious background?"

"My parents have been a lot of things. My grandfather, my mother's father, was a Christian Reformed minister. My father's parents belonged to a different branch of the Reformed church. And then they were thrown out of the Reformed church because I had a brother who was mentally retarded, and the Christian school didn't wanna take him because he was retarded but the public school did. But if you're Christian and send your kids to a public school in Holland, that's considered a big sin. Then we became involved in what was called at the time the Revival church, which later became the Pentecostal church in the late fifties, early sixties. When I was born my parents were involved in the Pentecostal movement, so I wasn't baptized, I was blessed as a child since they didn't baptize children in that church. As I grew up we were Free Evangelical and then we became Dutch Reformed, which is when I got baptized and confirmed."

"That's interesting." James rolled down the window to spit snuff. He retrieved another Budweiser from the bag between his feet. "We moved to Milwaukee from St. Louis in sixty-one because of racism. My sister and I couldn't go to the academy in St. Louis, so they sent us to the one in East St. Louis, which was just as bad. In the name of Christ, black children couldn't get an Adventist education in St. Louis. All in the name of Christ."

They were driving through Chattanooga now. From the highway, James pointed out the apartment where he and Sonja lived back in 1992. As they passed by the long row of buildings, Craig's cell phone rang. It was Sonja, as if she sensed exactly where they were. She called to ask how close they were and would it be possible for them to wait until her arrival the next morning before they went to meet Jennifer. She didn't want, she said, to hear any anecdotes after the fact—she wanted (no, *needed*) to witness the meeting with her own eyes. Was this woman out of her mind? Who did she think she was? How on earth could she think that he would wait for her, a woman he'd never even met, before seeing the face of the woman who brought him here, the face he'd been dreaming about for as long as he could remember dreaming? Before he asked her these questions, or worse, put her in her place, Craig handed the phone to James, who talked to her for the next two hours, which included the remainder of the drive and the first minutes of the meeting she wanted to witness with her eyes.

When the three men finally arrived in Roswell, they stopped at a gas station to get directions. Back in Milwaukee, Craig had gotten the address from a reverse phone directory on the Internet using the number England had given to James. The friendly black man inside the gas station gave them good directions. With no trouble, they located the apartment compound at 1902 Greenhouse Drive. At the entrance to the grounds stood a sign emblazoned with the words: WELCOME HOME.

The time was near.

THEIR EYES WERE WATCHING GOD

1 It is dark. It takes them a little while to locate the right unit. Craig anticipates what's about to happen, his anxiety stiff and peaked like whipped egg whites. What will she look like?

The time is near.

Will she recognize him?

The time is near.

How will she react?

The time is near.

They find the right unit. Uncle James, still talking on the phone with Sonja, knocks on the door. Job aims the video camera at the door.

Craig stands away from the door, away from his husband and uncle. James knocks again.

"Who is it?" a voice replies. Is it hers? Or his sister's?

"It's Uncle James."

The door opens. She appears in blue-green shorts and a white T-shirt. Her face shrouded with hair.

"It's the CIA." James laughs his shrill and infectious laugh.

"I thought you weren't coming until tomorrow."

"Well, I'm here now. Mind if I bring my friends in with me?"

"Not at all. Who are your friends?"

They exchange pleasantries.

Craig shakes her hand, quickly, and steps inside, trembling.

"So who are your friends?"

"This is Job." Job shakes her hand.

"Job's full name is Jacobus, which means James." Cell phone still live

with Aunt Sonja, Uncle James steps inside and away from Craig.
"Who is this?"
"You know who he is."
"No, I don't."
"Yes, you do."

With the back of her right hand, she pushes her long hair out of her face. She studies Craig's face. He has her protruding bottom lip. She studies closer. He has her exact caramel-colored skin with the reddish tint.

Closer.

He has that slightly squinted left eye that reflects her tightly squinted right eye.

And closer still.

She cocks her head subtly to the right, but not so subtly that he doesn't notice, and furrows her brow.

"It's been thirty-three years."

But she doesn't hear Job, because she already knows.

"My *son?*"

He nods.

"*Wow.*" She raises her right hand. "Joseph."

He nods again.

She steps forward to hug him. He clenches her.

"Oh, my God."

His water breaks.

"Oh, my God."

His earth quakes.

"Oh, my God."

His bow breaks.

"Oh, my God."

His heart aches.

"Oh, my God."

He can't let go.

"Oh, my God."

He won't let go.

"Oh, my God."

She rocks him slowly side to side.

"Oh, my God."

"It's okay," she whispers.

"Ohm'God."

"It's *okay.*"

"Ohm'God."

He buries his head in her shoulder.

"Ohm'God."

She strokes his head.
"Ohm'God."
She rocks him slowly and strokes his head.
"Ohm' God."
His earth quakes.
"Ohm'God."
His water breaks.
"Ohm'God."
And he wails three decades and three years of tears.
And time stands still.

NO SLEEP BLUES

1 Three days after arriving in Georgia, Craig and Job checked out of the Embassy Suites Hotel in Roswell and drove to Tanzania's apartment to see Jennifer before driving back to Boston. Talking on the phone to her mother when she opened the door, Jennifer put the small green-and-black Samsonite bag, which the door had slapped to the floor, back on top of the matching suitcase, which stood upright. Craig inspected the luggage. Both pieces were fully packed. He raised his eyebrow. Jennifer noticed. She took the phone from her ear. "I told you I was gonna visit you in Boston sooner than you thought. You didn't think I was just gonna let you walk outta my life that fast, did you?"

The whirlwind three days had spun him round like a top. Time didn't so much stand still as it seemed to lurch forward approaching the speed of sound or light or something way too fast to sense or comprehend. Craig looked to Job's face for guidance but couldn't read Job's expression, an expression Craig had never seen before. Craig couldn't bring himself to answer her. While she continued on the phone, he stood there, mouth open, and relived all of it in his head.

2 Jennifer's on the phone talking to Mama on the phone and Jennifer can't say my name can't say my name won't say my name   and is it Rwanda or Burundi I'm talking to now   and who wants to know if I'm a Seventh-Day Adventist and who really cares anyway and if someone really *does* care then why   and Tanzania is lighting candles and talkin bout Oprah moments and talking on the phone to someone she calls Twin

No Sleep Blues / 57

and is it Burundi or Rwanda who she tells   guess what   Mom's son is here yes right here in my living room with Uncle James yes right now and there's some tall thin white guy with a video camera   and why won't Uncle James put the cell phone down put the cell phone *down* hang up the damn cell phone and stop running up all my minutes talking to your wife who wants to listen in on all of this   and Jennifer shows Job pictures of her grandson Tanzania's son Quincy who is already sleeping in the back room and pictures of a little girl on the wall who belongs to Tanzania's husband Soldier but not to Tanzania   and where are we gonna stay honey I'm so tired   Jennifer smells funny her odor's funny and it lingers on me from the hug not funk or must or bad hygiene nothing like that but something different something deeper something smells off about her   *way* off but I try to put this out of my mind   and she calls Joshua and puts me on the phone and I say hello and he says   wow   just like she said   wow   they both said   wow   and then he is silent   and England gets on the phone and she asks how and I tell her a different version both of them true but this one different   I tell her the story of how she helped   and she asks is that so   and I say that's so   remember that guy what was it now just last week calling you up and looking for your son James   and she says yes   and I tell her the caller was me the caller was *me* and I tricked her with all that world-weary evil spread through her voice thick as tar   and she says I see   and I say I know you see and hand the phone back to Jennifer whose eyes are so closed and why are her eyes so closed up she doesn't look anything like the pictures Uncle James showed me with her eyes so closed up   and Tanzania still talkin bout Oprah moments shows me her wedding ring which is exactly like my wedding ring the exact same wedding ring and says you got good taste and she got married in August just like I did and all my daughters was married in August says Jennifer and now so is my son   and we need to get to a hotel honey because I'm tired and where should we stay   so Jennifer takes me in her car and Job drives mine and we go to a hotel an Embassy Suites or Luxury Suites or something like that   and on the way Jennifer tells me she understands   why I did it why I chose it   my lifestyle that is   knows and understands so much about me in the first few hours she understands why I chose my lifestyle and I wonder why she chose hers why she still wrapped up tighter than a new CD in her religion   I guess that's why she can't open her eyes no more but she understands me understands all there is to know about me and my lifestyle and my choice you wanna know why she says and I say why I'll tell you why son because I wasn't there for you son   your mother wasn't there for you son   so I understand your choice son your mother understands   and what the hell is this woman talkin bout   and I can't wait to check in cuz I just wanna sleep but Job just wants to talk so we check in and we talk and talk and we talktalktalk and it's latelatelate it was too late three hours ago and Rwanda calls and says she's on her way from Huntsville right now right *now* God damn it I added that part God damn it that is and it's already three or four or five in the morning and I need to sleep but Jennifer says you need to see your sister you'll have to get your rest later she's gonna meet us at Tanzania's so we can let Job sleep but your sister's already driving and she won't wanna wait till tomorrow and I can see her now speeding and sure enough in she walks at four or five or six in the morning with an 89-mile-per-hour-going-up-a-hill ticket and I wake up from a drowsy place not a sleeping place but a drowsy place oh how I wanna sleep and there she is ticket in hand and she looks like a little little girl her face is so startled and blank and she asks me how and I tell her how not the long version but the short version and I fall drowsy again and Jennifer takes me back to the hotel to my husband sleeping in the bed and he's so peaceful sleeping in bed and I'm so tired but can only fall drowsy but not asleep and the next morning or the same morning however you wanna look at it comes too soon the sunrise comes too soon and it's time to pick up Sonja at the airport and we all crowd in the Jeep all of us Jennifer and Rwanda and Tanzania and Quincy and James and Job and I'm driving and we get Sonja and Job sits all the way in the back scrunched up in the back videotaping the whole thing still from the back and crying and Burundi keeps calling every ten minutes she calls Jennifer on her cell phone trying to get a blow-by-blow every ten minutes she can't stand that she's not here to see it all herself and Jennifer talks to her and tells her what's going on and wants me to talk to her but I'm driving so I don't take the phone and we sing BLESSED ASSURANCE with Daryl Coley blaring from the car stereo and we sing and laugh and have church in the car and Uncle James cries and cries and Mommy I'm hungry says little Quincy five-year-old Quincy and so it's time to eat and he wants IHOP so we hop to the I and we eat and I'm so tired so tired and I wanna take a nap and so we go back to the hotel and I can almost taste the taste of sleep and just as we go in Jennifer speeds up in Rwanda's car and says you gotta get your rest later because I just got off the phone and Joshua and Nana are coming down right now on their way down right *now* son from Dalton and I guess my mother didn't go to church this morning she always goes to church but she didn't go this morning so she must *really* wanna see what's going on and in walks England bearing yearbooks and pamphlets and pictures of Frank and says Frank East is your father as if I didn't already know but *she* wants to know who helped me at Oakwood College who told me about them because I couldn't have found out without someone breaking her secret and Joshua hates secrets so he says at least ten times while I'm showing them how the long *long* version this time and they listen and I talk and I'm so tired all I wanna do is sleep will anybody let me sleep   and why can't I just tell them I need to sleep and we take pictures and Job puts the video camera on the tripod and starts talking to Joshua about medicines and treatments and children's ailments and England keeps staring at me like I'm Will Smith in SIX DEGREES OF SEPARATION but I ain't even though so many say I look like him but I ain't him   ain't no con artist come up in here to take yo money and I'm so tired and finally the last picture is taken and they leave and I sleep   finally   I sleep   and when I wake up Jennifer is back in my hotel suite and I call Frank East and Jennifer talks to him like old friends and I say hi dad he says well well and tells me it's not my fault   as though I think it is   but he says no   uh uh   no siree   what happened in 1967 is not my fault and he's glad that I sound good and tells me about brothers and sisters and ancestors from Jamaica and I give him back to Jennifer and she catches up on old times and hangs up   and now it's time to take a long walk in the park after dark with Jennifer and she tells me her whole life story   as if she could   and I tell her mine   as if I could   but we walk arm-in-arm near the Chattahoochee River right where she used to live before the hysterectomy   the hysterectomy that made her wish I was there and Soldier going off to war in Bosnia and leaving Tanzania and Quincy with nobody but her to help them in life   nobody but her   and that's why she lives there with them right now   and the next day we have lunch at Thank God It's Friday's before we go to Dalton to Uncle Josh's big old house on Ella Lane in Dalton about an hour from Roswell and Tanzania gives us a big tour so I can see the house that led me to them and I meet Joshua's youngest son Christian who's getting ready for college next year who's getting ready for something else right now looking at gay porn on the Internet and nobody sees this but me and him   and he sees me see it and then we go in Uncle Josh's gigantic red Excursion to see his old office and his current office and his brand new office where he doctors most of the children in that part of Georgia   and then we go back to the house on Ella Lane and England has made all sorts of veggie foods even though nobody is hungry but Job eats her sandwiches to try and make her feel good seems like everybody is doing stuff to try and make her feel good but she don't feel good sure don't look good got evil all over her face   all the time all over her clothes   all the time   all in her walk   all the time   and she won't look at the pictures Mama gave me to show her but I look at all of her albums and photographs and books and she gives me some pictures of Jennifer to take and she's just like Mama well not quite like Mama not in the ways that matter and Rwanda's ex-boyfriend Charles is in town and so is his mother who speaks with an Island accent and Rwanda tells him who I am and Jennifer tells his mother who I am and they can't believe it and Charles says you mean you gave up your firstborn son and he came back to

you after thirty-three years *thirty-three years* just like   and the phone rings and it's for me   and who one earth would be calling me here   and it's Joshua's wife Crystal who's out of town and oh how sorry I am she says that I can't be there but I know I'll meet you someday and this must be such a joyous time for you and good talking to you   and so I tell Jennifer what Crystal said and Jennifer says that's not like Crystal that sure don't sound like Crystal   but like her or not that's what Crystal said   and it's time to go finally it's time to go this is too much and I see what I wanted to see and got what I came to get whatever it was I came to get and I just wanna go home not home to the hotel or the apartment in Roswell but home to Boston where I can rest and sleep and wake up and pinch myself and pinch and pinch and pinch   and so I say it just say it   right here and now out of nowhere   I just say it we're going back to Boston tomorrow so Job can go back to work and they all realize it's about to end   all of it is about to end   and England says a prayer hides behind a prayer and keeps calling me Cedric not Craig not Joseph but Cedric and Jennifer keeps calling me Joseph not Craig because she can't say my name can't say my name won't say my name because three days ago she asked Mama for permission to call me Joseph and what did she think Mama was gonna say over the phone over the phone over the God damn cell phone three days ago   never talked to the woman a minute before but asked for permission to slap
her   face
and what about me you didn't ask *me* if you could call me Joseph not once did you ask me   but that's what you call me that's what you tell everybody my name is that's how you introduce me and that's what I allow and so lady
how
could I think about what you're gonna let me do as if you could *let* me do anything at all?

BELOVED

1 "How long have you been vegetarian?" Gail and her girlfriend, Tara, had house sat for Craig and Job, watching their dogs, J.B. the Rhodesian Ridgeback and Tanner the Silky Terrier. On the evening of Craig and Job's return, Gail prepared a welcome-home meal of fried chicken, collards, macaroni and cheese, and cornbread.

"Ever since I was eighteen months old," replied Jennifer, enjoying the macaroni and cheese and cornbread. "After we became Adventists, we became vegetarian."

"I'm so sorry," said Gail. "If I had known you were coming back with them, I would have prepared something special for you."

"You never have to worry about making anything special for me. I can always find something to eat."

While the five of them ate Gail's special meal, Joseph, Craig's beloved friend and next-door neighbor, walked through the front door. They heard his voice before they saw him. "Welcome back. I saw your car out front and I..." He was standing in the dining room when the sight of her stopped him. "Oh, my God." His tears—reflexes.

"Joseph, this is Jennifer," said Craig. Jennifer rose from the table and hugged him.

"Umph, umph, umph," was all Joseph could say. "Umph, umph, *umph-umph-umph*." He sat down at the place Gail had set for him. He looked at Craig and shook his head. If you could read his face, the poetry would be powerful. He filled his plate and joined them in breaking bread.

The six of them ate in the peace-filled quiet of people eating good, good food.

2   The next day Job went to work. Craig walked Jennifer around his neighborhood and told her about it. Roslindale had changed considerably since Craig moved in four years ago. Once a suburb of Boston, Roslindale Village had become the home of many first- and second-generation Brazilian, Puerto Rican, Haitian, Bajun, Jamaican and other Caribbean immigrants. Many of them became homeowners and lived with their extended families in restored, two- and three-story Colonial Revival and Mansard houses. Their simple yet intricate architectural details provide canvasses, ripe with possibility, for the beautiful, saturated palettes of the instinctively creative. Their new owners covered the clinical whites, pale grays and standard yellows they found with burnt siennas, ripe peaches, smooth burgundies, citrus greens and yellows, aqua blues and rich purples.

Craig took Jennifer to Americas' Food Basket, a large neighborhood supermarket near his house. It featured foods and spices of the Caribbean and the cheapest sweet potatoes and collard greens you could get your hands on. Hardly anyone in the store, customers and employees alike, spoke any form of English. The music of Creole and Portuguese harmonized with the cadences of Spanish and French, while Latin rhythms blared throughout the aisles from the speakers above. There were no white people there.

Gradually, many of the empty-nested white families moved, presumably, farther out into the suburbs—perhaps to Milton or Dedham or Brookline, the first home of the Kennedy clan. FOR SALE signs erected on many front lawns punctuated the neighborhood's expansive, hilly landscape. Real estate values in this part of Boston were increasing fast, quick, and in a hurry and homeowners were taking advantage of the market.

On the way back from the store, Jennifer's cell phone rang. It was Rwanda calling to give an update on Uncle James. Yesterday, while they were driving back to Boston, he had a manic episode. James locked Rwanda, Tanzania, and Sonja in the apartment on Greenhouse Drive and broke the telephone. Somehow, Tanzania took Quincy and escaped to a pay phone where she called Jennifer first and then the police. Sonja also snuck out and disappeared. Rwanda, whose nursing career up until then had included several stints in psychiatric wards, stayed in the apartment with James till the police arrived. Sonja miraculously reappeared after James was taken to a nearby hospital for observation and treatment. Now, Rwanda was calling to tell them that he'd just been released from the hospital, and instead of going to the Bahamas, which Sonja had actually arranged so her story to Jennifer wouldn't have turned out to be a complete lie, they would return to California later the next evening. Yesterday, when Rwanda spoke with Jennifer about her uncle's episode, she'd said, "Joseph isn't gonna wanna have anything more to do with us."

"You don't have to worry about that," Jennifer had assured her. "Joseph is all about family. Family is the most important thing to him and he'll be able to handle whatever he's confronted with."

3 The next morning, Craig was sitting at his desk in front of the computer catching up on email correspondence when Jennifer walked in wearing a shower cap and a red robe. She'd just gotten out of bed. "Joseph, show me that letter you wrote to Dorotheola Richardson at Oakwood." She sat down at Job's desk, which faced Craig's.

Craig looked up the file on his computer and printed it out. Craig watched Jennifer as she read what was now in her hands:

Dear Ms. Richardson:

I am not exactly sure why I feel compelled to write you this letter, but I do know that it's not in my hands now.

When I first contacted Oakwood College Archives, I told either you or Faye that I was looking to do some research on a family book project and that I had some photographs I was hoping to cross-reference with pictures from Oakwood College yearbooks.

That was not exactly true. For that I apologize, because I know that lying is not divine and I was raised to tell the truth.

Imagine my surprise when you said to me over the phone that you thought my mother attended Oakwood College! I never told you that, and so I took this as a sign that I was doing the right thing.

As it turns out, my birth mother did attend Oakwood College, as did my birth father, although documents from my research to date indicate strongly that he might not even know I exist.

Let me explain.

My birth mother was a freshman at Oakwood College in 1967 when she became pregnant with me. She left college at the end of the school year, went home to Wisconsin where her mother had her sent away to a boarding house in a small town so no one would know she was pregnant. I was born in December of 1967 and placed in foster care 6 days later. Sixteen months later in 1969, a family in Wisconsin adopted me and raised me to be who I am today.

But something has been missing all my life.

I am a 33-year-old black Harvard graduate and corporate manager with a good marriage, home, and relationship with the Most High. I was even briefly "famous" as a performance poet and theatrical artist.

But there is still an empty place inside. All my life, I have longed to know more about my birth mother and father, and their families—my roots—and so I started to search for them about five years ago.

All my life I have wanted to see at least a picture of them just to see which one of them I might look like.

Well, thanks to you and Faye, you have made that part of my dream come true.

I was able five years ago to get a collection of documents from the agency in Wisconsin that handled my adoption. In these documents, I was able over the years to figure out that my birth mother was also from Wisconsin, that she attended a college in Huntsville, Alabama, that her brother attended the same college, that my birth father attended the same college, that her first name was Jennifer, that her last name was five letters ending with the letter e, and that my birth father was from Florida. I also knew that she named me Joseph Bernard when I was born.

That was about it, because anything else in these documents that might remotely give me a clue as to where she lived, her birthday, her last name, her parents' first names, her grandparents' names, who my first doctors were, who my foster family was, where they lived—all this information was blacked out.

Imagine reading about your people, your life, and seeing long black streaks that render you anonymous.

But I didn't give up. I called the agency. I convinced the social worker to tell me the states where my great grandparents lived, but she refused to give me more information because Wisconsin adoption laws are rigid and archaic and don't seem ready to change any time soon.

I couldn't imagine that my mother, after all these years, if she were still alive, would not want to be found.

I couldn't imagine that she had not thought of me many times. I have no intentions of turning her life upside down or making any demands on her. I just want answers to so many questions; she probably wants the same.

So here I am. I have been denied information by anyone who holds the power to give it. I haven't been able to get her birth date, place of birth, last known address, social security number, or anything that might assist me in my quest to find her.

But I haven't given up, and I don't intend to.

I have posed as private investigator, genealogist, doctor—anything I could think of to persuade those with the information to give me what I wanted—but with no success.

I guess that's why, in the beginning, I posed as a researcher with you for fear that if I told the truth, another door would be slammed in my face.

Well, I hope you and Faye understand and accept my apology.

But more importantly, I want to thank you both from the bottom of my heart for giving me a picture of my birth mother, whose face I have now seen for the first time in my entire life.

And I look just like her.

I am enclosing some money so that you can copy the entire yearbook of 1967 and send it to me, and maybe I will be able to find a picture of my birth father and uncle as well.

Because this is so important to me, please do whatever you have to do to make it the best quality possible.

Maybe someday I will visit Oakwood College to experience firsthand the place where I was conceived, where my birth parents once walked.

In the meantime, I look forward to the yearbook. I thank you both so very much for what you have given me, and wish you nothing but blessings.

I am certain I will speak with you again soon.
    Very truly yours,
    Craig V. Hickman (born Joseph B. White)
    Boston, Massachusetts.

"That's deep, son. Did you ever talk to her after you sent the letter?"

"No, but she called me and left a message on my work phone." Craig opened the top drawer, flipped through a half-dozen micro cassette tapes till he located the one labeled:

RICHARDSON MSG.

"Here, you can listen to it," he said. "I forwarded it to my home phone and recorded it." He put the tape into the player that sat on the desk and pushed the play button. Her voice, mid-toned and sophisticated, had the cadence of a slight drawl:

"Craig Hickman, this is Dorotheola Richardson at Oakwood College in Huntsville, Alabama. We just received your letter this afternoon, which is Tuesday afternoon, about five o'clock, I opened my mail and I found this very fine letter which you wrote to us.

"My heart strings have been just pulled with emotion about your letter and I want you to know we are just thrilled to know that we have been a part of making your life much more sweeter and happier.

"Let me tell you, this will be confidential information; we will not share it with anybody unless you desire for us to share it. But we are here to help you with any other method we can help you with.

"But I'm just thrilled that you at age thirty-three have found a missing link into some of the situations that you have been wanting to discover.

"And God bless you for leaning on us for support in this cause and we are here to continue to support you.

"We pray for you and your family and we will continue to work toward helping you find the rest or put the other pieces of the puzzle together.

"God bless you. You have me crying, but I am so happy. And we are going to send you the whole yearbook. We had an extra one, and we are mailing the entire yearbook to you.

"God bless. Let us hear from you. Bye."

Craig handed Jennifer the yearbook off the desk. "Check out the Post-it notes stuck to the inside front cover." Jennifer opened the yearbook. Written longhand, the notes, dated March 28, 2001 read:

> *Craig, we decided to send you the copy of the '67 since we had an extra one. We are so happy that we had a part in you locating the picture that you were looking for and we hope and pray that you will have a very happy ending to your project. May God continue to bless you and your family. Faye Jenkins*

"That's beautiful, son. Just beautiful. It sounds like Dorotheola Richardson gets a lot of requests like yours, that's why she told you she would keep all the information confidential. I wouldn't be surprised if there have been many, many Adventist girls who left Oakwood to have babies. You know your Uncle James got a girl pregnant at Oakwood. Lolita Johnson was her name, I think. She left Oakwood and James never heard what happened to her or the baby."

"Yeah, he told me. Sooner or later, I guess all that repression gets up around the collar."

4 The next day, Jennifer asked Craig to share his art with her. He gave her his performance scrapbook, and two books of poetry he'd written and published.

She wanted more.

"What other books do you have that might help me see and understand homosexuality the way you see it, son?" He gave her Essex Hemphill's BROTHER TO BROTHER and CEREMONIES, and Leslie Feinberg's TRANSGENDER WARRIORS. She wanted more.

"Tell me about all of these, son." He gave her the story behind every framed award, poster, flyer, or announcement on the walls of the office.

She wanted more, more, more. Actually, she wanted all of him, wouldn't be satisfied till she had all of him, couldn't be whole till she had *all* of him. At least that's how it seemed to Craig. Who could blame her? Whatever her reasons, who could know what she had lost when she gave him away? He would give her back as much as he could.

He gave her four videos of his performances to watch. There was the one from the National Black Arts Festival, the one from OutWrite, the one from the Metropolitan State College of Denver, and the short documentary film about him that a woman had made for her final project at a Boston film and video institute.

She wanted him to watch them, at least one of them, with her.

Unable to look at his performances, he had only seen glimpses of the videos he gave to her and none of the dozen others he kept in the archive closet along with ceiling-high stacks of newspapers and magazines that contained interviews, articles, or reviews. They went downstairs to his basement healing room, which doubled as a den when he wasn't laying hands on clients, something Craig had done all his life, something he recently started doing for business, something he'd do a lot more of now that he was free from corporate madness. Craig decided he would try to watch the performance at 1996 OutWrite, a national conference for writers who were in the life. The conference was held at the Park Plaza Hotel in Boston, and Craig performed the closing plenary session in front of fifteen hundred people in the hotel's Grand Ballroom. Jennifer asked who the buzzed-cut, tie-wearing man in the black double-breasted suit with the deep voice who sat on a stool to introduce Craig was.

"That's Leslie Feinberg. She lived as a man in Buffalo, New York, during the sixties. She's a leader of the transgender movement and wrote a few books that she included me in, one of which I already gave you. At the twenty-fifth anniversary of the Stonewall riots in Greenwich Village, she invited me to perform with her. That was ninety-four and if it hadn't been for her, I wouldn't have gone. That was the year I lost too many friends in too short a time, and by the time the anniversary rolled around, I wanted to curl up and die, too. The Gay Games were also in New York that summer. It was intense, and I felt like I was sleepwalking that whole weekend. But anyway, Leslie's also a member of the Worker's World Party and she lectures around the world. Someone else from the OutWrite conference planning committee was supposed to introduce me, but Leslie told me she would find out who it was because she was gonna do the introduction herself in order to put me, as she said, in my proper place in history."

"My son, my son, I can't believe I'm about to watch one of your performances." Jennifer was ecstatic. She slid her hips over on the couch and patted the cushion next to her. "Sit down, son. Close to your mother."

Craig did what she told him. Leslie began her introduction. While she spoke, the audience responded like a Pentecostal congregation to good preaching.

"Please forgive me for not standing, and for speaking with a trembling voice," said Leslie from the television screen. "I am ill, and I hope to be able to convey through my words, however trembly they may sound, what an honor it is for me to introduce Craig.

"I've seen drag performance since I was fourteen-years-old. But when I first saw Craig's performance at the Northampton Pride festival several years ago, I was transfixed by talent. Since drag has been driven underground in this country for almost seventy years now, and since this is, as far as I know, the first drag/transgender performance in a plenary in its own name at OutWrite, I would like to just very quickly tell you what tradition I think Craig Hickman is a part of.

"Evidence of transgender in ritual dates back to the Paleolithic period on every continent on the planet. In those societies based on cooperation, Craig Hickman would have been respected and honored as being sacred. That's right. And as that ritual has continued in oppressed cultures even in this decade, Craig Hickman might have danced carrying the double-edged axe that we associate with the Amazons, worshiping the god Shango, the deity Shango, which represented all the sexes.

"It was with the first division cleavage of society into haves and have-nots that the powers that be co-opted the popularity of transgender in performance evolved from ritual. But with this difference—that transperformance, whether male or, later, female, had to be *impersonation* of the opposite sex—trans-expression could no longer take its place on the stage. And I believe since women were banned from the stage, and male transperformance could only find an honored profession in the theater, that it was one of the first attempts to drive a wedge between women and transpeople who are natural allies in the struggle against sex and gender oppression.

"By the nineteenth century, in English-speaking countries, male and female drag performers took center stage. But they were white performers, not African-American. And yet, if they stepped out of the theater in drag, they were arrested. You may or may not know that at the turn of the century in this country, drag was in its golden heyday in performance; it was considered acceptable entertainment for women and children. But what changed, you see, was that drag performance, particularly female impersonation, was thought of to be like a magic act—it was the art of illusion that only took place on the stage. And when in nineteen twenty-nine, Mae West put on the play PLEASURE MAN that showed that transperformers were just as trans off the stage as on, and even loved people of the same sex, the police stormed in and closed it, and began the first raids that drove drag performance underground in this country. And yet we know that the police brutality and mass arrests were not completely successful. For example, in the Hamilton Lodge drag balls in Harlem, which dated back to eighteen sixty-nine, attendance grew to eight thousand in nineteen thirty-seven.

"When I speak of drag culture, I say drag *cultures*, because, of course, drag and transpeople represent many nationalities, some of which face super oppression in this country, of which Craig Hickman is one. And so, I say that all cultures that are driven underground suffer from isolation. And yet, from drag and trans-oppression has come exquisite performance. Drag history is not the history of the Bohemian Grove where rich, white, straight men put on dresses in acts that as cruelly mock drag people and are as gender phobic as they are misogynist. Drag performance is the cultural presentation of an oppressed gender expression.

"So where do I place Craig Hickman in this long and proud history? I believe that Craig's writing and performance is the highest artistic expression of drag in history. Yes. And that together with Kate Bornstein, Craig Hickman and Kate are the most brilliant transperformers in history. That's right. Craig Hickman is Mother Father Sister Brother. Mister Sister to you. He is the living legacy of Harlem's drag and trans-history. She is the spirit of Stonewall. He is a transgender warrior. And she is too fierce! When I say that Ms. Hickman is the real thing... *trust!*"

The congregation roared as Craig walked onstage and gave Leslie a long hug.

"I don't remember all of that," said Craig, awestruck and shaking. "I just remember feeling like I couldn't possibly go on, couldn't possibly live up to whatever it was she had said about me."

"Of course you could, son. Of course you could."

"I didn't think so. That day was so intense. Black balloons hovered over the stage the whole time. I don't even remember performing. The audience wanted an encore. They wouldn't stop applauding. I was simply not there. When it was over, I was like, 'What just happened?' Seemed I must've channeled the whole performance. I haven't even been able to watch this video. After the performance, I was sitting with some friends in the hotel lounge and my friend Thomas and I saw an apparition of our friend Essex Hemphill, who'd written a poem about black balloons and who'd died the year before, walk right into the lobby of the hotel. We both got up and ran down to see him. By then, Essex was already on his way back out. Thomas said something to him, I don't remember what, and Essex got into a red car that was pulled up to the curb out front, smiled at us, his eyes sparked like a struck match, he rolled up his window and drove away."

"Thomas is one of the Brothers du Jour who you did THROUGH THE FIRE with right, son?"

"You've been doing your homework."

"Your mother is deep, son. I told you I wanted to know everything. Of course I read everything in your scrapbook already. I know Jeffrey died in ninety-four, but is Thomas still alive?"

"Yes."

"I also read in a review of one of your performances that people were crying in the aisles when it was over. Is this the one?"

"This is the one."

They turned their attention back to the television. Craig stood in the middle of the stage wearing a sarong and a gold blazer. His silver hoop earrings matched the choker around his neck. His just-below-the-shoulder-length dreadlocks, which Job would cut off in 1997, were rolled up and back, pompadour-style, away from his face. He looked like he was wearing a crown.

"You look just like me, son."

Craig saw himself start a monologue as April Marie Lynette Jones. April, a fast-talking weave stylist, was a persona that had come to Craig on the wings of a divination he couldn't explain. One morning—back in 1993—she'd woken him up talking. She couldn't stop talking. Smart talking. Back talking. Walking talking. Craig turned on his computer, opened a new file, and typed everything she'd had to say.

Now, not even two minutes into April's tale, Craig rose from the couch and said, "Sorry. I can't watch this. I just can't. But you enjoy and if you wanna talk about any of it later, I'll be glad to."

Days earlier, on April 22, when Jennifer sat with Craig on a park bench next to the Chattahoochee River and told him parts of her story—that her mother had named her after the actress Jennifer Jones; that she'd done hair at college in Lincoln, Nebraska, after he was born; that her daughters always told her she should write a book—he came to believe, right then and there, that April was an aspect of her. A part of his very own birth mother—perhaps a part that she wouldn't, couldn't, did not want to embrace—had come to him, in the month of April, as April Jones, all chatter and self-ordained authority. Right then and there, he told her that. And then he asked her, "Do you believe it?" and she said, "At this point, I could believe just about anything, son. Just. About. Anything."

And now he—he who was he *as* she—talked from the television while *she* sat on his couch in his basement healing room and watched—believing, perhaps; perhaps not—the part of herself that had come to her son, come *through* her son.

Oh, it was too much, all right. Just. Too. Much.

Craig had to get up.

And go.

COMMENCEMENT

1 The last time she came to America, she came alone bearing an aura of sunshine. Her son was getting *married*, for heaven's sake, and oh, how she loved the man he was marrying. After all, he was the only one of all her son's love interests who was willing, and actually wanted, to learn Dutch.

This time, her son was going to graduate from Brandeis University in Waltham, Massachusetts and receive his doctorate in health policy. This time, she came with her boyfriend, Rinus, and from the first day, her sullenness weighed everybody down. Whatever nourished the root of her gloom, it was clear to Craig that her love for him had turned rancid.

Almost three years had passed since Betsy's last visit. She had broken her hip, her middle son, Gerrit, had succumbed to brain cancer, and her youngest son, who was also her youngest child, had turned forty. Since Betsy's last visit, a lifetime had passed.

"For the first time in my life, my mother seems *old* to me," Job said while he took off his clothes for bed.

It was the first night of his mother's visit. Craig was already in bed, staring up at the cobwebs on the guestroom ceiling that he'd missed when cleaning yesterday. "I have no perspective on that. She looks exactly like she did the last time I saw her, as though somehow, she's been able to halt the aging process. But something else has changed about her in relationship to me," said Craig. "Didn't you notice how distant she was when I told her at dinner tonight how glad I was that she was back in our home? It's almost like she didn't even bother to pay any attention to what I said."

"My mother has always taken pride in her mobility. She loves to walk and to travel. To ride her bike. That's what's so ironic, that's what's so sad:

that she fell off of her bike when that dog jumped out of that car and ran in front of her."

Job was naked now. Craig so loved his long, sinewy legs, steeled from all that bicycle riding back in Holland, the world's bicycle riding capital.

"She was *always* on the go," said Job. "Now she's not as free to get around like she used to and I think it's taking a big toll on her. She definitely seems more depressed. She whines all the time now, even more than she did before."

"I wish I knew what was really going on. Or what else was going on. You can act like it's just her hip all you want. But I'll find out what else it is. I'll definitely find out."

2 Two days later, Job and Craig took Betsy and Rinus out for Mother's Day brunch. They also took Gwynneth whose two-and-a-half-year-old son, Justin Matthew, was their godson. Not if you asked Gywnneth, however. She would tell you that only Job was Justin's godfather. "I don't want my son to have anything to do with him," she'd say about Craig. An improbable wish, as long as Job was in Justin's life, as long as Craig was in Job's. Seven months pregnant, Gwynneth had stood up as a person of honor at their wedding. Her vocal and obvious disdain for Craig, even before the ceremony, boiled Craig's blood. How dare she stand before their wedding altar and feign support for their lifelong commitment? How dare she lie like that?

Apparently, playing the role of Job's best friend was easier for Gwynneth when Job had no one around who could see all her costumes. Gwynneth was one of the daughters of the late award-winning film actor who became most well known in a series of movies named after a pastel-colored feline. Like Craig, Gwynneth was adopted as a baby. Like Craig, she had in Job a man she considered a confidante. Like Craig, she would, for Job's sake, overlook her dislike of *that* one and would act—unconvincingly—like she was comfortable in that one's company. Job enjoyed a furtive thrill watching Gwynneth and Craig try to get along.

Craig wasn't exactly sure what, if anything, he had done to deserve such acridity from her. As far as he was concerned, which, regarding her, wasn't very far at all, she was pained by envy. Envy for his place in Job's life, in Job's heart. Envy for the amount of time she was once able to spend with Job whose previous two boyfriends got along well with her.

At their Mother's Day brunch, little Justin, with his permanent smile and nascent vocabulary, kept everyone entertained. Except Betsy. Craig could see that her mood was weighing Job down. For her, Job tried to keep up his spirits.

3

When they returned home from brunch, Craig called Jennifer while she was driving with her daughter, Tanzania, back to Roswell from spending the day in Dalton with her mother England.

When Craig's number flashed on her cell phone's display panel, Jennifer pulled over to the side of the road. Tanzania took the driver's seat while her mother, fully expecting the call, read Craig what she had written:

"Hello, son. Happy Mother's Day. Thank you, Joseph. I love you and I am proud to have you as my son and firstborn child. Now, I want you to listen to me for just a few minutes. I have some words for you, okay. Please don't interrupt me until I am finished. I love you more than words could ever say. I have missed you so much for thirty-three years. I am so glad you found me and are in my life until death do us part. I am so sorry for not being there for you as a child growing up, holding you when you were sad to support and teach you the things that mothers do. To see and hear you laugh and cry. To look at you and be happy and to see you sad. I missed helping you with your school work, your plays, your term papers, your science projects, your fundraisers, your sports games, and giving you money for your first prom, for the flowers, the limo, the tux.

"I missed you going on-stage to receive special honors and give your valedictorian speech and receive your grade-school and high-school diplomas. I missed being a proud mother as you grew into a handsome young man. I missed taking you to Harvard and being there to support, give advice, and guide you through much of the challenges that you faced in college. I missed you walk across the stage and receive your degree in government from Harvard. I missed the excitement of getting your first job, watching you perform your art and writing and your plays, novels, and books.

"Most of all, I missed helping you prepare for finding your partner in life. I missed helping you with your wedding plans and being able to counsel and guide you as you made the most important step in your life to be a partner to Job.

"Only God knows how truly sorry I am for not being there for you those thirty-three years of life. I can never make them up, son. Mom is healing now. I will be with you always and be able now to enjoy the present and future achievements of your life.

"I am so very sorry for not being there as a mother to you. Please forgive me, son. I have always loved you and prayed for you. Even when I told people I had three beautiful daughters, I would always say silently, And one handsome son.

"I love you so much, Joseph. Please accept my love for you as we begin a new life as son and mother together. May God bless and keep you. You have given me the best Mother's Day present a son can give by finding your mother. Love always and eternally, your Mom."

4   The next weekend, Jennifer came to Boston for Job's commencement exercises. Job's graduation ceremony was as uninspiring as any Craig had ever attended, including his own. The most memorable part was when another graduate mistook Gwynneth for Job's mother. Though Gwynneth was somewhere between the ages of Craig and Job, her carriage seemed ancient, her European-accented voice, gravelly and low. Dull hair the color of dirty dishwater was pulled back from a face hard as granite. When she heard, "Is this your mother?" her cloudy eyes darted down, her face flashed a panged look as vulnerable as any Craig would ever see from her. In that moment, he actually *felt* for her. After a weighty pause, Job clarified Gwynneth's identity. The mistaken woman made a quick departure, and the day's exercises proceeded to their lackluster conclusion. Thankfully, the event was scheduled near sunrise. It was out of the way and the rest of the day could be enjoyed instead of tense with anticipation.

And what a lovely day it was to enjoy. The sun smiled at the backyard lawn party and barbeque attended by forty of Job and Craig's friends. The last time they enjoyed a lawn party—just last summer—Job had turned forty and Gail helped with all the food. This time, Jennifer helped Craig prepare food all day the day before. A few guests took to screaming and dancing when they bit into Jennifer's cheesecake. Betsy had just witnessed her son walk across the stage and receive his last and most advanced degree. But not even Jennifer's cheesecake could break whatever spell Betsy was under. Her morosity competed with the sun's rays and almost won.

The day before, when Job and Craig had come home from a reception for graduating students in the doctorate program given by the university at the Heller School dean's house, Betsy, Rinus, and Jennifer were sitting in the kitchen debating the merits of selling the quilts Betsy quilted purely for hobby. Jennifer thought anybody who created something so beautiful other people wanted it should sell the creation, no matter how inexpensively. Betsy maintained that selling her quilts would dilute the joy she enjoyed simply by making them. Rinus agreed with Jennifer. Craig agreed with Betsy and told her so, in Dutch. Job said nothing.

After Job, Betsy, and Rinus said their good nights and retired upstairs, Craig prepared hot chocolate. "I'll have some of that," said Jennifer. Craig added more milk, sugar, and Droste Dutch cocoa to the saucepan. "How was the reception, son?" While he stood over the stove and waited for the milk to heat, he told her what a good time he had, how nice it was to meet Job's professors and his dissertation committee. When the milk started to climb the sides of the pan, he turned off the stove, poured them each a mug and sat down at the table across from Jennifer. "Job's mother doesn't like me at all, son. I can just tell. I could tell that Rinus likes me, though, so maybe that's why she doesn't like me."

Craig blew ripples across the thin film that covered the steaming chocolate milk. "Ma doesn't seem like she likes anybody right about now. I've never seen her quite this melancholy before. She's like the weather in Holland this time of year—overcast and chilly with patches of annoying drizzle but not full-out rain. The Dutch call that kinda weather *kut weer*, which means 'cunt weather,' I kid you not. Crude words for body parts show up in many of their figures of speech. But anyway, his mother's gloom and doom is tough on Job. He wants to talk to her, but he also doesn't wanna be annoyed by her fine, misty rain. He's actually been working longer days than he normally does and spending as little time alone with her as possible. I also think he's still upset that she didn't come to his birthday last year, and she knows it. But as is the case with them, instead of talking about it, they act as if everything is fine, when it's obviously not."

"That's a shame," said Jennifer, stirring her cup once more but taking no drink from it. "She comes all the way over here from Holland to see her son graduate and they can't even talk. Your mother would never allow that, son. Never. I'll tell you right now, son, if you ever have anything to say to me, no matter what it is—good, bad, or otherwise—your mother wants you to say it. You understand, son?"

"You can count on it." Craig finished his hot chocolate, gave Jennifer a kiss and went to bed. They had to be up by six to get ready for Job's big day.

5   The morning after Job's graduation, Betsy and Rinus took the subway downtown to walk a small part of the Freedom Trail. Jennifer was sitting at the kitchen table watching Craig prepare crab cakes for Job. It was one of the few days when Job had a break from clients in the middle of the day and could come home for a quick lunch. "What are you gonna do about work, son?"

"I don't know," said Craig. He finished dicing the onions and started to chop the celery. "I have a feeling my boss is gonna try to block my unemployment claim, but I'm sure I'll end up collecting after all is said and done. I can't imagine him showing up at the unemployment hearing having to look at my face after how he did what he did. All I did was ask the man for an assistant and, if not that, then a raise, and out of the blue he responds with a written warning pointing out all these things that made me the worst employee he'd ever hired. I had no idea about half of them, and the other half were blatant lies." Craig searched the pantry for canned crabmeat, in the cupboard above the stove for the Old Bay and the Colman's Dry English Mustard. "But if I were so incompetent, why had he just let me oversee the entire office build-out and coordinate the move to his power State Street address? Why was I doing all the human resources, overseeing the PR agency, designing his company's new collateral material, handling immigration visas, recruiting all the employees, administering the entire computer network, all the while keeping the books? I had just prepared that man's business *and* personal taxes. He couldn't even fire me to my face. A guy at the payroll service the company used told me that I was fired—on my cell phone, no less—when I was on my way to Milwaukee to find you."

"That's the way it always is with us, son. I had to go through it with one of my companies. After I saved them a ton of money and got all their marketing practices up to snuff, they fired me. I got a good settlement out of them. Your sister, Burundi, has had to deal with it, too. There aren't too many black biochemists in Texas. They see we have talent, and before you know it, we're running everything. Problem with that is, if you make the tiniest mistake, or if a key employee in the office feels threatened enough to go to the boss and tell him you're ruining morale—don't you just love that one?—the next thing you know, you're being blamed for everything."

"Ain't that the truth." Craig's tone of voice could only mean amen. "It's not unlike what seems to be going on with me and Job's family. Well, let me be more specific. With Job's mother and sisters, Els and Nelleke. Wilma and I get along fine. But the others—first, they loved me, and now, I get the cold shoulder. And I have no idea why."

"Wouldn't you like to know, son?"

"I guess, but it's nothing I can worry about too much. Whatever the reason, if I'm supposed to know, if it's something essential for my growth, then, sooner or later, it will be revealed to me. It's not gonna stop me from loving them." Craig turned up the flame under the cast-iron skillet. "As far as work is concerned, though—you want me to run your company's operations one day and then try to force me out or fire me the next—I'm over it. I'm all done with that. Basically, for ninety-nine percent of the jobs available in this economy, I'm unemployable. I can't stand rules that don't make sense, rules just for the sake of rules, and I'm done working in an environment where expressing an opinion is considered insubordination. So I'll collect the unemployment I've earned after years of corporate bullshit—excuse me, bullcrap—and assess my options."

"You ever think of going back to school?"

"Are you kidding me?"

"Son, a mother's job doesn't end just because her children are grown. A mother must continue to encourage her children to reach their full potential. Your mother can see that you need people to *get* it, to understand. You love to argue, son. I think you'd make a great lawyer."

"Yeah, yeah, yeah. Or a teacher or preacher or counselor or any of the other things people throughout my life have said I'd make a great one of. I'll tell you the same thing I've been telling all of them for the past nine years:

I'm an artist. That's all I really wanna be, no matter what else I get myself sidetracked in." Craig rolled the crab cakes in flour and placed them carefully in the hot olive oil. He rinsed several fronds of romaine and arranged them on a salad plate. "As an artist I get to teach, preach, *and* counsel. And unlike most lawyers I've met, I get to argue for truth. I'm most satisfied when I'm working for myself or doing something mindless for a paycheck while I'm putting all my creativity into my art."

"So, son, why haven't you been as dedicated to your art as you once were? You're very talented, son. You move people. I couldn't believe how much your audiences cheered for you on the videotapes I watched. Why did you stop?"

"Well," said Craig, pausing to turn the cakes over, "that's a whole *other* story."

Jennifer leaned back in her chair, crossed her legs and held on to her raised ankle with both hands. "I have all the time in the world, son. Remember, son? Until death do us part."

MARRIAGE

1 In 1982, Job went up from Middelburg, in Zeeland, a watery region in the southwestern part of the Netherlands, to Kananga, Zaire, in the heart of Africa. There, he would heal little children. He pondered this leaving, and even though he knew he had to leave, he felt enormous guilt for leaving so much behind. He left his sisters Nelly called Nelleke, Wilhelmina called Wilma, and Elizabeth called Els. He left his remaining brother Gerrit, who called him Job. As is common with Dutch children, Jacobus was officially given a name that he would be called. So his mother named him Sjaak, which sounds like "shock," but Gerrit, who was gifted in a way that most people could not see, was unable to pronounce Sjaak, so he called him Job, which sounds like "yawp." But most of all, Job left his mother, Elizabeth called Betsy. Betsy had recently buried her husband, Johannes called Han, who had smoked himself to a cancerous death on November 13, 1981, the day of their thirty-fourth *trouwdag*, which means wedding day. Job was the only one of her children at home to help Betsy take care of her husband in his latter days. Two males of the family already gone, his older brother Hans had drowned at fifteen in 1967, Job was the only one left who was able to take care of his mother, Gerrit being gifted in a way that needed so *much* of her care. But Job left his mother anyway. He had to. If he were to ever grow up. And so on July 18, 1982, Job took his one-month-old *Fysiotherapeut* degree with him to Kananga, Zaire. Two days earlier, while the sun traversed the middle days of Cancer, Jacobus called Job had turned twenty-two.

Centres Pour des Enfants Handicapés needed a physical therapist to work with children crippled by polio. Terre des Hommes hired Job for a project run by a mission of American Presbyterians and Belgian and Dutch Catholics in the West Kasai Province. He worked in the Tshikaji Hospital just outside of Kananga and in the rehabilitation center called Jukayi, which means stand up in Tshiluba, the language of the Baluba and Bene Lulua people of the Kasai. After three years there, Job moved to the states, which suffered from a shortage of physical therapists. He considered a private practice in Connecticut but accepted a position in Boston instead. Carney Hospital sponsored him for his work visa and eventually his green card.

In 1988, Job met Craig at Chaps, a popular nightclub in Copley Square. Craig was playing pinball and Job stood against a wall, smiling. He couldn't stop smiling. Looked like David Bowie with both eyes blue. Craig finally said hello and after a superficial conversation they went to Craig's dorm room and spent a rather forgettable time. But there was *something* between them, something dense and full of static, something both of them felt but couldn't shake. But nothing could come of the static because Job, as Craig would find out much later, was involved with someone else. Over the next several years, they would cross each other's paths here and there, have a quick catch-up conversation, if that, and go their separate ways.

On Sunday, January 12, 1997, Craig was searching for colleges in Huntsville, Alabama, the place where the Documents of His Genesis said Jennifer had attended college. Craig took a break from his research and checked out a few profiles on an Internet meeting place. A guy with the screen name Mulume had ended his profile with a personal quote: "Some people quietly come into your life and go. Others stay awhile and leave footprints on your heart and you are never the same." Craig thought immediately of Roy, whose wallet-sized portrait sat on top of the computer, stuck in the groove between the monitor's face and back. Craig thought also of Job, who he had not seen in years, whose business card sat inside his top desk drawer announcing a number Craig could never bring himself to call. Craig, signed on under the screen name Blklkme93, sent Mulume an instant message telling him how much he liked his quote. At the end of the chat session, Mulume revealed the he was the very same Job Craig hadn't seen in years, the Job who'd left footprints on Craig's heart. Later that afternoon, Job came over to Craig's Harvard Square apartment for coffee. Craig opened the door, Job stepped one foot across the threshold, and they kissed. Neither had any thirst whatsoever for the coffee that wasn't brewing on the kitchen counter. Eight months later, when Craig's roommates, Darlin and Gail, moved to San Francisco, Craig moved in with Job. Three months after that, Job took Craig to Holland to meet his family and to Paris where he proposed to him on the Eiffel Tower.

On August 22, 1998, Craig and Job got married in their back yard. In front of a hundred witnesses and eight people of honor, including Betsy,

Mary, Hazelle, Gina, Thomas, Gail, and Gwynneth. (The eighth was a man named LeRoy whom Job considered a close friend, although Craig had only met him a few times. After the wedding, Craig and Job never saw him again.) Job, dressed up sharp in bow tie and black tails, and Craig, draped in white Nigerian garb and ornaments, announced to their closest friends that death was the only way out. Nina Davenport, a friend of Craig from Harvard, and Martha Tompkins, a woman Craig met at the Massachusetts College of Art when he'd given a presentation a few years prior, documented the nuptials on videotape. Hazelle sang. Mary and Betsy cried. Gina humorously lamented that her younger brother beat her to the altar. She was off to a modeling gig somewhere across the country shortly after the reception wound down.

2 It seemed that as soon as Craig and Job carried each other across the threshold, leapt over the broom stick into a united life, their relationship broke down. As though the weight of their promises was too heavy to bear. The people of honor who stood up for them and signed their DECLARATION OF LIFELONG COMMITMENT, agreeing to help them in times of need, seemed so far away when skirmishes arose about underwear on the bathroom floor and dishes left too long in the sink and you never let me finish what I have to say and why don't you ever initiate sex anymore and when's the last time you stood up to someone for me you never have my back you coward and when are you gonna get a *real* job and why you always running over to Gywnneth's when we fuss and fight putting all our business in the streets when you know she can't stand me and it would be nice if you could just *say* what it was that pissed you off when it happened instead of waiting for me to tell you what's pissing *me* off and using my time to throw your shit back in my face and you ain't the only one who can play childish games and you were right I was wrong and I'm sorry I won't do it anymore and I love you honey I'll be better about that and I miss your touch please come back to bed I don't wanna sleep alone tonight.

Still caught up in his past lovers' con games, Job refused to put Craig's name on the deed of their house lest history repeat itself. That wasn't the reason Job gave, mind you. He'd convinced himself it was more about points and interest rates. Job thought the only way to add Craig's name was to refinance the house. Craig wasn't convinced that adding his name to the deed even required a refinance, but Job refused to get clarity on the matter. Before they remet, Craig's credit had taken a beating after his first agent's ill affairs required a bankruptcy filing just to make ends meet. If refinance was required, surely, Craig thought, a few points over a thirty-year loan were worth it for the sense of equality that joint ownership enabled. Besides, with real estate values what they were around the nation at the turn of the century, Craig believed their house was already worth at least twice what Job paid for it back in 1994.

Sometimes Craig thought that Job, deep down, didn't really believe they were married.

He also thought Job didn't have the patience to support Craig's artistic endeavors. Not, as Job would swear to God, for any lack of belief in him. But the income generated from performance or writing was, at best, unpredictable and at worst, non-existent. Whenever Craig would settle into his next pursuit, Job would fret about money. Craig would abandon his project and return to corporate misery. He pulled more weight than was his share to pull, a pulling that spasmed his spirit, if not his back. Thankfully, Job was able to sleep again. Craig did not despair for he had more patience than Job. Craig would continue to do whatever he had to do to allay his husband's fears. But he also knew there would come a time when he would do whatever it took to honor the commitment he'd made to his art six years before the one he'd made to his husband. Would come a time when no amount of fret would stop him.

Meantime, chaos trumped order. Counseling—individual and couples—offered no viable remedies. Job and Craig were two-of-a-kind, willful, stubborn, always right, and nobody could tell either one of them anything. Certainly not the other. And yet, they were as different as fire and water. Craig, the flame that could change the state of things, direct and scorching, with no care whatsoever for what anybody thought. Job, the fluid requiring the container of other people's approval to define his shape, lest he spill forth and gush free, knowing not which way to flow, afraid of what he might truly become without it.

But when push came to shove, they could count on each other, always, in the ways that only those who fight for a better love could. When Craig's grandmother, Mary's mother Magnolia, died in the first month of 1999, Job said, "If you need me to go with you to the funeral, I'll go."

"I'll go alone," said Craig. "I wasn't all that close to Grandma Maggie because I didn't really know her very well. I only met her once as a child. She came to visit us on Twenty-Fourth Street. I couldn't have been older than three. She was a big woman. Like a tower. At least that how's she looked. I can see her standing on the porch in a white blouse and a green skirt looking down at me. I was thirsty and she went in the house, came back, and gave me some lemonade in a red plastic cup. I was so thirsty, I took the cup and gulped the lemonade down as fast as I could. 'You too smart not to know how to say thank you,' she said. 'Thank you, Grandma,' I said as I handed her back the cup. And that's it. The only memory of her that I have. Mama swears I was too young to remember her, but I do. White blouse, green skirt, red cup. Her blouse even had a bow at the top, left side. My left; her right. I see it now sure as I'm sitting here. The last time I saw her at the family reunion five years ago, she'd had so many strokes she could hardly recognize her own daughters who were taking care of her every day. Her passing will be tough on my mother and aunts and uncles and the cousins who were much closer to her than I was. But I'll be all right. Just keep the good energy and love flowing toward us, and everything'll be okay, baby. But I *do* need you to wait for me. Just because we've opened things up lately, doesn't mean that it's a free-for-all. Wait for me to come home, you understand what I mean?"

"Absolutely. I couldn't see myself doing anything with anybody while you were away burying a member of your family, whether you were close to them or not. That just wouldn't be right."

Six months later, when Craig came home from the office feeling betrayed by his boss over some office politics and overblown egos, Job broke the news that Granny Alma had died. Not even a week earlier, when they were on their way home from somewhere, Job had asked Craig how he would feel when Alma Leigh, who suffered from Alzheimer's in a nursing home, died. "She's my Granny. She's the only grandmother I really knew. She helped raise me. She's my Granny. I'm the first of any of her grandchildren—the first one, period—who called her Granny and she liked it so much that she told everybody else to call her Granny too. Mama even called her Granny sometimes. That one will be tough. I can guarantee it. Her death will be very tough on me."

It was tougher than he thought. The day after Job broke the news to him, Craig drove to Milwaukee, alone. The morning after his first night there, Craig woke up with a neck so stiff and sore, he knew something in his universe was misaligned. He spoke with Job about it over the phone, but nothing out of the ordinary was going on with him. At least that's what Job said. Craig stayed in Milwaukee for four days, eulogized his Granny, helped his mother (other than the nursing-home staff, she'd been Granny's primary caretaker in her latter days) hold it together as best he could, and returned to Boston. As soon as he walked in the house, the energy slapped him cross the face. Hard. The source of his sore neck five days earlier was still thick in the atmosphere. Job tried to comfort him, tried to take his mind off his grief by trying to make love to him, but Craig was too caught up in the thickness. "Job, did something happen while I was away?"

"What do you mean?"

"Whatever it is, just say it. Don't make me ask you again."

"Well, I bumped into Mark on the Internet. I didn't mean to, I was just checking my email, and an instant message popped up and it was him and I always wanted to get with him again, and one thing led to another and so I went over there, and it was all right, nothing special. I didn't stay overnight, though, I came home. And that was it. That's all. Nothing major."

When betrayal enters the soul, the heart explodes.

Craig almost talked himself out of his outrage, out of his exploding heart. He unpacked his bags, ate dinner, and turned in early. But when he came home from work the next afternoon, he could contain his rage no longer. "If you don't get out of here, I'll kill you. I swear it. How could you? How *could* you? Where'd you toss your morals so fast, huh? All your love for me just thrown out the window, huh? Is that it? You can't stand me no more and this is how you show it?" He tried to remain civil, but he felt as though all the blood in his body had turned to acid. He started shouting. "Seems like it was only yesterday you asked me about him and I *told* you he still made me uncomfortable, that I couldn't understand why you wanted to get with him again in the first place after our experience, and you promised you would talk to me *before* you got with him. It hasn't even been six months, not six months since I buried one grandmother and now my Granny is gone and you go and do this? And of all people you just had to pick *him*? What the hell happened to your morals, your ethics, your respect? What happened to 'That just wouldn't be right?' You're a liar. I hate you I hate you I hate you! How could you do this to us? I don't wanna see your lying face, you liar. You better get outta here I don't know who you are anymore I can't believe this I can't believe you you're a fraud I hate you you liar go to Gywnneth's she'll be glad to take you in I'm sure or go to I don't care where you go just get *out* go anywhere you liar liar *liar* just go to *hell!*" Craig threw framed pictures and books and shoes and half-full glasses. On his way out the front door, he shouted, "As far as I'm concerned you don't live here anymore and when I get back you better be *gone!*"

Job went to Gywnneth's and stayed for two weeks. One week after that, on the morning of Job and Craig's first wedding anniversary, Betsy called to tell Job that his brother, Gerrit, who'd battled an inoperable brain tumor for two years, had died.

"Help me," was the first thing out of his mouth when Gina picked up her cell phone.

"What's going on, Craig?"

"I need you to come here as soon as possible. Job just got on a plane to go to Holland. His brother died, and I want so badly to get him back for what he did to me when Granny died. But the energy is too messed up between us, and I don't wanna mess it up even more. But I will, I just know it. I don't trust myself right now, Gina. Please. Can you get out here? I swear to God, I'm about to lose it."

Gina was on the first available flight from General Mitchell International Airport.

3   It would be a long way back. For more than a year, Job and Craig walked on a plantation of eggshells. Like a bookkeeper keeping accounts of debts overdue, Job held onto silent resentments. Craig wouldn't put down his artillery or his armor. Soon, Job would turn forty, and Craig could hardly bring himself to care.

Job's family was coming to America. In Holland, birthdays are more celebrated than Christmas and the crown years, the birthdays ending in zero or five, are the ultimate milestones to be honored with huge gatherings of family and friends. Job missed one crown-year celebration of all his family members since moving to the United States in 1986. He would almost always go to Holland to be with his people on their special day. In addition to Betsy's seventy-fifth, Craig had attended Els' fortieth and Nelleke's husband's fiftieth. Job's mother, his three sisters, and his nieces and nephew had all planned to attend Job's fortieth. But a broken hip slow to recover kept his mother from coming. Els offered no compelling reason for not showing up; she simply changed her mind. Her daughter, Bianca, went to Spain instead. Matthijs, Nelleke's son, stayed home.

And so it was that Wilma, Nelleke, Job's niece, Eliza, and Marinka, a distant cousin from Eliza's father's side of the family, came to America for the big four O. Happy to see them all, Job was crushed that his mother was not with them.

THE QUEEN ELIZABETH VERSION

1 In the time it took for him to tell her, among other things, why he had brushed his art aside, Craig threw together a Cajun remoulade to dress the top of the crab cakes, which were nestled in the hearts of romaine. Around the croquettes, Craig arranged some mixed berries left over from the barbeque. Perfect timing. Job came rushing through the front door, apparently with less time for lunch than he had anticipated. "Every time I come in, even in the late afternoon, you two are sitting at the table, still wearing your lounge clothes, talking, talking, talking." He sat down immediately and inhaled his lunch. "Don't you ever get out and go anywhere?"

"We've been to the grocery store a few times," said Jennifer, laughing. "I'm getting to know my son. How else can I do that if we don't talk? I'm in no big hurry to see Boston. But I promise you, next time I visit we'll get out of here. I might be able to come back for Memorial Day weekend and do something touristy. I really wanna see Harvard, see all its history, see where my son went to school, but that's not gonna happen today. I have to start packing soon. You know I'm leaving later this afternoon."

"Oh, that's right. I completely forgot." After he swallowed his last bite, Job rose and gave Jennifer a hug. "Have a safe trip and we'll see you again soon." He turned to Craig. "Thanks for the lunch, honey. It was good." He kissed his husband on the forehead. "I'm outta here."

The next morning, Betsy and Rinus awoke early and went for a walk. Right before he left for work, Job stood in the guest room doorway and asked Craig, who lay in bed, to do him a big favor. "What? Are you kidding me? Whoa, whoa, whoa. Wait a minute," said Craig in his hoarse, early-morning drawl. He got out of bed, rubbed the sleep from his eyes, and took a long look at the man standing in the doorway as though he were some stranger come to call. "Your mother asked Rinus to ask you to ask me to do *what?*"

"It's not that big a deal, Craig. She'd do it herself, but she can't climb the basement steps because of her hip."

"Job, has your mother said something to you about me?"

"Not really."

"Not really? What did she say, Job? Don't mess with me."

"Well, when you got back from the airport yesterday and took a nap, I was downstairs folding the laundry and she asked me why I had to go out and work all day and still come home and fold the laundry while you're upstairs sleeping?"

"I sure hope you told her it was the first time you raised a finger to fold a single piece of laundry in months." Craig began quietly, civilly. But as he went on, his voice rose in pitch and power. "I also hope you told her that I'm the one who thoroughly cleaned and deodorized this whole house, washed, dried, and pressed the sheets, and made the bed better than a hotel chambermaid so she could be comfortable in *our* bed while we slept in the guest room."

"When your parents visit, they sleep in our bed, too."

"Don't even go there, Job. That's not the point. Besides, my mother would never ask you, under any circumstances, to wash her underwear."

"Well, I told Ma that my folding the laundry was no big deal."

"No big deal? Wait a minute. Why are you even telling me this? And don't say it's because I asked. Lord knows I ask you to tell me lots of things you refuse to tell me. Is what she said how *you* really feel? If so, you better own it. And who the hell does she think she is anyway? Queen Elizabeth? Where does she get off being a guest in *my* house and have the audacity to question my contribution to the chores around here? Oh yeah, that's right; it's not really my house, is it? It's only *your* house, and I'm just—who does she think I am, Hattie McDaniel in GONE WITH THE WIND? I can't even remember the last time I slept, and in case both of you have forgotten, I've just been on quite a ride. If I need to sleep all day, everyday, for the next month, that's exactly what I'm gonna do. And anybody who don't like it— well, that's just too bad."

"I went on that trip with you—"

"Well, pardon me for not being sensitive to *your* feelings, dear. I'm way too pissed off right now for any of that. And in case you *also* forgot, I'm the one who got fired from his job for some racist, homophobic mess just before you went on that trip with me. That you would even stand there holding a bag of your mothers dirty drawers and ask *me* to wash them knowing full well what she said to you yesterday about the laundry makes me wanna *scream*"—and so he did—"and now I know why she felt she had the right to have her boyfriend ask her son to ask his maid to wash her drawers. Talking about she would have done it herself, but because of her poor, poor hip she couldn't go up and down the stairs. She didn't seem to have a problem getting up the stairs to go to bed last night, or the night before that, or the night before *that*. Now all of a sudden she can't climb the damn stairs? What in hell has gotten into her? Job, c'mon, man, come *on*, can't you see what she's doing? I swear to God, man, your mother is out of her mind and if you don't talk to her, I will."

Craig slammed the door. He heard the tissue-paper sound of plastic hitting the floor and moments later, the squeak and bang of the front door opening and closing. Craig stayed in the guestroom with the door closed all day. He didn't eat, drink, or go to the bathroom. When Job returned from work early that afternoon, Betsy's undergarments remained in the plastic bag in front of the door, exactly where he'd left them.

2 Two days later, just after dinner, Craig was standing over the kitchen sink when a pain knifed through the middle of his chest. When he laid his right hand where the pain was, he could feel his heart beating so fast it shocked him. Minutes earlier, Craig and Job had exchanged more words about his mother and Job slammed down the coffee pot from which he was about to pour his mother a cup and left the house. Craig had no idea where he'd gone and he wasn't answering his cell phone. Craig called Joseph next door to come over right away and drive him to the emergency room.

By the time Job got Joseph's message and drove to Beth Israel Deaconess Hospital, Craig's heart rate had slowed to 104 beats per minute—still too fast—and the pain was gone. Job called Jennifer to tell her about Craig's heart, to tell her that he thought they were both going way too fast, trying to flesh out too much, too fast. He even suggested, almost ordered, that she not come back for Memorial Day, but at another time, perhaps a little later in the summer. What he heard shocked Craig more than his fast, fast heartbeat. Job was telling someone—directly, no less—what he thought, what he felt. Practically told her to do something different than what she had already expressed an interest in doing. What drugs had he ingested? What was it about Jennifer that invited such uncharacteristic bluntness?

✍

Two days later, Betsy and Rinus went back to Holland. Before she unpacked her bags, Craig had no doubt, Betsy wrote an email to Job telling him what a horrible time she had and how badly Craig had ruined her visit. How Craig hadn't allowed her to spend any time with her son. How Craig must have planned his hospital emergency on the one night she had planned to go see a movie with Job just to keep her and her son apart. How Craig had hardly anything to say to her, making her feel so unwelcome. An expert fisher, Betsy hooked the bait, cast the line all the way across the Atlantic Ocean, and like a starving little scrod, Job bit. He became convinced that Craig had actually *done* something to her. Each day for the next few, Nelleke, Job's oldest sister, called him and sent at least one email. Nelleke called Job once every six months, if that, and sent an email only if she had some news about her grown children to report. Each day for the next few, Job grew more ornery, more distant from Craig. The farther away he grew, the more he smoked.

Sure enough, it was beginning to be revealed. Soon, Craig would have to send his own missive to the queen and her minions across the ocean.

VERITAS

1630-1930
CAMBRIDGE

LOCATION CHOSEN IN 1630 TO BE THE CAPITAL OF THE MASSACHUSETTS BAY COLONY. SETTLED IN 1631 UNDER LEADERSHIP OF THOMAS DUDLEY AND CALLED NEW TOWN. THE COLLEGE ORDERED TO BE HERE, 1637. NAME CHANGED TO CAMBRIDGE AFTER THE ENGLISH UNIVERSITY TOWN, 1638.
MASSACHUSETTS BAY COLONY
TERCENTENARY COMMISSION

---

1 It was May 29, 2001, the day after Memorial Day. Exams were over, the halls were empty. The only students left on campus were the dormitory cleanup crew and those awaiting their commencement exercises in just over a week. The main event would take place on the steps of Memorial Church, where Jennifer and Craig now sat, looking across the Yard at Craig's favorite Harvard building. "I'm tired," said Craig, sighing. "I feel like a member of the Crimson Key Society."

It had been a long, long day that included a moment a long time coming. Jennifer and Craig had arrived in Harvard Square at nine o'clock that morning. Harvard Square's original 1630 street plan, all labyrinth and meander, has survived almost intact. The Cambridge Common, where animals once grazed and Cantabrigians once voted, remains as a park. Across Garden Street, the steeple on the First Parish in Cambridge pointed up to a cross at the top. Every time Craig visited Harvard Square, he was astounded at the absence of The Tasty, an all-night, greasy spoon diner. The place was as small as a large closet with a tiled floor and stationary round stools lined along a counter that stretched from the entrance to the back. Posters hung on the walls proclaiming it older than Harvard itself. In the mid-nineties, The Tasty was replaced on the corner of JFK and Brattle streets by a high-end chain clothing store. Back when Craig attended Harvard, he and his friends had spent many a sunrise there gobbling steak fries and tuna melts, onion rings and greasy double cheeseburgers.

The atmosphere around Harvard radiated a certain splendor even when clouds loomed above. However, on this long, long day, the hundred-seventy-five-foot white spire of Memorial Church broke clean through the giant elms against a clear sky and glimmered in sunlight. Craig's Parking Fairy, as he had come to call his good luck finding a place to park in high-traffic areas, provided a spot on Brattle Street, across from the Loeb drama center, home of the American Repertory Theater. Craig and Jennifer walked down Story Street almost to the end where Craig pointed out the boarding house run by Harriet Ann Jacobs from 1873 to 1876. "Harriet was a runaway slave who wrote INCIDENTS IN THE LIFE OF A SLAVE GIRL after she freed herself by hiding out for seven years and eventually reaching New York," said Craig. "It was one of the first books we read in my black women writers class during my freshman year." Craig walked them to the end of the street where he pointed out the Charles Hotel, the top of which could be seen across Mt. Auburn Street. "That's where I waited tables at the Bennett Street Café throughout most of college and for a year after. Lots of celebrities who didn't want to deal with the congestion of Boston would stay there. I waited on the likes of Vincent Price, Jane Fonda and Ted Turner, Debra Winger, Michele Pfeifer, Jack Nicholson, Susan Sarandon, and Maya Angelou. I waited on John Kennedy Junior a few times, and my most vivid memory of him is that every time I saw him, he had a cast on one of his feet. I believe he had a cast on his foot or had just come out of one when his plane went down." Craig and Jennifer backtracked down Story Street, crossed Brattle, and headed up Church Street, passing by the Harvard Square Theater on the right. At the end of the street on the left stood the First Parish in Cambridge. Built in 1833, First Parish held Harvard commencement ceremonies until 1873. The first Meeting House of the First Church in Cambridge, an earlier incarnation of First Parish, held the sessions of the General Court of Massachusetts, which ordered the founding of Harvard College in 1636. Next to the church and directly across Massachusetts Avenue from Johnston Gate, the main entrance to Harvard Yard, was an ancient cemetery. A light-blue oval plaque, which marked sites of historical interest around all of Greater Boston, was affixed to the wrought-iron gate. It read:

OLD BURYING GROUND
BURIAL PLACE OF EARLY SETTLERS
TORY LANDOWNERS AND SLAVES
SOLDIERS · PRESIDENTS OF HARVARD
AND PROMINENT MEN OF CAMBRIDGE
1635

The late spring light illuminated the slate headstones, many engraved with Puritan-influenced skull and bones. Craig directed Jennifer's attention to the headstone that marked the grave of an early Cambridge girl:

> HERE LIES THE BODY OF CICELY, NEGRO
> LATE SERVANT TO WILLIAM BRATTLE
> SHE DIED APRIL 8, 1714
> BEING 13 YEARS OLD

After they viewed all of the headstones, they crossed the street commonly called Mass Ave. Erected on an island in the middle of the avenue, was a giant statue of William Sumner, seated. It was the work of Anne Whitney, one of America's most distinguished sculptors. At the age of sixty-seven, she won first place in a competition for her memorial to William Sumner. But when the judges discovered the winner was a woman, they denied her the commission, even though Whitney had already won, years earlier, a commission for the statue of Samuel Adams, which the Commonwealth of Massachusetts contributed to the national capitol building. Using her own resources and the donations of friends, Whitney completed the Sumner memorial when she was eighty and donated it to the City of Cambridge. When they walked by the statue, Craig said, "The same artist who sculpted this statue sculpted a statue of Leif of Norway that stands in one of my favorite parks in Milwaukee."

"Then you'll have to show it to me when we go to Milwaukee, son." They walked into Johnston Gate, the oldest of the gates built into the iron fence enclosing the entire Yard. The gate was the first Harvard structure to use handmade and wood-burned Harvard Brick to resemble the brick used in earlier buildings. Craig walked Jennifer by Massachusetts Hall, the oldest building on campus, to Straus Hall, the first dormitory on the right that bordered Massachusetts Avenue. "Most of the freshmen live in the Yard and this was where I lived," said Craig. "Straus D-32 up on the third floor. My room overlooked Harvard Square."

"How many roommates did you have?"

"Three. Jeremy, the Jewish boy from Philadelphia who thought he was a Beastie Boy, was excited about the prospect that his one black roommate would love rap music as much as he did. To his disappointment I broke the news that I didn't like it much at all. My father thought he was the funniest one. Ray was a hippie-type from South Africa by way of Northampton, Massachusetts, the state's granola capital. He was totally allergic to the concept of bathing. Our whole dorm room was always musty with Dave's funk, and I'm *not* talking about music. Daniel, my bunkmate, was a reserved Jewish intellectual from Montreal who drank red wine or white wine or pink wine twenty-four-seven. Daniel used to steal my quarters off the dresser. I guess he didn't think I'd notice because I kept so many. One time when he was drunk, I got him to admit it and he paid them all back to me in dollar bills."

They walked past Weld Hall, which stood parallel to Straus and close enough to form a courtyard with it, and into the first open part of the Yard called the Old Yard, a long, rectangular lawn with crisscrossing footpaths. Colorful tents covered the lawn in the Yard between Thayer Hall and Weld Hall. People had gathered—apparently some had slept over in the tents—for rallies and demonstrations to get Harvard to support a living wage for its employees. "Daddy Hazelle brought you to Harvard, son?" asked Jennifer.

"That's Harvard Hall," said Craig, pointing to the first building to the right of Johnston Gate, facing it. "I took my favorite government class there. It was a political theory course taught by Harvey Mansfield. But yes, my father came with me. Since he doesn't fly, we took the train. My back hurt so bad after we got off that Amtrak, I told myself I'd never travel by train again. When we got to Boston, he rented a car for the trip over to Cambridge. Within five minutes of driving amidst bats-out-of-hell drivers down streets with medieval angles that could turn, with no notice, into one-way streets right in front of you, he gave me the wheel. I just did what I'd heard someone say about driving in Boston the first time I came here for Model United Nations while I was still in high school: turn your rearview mirror up and don't bother using the side ones." They arrived in front of Holden Chapel. "This is the chapel where my friend Dawn and I decided to start the Callbacks, a co-ed *a capella* singing group. A *capella* groups were all the rage in college. They have a long tradition in the campus life of many colleges. The first one was formed at Yale in the early nineteen hundreds. It was an all-guy group called the Whiffenpoofs. Anyway, Dawn and I had tried out for almost every singing group, but were rejected. I even auditioned for the Glee Club and she for the Radcliffe Choral society. Since we had the high voices both groups needed at the time, we where sure we'd at least get into the bigger choral groups. No such luck. So we stood right here late some evening looking at lists that didn't include either of our names and decided we would start our own group. And we did. And since we had made it to lots of callbacks, that's what we decided to call our group. As it turned out, all the members of that first group had made it to the callbacks for other groups, but didn't get accepted. The Callbacks are still going strong. In fact, they've become one of the premier groups a lot of the undergraduates wanna get into before any of the others. I still come to their concerts every now and then. In fact, the weekend I went to Milwaukee and found all of you, I missed our fifteenth-anniversary concert."

"Then you must've really needed to come and find me, son. The Lord knew the timing was right."

"They actually celebrated the anniversary a semester too early and I wasn't terribly happy about that. I'm sure they had a reason, but I can't remember what it was." Craig wanted to go to the statue of John Harvard in front of University Hall, but a tour group stood around it, so they cut across the Yard, passing by Matthews Hall on the left, and walked toward the Science Center instead. "We wouldn't have turned fifteen until the semester coming up and I consider it bad energy to celebrate any anniversary before it actually happens. I've never even celebrated my own birthday before the eighth."

Between the Yard and the Science Center, Craig pointed at a patch of lawn that stretched toward a building that looked like a huge cathedral. "That's where the Callbacks now sing all their concerts, but it was tough to convince the dean of students in my junior year that our group should be given the opportunity to sing there. The year I arrived, Harvard was celebrating its three-hundred-fiftieth anniversary. That whole lawn area was covered with a huge tent and the black-tie anniversary ball was held there. I was completely overwhelmed by all the pomp and circumstance. I couldn't believe I entered Harvard during such a milestone year. It was quite the momentous occasion to take part in." He turned their attention to the Science Center. "If you look closely, you can see that the Science Center was designed to look like a camera."

"It sure does, son. I can see that. What's that beautiful building with all the columns over there? Is that the big library?" Jennifer pointed to a building that looked as though it could be near the Mall at the nation's capital.

"No. That's the Littauer Center for Public Administration. That's where the government and economics departments are."

"Let's go there next. I wanna see the department where you got your degree."

"Nothing special about the gov department, but, if you wanna see it, let's go."

In the basement level of Littauer where the government department offices were located, Jennifer walked around the department's lobby area and then through the graduate student cubbies as if she were looking for something. "Did you have any classes in this building?"

"No. Wait a minute. Yes I did. Up on the second floor, I had my junior tutorial. Religion and politics in the Middle East. Worst class I ever took. Not because of the subject matter, but because the tutor who taught it accused me of plagiarizing my final paper."

"Oh, mercy."

"Exactly. I knew he didn't have a case. Maybe he thought I plagiarized it because he couldn't bring himself to believe that I could've written it. I don't know. He never even showed me exactly where in my paper the alleged crime occurred, but I wasn't about to go before the Ad Board. I had heard too many horror stories about that. If he'd taken me in front of the Ad Board and they found me guilty, I would have been suspended for a year or expelled. I thought to take my chances, but I also knew that if I got suspended, I never would've come back and finished. Besides, my parents had already booked their train tickets for Junior Parents' Weekend the next semester and I certainly didn't wanna chance ruining that."

"So what happened?"

"He gave me two choices. He would fail me or I could write another paper on a topic he chose for me. I had to photocopy every single page of research material and highlight in the text of my paper *and* on the copy of the research all the direct quotes that I included and anything that I had paraphrased. If you wanna get a degree in a field of concentration, you have to get better than a C minus on all required courses or you could only get a degree in general studies. So, I completed his little exercise in I don't know what and got a C minus."

"Were you the only black in the class?"

"Yes. At least I was the only one who looked black."

"He must've been racist."

"Perhaps, but he didn't like me from day one. My gut told me to transfer to another tutorial, but I didn't listen to it and I paid the price. He always put me on the spot, so I never had much to say in class just to spite him, even though participation in class discussion was part of your grade."

"I'm proud of you, son. Proud that you could get through that and finish and still get your degree with honors."

As they left the building, Craig took a picture of Jennifer standing in front of the columns and then she took one of him. She asked a woman coming up the steps to take a picture of them both. After the photo session, they walked over to the entrance to Paine Hall, but before they went inside, Jennifer wanted to sit down. "Let's just sit here for a minute out in the sun on this beautiful day, son." And so they did.

Jennifer wept.

Moments after they sat down, Craig watched in awe as Jennifer wept, and wept, and wept. She who had not shed a tear when her firstborn came walking through her door; she who had rifled through the pages and pages of her son's adoption papers and uttered no words; she whose mother told her on the day she got into her son's car to travel north—that her sire, an abomination before the Lord, was exactly what she deserved for spreading her legs before wedlock—and made not a sound. Now—all of a sudden, all at once—before the sun, her sire, and the strangers passing by, her floodgates split open, her walls came tumbling down.

And Jennifer wept.

"I just didn't know that you would've gone through so much pain," she moaned—through her tears, through her heaves—to the sun, she moaned, "so much pain, so much pain, I never would've thought that you would've gone through so much *pain*, and I wasn't there for you, son, and I'm so sorry, son, and, Lord, what do you want from me, Lord, what do you want, what do you want from me, Lord, what do you want from me, Lord?"

Craig could not speak. What could or should he do? Jennifer threw back her head, the sunlight anointed her face. Craig said nothing and watched as all of it—the light, the tears, the snot—dripped from her face, slid down her chin, and drenched the collar of the navy-blue dress she wore.

After what seemed to Craig to be a long, long time and a long time coming, her tears dried, her heaves returned to breaths. Jennifer reached into her small leather purse and retrieved a clump of tissue, a compact, and an eye pencil. Like an actress between scenes, she swiftly completed the reassembling. "There," she sighed, smoothing back and shaking out her henna-rinsed hair. "I'm ready to see the rest now."

They walked through Paine Hall, where the Callbacks sang their first concert. The concert hall was closed, but Craig found the custodian, who just happened to have a wife, who just happened to be adopted, who just happened to be searching for her birth mother. The custodian gladly opened the hall and told them they could spend as much time there as they wanted. And so they did. Afterwards, they walked through the music department, entered the Science Center from the back, and went to the Greenhouse Café for lunch.

"This was where I used to buy chocolate-chip cookies almost every day," said Craig, enjoying the one he was eating.

Jennifer finished her veggie roll-up and sipped on her Dasani. "Tell your mother about Harvard, son. The experience, I mean. Seeing all these beautiful buildings is great and everything but I want you to tell your mother how it *was*."

"As I've often said, Harvard was the place that cracked whatever illusions I still had about life."

"How so?"

"You have to stand on your own two feet, there's no other way to look at it. You had to advocate for yourself, you had to fight for yourself. It was not the space for the weak of spirit, let me tell you. It was so competitive and I don't mean academically either. I'm talking about all the extracurriculars, all the social activities. You had to comp—as in compete—to give campus tours. You had to comp to write for the papers, you had to comp for everything, and either you could handle it or you couldn't. And a lot of people couldn't. I couldn't for the first six months. Many students ended up in mental health and the infirmary. The wealthiest students went to McLean's for a stint. I had to go back to Milwaukee a week before Thanksgiving for a weekend because I felt anxious all the time."

"What was the problem?"

"I'm not sure, really. I've read that people who are adopted can have a hard time being away from home for long periods of time. I don't know if that's what was going on or not, but I was completely overwhelmed. I didn't feel like I really belonged. But when I got back, I figured I had to kick in and learn how to do this, so I started competing. And that's why I started a singing group because I was sick of the rejections. And that's where I focused ninety percent of my energy for three-and-a-half years. Not in academics, because, quiet as it's kept, that's not why anyone really went to Harvard."

"Why didn't you feel like you belonged, son?"

"Many of the black students seemed like they were trying to pass. Not the way those of mixed-race would pass a hundred years ago, but in a way that could only be possible in this era. The thing I didn't like at Harvard—and this is that whole divide and conquer thing we've been doing to ourselves for years—was that so many black folk seemed to reject their blackness and stay away from anyone or anything with color. And I wasn't mature enough to accept that. And then, there was a whole other group of militant wannabe black folk who called the self-rejecting folk Incognegros."

"Incognegros?" Jennifer laughed.

"That's what the wannabes called them. I didn't really wanna have anything to do with them, either. I knew that a lot of my friends were white, I had relations with white men, so I knew enough about myself to know: I couldn't go over here, I couldn't go over there, so I felt caught in the middle. I eventually met some black students that also weren't trying to identify with either of those groups and a few of us became friends. But, I don't know, I just didn't feel like I belonged. The Callbacks was the only place I felt like I fit. Maybe because I created them. I don't know. But they gave me a sense of grounding, I suppose. They, along with my friends Vicki and the two Ians, were my college family."

"Thank the Lord that you finally found your *real* family, son. Thank the Lord."

✍

Jennifer and Craig walked up to the building that looked like a huge cathedral. Hanging on the door to the entrance of Memorial Hall was a flyer announcing a film about adoption that was screening at the Harvard Film

Archives just around the corner. Jennifer pointed out the flyer to Craig. They both looked at each other, but didn't say a word. They walked in. The Memorial Hall side was open; the Sanders Theater side, other than its huge, cavernous vestibule, was not. Under a dome of light filtering through a kaleidoscope of stained glass, Jennifer and Craig read the lists of names that covered the walls of the vestibule.

"Look here, son," said Jennifer, pointing to one of the engraved plaques under the year 1863. "This one here's from Marietta, Georgia. You remember that's the next town over from Roswell where I live? Take a picture of this one, son. I know your grandmother would like to see that."

After the Civil War, Harvard sanctioned a group of alumni who had petitioned the college to let them raise funds for a memorial to the Harvard graduates who had fought for the Union. The group suggested that the memorial take the form of a building, one that would commemorate those who died, as well as meet the college's needs for a theater and an alumni gathering place. Coincidentally, Charles Sanders had bequeathed to the College substantial funds for the purpose of erecting a hall or theater that could be used for many occasions: commencement, alumni reunions, exhibitions, and public literary, music, or celebratory events. The two projects were joined, each complementing the other.

Jennifer and Craig left Memorial Hall and Sanders Theater and walked back into the Yard. "Now, I'll take you into Memorial Church and show you where I sang in the choir."

"I thought you didn't make it into any of the choral groups."

"I didn't. Not until my sophomore year anyway. Dawn told me about University Choir. She said the auditions were rather straightforward and they were always looking for tenors. And on top of that, you got paid. I guess it was the only way to get the choir to church at eight o'clock every Sunday morning." Craig chuckled.

"You got paid to sing in the church choir?"

"Sure did. All the members of University Choir became employees of the University and received, I can't remember, something just above minimum wage for rehearsals and Sunday performances. I guess that makes me a professional singer after all." They laughed.

Craig walked her through the side door and into the choir loft, which was situated behind the altar, behind a thick, carved wooden screen. "That's where I sat." Craig pointed to the first row of pews on the right half of the loft. Jennifer sat in the pew where Craig sat every Sunday while classes were in session. She snapped a photograph of the organ pipes, giant towers that seemed to stretch up toward infinity. Then, Craig took her downstairs to show her the room where they used to rehearse. They walked back to the church offices, into where Craig had just seen the Reverend Peter Gomes walk minutes earlier. Craig asked the Reverend's secretary if he could introduce Jennifer to him, but she said that he'd just gone into a meeting. As Craig and Jennifer turned to go, Reverend Gomes emerged from the door behind the desk and came into the lobby for something, so Craig was able to introduce them after all. "He's an openly gay minister," said Craig, "who had the courage to pronounce out loud his love for men several years ago, God bless'm. He wrote THE GOOD BOOK, which, among other things, examines what the Bible *really* says about same-sex love." Jennifer didn't respond.

Upstairs, inside the church, Craig and Jennifer looked once again at walls of name after name, inscribed in marble, on each side of the church. Dedicated on Armistice Day 1932 in memory of those who died in World War I, Memorial Church was a gift of the alumni to the University. Since then, memorials had been added to remember those students or alumni who died in World War II, the Korean War, and the Vietnam War. After Jennifer and Craig took an entire film roll of pictures from every angle of the main floor and balcony with each of them in the photographs, Craig said, "Now we can go see where I graduated." They walked around to the side of the church that faces Craig's favorite Harvard building. There, they sat down on the steps.

✍

"What's the Crimson Key Society, son?"

"A group at Harvard that gives campus tours and runs freshman orientation and ushers commencement services and other hosting-like activities. They act as the college hospitality committee."

"Were you ever a member?"

"No, I drew the line. I refused to comp for a group that gave campus tours. But I can't remember them back in my day telling us that Widener Library, that big old beautiful piece of building standing right there, was designed by a black man."

The Harry Elkins Widener Memorial Library is the second largest library in the world after the Library of Congress. Built in 1915 with a gift from Eleanor Elkins Widener, it stands as a memorial to her son, Harry, who graduated in 1907, a book lover who died on the Titanic. Widener selected architect Julian F. Abele, chief designer of the firm, Horace Trumbauer & Associates of Philadelphia, to design it. Abele had studied at the Institute for Colored Youth before entering the University of Pennsylvania in 1898. He was the first black to graduate from the Pennsylvania School of Fine Arts and Architecture in 1904. Trumbauer invited Abele to join his firm and sent him to Paris to study at L'Ecole des Beaux Arts. By 1908 Abele became chief designer.

"So this is where you graduated?"

"Right here, indeed. Thousands and thousands of chairs are lined from University Hall to Sever Hall. A huge black and crimson tent hovers above here just in case it rains. They call this the Tercentenary Theatre, which used to be the New Yard. It'll be eleven years in June. The year I graduated, Ella Fitzgerald received her honorary doctorate. My father almost had a heart attack. When she came up here to receive it, a lot of people chanted for her to sing. I have a picture at home with her and my family and me that I got somebody walking by to take of us. Remind me to show it to you when we get home."

They crossed the Yard and walked up the steps to the main entrance of Widener. When they tried to get in, the woman sitting behind the entrance podium asked to see a Harvard identification card. "I don't have one anymore," said Craig.

"You an alumnus?"

"Yes."

"Well, then you can apply for an ID for unlimited use of the library, but you can't get in without an ID."

"I thought you only needed an ID to get into the stacks. Tourists can't even get in anymore?"

"Not anymore."

"Wow. When did that change?"

"A few years ago. Around the time when all the renovations started, I think."

"Ah. I see. And you can't make any exceptions, not even for my long lost birth mother whom I found just last month and who missed all of this?"

The woman's face said, Yeah, right. Nice try. "I'm afraid not."

"Oh, well." They walked back out onto the steps. "Sorry. I wish you could've seen inside. I can't even begin to describe what it looks like. But it feels so big and so grand. So *old*. It's not even a hundred years old yet but it feels ancient."

"Well, son, you're just gonna have to apply for your ID and bring me back someday. That's all. Get someone to take a picture of us in front of these big columns."

He did what she told him.

Just as well they couldn't get in. Craig was ready for a nap. Before they departed, Craig took a few pictures of Jennifer standing by the John Harvard statue in front of University Hall.

They drove down Massachusetts Avenue toward Boston. Just before they passed Cambridge City Hall on the left, Craig pointed out the tall, gray concrete building on the right where he lived for almost a year after college. They drove through Central Square and a few blocks down on the right, Craig pointed out The Paradise, the bar where Craig played pool during college. Just before crossing the Charles River into Boston, Craig pointed out the Massachusetts Institute of Technology on the left. "That's a place I'm sure your sister, Burundi, would like to see given her interest in the sciences," said Jennifer. "And speaking of which: when are you gonna meet your sister? Son, I want all my children to get to know one another, so you need to meet Burundi soon. I also think it's time that we go to Milwaukee. If you felt like a tour guide today, son, just wait until you see how you feel when we go to Milwaukee and you show me your life there."

"That'll be intense."

"I know it will, son. But it's time, son. It's time. I was thinking that maybe at the end of next month, you could come down to Atlanta and meet Burundi. I don't think Rwanda will be able to make it there from Barbados, but we'll see. If she can, it could be the first time in my life that I have all my children together. After that, you and I could head straight to Milwaukee and celebrate the Fourth of July with your family. There's a lot I wanna talk to you about, but only when we get to Milwaukee."

"We talk about so much now. What can't we talk about here that we can only talk about in Milwaukee?"

"You'll see, son. I promise you it's nothing bad, but I don't wanna talk about it until we get to Milwaukee. I wanna see where and how you grew up first."

Now Craig was intrigued. He hadn't planned on taking her to Milwaukee to meet his parents and sister any time soon. He feared his mother wouldn't be ready for all of that. He wasn't even sure that he was, quite frankly. But Jennifer had hooked his attention. After she returned to Roswell the next day, he would ask her in email after email what it was she wanted to talk about. But she always had the same reply: "Wait till we get to Milwaukee, son."

And so he waited.

EVA NAOMI'S ROOM

1 Every single thing about Burundi was enjoined by perfunctoriness. Her eyes. Her smile. Her voice. The way she moved her mouth when she mumbled. Which was each and every time she moved her mouth to speak. Her gait. The dim, cool light coming from the heart of her. Jennifer had described her as the only one of her daughters who had an hourglass figure. That Jennifer could say that of all her children, Craig was most like Burundi, struck Craig, now that he'd laid eyes on her, as inane. There must be more (mustn't there?) but in her case, there didn't seem to be more to her than met his eye. And there were many, many hours in that glass.

A moment after he met her, Craig was already ready to move on to Milwaukee. But he and Jennifer weren't scheduled to make that trip for another two days. By then, Burundi and her husband, Zion, would have driven back to Fort Worth and Job would have flown home to Boston. By then, the five of them would have piled into Burundi's car and visited England in the back of the house on Ella Lane. By then, Craig, alone, would have gone upstairs in the front of the house to listen to Joshua, an uncle eager to tell his nephew a side of the story Craig could not have heard from anyone else.

But now, the five of them traveled the two hundred miles to Huntsville where Burundi introduced Craig and Job to Zion's parents over a Sunday dinner. After a meal that featured a meatless meatloaf, the five of them traveled around the corner to see Eva Naomi. A small woman with close-cropped hair that showed off her perfectly round head, Eva Naomi wasn't expecting them but she was mighty happy to see them. She welcomed the five of them into her small bungalow, which seemed to Craig no bigger than a big room. "Look closely, Eva," said Jennifer before she introduced Craig to her. "Do you know who this is?"

Eva squinted and looked at him. "Well, no, I don't think so, but he does look familiar."

"This is Joseph."

"Well hello, Joseph."

"This is my and Frank's son."

Eva's jaw dropped, her eyes bulged, and her face solidified quicker than candle wax drooling from a guttering flame. Quicker than that—it cracked. Her tears came, wetting her molasses-colored skin. "Come *here*, baby," she said and reached out her arms. Eva and Craig embraced.

"I wish you had your video camera," Jennifer said to Job, "I would love to see that look on her face again."

While Job went to retrieve the video camera from the car, Jennifer introduced her daughter and son-in-law to Eva. Four of the guests sat down on Eva's two sofas, Craig on a chair next to the sofa where Eva and Jennifer sat. Craig began telling Eva the story of how he found them all. Job returned, aiming the camera at Eva.

"Don't you dare take no picture of me sitting up in here slinging snot," Eva ordered in a singsong voice that sounded like an elementary school teacher's. They all laughed.

"You should've seen how I looked when they found *me*," said Jennifer,

"You don't have to have nothing on but love," Craig said to Eva.

"Let me get another hug, child." Eva and Craig stood and she swallowed him once more in her arms. "This is just too much."

"I recognized you from your sixty-seven yearbook picture." Craig sat down on the couch between her and Jennifer. "You still look the same, Eva."

"If you don't turn that camera off, I'm gone whoop you."

"This is gonna be on Oprah one day," said Job, laughing.

"Better not be," said Eva, sniffling and drying her eyes with a napkin.

As Craig continued with the story, underscoring all the coincidences, which by now didn't seem like coincidences at all, Eva kept shaking her head and saying, "Get outta here," and, "You've got to be kidding me." Burundi and Zion sat quietly on the other couch, not even bothering to feign interest in a story they had already heard several times by now.

Eva sat up, looked at Jennifer, at Craig, then back at Jennifer, and said, "And you know, yall look just alike. That is *your* child, Jennifer."

"As soon as we saw her picture in the yearbook, we knew it was her," said Job from behind the camera.

"And who are you?"

"I'm his better half."

"You're his better half?" She let the coin drop. "Good. Congratulations." Eva turned back to Craig and slapped him on the thigh. "*Baby*. How old are you?"

"Thirty-three."

"Has it been that long? It has been hasn't it?"

"Eva's the only person that I called, the only one that I told," said Jennifer. "She was the one who had to call Frank and tell Frank because I wasn't able to find out where he was and I knew Eva would know."

"I met him, too," said Craig.

"Did you?"

"Uh huh. Earlier this month, Job and I went down to Miami for a little vacation, but flew in and out of Ft. Lauderdale. When we flew back on Father's Day, I called Frank and he met us at the airport."

"What's he doing?"

"Farming, selling herbs—the medicinal kind—doing production management for some small bands and raising collard greens and melons and sweet potatoes and okra. And he works at a liquor store. And he drinks. Says he wakes up at six in the morning slides a few cocktails down his throat and heads out to the fields." They laughed. "He has a wife. His father lives with him, and his brother Bernard does as well from time to time."

"He and Verita got divorced," said Jennifer.

"I didn't know that," said Eva.

"I didn't either. But he's been remarried and has, how many kids, son?"

"He doesn't know. At least eleven, including me. Nine boys and two girls. Most of the boys are between the ages of thirty and thirty-four, so he was pretty busy for those four years."

"What's he trying to have, a coupla basketball teams or something?" They cackled. Then Eva sighed, "I feel like I'm gone faint. This is a miracle."

"Unreal but *for* real," said Jennifer.

"I'm scared to do that myself."

"Do what?" asked Craig.

"Seek my folks. I was raised in an orphanage and the woman who ran the orphanage ended up adopting me. But I haven't done anything about finding my folks. I don't know."

"I didn't know that." Craig looked at Jennifer. "You didn't tell me that your best friend from Oakwood was adopted."

"I didn't know either."

"My daughter wants to do it," Eva continued, "she would like to know her genealogy, but these searches can be expensive so I told her let's put our money somewhere else. If the Lord wants me to find this out, it'll happen." She turned her attention to Burundi and Zion. "Now how long have yall been married?"

"Two years in August," said Burundi.

"Yall happy?"

"Yes."

"Any children?"

"Not yet."

"Not now. That's right. Yall need a few more years to enjoy each other first." Eva looked and pointed at Job and Craig. "And how about you two? Yall doing good?"

"We've known each other for twelve years now, be married three years in August," said Job.

"Good. Yall take care of each other now, ya hear? Stay together." Eva dropped her face into her left hand and shook her head. "Lord have mercy on my soul." She raised her head. "What are yall doing here anyway?"

"Visiting my in-laws," said Burundi. "Zion's parents live right around the corner and we had dinner there tonight."

"You probably know his father, Eva. He used to be president of the central states region of the Adventist church back when it was still called central states. I don't know if he was around Oakwood back when we attended, but you probably would know him if you saw him. But we've been making the rounds. We'll be in Atlanta for a few more days and then Joseph and I go to Milwaukee to meet his parents."

"Where's your daughter?" asked Craig.

"She's at a wedding," said Eva. "She's in her friend's wedding. Her pictures are over there on the wall."

Craig rose and looked at two walls lined with framed portraits of a girl with stunning beauty. "Wow. This is your daughter?

"You better get your eyes offa her and put'm somewhere else," Eva said. "She ain't legal yet." They laughed.

"Hey, beauty is beauty. She's a covergirl. If not, she oughtta be."

"Eva was truly blessed because she thought she was never gonna be able to have any children," said Jennifer.

"I thought people were legal at twelve in Alabama," said Job, sarcastically, and a bit too late for anyone to get the joke.

"What did you say? You know I didn't hug you, honey." Eva rose from the couch. "C'mere and lemme give you a hug." Eva and Job embraced. She turned her attention back to Craig. "Lordy, I need to pour me a cocktail and then you can finish telling me how you got to her front door." They laughed. Eva didn't pour herself a cocktail, but she settled back into the sofa, into the story she still couldn't believe. Craig took her through the drive to Roswell, Sonja's plan, Jennifer's recognition and utterance of the name she had given him.

"You named him? I didn't know that." Eva shook her head at Jennifer.

"No, you didn't know that because I called you right after he was born."

"Did she cry?"

"No." Craig continued with the story. Zion struggled against sleep, so settled into the sofa he was, so full from his mother's healthy meatless dinner.

"How did you find your father?"

"Same way I found everybody else."

"Matter of fact," offered Jennifer, "on the second night when he met me, he called Frank and his wife Teresa picked up the phone and said Frank was occupied. So I told Joseph to give me the number and I called back and she told me the same thing—that he was tied up and sleeping or not available and I told her to tell him that is was important that I talk to him. I said, 'You just tell him that it's Jennifer White.'" She punctuated her name just as she had over the telephone.

"Lord have mercy, that man musta flew up outta his bed and snatched that phone outta her hands," said Eva. She and Jennifer shared a shrieking laugh.

"And I said, 'Hi, Dad.' He paused and asked me how I found everyone, gave me a quick update on the family, and told me that whatever happened wasn't my fault. In fact, he said he tried to get Verita to adopt me but I was already in the system. So has Jennifer told you why she named me?"

"No, we haven't really talked since then."

"I told you, son, after it happened I never talked to anyone about you. I just kept it in my heart. Eva wouldn't know."

"I've thought about you from time to time." Eva sat forward again and looked past Craig to Jennifer. "I've wondered about your son, too, but the few times we talked, girl, I thought, naw, uh uh, maybe that's a wound she don't wanna be opening, so I just left it."

Jennifer told Eva why she named him Joseph. Eva cried again.

Eva's covergirl daughter, Ariana, came back from the wedding and Eva introduced her. Then, after Eva asked, "Jennifer, isn't it funny how both the men we were in love with in college married other women?" they caught up on their former loves current lives, on what happened to a girl called City from their old high-school click. Her name was Frieda but they called her City, because she had the biggest breasts. And if there was a City, then Jennifer was Town, and Eva was Country because she had the smallest breasts. They talked about the apartment where Eva lived in sixty-seven, where Jennifer hid out after disappearing from summer classes when she discovered the baby in her belly. The apartment where her parents found her after the school had called them in Milwaukee to report her missing that summer. It was the first time, but not the last, that they would receive the missing-student call from their daughter's school.

The night Jennifer and Craig sat on the Chattahoochee, a few nights after he showed up on her doorstep, Jennifer told him about running away from Union College, an Adventist school in Lincoln, Nebraska. Pregnant again, this time she ran to Omaha, to the man then called Laurence, the father of the twins growing in her belly. When her parents finally found her there, her mother faced down Laurence and told him he was lucky she was a God-fearing Adventist because if she wasn't, she'd kill him. This time, Jennifer did not go with her mother back to Wisconsin. She stayed with the man who would become her only husband, the man that moved her to Tucson where Rwanda and Burundi were born.

Craig's thoughts came back from the river and he returned his attention to the stories Eva and Jennifer sent back and forth, back and forth over him, sitting on the couch in Eva's room. They shared laugh after laugh, update after update. Eva told Jennifer that she left the Adventist faith ten years ago; Burundi asked questions about the names of people she recognized in their stories; Job kept videotaping; Zion finally fell asleep. And then, out of nowhere, in response to no question, no request for clarification, Eva said it. She leaned forward, turned to her left, looked Jennifer squarely in the face, and said it. "Family is so important. Now you can go to your grave and not worry about it. You know your mother called my mother back in sixty-seven and asked her if she could take you into her orphanage in D.C. while you were pregnant. She sure did. But under the circumstances, you know, we being friends and all, my mother didn't think that was a good idea, so she told her she didn't have any room. But your mother definitely asked my mother about it. Yes she did."

Sitting between the two old friends, Craig felt the chill that moved back and forth, back and forth over him from both sides. How could this be so? Hadn't Jennifer said that her mother couldn't stand Eva, calling her the devil in disguise? Why would she then ask Eva's mother to take in her daughter? All the way out in Washington, D.C., no less? Wasn't Eva's mother somehow affiliated with the Adventist Church since she'd sent her daughter to Oakwood College? Wouldn't that defeat England's purpose of hiding her daughter's secret, keeping it out of the gossip-laden Adventist circle? And if it wasn't so, why would Eva tell her this now? In the middle of their chill, Craig came to realize he might not ever discover the answers, for he could bet his whole self that Jennifer would never confront her mother about the thing she'd just heard, to which she muttered, "No. I didn't know that," and then she cried. Softly, gently, she cried. Eva gave Jennifer a napkin to wipe her face. Burundi left her husband's side and squeezed between Craig and her mother, placing her arm around Jennifer and pulling her mother's head into her bosom. For what seemed a long time, no one spoke. Job turned off the camera.

"I think we need to go," said Craig, finally, "we still have to drive back to Dalton tonight."

But Eva wasn't finished. She wanted to tell more of a story it seemed likely she hadn't told to many, if any, and most definitely not Jennifer, about her and her sister's birth. About the big black limousine that picked them up when she was a little, little girl, and took her and her sister to a big house where a woman, whom she would later call Mama, also cared for other children who had no parents. About how she wondered growing up why and what for and how nobody could (or would) tell her where the mother who bore her might be; where her little sister, who left the big house when Eva was five, had gone. About how the woman called Mama had helped her try to locate her sister some years back but with no success. Somewhere during her story, Craig put his arm around Eva. When she finished, he offered to help her in any way he could should she ever decide to seek her people once more.

They rose from their seats, their stories, their pain, and their wonder. They said their so-nice-to-meet-yous and keep-in-touches and farewells and the five of them got in Burundi's car and began the silent drive back to Dalton. Sitting in the back seat between Burundi and Craig, Jennifer returned to her soft, gentle crying. "I can't believe it. My mother really wanted to get rid of me," her voice a whisper. Burundi reached her arm behind her mother's head to tap Craig's left shoulder. In the shifting expressions of her perfunctory face, illuminated by the light from the highway lamps that sliced across it, she told him to slide closer, why don't you, and put your arm around her, why don't you, and help comfort her already. Craig leaned his right elbow on the car door armrest, held his face in his hand, and looked, pensively, through the glass. Outside, night cloaked the hilly Alabama landscape. There wasn't a moon or a star in sight.

SECRETLY, THAT SUMMER

1 "It never even crossed my mind that we would be giving you away. Yes, you would be my nephew, but when you came home with us, you would be more like my little brother. Jennifer would go back to school, and I would help my mother take care of you. That's the way I thought it would be and I had quite a tantrum when it finally became clear to me that it wasn't gonna turn out that way." Joshua and his nephew are sitting in his second-floor playpen. Craig would bet money that this was the first room Joshua thought of when he drew up the blueprints for the house fifteen years ago. Reams of black felt line the walls of the huge room to absorb all the sounds Uncle Josh's toys are capable of making—huge floor-to-ceiling speakers connected to amplifiers, mixers, stereos, video players and more DVD players than you see on the shelves at Circuit City. A three-sided sectional couch opens in front of a giant-screen plasma television. Craig sits on a side of the couch where he can look at his uncle without turning his neck. Joshua sits at his desk, which is more like a cockpit, where he administers the computer network he has set up in his home, controls all the audio-visual equipment across the room, prepares Sabbath school lessons for his church around the corner, and searches the Internet for pictures of Halle Berry and pretty, pretty women with no clothes on.

Earlier, Joshua was screaming and hollering at his mother about any and everything and when Craig interrupted with, "Uncle Josh, I wanna talk to you," Josh answered, "It's not gonna help any," as though he thought Craig meant he wanted to talk to him about the nasty things he was saying to his mother. "No, no, I wanna talk to you about the past," Craig clarified.

"Oh, okay. It'll have to be later today because I'm going out of town tomorrow." Tomorrow, Craig will go to Huntsville to meet Burundi's in-laws. On the way back to Roswell, they will have to drive by Dalton and Craig was thinking *that* might be a good time to talk, since Joshua was so preoccupied with rage, but as it turned out, today was the best.

Joshua speaks with the cadence of an evangelist. Or a deejay. Stubborn as a child, his voice disobeys the felt-covered walls and reverberates anyway. Craig can feel it in his body. In a few hours, they will talk about their careers, about politics, about King David's relationship with Jonathan, Jesus' relationship with the disciple John, and about Joshua's thesis that agape between men can only become erotic if the devil enters and twists it. But right now Joshua is turning side to side in his chair while talking about 1967 because "Tell me about nineteen sixty-seven" was the first thing out of Craig's mouth when he sat down a minute ago.

"When I first found out that my sister was pregnant, I had absolutely no trouble at all believing it. From the time she was about twelve or thirteen, she was busy about the neighborhood, flirting with all the boys. If I saw it, surely my mother saw it, too. I'm sure my mother did whatever she could to discourage such behavior in Jennifer. But Jennifer has always done what Jennifer has wanted to do, especially if it went against what our mother wanted. And with sex, Jennifer could not be tamed. In fact, if you tell me you have trouble with sex, I would find that easy to believe. We all have had our problems with sex, and Jennifer was no exception.

"I stayed with my sister for most of that summer when she was pregnant with you. If she tells you she doesn't remember, it's because she was catatonic. Dead. Or, she may as well've been dead. That frozen look on her face sticks in my memory like good preaching.

"She could hardly do anything for herself. She got up; sat on the bed and stared out of the window all day; ate, read the Bible, and slept. That was about it. At the time, I didn't know what the plan was. Of course I knew she was pregnant, but I just thought she was in Madison to have the baby, and then we would take the newest member of our family home and that would be that. Not that anyone would know the baby was my sister's. I figured that was the whole point of my mother moving her away from home: so no one would know she was pregnant. But when the baby came home, it would still be *ours*, and we might make up some story that we adopted a child or were taking care of a child whose mother wasn't able to for whatever reason. But whatever story we would make up, the baby would be *ours*.

"It never once crossed my mind that we would give you away.

"I turned fourteen that summer and I was excited about having a baby around. I was the youngest, and I thought it would be nice if there were someone younger in the family who could look up to me. Jennifer and James were only a few years apart in age, but I came four years later, so I was somewhat on my own. Although being the youngest *and* a boy, I guess you could say I was closest to my mother. I would have to say that I gave my mother some of her best challenges. I challenged everything my mother told me. She'd say this had to be like that, or that had to be like this, and I'd ask, 'Why?' I had to figure out for myself the right and the wrong of it, and not just because she'd say, 'Because I said so' or 'Because I told you so.' I wanted to know how she came to her conclusions, whether or not her reasoning was sound, and whatever the case, even if I agreed with her, I would challenge her. Just for the sake of the challenge.

"I hate secrets. I've always hated secrets. And here we were making a secret out of this member of our family who wasn't even born yet. I always had a feeling when I was staying with my sister in Madison that you would be a boy. I don't know why I felt that, but I just did. And so I was rather excited about having a little nephew around, who would be more like a little brother to me. It didn't matter that my mother was so ashamed that her own daughter had actually gotten pregnant against her best efforts to raise a virgin. I wasn't gonna let my mother take that out on you. You were gonna be *my* little brother. Mine. All mine. James was going off to medical school and Jennifer would be finishing college and I wouldn't have to leave for Oakwood in quite a while.

"It never crossed my mind that we would be giving you away.

"I guess I could understand why my mother sent Jennifer away from Milwaukee where she could have the baby. No one in our church could know she was pregnant. In the Adventist circle, especially among the black churches, word spreads quickly since everybody knows everybody. A lot of people are connected through Oakwood College. Not wanting her business to circulate so quickly, my mother did what she had to do to keep her family's secret a secret, to keep the good White name intact. Shortly after my parents found Jennifer and brought her back from Huntsville, my mother made the arrangements, and they drove her to Madison.

"That summer stands out in my memory vividly even if my sister can't remember it, as traumatized as she was. She wasn't supposed to leave the room upstairs or be seen by anyone. The only time she could leave the house was on the Sabbath. Every Sabbath my mother and father came to Madison and took us to a nearby park where we had worship and a picnic. Jennifer wasn't able to go anywhere other than the park on the Sabbath with me and my parents.

"That summer left such an impression on me. I remember feeling the most pain I've ever felt in my life that summer, in that house. The owners were a black family who lived downstairs. I don't remember what they did or how my mother even found them. They couldn't have been members of the church; that would have defeated the purpose of Jennifer being there. Knowing my mother, she probably found them through an ad she placed in a Madison newspaper and paid them handsomely to house and feed Jennifer and keep her out of public contact.

"She couldn't even use the phone.

"Well, one time, since Jennifer wasn't to leave her room for any reason whatsoever, I went downstairs to make her some lunch. I think she must've had a craving for a tomato, because I remember looking all over to find tomatoes. I like my tomatoes with a little salt on them, but I remember Jennifer insisted that I didn't put any salt on anything. That summer, she didn't eat salt at all. Finally, in a small bin on the floor next to the refrigerator, I found some tomatoes, only a few, and I sliced them up nicely and for some reason, which I don't remember, I was in a mighty big hurry to get them upstairs to her. So I've got this little white saucer with these red cut tomatoes, and I'm running up the back staircase of the house to get to the room upstairs, and I guess I tripped on a stair and hit my shin hard, and I mean *hard,* on the front of one of the steps. Shards of white porcelain scattered everywhere and crushed tomatoes ran down the steps like blood and I was in the most physical pain I ever endured in my life. There was a gash in my shin, and I tried so hard not to cry, so hard, because I didn't want Jennifer to hear me, but I can't remember if I succeeded or not.

"It was the most physical pain I've ever felt.

"I'm sure my mother was in some of the most pain she'd ever felt, too. Her only daughter was pregnant, and the mere thought of it shattered her world. Who would help my mother now that her own daughter had strayed from the Lord? I'm not really sure that she needed help. But she had helped so many other young girls who'd gotten themselves into trouble. She helped so many other mothers with their children that when her daughter made the mistake of stepping out on her faith and bringing shame to the family name, she couldn't imagine who would possibly be there to help *her.* She took pride in her role as the matriarch who had done it all—perfectly. So proud she was to be able to help the children of so many other mothers who had not raised their children perfectly, according to the Good Book. That is how she tried to raise all of us. Except that the book had very strict guidelines, all of which had to be done perfectly, and in her mind, she had succeeded. How then could her very own daughter not be perfect? Or more importantly, how could she go on when everyone believed her to be the perfect Seventh-Day Adventist mother only to find out that she wasn't? And she would go on punishing Jennifer for years and years—she's *still* punishing her—for making her see that she wasn't perfect.

"My mother could get downright cruel and I mean *cruel.* When my boys were young, Jennifer and her girls; James and Brenda and their girls; Crystal and I and Christian and Little Josh; and my mother and father were sitting at a table eating. It might have been a Sabbath dinner, but whatever it was, we were all there and my mother was going on and on about how happy she was because I was the only one of her children who had finally given her grandsons. She sat there, knowing what had happened with you, knowing none of the kids knew about you, knowing none of us could or would correct her, and so she just laid it on thick. Jennifer sat there at that table, face frozen and looking as dead as she did the summer she was pregnant. I don't know that I've ever seen my mother so cruel, and she can be ruthless. That night, I told Crystal about you. I had to tell somebody because I wasn't gonna blurt it out at the dinner table. When I told her, Crystal said, 'Now it all makes sense.' Now she could see and understand so many things about Jennifer, about my mother, about what she saw in their relationship. Ultimately, I do know why my mother and Jennifer chose to give you away. Did I agree with it? Of course not. Could I do anything to change it? Of course not. I was very upset when it finally became clear to me that you were not coming home with us from that hospital in Madison."

"You were there?"

"Yes, I was there at the hospital when you were born. I even saw you after they carried you out of the room. You were wearing a little blue hat. I thought it strange to see a newborn in a hat. Maybe that was the hospital's way of identifying the babies who were about to become orphans. I know better now. But I was angry, and I yelled and kicked and screamed because I wanted you to come home with us. But everything had already been arranged and the sight of you in the blue hat was all I ever thought I would see of you. So on that Sabbath when Jennifer called to tell me that you had come back, I almost died. I was sitting with Crystal downstairs in the room off the kitchen. Jennifer told me that you were sitting right there next to her on the couch. I said, 'He's sitting where?' and she said, 'Right here, right next to me in my house,' and I thought it was a dream. It just had to be a dream. I was in a trance. I don't remember saying anything to Crystal, anything at all. And then you got on the phone and I heard your voice, and I couldn't believe it. I just got up, walked into my mother's apartment, and handed her the telephone. I watched her face twist and her eyes shrink to slits. She couldn't believe what she was hearing either. It was divine justice and I couldn't have been more satisfied. In the morning, after Sabbath school and instead of going to worship, she wanted me to take her down to Roswell, she couldn't wait another minute to go down to Roswell and see if, indeed, the voice she had heard over the telephone on that Sabbath sundown really belonged to the boy she had secretly sent away from us thirty-three years ago."

Book II

BRANCHES

Whoever wishes to become a truly moral human being must first divorce himself from all the prohibitions, crimes, and hypocrisies of the Christian church. If the concept of God has any validity or any use, it can only be to make us larger, freer, and more loving. If God cannot do this, then it is time we got rid of him.

—James Baldwin
THE FIRE NEXT TIME

MEET ME IN MILWAUKEE

1 "You're trapped," Jennifer said as Midwest Express Flight 1069 from Atlanta to Milwaukee made its final descent into General Mitchell International Airport. "You're sitting next to your mother, while your other mother is waiting for you at the airport. I told my daughters, 'Joseph has two mothers, you know.' They were like, 'That's true.' You're trapped and you can't get out, son."

Craig hadn't thought of it like that. Not yet, anyway. Now, all he could think of was that the woman who gave birth to him was about to meet his mother, a situation he'd never even let himself imagine. He would bet his own life that his mother hadn't imagined it either, even though it was she who'd said to both her children, "Someday you will wanna find your birth mothers. Surely, I say to you, you will wanna know where you came from. If you decide to find them, I'll support you. I'll even help you as best I can." Her son found first. After they finalized their plans to meet in Milwaukee, Mary grew stupid with the anticipation of seeing the woman her son came out of. As Craig looked out of the window and saw Wisconsin's coast carved out of the turquoise water of Lake Michigan, he thought about the email he had written to Jennifer in the weeks leading up to the visit.

> *Mama said she can't cook the food you eat so she will stand back and watch and learn! Daddy is excited. He will be getting the slides of my childhood together to share with you. Gina wasn't home, so I'm not sure where she will be. They will more than likely want to go to church on Sunday morning and introduce you to people. I have to admit, I haven't been to Siloah forever and ever, amen, but the school will probably be*

open for Sunday school and I can take you through it and show you where I had classes as a teensy child! I know you want pictures of everything, so I will bring the camera and try not to be too obvious! Oh, and please don't call me Joseph around my parents.

❧

Mary and her niece, Bernadine, met them at the gate. Mary, who stood at four-foot eleven, looked dwarfed next to Jennifer's five-foot-eight-inch frame.

"She's pretty, Craig. Isn't she pretty?" said Mary, battling back tears as she hugged Jennifer.

When they got to the house, Mary fumbled in her purse for the four keys needed to open it: a doorknob lock and a deadbolt for the iron screen door and another knob lock and deadbolt on the maple door behind it. Milwaukee had become a violent city in the last decade and Mary wasn't about to let no hoodlums break in her house, violate her sacred space. Uh uh. No, ma'am. No way. "Hazelle must be in the bathroom." Mary started bouncing while unlocking the doors. "Shoot. I'm gonna have to go myself."

"He's supposed to have the door open and ready for us. Come on Dad," said Jennifer, laughing.

"Well, it sure took you a long time to get to the door," said Mary as Hazelle entered the foyer.

"Enter and sign in, please," said Hazelle, jokingly. "It's about time yall got here."

Jennifer hesitated before crossing the door's threshold. Bernadine carried Jennifer's luggage up behind her. "You can go on in, Jennifer," she said.

"I know. It's just..." Bernadine looked her in the eye as if to say, I understand. Finally, Jennifer stepped into the foyer.

"Well, hello there, lady," said Hazelle. He hugged Jennifer and then Craig. "Come in, come in. Have a seat anywhere."

"It's very nice to meet you, Hazelle," said Jennifer. Hazelle sat down in his rocking chair. Jennifer fixed her eyes on the pictures hanging on the wall just beside the foyer: Craig, in his high school cap and gown, smiled from the wall; Gina, in the same garb, smiled above him. Jennifer couldn't stop her tears.

"Jennifer, will you sit down," Mary said on her way back into the living room from the bathroom. "Why don't you sit down, honey? Can I get you something?"

"Why does everybody want me to sit down? I can't sit down. I don't wanna sit down right now." She studied Mary's black doll collection displayed on an antique table in the foyer. Her eyes traveled to the matted and mahogany-framed poem hanging right next to the graduation portraits:

Petals

As I sit and reminisce
I am reminded of your
strength and courage in the
face of hardships. I

see a little boy safe under
your wings of love grown strong
from storms of broken dreams
blizzards of pain. But

you prevail, weary
but wiser to impart your
insight deep
within him. He

honors you such
a remarkable woman
unfaltering amidst
life's contrary ways. You

always see
tulip bulbs in
dense weeds
leaf buds on

bare trees foretelling
the mystery of rebirth,
reflecting all the
majesty that is you. He

hopes to return to you,
unyielding, the blessings
of your love
fully blossomed.

Cherishing, respecting
loving you
the little boy, grown-up
reveres his mama.

"I was just reading the beautiful poem Joseph wrote for you."

"Why, thank you," said Mary, proudly. "Craig gave that to me for Christmas one year when he was away at school."

"If you don't mind, I wanna walk around right now and see the house," said Jennifer. Mary didn't mind. "Joseph, you'll have to tell me how things were around here when you grew up."

Craig led Jennifer through the den and into the hallway that opened onto the kitchen at the back of the house. The hallway opened also to the bathroom, his parents' bedroom, and the bedroom he used to share with Gina, which they entered. She wanted to know what used to hang on the bedroom walls, which side of the dresser had he kept his clothes. Craig described each room as he remembered it when he lived there. They walked into the kitchen and Craig pointed out the chair from which he had called England two-and-a-half months ago. Where he sat for family meals, kneaded his first dough. They walked down the back landing off the kitchen hallway and outside into the yard. He pointed out Hazelle's green, green lawn; his garden; his flowerbeds of roses, petunias, and tiger lilies; the clothesline he hung for sun drying sheets. He told Jennifer about his favorite Mountain

Ashe tree that, to his dismay, Hazelle had cut down sometime during his freshman year of college because the birds that perched in the tree soiled the laundry waving in the breeze. He pointed out the area next to the garden where Chico, his German Shepherd Collie Poodle, used to do his business. Hazelle had since turned the area into a compost heap. They went back inside and to the basement, where Craig showed Jennifer his childhood playroom. The orange Tonka dump truck, which became his favorite toy after the mysterious disappearance of his Evel Knievel, still there. Jennifer sat down on the red cushions on top of a wide platform built out of the wall. "This is where I'm gonna sleep, son, right here where you played as a child, son. Go upstairs and get my things and bring them down here." He did what she told him.

Mary saw Craig with Jennifer's bags. "Where are you going with those?"

"I'm taking them downstairs, Mama. She wants to stay down there."

"Oh, no," said Mary beating Craig through the door and down the steps. "You will not come here," she said to Jennifer, "and sleep in no basement. I won't hear of it."

"It's fine, Mary. I wanna be down here where my son played. I told you I'm easy. You don't have to do anything special for me."

"Easy or not, I won't hear of it. I'll be insulted. You will not sleep down here in this damp basement. You'll catch a cold. You'll go right upstairs and sleep in Gina's room."

"I don't wanna put Gina out."

"Gina will sleep on the couch or at one of her girlfriends. And that's that. I don't wanna hear no more about it."

And that was that.

Gina slept on the couch and Jennifer stayed in Gina's room. Craig, who had planned to sleep on the floor in the living room, ended up talking to Jennifer through most of the night and fell asleep next to her on top of Gina's bed.

2

The next morning, Craig was in the basement looking through some of his sister's boxes. Gina hadn't unpacked everything after moving back from New York. Craig was hoping to find her adoption papers so he could help her find her people, as Mary wished. Hazelle was washing a load of laundry when Mary came downstairs and saw Craig searching through the box. "What are you doing?"

"Trying to find some of Gina's—"

"Oh, no you don't," Mary said emphatically. Craig wasn't sure why Mary didn't want him looking in Gina's boxes, but figured it must have something to do with the fight they'd had on some prior visit when she wanted back a box of her papers that he wasn't finished searching through. "Hazelle, come in here and take this box and put it away." When Mary's voice had her trademark don't-even-think-about-it tone, Hazelle always did what she told him. Craig snatched the box out of Hazelle's hands, ran upstairs with it, and proceeded to have a tantrum like none Mary had ever seen, even when he was a little, little boy. He was shrieking and wheezing and crying and screaming and squealing words nobody could figure out.

Jennifer rose from the living-room couch and tried to intervene. "This doesn't concern you," said Mary, sternly, "and if you don't like it, you'll have to leave and go stay at a girlfriend's house, that is, if you have any friends around here." Jennifer sat back down. Mary kept calling for Hazelle to do something, call Mr. Fate across the street, call the police, anything that might make her son calm down, but she knew he wasn't going to calm down until he felt like it. Mary tried one more time to get his attention. "Craig, listen here, you can't go on like this. You calm down, put the box down." She paused and then ordered, "And don't you dare curse at me."

Ah, yes. That's right. Once upon a time, Craig cursed at his mother—right to her face, mind you—and lived to tell about it. It was the last and final time he'd taken the bait. Every time Craig came home from college on a holiday break, Mary would pick a fight with Craig straightaway. The fights always started over something as trivial as dust, but by completion, an empire of resentment was unearthed. She resented that her son had grown up, was no longer the "little angel" who used to sit with her and tell her how happy he was to be her little boy and pat her on the head like she was his child. That he had grown away, so far away—eleven hundred miles away, to be exact—at the Ivy League school she'd never imagined he would choose because it was so far away from her. So far away she didn't even go there with him when he left. He resented that she missed him so much, not the him who was at school so far away, but the him who was her little angel. Deep down, he also resented that she never did anything, anything at all, to stop his father from picking on him when his father was drunk. Like that time when he was ten-years-old and Hazelle stumbled home at one o'clock in the morning, woke Craig up and ordered those dishes washed, dried, and put away. That she had feigned sleep through his refusals, his shouting pleas to "Tell Daddy to leave me alone!" and their knockdown, drag-out fight (the only time he ever wrestled with his old man) that ended with pots and pans all over the kitchen floor, a split lip, and a weary old fool passed out on the bed beside her, wide awake and praying. Craig would come to forgive Mary for not making Hazelle stop. For he knew exactly what she knew: liquor was most unyielding. When possessed by it, Hazelle would grant Mary none of her demands. But Craig would have more trouble forgiving Mary for resenting his growth.

In the meanwhile, they fought about dust. Craig didn't like connecting with his mother, especially when he hadn't seen her for a long time, in such an irritating and roundabout way. But he went along with it. Until he couldn't, that is. The last time he'd taken the bait, Mary overheard Craig ask his father for the car keys. She rose from the couch and walked quickly to the kitchen hallway where her husband and son stood. Hazelle dried his hands, which were wet from washing dishes, and reached into his pocket for the keys. "Uh uh, Hazelle," said Mary. "Mr. Criear might come over here later and take me driving, so you leave those keys right in your pocket." Mary had tried to learn to drive more times than Craig could count, but she never felt comfortable enough to drive after 1954 when she drove their '48 Ford Prefect into a parked car. Even though she stopped driving, she kept her driver's license renewed ever since. Just in case.

Craig turned to his mother. "Mama, what are you talking about? You're not even trying to drive right now," he said, impatiently.

"Don't try and tell me what I'm *not* doing." Her hands were on her hips and she waved her neck to dot the *i* and cross the *t*. "It's my car and so it's staying right where it is in the garage until I make up my mind."

"You're lying."

"What did you say?"

"You heard me."

"You gonna stand there and call me a liar?"

"I haven't called you anything, Mama." He hit the word *Mama* with a boxing glove. "But you're lying."

"You say that one more time, and I'm gonna—"

"You're gonna what? Huh? What're you gonna do?" Craig stepped closer to her, searing his eyes into hers from more than a foot above. "I can't *fucking* believe that you would stand there and make up some story about how you might wanna drive later just because... what? What, Mama? *What?!*"

Mary braced. "I didn't think I would live to see the day when my own son cursed his mother," she said, her voice reduced to a cracking whisper. "And his father just stands there and doesn't say a word."

"I didn't think I would live to see the day when my own mother told her son a barefaced lie." Craig turned away and walked into the back bedroom.

When he turned around, his father was standing a foot in front of him. "Son, you can't talk to your mother—"

"Daddy, I would step back if I were you," Craig cut in, rage running through his veins like poison. "I mean it, Daddy. Before I go outside and get me a switch off the tree and beat you both up and down the street like you used to do to us when we acted up." Hazelle looked up at his son and stared him directly in the eye. Whoever blinked first would lose the first tear. Hazelle retreated to the kitchen. Craig closed the door, sat down on the floor, and let his tears loose.

Now, Craig's weeping and shrieking grieved Mary, sent her far beyond her mind. She watched Jennifer trying to comfort him and "You're gonna have to get out of here and go stay with a girlfriend or something," shot out of her mouth again before she had a chance stop it. "Hazelle, maybe you oughtta go over and get Mister Fate if you can't handle the situation yourself. I just don't know what's wrong with him"—she looked at Jennifer—"I'm sorry, Jennifer. You don't have to go anywhere. He's gonna make himself sick with all that crying if he don't watch out. This is my house and I have a right to keep anybody's hands off of my things, including his."

"They aren't your things, Mama." Craig's words becoming decipherable again. "That box belongs to Gina."

"Mama Mary," began Jennifer, carefully, "would you feel better if we called Gina and asked her if it's okay for him to look through the box?"

"He's always meddling. I don't know what he's looking for, anyway. Always coming home and wanting to go through stuff. Takes my pictures and doesn't bring them back. I guess I oughtta just go sit down somewhere and be quiet." And so she did.

✍

Craig kissed Mary on the forehead before he and Jennifer left the house. Jennifer was ready for the tour she'd told Craig he would take her on when they got to Milwaukee. Craig was eager to hear what Jennifer wanted to talk to him about, but she still wasn't going to say a word until she saw everything she wanted to see, heard everything she wanted to hear. "First, I want you to take me to Juneau Park. When we get there, I want you to tell me all about it, son. About the man in the van, about Roy, about everything. Son, I've seen it all, heard it all. My daughters always tell me—they say, 'Mom, you see all, know all.' I want you to tell me everything, son." And so they climbed into his parents' white '88 Toyota Corolla and headed east toward the lake.

PARADISE

1 The sixth month of the nineteen hundred and eighty-third year. The Police's EVERY BREATH YOU TAKE was playing on the radio when Roy dropped off Craig in front of the number 62 bus, which was about to stop on the corner of Capitol Drive and Holton Street. Clouds loomed in the sky, blocking out the sunlight, and as he was getting out of the car, a spattering of raindrops slid down the windshield. Roy offered to take him all the way home, another mile or so west on Capitol and three blocks north to Twenty-Ninth and Roosevelt, but they both thought it best that, this first time at least, he get himself the rest of the way home on the bus.

It was still daylight, after all.

It might have been the last and only time Craig was in Roy's car. Thinking about Roy on that bus ride, Craig couldn't really know if he'd ever see him again, even as he stared at the phone number Roy had scribbled on the piece of paper retrieved from the glove compartment. 961-1447.

He would remember that number for the rest of his life, as clearly as if he'd just dialed it a moment ago. No needing to pick up a phone and ghost dial the numbers till it came back to him. 961-1447.

The number would always be there, perched at the precipice of recall like a dove, wings lifted. 961-1447.

Staring at that number the first time, he couldn't know then that he was looking at a number he would call regularly over the next five years, throughout high school and the first few years of college. He couldn't know then that the number he looked at belonged to the man who would become a rare friend and mentor; a confidant and teacher—a savior. He couldn't know then that the number belonged to his first true love. His only deep love for the next fifteen years.

Sixteen-and-a-half years stretched between them, a time span nearly equal to the age of his eyes looking at the number on the bus ride home. On the day they met, Craig was fifteen. Two days earlier, while the sun traversed the first days of Cancer, Roy had turned thirty-two.

Fifteen. Thirty-Two. Illegal. Taboo. That controversial and terrible taboo, one of so many, that represents the decline of human morality. Man-boy love, it's been labeled. Not just love, or Greek love, or May-December love. But man-boy love, complete with all those perverted connotations. Man-boy love... Or was it?

✍

At fifteen, Craig could hardly call himself a boy. Young man, perhaps, but certainly not a boy. He used to watch the Monday night television series JAMES AT 15 featuring the high-school trials of a pasty-faced, dirty-blond white actor whose career apparently ended the season after his character turned sixteen. Craig was a few years younger than the characters on the show. Yet, much of what was going on in his life matched what was going on in theirs—and then some. He'd had many emotional and experiential firsts at which their weekly dramas only hinted. They were stricken with all the changes and problems that accompany puberty. The television characters had troubles with girls and so did Craig. But his energies weren't completely focused on the sugar-and-spice-and-everything-nice gender.

Thanks to Ms. Krause, an encouraging and supportive seventh-grade teacher at Siloah Lutheran School, he enrolled in a watercolor painting class at the Milwaukee Art Museum the summer following seventh grade. Ms. Krause even paid for the class, so generous and moved was she by whatever he had done artistically to move her.

The museum was housed in the War Memorial, a characteristic piece of Frank Lloyd Wright architecture that loomed over Lake Michigan at the easternmost part of Milwaukee's downtown. If you stood on the Memorial's second-floor terrace, you could see Lake Michigan to the right stretching south toward Bayside, and to the left, a skyline that jutted out from a tree-lined hill stretching far into the distance until carved out by the tip tops of boats anchored in the McKinley Marina.

One sunny morning during the second week of class, Mr. Chevalier, the art instructor, took the class over to the part of the hill closest to the museum. There, he instructed his apprentices to paint a lakefront landscape from the grassy slopes of Juneau Park. Staring out onto the lake, Craig was overtaken by the splendor of the horizon and he saw himself soar toward it. He was reminded of the first time he felt himself fly and he got so lost in the memory for so long, another student had already outlined the lighthouse by the time Craig's attention returned.

✍

The Wisconsin landscape reigns over all Midwestern landscapes in the summertime. At the horizon, miles and miles of rolling hills, so steep sometimes they approach the height of mountains, edge long stretches of cornfields and undulating kingdoms of grain.

Most of northwestern Wisconsin, where the Hickmans went camping, was formed during the Ice Age by glaciers. Minnesota, which borders Wisconsin on the west, is called the Land of Ten Thousand Lakes, but Wisconsin's lakes are just as copious. They well up on the bottoms of deep canyons and valleys with their gleaming turquoise surfaces, reflecting the surrounding crags and the scintillating sun above, giving back the gift of light in all its magic and majesty. Among its many wonders of nature, Wisconsin boasts mile-long caves adorned with stalactites and stalagmites, and a thirty-mile, two-hundred-foot-high rocky ledge overlooking an eighty-three-acre marsh where geese flock called Horicon Marsh and Ledge. This was their favorite getaway. Two-and-a-half miles from Horicon Ledge Park sat the Playful Goose, the campground where they would go every weekend from Memorial Day to Columbus Day to worship simplicity. To get in touch with the earth again. To revive. Yes, they went to a brown brick building most Sundays from All Hallows Eve to Pentecost to partake in the rituals of Martin Luther, but the Playful Goose was where they really had church. How they so enjoyed driving on narrow country roads through wide rivers and sky-lit caverns of towering pines, hiking along steep cliffs, fishing in singing brooks clear as diamonds, chasing deer darting into the woods.

The camping group they belonged to featured families from almost every walk of southeastern Wisconsin life: The Santiagos, a Mexican family with a daughter and son from one of Milwaukee's poorest neighborhoods; the Kosciuskos, second generation Polish immigrants who grilled up the juiciest sausages and boiled the tastiest sauerkraut this side of the Atlantic; the Kiyotos, a Japanese and American couple with twin girls, Ai and Tai, who had eyes of onyx; and the Liebermans, who could trace their German ancestors back to the Middle Ages. These were the regular lot. Other families camped for a season, maybe two, and never came again. Craig would wonder what happened to Heather, a girl with Shirley Temple curls who didn't speak much, but always seemed to be looking for something she couldn't quite capture, like an unending hunger that could never be satisfied. The chili-mac potlucks, beans slow baked for two days in ground pits, the nighttime symphony of crickets and cicadas, and the folklore and fables with plots more tangled than any Old Testament tale told around huge campfires while roasting marshmallows for graham cracker and Hershey's chocolate bar s'mores: these were the flavors and sounds of a campground revival the Hickmans drove one hundred miles to in their white and green nineteen-foot Fan trailer hitched to their green '69 Ford Fairlane Squire wagon.

Gina Louise, sitting behind her daddy, humming the same song he whistled while driving, stared out of the window at countless miles of grazing cows. Craig always fell asleep in the seat behind his mama within five miles of Milwaukee on highway 43 headed north. Of all the memories Craig kept of those days when city folk turned pure country, he would hold most vividly, like a recurring dream, the night when he was nine and his sister was twelve.

Now, nights in the country are unlike any night a city boy could ever dream up. Away from the red-orange glow of bonfires and lantern-lit tents, there is nothing except a vast yawn of black and, if the skies are clear, the purest starlight and moonbeams the eye can see. But on an overcast night, like the one of this memory, there is only abyss:

Gina, Craig, Proserpina called Penny and Jesus Santiago, go for a walk into the warm black expanse of this country night. They come to the end of the gravel road that divides the section of trailers and campers from the tent area. "Let's see how far we can run before we get tired," says Gina Louise.

Her little brother has just begun running for the summer track club Milwaukee Striders. Kern and Big Joe, the club's coaches, discovered at a community track meet held at the Rufus King High School stadium that Craig ran as fast as a baby jaguar. Kern and Big Joe conditioned their runners hard, and all of them were in great shape. Gina Louise could chase down the fourteen-year-old boys who pulled on her thick, long hair in a game of cat and mouse the mice were certain to lose, a certainty that grew more so the longer the chase lasted. Hazelle and Mary Juanita were convinced their children were the fastest children alive. Up and down the block they would race, barefoot on concrete, getting to the finish line ahead of every other child in the neighborhood, and almost always side by side. And so Gina Louise decides that she wants to run into the night. Whatever Gina Louise wants, Gina Louise gets. "But it's too dark," says Craig.

"Don't be such a crybaby," she says, knowing he will do almost anything to avoid being called *that*.

"We won't be able to see the fire pits," says Jesus.

"Or the iron well pumps," says Proserpina called Penny. "I almost cracked my skull on one of them big old things in broad daylight."

They hear the sound of each other's breathing, all of it a bit faster than a few minutes before. "Just keep your eyes wide open," Gina says.

Eyes open, eyes shut, it doesn't matter: blackness is all there is.

No one brings a flashlight, making Gina Louise's wish even more attractive—to herself. Certain by now her brother will join her, despite the terror darkness stirs up in him, she hears without hearing Jesus and Proserpina called Penny's final attempts to talk her out of it. Not even the mention of snakes can do the trick: once any child of Mary Juanita and Hazelle makes up their minds, it would be easier to move pain than it would to move their minds. And so they run, just the two of them, into all that darkness. Far enough, fast enough for the tears that well up in their eyes to streak back on their temples and disappear into their hair. Far enough, fast enough for sidesplitting laughter to rush nonstop from their guts like rapids after the falls. Far enough, fast enough for their legs to become wings and they fly, free from the earth below, the moon behind the clouds above, the blackness all around. Side by side, they fly, afraid of nothing. Flying, flying, flying, until they tumble down together onto the dewy earth, still boiling with laughter. "How far do you think we went?" Gina asks her little brother, feeling her legs return, heavy as wet hay.

"I don't know," he replies, catching his breath, "and I don't care, as long as next time, we go even farther."

✑

Craig snapped out of his reverie and returned to the task at hand. While sketching the first of several landscapes, Craig couldn't help noticing all the pedestrian traffic in the distance. Juneau Park's beauty was intoxicating; it was certainly no surprise to see many, many people there on a sunny summer morning enjoying the light.

But there were men, lots of men, coming and going and going and coming up and down a little path that led into the trees on the side of the hill. It was an intriguing sight, and Craig loved intrigue. In fact, he loved anything slightly out of the ordinary. Lots of men, handsome men, appearing and disappearing into the trees was just enough out of the ordinary to hook his attention. And hold it. A few sunny afternoons later, after Craig laid out his watercolors to dry, washed his station, and rinsed out his paintbrushes, he decided to investigate the tree-lined hills of Juneau Park. He walked down that path, on the side of that hill, descending into the dark, cool, shady depths of lust, into the inner sanctum of Paradise. Where he found a kind of pleasure with which he was more than satisfied to acquaint himself. There they were. Men in groups of three, four... eight. Doing what men who come to the tree trunks of city parks and country parks and highway rest areas around the world do. He found every excuse he could to return almost daily to Juneau Park after completing the three-week summer class. Little did Craig know that his adolescent sexuality was taking root in a place where men frolicked at least as early as the nineteen hundred and tenth year. He wouldn't find this out until he read George Kennan's memoirs, but by then he was already in college. Kennan documented that tidbit of history, which might possibly be attributed in part to the presence in the center of the park of a large bronze statue of Leif, son of Erik of Norway. Sculpted in the eighteen hundred and eighty fifth year in Boston by Ann Whitney, an artist who loved women, and erected in Juneau Park as a reminder of where the first settlers of Wisconsin arrived, it has been maintained and restored by the Danish Sisterhood, the Swedish American Historical Society and the Nordic Council.

Leif strikes a pose, clad, it appears, in military armor, replete with a skirt fashioned from several vertical panels of bronze. His right arm akimbo, his left arm raised just above his forehead in salute to what you can only imagine, he looms above passersby, serene as Michelangelo's David. And very fey. Unbeknownst, perhaps, to his creator, Leif stood erect as a pleasant and honorable invitation to those who would find a sanctuary for their desires on the wooded hill behind him. On Leif's hill, Craig took his place—driven, focused, wide-eyed with curiosity, and armed with a raging teenage libido.

And so it was that, day after day, Craig rode his blue ten-speed bicycle east on Capitol Drive to the Centennial bike path and down to Juneau Park, so eager was he to partake in the communion of men. White men, that is. Or that is how it seemed. It didn't take long for Craig to notice that white men were the ones who usually approached him. Few men that looked like him frequented the bushes and those who did seldom looked each other in the eye and never, ever got close enough to touch one another. Now what was *this* all about? All his friends and dance partners going as far back as kindergarten were black. Now, here in this place, outnumbered by the white men, they wouldn't even look each other in the eye. Craig wanted to look at them, touch them, dance with them, but why didn't they want to dance with him? There awakened in him a feeling of lonesomeness, a sense of separation from all that he knew. Each time he came to the park, each time he and his brown-skinned brethren could not look at each other, his isolation intensified.

One day, Craig noticed a black boy about his age, perhaps a bit older, standing against a tree with a group of white men gathered around him, taking their pleasure. The boy was moved from one set of hands to another, turned, twisted, bent over, pushed down on his knees, pulled up by his armpits, bent over again and again, entered on both ends. The boy seemed to disappear, to become invisible, and all Craig could see were the boy's suitors, writhing, pushing their thighs forward, tightening their buttocks as they emptied themselves inside him. It was as though Craig were standing outside his body, witnessing him*self* in the midst of the voracious mob.

The image repulsed him, made him feel wretched. It aroused him, too. His eyes blurred and it was *he* who was taking whatever they were giving and feeling good about it. Before becoming completely lost in his dream, Craig blinked. The vision of the boy came into focus once more. The crowd of white men retreated, and the black boy was left, half-naked, alone under the tree.

The light filtering through the leaves from above shone on the boy and Craig caught a glimpse of his face, shiny with sweat and looking like a statuette of Snow White, with that same startled gaze. He watched as the boy clumsily, quickly, pulled up his shorts, picked up his shirt from the ground, shook it out, and put it back on. The boy walked farther down the hill and disappeared on one of the paths that led to the lakefront. Craig walked back up to the park, retrieved his bike from the post he'd locked it to, and rode home.

2 And it came to pass that, during the season of street parades and lakefront festivals, it rained. Every day, all day, for six days, it rained. Right in the middle of the longest days of the year—it rained.

The Summerfest grounds at downtown Milwaukee's lakefront hosted a series of summer festivals from June through September. Honoring the city's rich cultural and ethnic traditions, tourists could attend Afro Fest, Irish Fest, Polish Fest, Fiesta Mexicana, German Fest and Indian Fest. Summerfest, the biggest music festival in the state, kicked off the season with amusement park flair and included a small roller coaster and Ferris wheel. It seemed as if every Milwaukeean anticipated this first festival of the season more eagerly than summer itself. But in the nineteen hundred and eighty-first year, the rains that came without relent kept many disappointed city folk indoors.

Their cellar filled with rainwater so quickly, the drain in Hazelle's haven couldn't eliminate it fast enough. The water level climbed halfway up the hallway stairs leading to the first-floor landing. It took three days for the basement well to dry up. A whole week passed before everything dried up, assisted by fans and dehumidifiers. Mary Juanita and Hazelle, equipped with blue facemasks and yellow gloves, sifted through the wreckage like soldiers after a battle, snapping Polaroids for the insurance claim application.

"Why in heaven would the Lord send this plague into my home?" Mary said to herself as she rifled through an antique trunk, its contents grown thick with mold and mildew. Rarely did she cry. Now it seemed her tears came like the rains as Mary Juanita uncovered the remains of her son's baby book. She had brought her daughter's upstairs the past winter to share with Rose, a friend of hers, but had forgotten to put it back in the trunk downstairs along with the other memorabilia, scrapbooks, photo albums and keepsakes she had collected and assembled over the years. It was a time when her poor memory was a blessing. Unfortunately, for reasons she couldn't remember, she hadn't brought her son's book to show her friend.

She could never forget, however, putting his book together. She wouldn't ever say so out loud, but her son was her favorite. Of course she loved both her children. But she was a mother, after all, and what she felt for her son had more weight at the bottom of it, seemed to pull her into a deeper place where a love flowed with no conditions, no boundaries. Wasn't this the way it had always been for mothers of any age, anywhere?

Craig sensed this as early as three when he sat in the kitchen of their house on Twenty-Fourth Street. His mother had just finished bathing the young throwaway girl smelling of dried urine who'd knocked on the door earlier that morning. She gave her a blouse and pair of pants from her daughter's drawer and closed the bathroom door so the girl could dress. While Mary stood before the Frigidaire preparing some Cream of Wheat, bacon and toast for her, Craig said, "Mama, do you like being a mother?"

"Of course I do."

"Do you like being *my* mother?"

"More than anything else in the world, my little angel."

"I like being your little angel too." Mary Juanita finished stirring the pot, turned a piece of bacon, walked over to her son, and gave him his favorite kiss on the forehead. He kissed her on the cheek, raising his right hand to pat her on the head like she was his child. They both giggled.

Mother and son. Their bond was special, even sacred. In Leviticus, Moses wrote that Yahweh told him to tell the children of Israel that after she bore a son, a mother could be purified in half the amount of time than if she bore a daughter. Whether this was truth or the simple promotion of patriarchy, Mary Juanita had to believe it, for the Bible told her so, and she believed everything the Bible told her. Although her son had not come from her womb, he may as well have, for she loved him just the same and appreciated him even more.

"My little angel." Out loud, she would call Craig that for most of his childhood and in her prayers, for the rest of her life. When his adoption was final, the agency sent her three baby pictures taken during the sixteen months the foster parents cared for him. There was the one of him sleeping in the crib, covered with a diaper, a smile big as sunrise painted cross his face. There was another one of him in the arms of his foster mother, whose face rested out of the picture's frame. And there was her favorite: he was standing up by himself for the first time, a look of surprise in his eyes, legs bowed wide enough to roll a basketball through. "My little angel." She would get lost in these images as her son grew up way too fast and journeyed into the world, dealing with only God knows what. She wanted—no, *needed*—him to be her little angel forever, for that was a world close to her bosom, a world that made sense, a world she could control.

Regret stung her like bad news. Standing over the trunk, these images of him could only be seen in her memory, and poor as it was, she would never forget them. Despite her fear that time would also wipe them out of her memory the way the rain had washed them out of her hands. She wished she'd kept his book in the top drawer of the bureau closest to her bed. But she'd finally decided to store it in the trunk along with her daughter's, which she had moved there a few years earlier. And so it was that her tears kept coming.

3 After the plague, the sun lost the battle with the clouds for another week, and showers came intermittently. God was wringing out the clouds, sopping wet rags that held more water than they could.

On the day his mother cried, Craig took the bus downtown instead of riding his bike. The Grand Avenue Mall was crowded but not with the kind of company he craved. He left the mall and took the number 30 bus, which passed Juneau Park on its way up the east side to the University of Wisconsin at Milwaukee.

He could see the park from the bus, could tell that there weren't many men out strolling that day. He hadn't ridden his blue Schwinn to the park in a long time, hadn't danced naked with grown men under the trees. He rode past the park at least half a mile, the side of that wooded hill stealing his thoughts the whole time. Somewhere up Prospect Avenue, he got off the bus. Desire was the magnet that pulled him; under its spell he walked back, craving the naked dances. As he approached, he noticed a gray van in the parking lot at the park's entrance. A man was sitting in the driver's seat. Those eyes. Those penetrating eyes. Those misty-brown eyes charged with lightning, emerging from that white face, a face signifying, at once, the source of and refuge from Craig's private storm.

Craig entered the van and sat in the passenger seat. He looked at the man's green-and-white-striped T-shirt, his tan shorts, his boulder arms and tree-trunk legs. Neither one of them spoke. In the back of the van where the seats ought to have been rested a large mattress covered with a sheet, unmade. Shades were drawn down over the windows on both sides and in the back. Outside, daylight diminished beyond the trees and the inside grew darker.

Silence. Deafening silence.

Craig shifted in his seat, his forehead anointed with sweat. Something tasting of dread moved up from within him and his gut twisted. He wanted to leave but fear paralyzed his limbs quicker than a broken neck. The man wrestled him from the seat and forced him down face-first onto the mattress. Holding Craig's head down with his arm across Craig's neck, the man pulled down Craig's shorts and entered him.

Short of breath, sweat stinging his eyes, he could make no sound whatsoever. He tried to scream, but only silence escaped. His body cried out, *Mama, Mama, please!* like when he had fever, *Mama, Mama, please!* like when his Daddy couldn't control his liquor, *Mama, Mama, please!* like that night he felt the presence of spirits who slapped his hands and called him a living abortion. The pounding of the hammer down and up into him was so much louder than his heartbeat, so much louder than the rain beating against the van, so much *louder* than his pleas toward heaven for release. Finally, the hammer stopped. The man snatched out his weapon, but before his target had a chance to dress, he slid open the van door and threw Craig and his clothes onto the rain-wet pavement and drove away.

Craig gathered himself, put on his clothes and looked around. As far as he could see, no one saw him. How grateful he was for that. After he arrived home, he avoided his parents and soaked in a hot bath for what seemed an eternity, trying to soothe the pain. He finally got out and began drying himself off, careful not to touch right *there* too hard. When he was drying, he noticed the dark stain in his underwear, which lay on the floor in front of the heating vent. Blood, sure enough. He skipped dinner, telling his mother that his stomach hurt and that no, there was nothing she could give him to make it feel any better and no, he didn't want to look through any of her photo albums with her. "All I wanna do is sleep, Mama." And so he stuffed the bloody underwear under his mattress, certain he would remember to take care of them the next day. If he woke up.

4

Paradise became Gethsemane. There, a part of Craig was captured. His journey out of captivity would be long and arduous. He vowed never to return to Juneau Park. But his vow was borne more from desperation than from commitment; he would, therefore, inevitably, break it.

It wasn't as if he didn't try, though. But the spell of desire was too deep. His spirit was willing; his flesh, weak. And so he found other places: bookstores, backrooms in bars, rest areas, picture shows, other parks. He was driven. He would now control every encounter, or at least he would in his mind. He was the aggressor. Never, no, never, would he do *that* to someone—never, *ever*—but he made sure to put himself in a position of power in every situation. The effort made him tired. But more than that, it made him blind. He could not see how this need would make itself at home in almost every aspect of his life.

Late the next autumn, the one when he entered high school, he finally went back to Juneau Park, searching for freedom in the very same place that held him hostage. If there was something there, anything at all, that he could vanquish, no matter how small or insignificant, perhaps he could get some relief from bondage. But the angry trees grew crooked in autumn's gale. The wretched branches hung heavily overhead—naked, cold, sterile. Beneath his skin, the bitter core rotted, while the willows wept.

5 School was out for the summer, and Craig missed Juneau Park more than he realized. Even though it had betrayed him, it was *his*. He still believed that he could reclaim what he lost there. Less than a year had passed but he felt much older, so much stronger. How could he let Juneau Park continue to defeat him? Continue to make him feel so isolated from everyone else? So cut off from himself? He couldn't and so he returned. He spent less time on the paths, and more time in the park, enjoying the way the light turned the surface of the lake into a newly polished silver platter. One day, he walked the path from the park's northern entrance to the War Memorial Art Museum, which framed the view at the south-easternmost point. About three quarters of the way along the path, just past the bathroom building and the statue of Solomon Juneau, which reminded Craig of photographs of the Lincoln Monument in his history books, the trees along the side of the hill gave way to a sloping lawn. From here, the park provided a clear view of the lake on the east. Out of the lake rose a lighthouse at the end of a half-mile-long promenade. Upon glimpsing the lighthouse, Craig's feet froze, then thawed just as quickly. He turned to the east, his glimpse becoming a gaze. His concentration heightened his trancelike demeanor as he walked, slowly, halfway down the hill, never averting his eyes from the lighthouse. Although it was the same lighthouse he had captured in his first watercolor landscape, it became a vision he'd never seen before. It must have been noontime. Yet, the lantern room of the lighthouse beamed brighter than the star of day, which hovered high above his sightlines. Soon, the light transformed and he was able to see vivid auras of color—green, orange, violet, amber, coral, maroon, indigo, gold—emanating from the tower. Suddenly the light exploded, bursting into a myriad of distinct particles.

He could see each and every one of them.

This new awareness of the light wasn't something he would analyze, something he would explain. It simply *was*. He never told anyone about it for he was sure no one would believe him. Just like no one believed him when he was three-years-old and sleeping on his bed in the house on Twenty-Fourth Street. It was the middle of the night and the covers were pulled over his head. His arms were outside of the sheets, stretched out from his sides, the palms of his hands face up. The door to the bedroom opened and a draft swept through the room. In a moment, he felt the monster standing over him, heard the monster call out, "You big old crybaby," cackling and slapping Craig's hands, "you living abortion." Craig knew what a crybaby was, had no idea what an abortion was, but was scared anyway. He heard the monster eat his Evel Knievel motorcycle and doll, his favorite toys, which he'd put on the cedar desk next to the closet. The monster disappeared into the closet, slamming the door. After trying in vain for minutes to scream, Craig finally yelled out, "Mama, Mama, *please!*" Mary Juanita and Hazelle, asleep in their bedroom across the hall, woke up and rushed into their children's room. Craig, flirting with hyperventilation, told them what happened.

"Honey, please. Calm down. There was no monster in here," said Mary, wiping the sweat from his forehead with her hand.

"Yes, there was," he shrieked and pointed. "It was right *there*. It took my Evel Knievel, my Evel Knievel into the closet, into the closet and ate it, Mama. Yes it, yes it did. Mama, I heard it, I heard it. The monster did it. If it wasn't there, then where is, where is my bike?"

"Are you sure you didn't leave it outside? Didn't you take it outside today? You probably just left it outside."

"I put it right there, right there every night, every night and now it's gone. The monster ate it." Craig was jumping up and down now.

Hazelle opened the closet and looked around. The daredevil doll and his bike were nowhere to be found—not on the shelves or under the bed or in the desk drawers.

"Are you *sure* you put it there tonight?" asked Mary, holding Craig at the waist.

"Yeessssss."

Gina Louise, who slept in the upper bunk and would usually awaken if her brother sneezed too loudly, stayed asleep throughout the entire episode.

They never found the bike or the doll.

And so it was that the next spring, they moved to Twenty-Ninth and Roosevelt.

6 And it came to pass on the twenty-eighth day of June in the nineteen hundred and eighty-second year, that the clouds loomed in the sky, blocking out the sunlight and Craig took the bus to the park. He sat on the hill just below the statue of Solomon Juneau and studied the lighthouse for

an hour, a ritual he began shortly after the first vision. Later, he was swinging on the swing set in the sandbox near the building that housed the restrooms. A tall, thin man with short, dark-brown hair, wearing gray sweatpants and a matching jacket walked past the sandbox and into the bathroom. He's kind of cute, thought Craig, already walking toward the bathroom. The man was at the urinal when Craig entered. By the time Craig situated himself one urinal away, the man had already finished his business and walked to the sink. While the man, who had not even looked at him, washed his hands, Craig zipped his pants and on the way out of the bathroom, walked close enough to the sink to firmly press his arm against the man's butt just before walking through the door and back to the sandbox. A moment later, the man walked out of the bathroom and headed down the main path on the side of the hill. Craig followed him down the path and tried to guess which trail the man would take to which hidden clearing. But the man kept walking, never once looking behind, turning down no trails in search of a place for them to begin their private, public dance. Craig knew where the main path ended, but he seldom got that far, and when he did, it was only to exit. Now, this man with the mystery eyes, this man that was drawing him like the pond draws the loon, this man was going, going, going, and there would be no dancing today.

At the foot of the hill, the man stopped and sat down on a huge tree trunk that had fallen across the path, probably during a lightning storm. When Craig saw him sit, he slowed his pace. What am I gonna say? Craig asked himself. He couldn't just walk right up and touch him again, for the clearing at the foot of the path was too large, too open. He stopped and turned around. Should I just go home and forget it? The man still would not look back and it seemed he hadn't taken the bait in the bathroom. He must not be interested. Of course, he's interested. Why wouldn't he be interested? This is too much work today, thought Craig, as he started up the hill. He also thought that he couldn't think of the last time he capitulated so quickly.

And so it was that Craig turned right back around, walked deliberately to the tree trunk, sat down, straddling the bark with his long legs, and confronted this man whose name he didn't know, this man whose face he'd never seen, this man who already stoked the fire in him. "My name is Craig and I think you have the most beautiful eyelashes I've ever seen."

"Thank you," the man replied, smiling. He reached into the pocket of his sweat jacket, pulled out a pack of cigarettes, and lit one.

"A Marlboro man, I see."

"Oh, I'm no cowboy. My name is Seldon, but you can cuh-cuh-cuh-call me, call me Roy."

"Seldom?"

"Seldon. With an *n*. It's my fuh-fuh-fuh-father's name. An old German name I buh-buh-buh-believe. It means rare."

"Nice to be rare, I guess. But I like Roy better. It means king. How old are you?"

"I just turned thirty-two. Two days ago."

"Happy belated birthday."

"Thanks. And you? You must be twelve."

"Fifteen. But I don't look a day over fourteen."

They both laughed.

"That makes you, what, a suh-suh-suh-sophomore?"

"I will be this fall. I go to Rufus King."

"Do you like it?"

"I think so."

"You think so?" Roy laughed. He took a long, deep drag on his Marlboro, bent back his head and blew the smoke up. "What do you think, do you *think* are your favorite subjects?"

"Latin, algebra, history. I can't really stand English. I love numbers. Next year I have to take geometry and I can't wait to get into physics. I think I wanna be a mechanical engineer. What do you do?"

"Ever known anyone who had a cruh-cruh-cruh-*crown* or a pair of, a pair of dentures?" asked Roy. Craig nodded. "I make those."

"I never met anybody who made those. What do you call somebody who makes those?"

"A dental lab technician. I live right above the dent-dent-dent, the *dentist* office where I work."

"How convenient. Must be nice, but you have no excuse for ever being late for work." After a stretch of silence, Craig looked up and started to sing, his Motown falsetto soaring into the branches above them. Craig stopped and asked, "Do you think the sun is gonna come out any time soon?" wiping a raindrop from his arm. He continued his song. "*Doo waah, doo bee doo...*"

"Who needs the sun when you can hear a voice like that?"

Craig stopped singing, and dropped his head. But he couldn't hide the smile that broke open his face, like morning. "Are you always this good?"

"Only when inspired," said Roy with a wink in his voice and a glint in his eye.

Craig found no words to fill his moving lips. The force of Roy's stare penetrated his skin like olive oil. He could feel himself blushing, even if Roy couldn't see it. Craig shifted positions on the log, readjusting his engorged bulge. Finally, Roy asked, "How did you get here today?"

"I took the bus."

"Where do you live?"

"On the north side. Twenty-Ninth and Roosevelt. You know where that is?"

"Sure do. I see you have no uh-uh-uh-um-*brella*. How about, how about I give you a ride home?"

"A ride to the bus is fine, thank you. Can you take me up to Capitol Drive, or is that out of your way?"

Roy stood up and stretched out his hand. Craig rose and took it. They walked back up the path through the park to the parking lot. Roy had parked his silver Honda Civic only a few spaces away from where the gray van had been parked last summer. Roy opened the passenger-side door for Craig and closed it behind him after he got in. While Roy drove up through the east side and west on Capitol Drive toward Twenty-Ninth Street, they spoke little. Mostly, Craig sang along to his favorite song playing on the car radio and fantasized about being his king's favorite little prince. "*Every breath you take, every move you make, I'll be watching you...*" Somewhere along the way, Craig put his left hand on Roy's right leg. Roy laid his right hand, gently, on top of Craig's, and they held hands for the duration of the trip. As they approached Holton Street, Craig said, "This is good enough. We passed the bus a few blocks back. I'll get out at the next light and take the bus the rest of the way home."

"You sure? If you don't want me to druh-druh-druh-drop you off in front of your house, I can at least take you to Twenty-Ninth Street."

"Thanks, but I'll get out here. It's probably best."

Roy nodded and pulled over. With eyes at once tentative and furtive, each one looked at the other. Craig leaned over, Roy leaned, too, and they kissed. After their lips parted, Craig giggled. Roy smiled. "Would you like—can you like—I'd, well, you know, luh-luh-luh-like it if you would call me suh-suh-suh-sometime, you know, that is, if you wuh-wuh-wuh-*want* to." Roy retrieved, quickly, a pen and a piece of paper from the glove compartment and wrote down his phone number.

Craig took the piece of paper dangling from Roy's outstretched hand. "Very nice to meet you today. Thanks for the ride. And the kiss." He got out of the car, closed the door and motioned for Roy to roll down the window. "I'll call you," Craig said, leaning into the car from the sidewalk. "You can count on it."

COMMON UNITY

1 After Craig told her all about it, Juneau Park pulled in a man with a picked-out afro who rode toward them on his bike. As he got closer, Craig recognized from a long time ago the tall, thin man who'd always reminded him of Arthur Ashe. Craig waved to him as he rode by. The man smiled, braked, and, straddling the red bike, walked over to them. "Long time no see. It's been years and years since I saw you last."

"You still look the same. I forgot your name though."

"Josh. You're Craig, right?"

"And I thought I had a good memory. This is Jennifer."

"Well, hello, Josh."

"Nice to meet you, Jennifer," he said and shook her hand. He turned his attention back to Craig. "Where you been, man?"

"The short or long version?" They all laughed. "The short headline," Craig continued, "is that I went to Boston for college and I've been there ever since. Now, I'm back visiting my family. Things sure have changed a lot around here. The hill has eroded and there aren't as many people hanging out anymore."

"So many of us are gone now," Josh said solemnly. "Do you remember the big guy who used to fly his homemade kites, two, three, four at a time?"

"Sure do. He always flew them right over there." Craig pointed to the hill in front of the Solomon Juneau statue. "He wore the brightest shirts."

"He just died a little while ago. A few months, maybe."

None of them spoke for a few moments. Craig stared into the sky and tried to visualize soaring kites bright as shirts. "We're taking a walk down memory lane today. It might be nice to have a picture of this chance encounter when I look back on it. Mind taking a picture with me?"

"Not at all."

Craig gave Jennifer the camera and she snapped a photograph of them standing in front of the bike, arms around each other, looking like brothers.

"Thanks a lot," Craig said, "and it was nice running into you."

"You too. Enjoy the rest of your visit," Josh said. He rolled the bike forward, stepped his left foot on the pedal, tossed his right leg over the seat and rode down the main path toward the War Memorial.

"Wow, son, that was deep. He's even got my brother's name."

"Josh used to come into McDonald's when I worked there in high school. I can take you by there if you wanna go. It's not too far from where Roy lived. You ready to go?"

"Not yet. Before we leave I want you to tell me how Roy saved you. You call him your savior and I wanna know what you mean. Remember, your mother's deep, son, and I've heard it all,"—how many times was she going to say that? Craig thought—"so don't worry about saying anything that might offend me."

"I can't remember the last time I worried about offending someone. But I don't know exactly. I mean I don't know if it was any one thing he did, or the way I saw him in my life, or just how I feel. Maybe it's all of the above. It's hard to say. I wouldn't even know how to explain it."

"Try, son. Just try."

"I'll do my best. But in the car. I'm ready to get out of here."

GRACE

1 And it came to pass on the seventeenth day of June in the nineteen hundred and eighty-fourth year that Craig first heard about it. Roy was rolling a joint when the evening news came on. Roy usually rolled a joint when the news came on, for after the news anchor fed the fear-greedy viewing audience the last warnings of the eve, Roy would lead Craig to his bed and dance with him on a plush blanket of lions.

And what exquisite dances they danced. Roy was smooth, lean, tall, and graceful with a sternum that bent forward like a bird's neck. Craig would rub him down, lick him up, and turn him over and back. Roy allowed Craig to do whatever he wanted and when Roy was ready, he'd make no mistake. "Now, you're gonna fuck me." And so Craig would do exactly what Roy told him. For as long as he wanted to do it. It was Craig's reward, Roy would say, "For making me feel mighty, mighty real."

But on that June evening, Craig, who usually let the bad news from the Magnavox float right through him, sat straight up on Roy's brown tweed loveseat and choked on the headline that spilled from the anchor's mouth:

"Next up: deadly syndrome becoming epidemic among homosexual men in New York and San Francisco. Stay tuned."

They stayed tuned.

"I've been to New York *and* San Francisco," Roy said. He looked right at Craig, right into him. "I cuh-cuh-cuh-could have it, Craig. I could *have* it."

Craig said nothing. Roy smoked the whole joint. Craig had never seen Roy smoke a whole joint. They didn't dance that evening. Roy refused.

No matter how much Craig would plead, Roy refused to dance with him ever again. Not even with a condom.

2 And it came to pass on the twenty-second day of July in the nineteen hundred and ninety-first year, just after midnight, that the last man got away. Tracy Edwards, a thirty-two-year-old black man, had been handcuffed and threatened with a knife in the bedroom of the thirty-one-year-old white man's apartment. Realizing that there was more to their encounter than an S&M scene, the small, thin man with the dark-brown skin, handcuffs dangling from his wrist, ran out of Apartment 213 of the Oxford Apartments at 924 North Twenty-Fifth Street near Marquette University. Two Milwaukee police officers that had been patrolling the area saw Tracy, stopped him and asked what was going on. Tracy told them what the guy in the apartment had done to him. The officers decided to check out the story.

When the cops arrived, the blond man with the wry smile and calm demeanor opened the door. The officers were stunned by the strange stench that hung in the dense, unmoving air. The stifling heat, the oppressive humidity, typical of a Milwaukee summer night, intensified the stench, refusing it the faintest breeze on which to sneak away. In the bedroom, photographs of dismembered human bodies and skulls in a refrigerator popped the eye sockets of one of the officers. He yelled at his night-watch partner to place the blond man under arrest. The man was Jeffrey Dahmer.

After they subdued him, the officers shrieked again and again and again at the horror they uncovered. The Arm & Hammer in the refrigerator had no answer for the odor of a decomposing head. The freezer held another three stored in twist-tied plastic bags. Behind a deadbolted door, which one of them shot open, the officers uncovered a stockpot with returning-to-dust hands, containers of chloroform and alcohol, glass jars of male organs preserved in formaldehyde, and Polaroids of men, all of them black, in pre- and post-death poses. One of them had been cut open from the neck to the groin, like an animal butchered and gutted after slaughter.

The Milwaukee Police Department, the entire city of Milwaukee, the media and much of the rest of civilization, but most importantly, Jeffrey Dahmer's family and the families of the murdered missing, tried to understand what had really happened in Apartment 213. Theories and analyses, assumptions and lies—conjecture, all of it—flooded the media outlets with an unparalleled sensationalism.

Craig couldn't watch or read about much of it. He used to run track with Tracy Edwards' younger brother and the blond man with the penetrating blue eyes looked entirely too familiar to him. He turned off the television and went to take care of his garden.

Craig lived alone in his one-bedroom apartment on Park Drive across the street from the Victory Gardens in a neighborhood of Boston called the Fenway. Fenway Park, where the Boston Red Sox played their home games, loomed just around the corner, and every baseball season, the area around

Craig's apartment was so congested, it could take an hour to travel two blocks by car. The Victory Gardens, also known as the Fens, abutted a shallow, curving stream whose banks were overgrown with tall reeds. Day or night, men would come to the Fens, just as they would come to Juneau Park, craving their public, private dances, falling on their knees, faces up, throats yawning to the heavens. Craig thought it more than coincidence that an exact replica of Leif—sculpted by the same Boston artist—which stood in Milwaukee's Juneau Park, stood also on Commonwealth Avenue one block away from the Fens.

It was in places like these that Craig, two years later—when his mentors and friends fell like dominoes—in his role as an HIV educator and outreach worker, would distribute condoms and lube and pamphlets to his brothers. It was in places like these that Jeffrey Dahmer lured his kill.

Craig finished tending his plot of vegetables and flowers in the Victory Gardens and walked around the corner to the White Hen Pantry on Boylston Street to buy a pack of cigarettes. Before he got to the checkout counter, the face that stared from the cover of NEWSWEEK on the magazine racks diverted him. He walked over to the display, reached out to pick up the magazine, but pulled his hand back before he touched it. Oh, my God, thought Craig. That's him. Craig might forget your name, but never your face, and never—ever—your eyes. That's definitely him. It was the man who'd opened the door to his suite at the Hotel Wisconsin that sweltering evening four years before.

※

It was the nineteen hundred and eighty-seventh year, during the summer after Craig completed his freshman year of college. He returned home to work as an intern for the Milwaukee County Department of Administration Division of Fiscal Affairs at the Milwaukee County Courthouse. After working late one evening, Craig walked to the Grand Avenue Shopping mall not too far from the courthouse. The stores would close soon and the restrooms would be full of men who'd come to the mall with no intention of shopping. Craig walked into the downstairs restroom. Surprised, he found it empty. No matter; he really had to use the bathroom anyway. While sitting on the toilet, he saw a note written neatly in black against the blue paint of the stall:

For a good time call 271-4900 Room 563

He memorized the number as quickly as he read them. When he finished his business, Craig called from the Wisconsin Bell pay phone outside the bathroom. After the man on the other end said he was right across the street at the Hotel Wisconsin, Craig decided to go and meet the man with the neat handwriting who offered a good time.

Situations like this excited Craig but never made him nervous. When the man with the blond hair and the penetrating blue eyes opened the door, Craig's whole body stiffened.

"Why don't you come in?" the man said.

"I don't think this is such a good idea."

"Sure it is. Best idea you've had all day," he said, looking Craig up and down. "You're cute. Really cute. Come on in, we can relax, unwind, have a drink and then have some fun."

Craig stepped, slowly, into the hotel room.

"Please, make yourself comfortable. You're *such* a cutey. You must be really photogenic. You ever done any modeling?

"No."

"Not yet. Now sit down and make yourself comfortable. I'll get us a drink."

His eyes were glassy and he smelled like a distillery, but he didn't walk across the worn, brown shag carpet to the kitchenette like a man who was drunk. While the man made their drinks, Craig studied the drab room. The late evening light couldn't peek through the barred windows' pulled-down shades. The television, which flickered toward the bed, had to be as old as the one they had when he was a little, little boy. There was a Polaroid camera near the foot of the big bed. The bed was turned down.

"C'mon over," said the man, who returned with two plastic cups and sat down on the old gray sofa, "and have a seat."

"You know what? I think I better go."

"C'mon, cutey. At least have a drink first."

Craig eyed the cup the man had put on the cocktail table. It was brown, perhaps a few shots of liquor mixed with Coca Cola or Pepsi. The man hadn't bothered to ask him what he wanted. Craig could hear Mary's voice as clearly as if she were standing behind him: *Never accept a drink from anybody you don't know and never leave your drink unattended.*

"Thanks, but—No. Thanks. Sorry to have wasted your time."

Craig turned and ran out of the room, down the hallway. He wasn't sure why he was running. He arrived at the elevator, pushed the button for down. Craig heard the elevator clunk loudly in its shaft, but he couldn't wait. He looked around for the stairwell and when he located the exit sign, he ran through the door, down the stairs and out onto the sidewalk. He inhaled the muggy air, sighed relief. He loosened his tie and unbuttoned the top of his shirt. He ran a few blocks, still not sure why he was still running or where he was running to.

He got on the number 30 bus and headed up the east side to Roy's apartment. Roy could see that Craig was startled, but Craig wouldn't tell him why. Roy had never seen Craig like this before, but he knew well enough to be silent when Craig didn't want to talk about anything. Roy served Craig a bowl of the chicken stew he had just prepared and poured him a glass of orange juice. After they ate, Roy took Craig home. All the way home. Dropped him off right in front of his house. Roy didn't drive away until he saw Craig go inside.

✍

Craig had had enough of the NEWSWEEK cover's penetrating blue eyes when he finally moved himself to the checkout counter. He bought a carton of cigarettes—he'd never bought a carton before—ripped it open before the cashier could hand him his change, opened a pack, and lit one just before exiting the store.

In the lobby of his building, he opened his mailbox and retrieved his mail. As soon as he entered his apartment, he sorted through it: a telephone bill, three free circulars, and the Siloah Lutheran Church and School bulletin. He had asked Mary several times to stop updating his address in the church's membership directory, but she'd refused each time. "What do you expect me to tell them," she'd asked, "that my only son isn't interested in the Lord anymore?" Craig usually tore up the bulletin right away and threw it in the trash. This time, he sat down on his overstuffed cream-colored sofa and opened the light-blue cover with the line drawing of the church on it. "A Letter From Your Pastor," the first item of every issue, blindsided him. Craig lit another cigarette as he read Pastor Westendorf's diatribe on the homosexual community, a perfect example of what happens when God's word is ignored. All of Jeffrey Dahmer's victims had brought it on themselves because of their sin against God. Jeffrey Dahmer must not have been raised up in the ways of the Lord, and his perversion took the most extreme turn. As Craig read and smoked and smoked and read, he asked himself why *this* had to be the topic of the Pastor's letter this month. Wasn't the magazine cover at the White Hen Pantry enough? He turned the page and found his answer. Curtis Straughter, a boy from Craig's second-grade class, had been revealed as one of Jeffrey Dahmer's victims.

Immediately, the tears came. He lit another cigarette.

Through his smoke and tears, he could see Curtis' face with its blank expression, immovable as a bust. Curtis was a shy, quiet, smart boy who only attended Siloah for a year. Craig lit another cigarette and returned his attention to the letter, which ended with a prayer for every homosexual's salvation.

On the next page was the article where the staff and congregation said farewell to Mister Floyd Hermann, a teacher at Siloah for twelve years, who had taken the principal's assignment at a Lutheran school in Arizona. Throughout his tenure, Mister Hermann taught several grades, but he began with the fifth grade, which he taught for the most years. Craig was in the fifth grade during Mister Hermann's first year at Siloah. Even then, Craig knew his teacher, a divorced man who kept a picture of his son and daughter on his desk, was in the life.

It wasn't until Craig was in high school that he verified his feelings. After some Saturday afternoon church group, when everyone else had departed and the coast was clear, Craig tackled Mister Hermann in the church office. They wrestled for a few minutes, and sure enough, Craig could feel the gorge growing in Mister Hermann's groin. Craig stopped and got up. He reached down his hand to help up Mister Hermann, whose face had flushed red. Red from arousal, from embarrassment, or both, Craig didn't know. All he could see on Mister Hermann was a red face and a pair of plaid trousers tented near the zipper. Craig kept his laughing internal. "See you later, Mister Hermann," he said with a sing in his voice and went home.

A few weekends later, Craig showed up unannounced at Mister Hermann's apartment on Twenty-Ninth and Atkinson, two blocks down the street from his house. There, they danced and wrestled and wrestled and danced regularly on the weekends until Craig left for college. After that, Mister Hermann moved down the street into the upstairs unit of Mary and Hazelle's two-family house. That's where he lived when Siloah—when Craig's parents—praised him in print and wished him blessings in his new ministry.

Now, Craig was angry. The pastor's dogmatic exegesis of homosexuality on one page, the entire staff's praise of the homosexual teacher as the best thing for Siloah's members since the Resurrection on the next, and the discovery that he was way too connected to the man with the penetrating blue eyes—all of it turned Craig's insides to granite.

✍

A day and three packs of cigarettes later Craig called his mother and father and told them about everything—about Juneau Park, the man in the van, Jeffrey Dahmer, Mister Hermann—everything. He even told them about Roy. They told him that they loved him—no matter what—that they would come to visit him soon.

A few days after that, Craig was rummaging through a box of pictures when he saw the wallet-sized portrait of Roy. Craig couldn't remember when Roy had given him the picture. Craig turned it over, but there was nothing written on the back of it to remind him. In the photograph, Roy was wearing a gray, pinstriped three-piece suit. Slanted stripes of black and white and blue made up the thick, double-knotted necktie. Roy was sitting on a stool, face forward. His torso was turned slightly to his right, his legs open. His hands rested on his right leg. His left arm crossed his body, and his right hand looked as though it might be massaging ever so slightly his right wrist. A wide forehead and two bushy eyebrows away from a widow's peak, Roy's gray eyes looked right at you. His thin lips were framed from above by a well-groomed, thick brown mustache and from below by a soul patch pointed at his long, round chin. Though he wore no smile, the look on Roy's face reminded Craig of Roy's laughter. Craig put the photograph on the cocktail table next to the phone. He lifted the receiver and dialed the number.

1-414-961-1447.

Roy picked up on the third ring. When Craig told him who it was, he heard Roy smile through the phone.

"My goodness, how're you doing?" said Roy. "To what do I owe this pleasant surprise?"

"I'm fine. Been thinking about you a lot. Even more so now with everything that's going on in Milwaukee. It all seems like a bad, bad dream. Unreal. What's it like around there right now?"

"Well, I can't really tell you. I don't know. I huh-huh-huh-*haven't* been out too much lately. It's been about a year."

"Why not? What's going on?"

There was a silence.

"Let's just say that I have health issues." There was another silence. "Uh-uh-uh-I'm gonna beat this though. I have the best doctor in Milwaukee and I just know I'm gonna beat this, Craig."

"Are you still working?"

"No. They wouldn't let me do my job anymore after they found out. I had to tell them. I didn't wanna wait for them to suspect anything and then catch me off guard. I wanted to be in control of what was gonna happen. I worked for that dentist for over fifteen years."

"You're still the only dental lab technician I've ever met."

Roy laughed.

"How's Eric?"

Eric was Roy's longtime companion. Although they never lived together—Eric lived with and took care of his mother who suffered from multiple sclerosis—they would remain each other's firsts till the day they died. Craig had met Eric only once.

"He's not doing too good at all, Craig. He's in *way* worse shape than I am. I kept telling him to get himself checked, because if I had it, he huh-

huh-huh-had to have it too. But he waited and waited. Said he didn't wanna know. Now, he's got wasting. He lost fifty pounds in two weeks. I don't think it's gonna be much longer."

Craig took a deep drag from his cigarette and exhaled loudly enough for Roy to hear.

"Are you smoking?" There was a parental tone in Roy's voice.

"Uh. Yeah."

"Well, what duh-duh-duh-did you go and start doing that for? I told you not to smoke."

"You gave me a lot of good advice that I didn't take and a lot more that I did. I'm sure I'll quit someday." There was a silence. "I finally found out for the first time last year that I'm fine," said Craig, sensing that Roy wanted to know but didn't want to ask. "I don't blame Eric for not wanting to know. I didn't wanna know either, because I just figured I had it, and what could I do except wait to get sick? But I'm fine, and I'm gonna do my best to stay that way."

There was another, longer silence.

"Uh-uh-uh-uh I'm really glad to hear that, Craig. How's your family?"

"Everybody's doing well. I think my parents are gonna come and visit me soon. They haven't been back out this way since I graduated college, and now I live on my own, so they wanna see my apartment. Gina's fine. She works over at Bay Shore at Rogers & Hollands Jewelers. How's your mother? Does she know what's going on with you?"

"Old biddy'll probably outlive all of us," said Roy, laughing. "Yeah. She knows. I get down to Illinois to see her a lot more than I used to, since I huh-huh-huh-have so much time on my hands. She told me I might as well just move back home, but I don't think that would be such a good idea. I need to stay right where I am. My doctor is here. My friends are here. I need to stay in my life the way it is now, you know wuh-wuh-wuh-what I mean, Craig? I believe I can beat this thing, Craig, I really do."

There was an even longer silence.

"Roy, I want you to know something. All of your friends told you that you were a fool to get involved with me, as young as I was when we first met. But you didn't take their advice, you followed something in your gut that told you what you were doing wasn't gonna end in disaster. Somehow you knew I wasn't gonna report you, have you arrested, or blackmail you. I guess a person who thought they were somehow being abused, or felt like they had no control over the situation, or someone who just wanted to take advantage of you, might do such things. I want you to know that I have only and always felt nothing but love for you. I've never felt fear for you or about you, and even back then, I held you in the highest regard. You were my mentor, my lover, and my friend. I guess, after all, you really were my king,

Roy. You came to me during a part of my life when I was very unhappy. I wanted to quit school, but you encouraged me to stay. You always told me, just like my father, whose words I couldn't hear at the time, you always told me I could do anything I put my mind to, that if I kept my mind in the toughest game, I'd never lose it. You told me that I was special, and even though I didn't feel special, I believed it because you said it. And I wanna thank you. Thank you for being a part of my life and for loving me. But most of all, I wanna thank you for caring so much. I can only hope to meet someone who cares as much as you did. I don't know where I'd be if we hadn't met, but I know my life is better because we did."

Then there was the longest silence of all—it could have been two minutes or two hours. The air sounded dead, but it wasn't dead. It was alive. Alive with something both of them took time to share—to savor—without speaking.

Finally Roy said, softly, "Thank you. Thank you, Craig."

"If I come to Milwaukee for Christmas, I'll definitely come and see you, it's been too long."

"I'd like that. I don't look like I used to though. As you might guess, I'm thinner. I'm in no way gaunt, but I'm much thinner. Huh-huh-huh-how about you? Have you grown into the handsome man I told you you'd become? Have you lost any of that cute baby fat in your cheeks and developed those sculpted cheeks I said you'd get?"

"I don't know. You'll have to tell me when you see me." Craig held the phone in the crook of his neck. He snuffed out his cigarette in the ashtray next to Roy's picture. He picked it up and held it in his left hand. He circled his right forefinger over Roy's face and lips, ran it down Roy's torso, fondled Roy's left hand and right knuckles, touched the creasing shadows between Roy's legs.

"I told you that you looked like your father and when you grew up you would look like your mother. Remember when I told you that?"

Craig brought the picture to his nose. He closed his eyes and took a deep whiff. He could've sworn he smelled Lagerfeld, Roy's favorite cologne.

"We were resting on top of a picnic table in Brown Deer Park," Craig finally replied. "It was the only time we ever took a bike ride that far together. I remember feeling like I was on top of the world. I felt like I could tell you anything. You told me all about your family that day. I told you all about mine. I told you that I wish I knew who I looked like. And you told me. You said that I looked like my birth father and as I got older, I'd start looking more like my birth mother. And you said it so matter-of-factly it was as if you had just *seen* them. Maybe you had. I believed what you said. I still do. I think of what you said almost every time I look in the mirror, Roy."

"Do you thuh-thuh-thuh-think you will ever look for them, Craig?"

"I don't know, Roy. I just don't know. I don't wanna hurt my parents."

"Follow your heart, Craig. Follow your heart wherever it leads you. Craig, your heart will never fail you. It will never let you down."

Other than the goodbyes that ended their conversation, those were the last words Craig would ever hear Roy say. Craig did not go to Milwaukee for Christmas.

And it came to pass the next spring, on the fourteenth day of May in the nineteen hundred and ninety-second year, that Craig was walking past the Victory Gardens on his way to the first rehearsal of his first play. He stopped for no apparent reason and turned toward the Fens. Wearing a pair of gray sweatpants and a matching jacket, Roy emerged from a coppice of budding rhododendron. Craig waved. The sunlight passed through the prism of Roy's wide smile and bent toward Craig, flooding his sightlines with bands of color more vivid than any rainbow he'd ever seen. When the colors melted into the deep green of mid-spring foliage, Roy was gone.

Craig smiled and said out loud, "At least this time, I had a chance to say goodbye."

UP AT THE NET

1 As he tried to explain it, Craig drove Jennifer past St. Marcus Church and School where Gina went for a few years before transferring to Siloah. They drove by Roy's apartment, past the McDonald's where Craig once worked, and then back down to Brady Street East, the part of town once known for thrift shops, vintage clothes, good restaurants, bohemian artists, and cheap rent. Now, the restaurants were called bistros, thrift shops became boutiques, and the bohemians couldn't afford to buy the condos. Just off Brady Street on Franklin Place stood the old Boys Club building where Craig had been a member from third through sixth grade. As they drove by the building, which had become an African Methodist Episcopal Church, Craig recognized the man a few houses down watering his front lawn. Craig slowed down. "Hey, Winthrop," he yelled, "you missed a spot."

The man turned off the hose and walked toward Craig's car. "Craig? Craig Hickman? What on earth are you doing back here? Finally got sick of the East Coast?"

"Well, let's just say that I'm showing a very special person what my life used to be like. Winthrop, this is Jennifer. Jennifer, Winthrop." They spoke to each other.

"This is Winthrop Woodruff," Craig said to Jennifer. "He publishes one of the news magazines here in Milwaukee that I've written for. But I met him a long time ago in Juneau Park." Craig turned to Winthrop. "It's okay, dear, she won't tell. Do you remember that I'm adopted?"

"Now that you mention it."

"Well, this is my birth mother whom I found a few months ago. She's in town meeting my parents, taking a look at the life she missed."

Winthrop widened his eyes and opened his mouth as if to say: *wow*. He looked at Craig, then Jennifer, then again at Craig and said instead, "You do look like her. I'm honored to meet you, Jennifer." Jennifer smiled. Winthrop reached over Craig to shake Jennifer's hand.

"Well, we're heading back home now. Nice running into you and give my regards to your hubby."

✍

Rufus King High School was built like a prison with a gigantic stone stadium out back that recalled the ancient Coliseum. Named after a Union Civil War general, it was rumored that King had in fact been a prison. Despite its ominous appearance, this was only a rumor. King had been built as a high school, with a twin structure on the south side of town known as Pulaski High School. Craig drove Jennifer by Rufus King on their way back home from the east side. As much as Jennifer had wanted to see inside, school was out for the summer so the best he could do was show her around outside. The stadium had been torn down and replaced by open stands that surrounded the track. They sat down together high up in the stands.

"Your Uncle Josh used to play basketball right over there." Jennifer pointed across the track to the fenced-in basketball courts on the other side. Four tennis courts were situated next to the basketball courts. A black man and woman were playing on one of the tennis courts. The woman was the more skilled player, hitting balls, like a coach or an instructor, primarily to the man's backhand side. He hit several balls over the fence.

"I always wanted to play tennis."

"Why didn't you, son?"

"Too expensive. North Division, where Mama went to high school, and where I ran summer track, had a decent summer tennis program, but we couldn't afford all the equipment and all the travel. There were probably some sponsorship programs we could've applied for, but I never got my game anywhere near a level where I could convince a sponsor to back me."

"You excelled in most sports, son, just like your father. Frank was the captain and quarterback of Oakwood Academy's flag football team."

"At Siloah I was, too."

"What made you wanna play tennis?"

"I can't say that I excelled in basketball, and I was a pretty poor swimmer. Actually, I'm terrified of water, almost as much as I'm scared of the dark, but I swam anyway. I almost drowned three times when I was little. But I swam anyway. I set records in track and field when I was young, but when I grew so fast—a whole six inches in the summer between elementary and high school—my knees couldn't keep up and I slowed down. As for tennis—I'm not really sure why I wanted to play. I always liked the matches between Chris Evert and Martina Navratilova. They had totally different approaches to the game, Martina was always up at the net, Chris always back at the baseline hitting passing shots that Martina couldn't touch. I liked John McEnroe and Jimmy Connors, too, but that's because they were so passionate about what they were doing. Anyway, I guess I liked the notion that on the tennis court you're all you've got. With basketball, you had your whole team to help you win a game. Even if you weren't playing so well, you had others to fall back on. Running track and swimming were different. In track, at least in the individual events, you're never really competing *against* anyone. You ran your fastest and you won or you didn't. You swam your fastest, and someone else might swim faster and beat you. You jumped the farthest or the highest and you won the event or you didn't. You didn't have to really use your mind. But in tennis your opponent could have quite a bit to say about how well you played. It was you against them. Unless you and your opponent are entirely mismatched, you have to figure out how to win the match while you're playing it. No coach to turn to during the match. You might have a game plan, you might not. It almost doesn't matter. Either you have the ability to read the game or not, and if you have that ability—to figure it out as you go—then you better hope you have enough weapons and enough variety in your game to back it up and make the right adjustments. It's like life. Life is what's happening while you're making plans. You adjust to the balls life hits back at you, step into the court and dictate what's in your power to control, or you lose. You can have all the friends in the world, but when push comes to shove, all you really have is *you*. You have to figure it all out for yourself."

"Not if you have a strong and close family, son. That's what families are for. Your family is there to help you figure it out. Your family is there for you to lean on when you can't stand on your own."

"At the end of the day, you fall down alone. You stand alone. Someone might hold out his or her hand for you, but you have to want to grab it. It's up to you."

"Well, I want you to know that now that you've found your family, you don't ever have to be alone again."

"I don't think you see what I'm saying."

"I know what you're saying, son. I'm the mother. I'm *your* mother and I'm here to tell you that you won't ever have to feel alone or be alone again. Joseph, I'll always be here for you, son. Always." Jennifer put her arm around Craig's shoulder. "Now tell me, son, tell me about your high school friends. Tell me about your girlfriend, Kitty. Wasn't that her name? Joseph, your mother's here for you now, son, and I want you to tell me everything."

SARAH AND JOSEPH

1 And it came to pass that in September of the ninety-hundred and eighty-second year, Craig was assigned to Mr. Yosowsky's homeroom at Rufus King High School for the College Bound. Because of this designation, Rufus King boasted a mix of students from all over the Milwaukee area, even though it was situated in the inner city, only a mile from his house. To the neighborhood parents' dismay, middle school students had to apply to get into King, and that could mean that children who lived right down the street from the school were unable to attend it.

In the same year, Gina entered the senior class at Wisconsin Lutheran High School in the far-out suburb of Wauwautosa. Wisco, as it was called by many of the Wisconsin Synod Lutherans in southeastern Wisconsin, was the high school of choice for any child who had attended any of the elementary schools in the synod's school system. But Wisco's tuition was expensive; Hazelle and Mary could only afford to send their oldest there. Just as well. Craig had already become frustrated with the lack of debate about the word of God engendered by his elementary-school teachers and church pastors. As early as the second grade, he could see that none of them were interested in the challenges he introduced in Catechism class, and he didn't look forward to enduring any more of that nonsense for another four years. As it was, Craig didn't really want to be in *any* high school, and if he could've had his way, he would have flapped his big wings and flown east, chasing the sunrise. Instead, Craig showed up in Mr. Yowosky's homeroom everyday of his freshman year, never tardy, even if he woke up with a stomachache, as he had so many mornings that first semester. Encouraged by Mister Gallagher, his freshman gym teacher and basketball coach, he got to school an hour early every other day of the week to lift weights. Enduring the rigor and sore muscles of Gallagher's warden-like workouts, Craig's naturally thin frame and long limbs bulked up in no time at all.

Craig busied himself with an overabundance of extracurriculars. In addition to basketball, he joined track and field, student government, math track, and debate. Over the next three years, he would switch from basketball to swimming during the fall semester, and joined forensics, yearbook, choir, swing choir, student government and national honor society. Throughout all of it, his grades remained perfect, and he enjoyed being atop the honor roll every marking period when it was posted on the second-floor bulletin board right outside room 214 where he took Latin, his favorite class, taught by Miss Link, his favorite teacher. He devoted more energy trying to astound his teachers, coaches, and guidance counselors than trying to impress his classmates, and when freshman year ended, he could not think of a single person he could call friend.

2 Joseph Heinemann was proud of his heritage. Although his mother was not Jewish, his father was, and he identified with that part of himself so much that, "I'm Jewish," was one of the first things about himself he told his new friend on the school bus ride to their first swimming practice over at Riverside High. Since King had no pool, the team used the facilities at Riverside, which was right around the corner from Roy's house near the corner of North and Oakland avenues on the east side. Craig found Joseph goofy in an endearing way. Joseph's big front teeth reminded him of Roosevelt, his first best friend from elementary school, but his body—broad shoulders that tapered to a svelte waist and long sinewy legs—could have been the subject of a classical sculptor. An honor roll constant, Joseph asked a lot of questions—a lot of the time. Craig found his interests in philosophy and humanity comforting and attractive; they became close friends. Craig called him Joseph the Jew and although Joseph knew the name Craig's parents gave him, Joseph called him Craig van den Landenberg Hickman, a name with a bit of Dutch in it.

"You taking the bus back to school today?" Joseph asked Craig after swim practice one evening.

"Not today. I'm meeting my friend Roy."

"Who's Roy? What high school does he go to?"

"He's not from any high school. I met him downtown last summer."

They were the last two in the shower and Craig felt like testing the waters. "He's actually a guy that, well, I guess you could call him a very special man. He's a very special man to me."

Joseph rinsed the shampoo out of his eyes and looked squarely at Craig.

"What are you talking about, van den Landeberg? Are you trying to tell me that he—that *you*—?"

Craig raised his eyebrows and looked directly into Joseph's eyes. "Don't even try to tell me that you're surprised."

Joseph was the only person in high school to whom Craig confided all his truths. Joseph was also the person that made Mary confront the part of her she'd suppressed with all her might—and when might wasn't enough, she'd called on her Savior for reinforcements—since the day nine years before when Miss Kado had called her and her husband to their son's school to show them what she'd found on the floor next to his desk the day before.

"Son, let me ask you something," she prefaced while organizing the magazines on the cocktail table in the living room one Saturday afternoon a few weeks after Craig and Joseph's shower conversation. Craig sat rocking in the chair that had belonged to his grandfather, the rocking chair his Granny Alma gave them, the chair that became his father's favorite place to rest while awake. "Now I'm your mother and I feel I should know whether or not you are—are you a homosexual, Craig?"

"I can't be *a* homosexual, Mama, cuz homosexual is an adjective. Well, that's all it needs to be, anyway. Why do you ask?"

"You don't have no girlfriends, you don't talk about no girls anyway, you're on the swim club, and as far as I know, only boys call here. That Roy calls sometimes, but that Joe Heinemann; he calls almost everyday. You two must be mighty, mighty close. He's part of your swimming club, right?"

"Joe and I are best friends, Mama. Can't I have a best friend?"

"Certainly, son. But I'm your mother. Wouldn't you want me to know? I would think that, as your mother, I should know. Better that I ask you, son, don't you think?"

While she was mining her son's world, Mary Juanita straightened up the entire living room, closed and opened the front curtains at least four times, and dusted and buffed the television screen to a gleaming gloss.

"I guess. You can ask anything you want." Craig paused and then declared, "I'm a teenager, Mama. A *teenager*. That's enough, isn't it?"

"I guess it is, son. I guess it is."

3 The next semester, Craig warmed up to Sarah Katherine called Kitty, the short, petite, glamorous East Indian girl with the starlight smile and the bouncy breasts. She told almost everybody on the swim team that she had a crush on him, hoping his teammates would eventually convince Craig that he should ask to carry her books to class. Craig thought she was the prettiest freshman at Rufus King. She seemed older than the other girls

in her class, and wouldn't she be the cat's meow among her friends for going steady with a *junior*, couldn't you just die? Her sister, Bethany Dionne, who had jet-black hair longer and thicker than Gina's, was the offspring of a black soldier and a Vietnamese girl. Her brother, Nathaniel, was a full-blooded black boy whose coal-colored skin was always ashy. Just like Craig and Gina, all of them were adopted as babies. Kitty's parents, both white professionals, were divorced when Kitty was seven. All the children stayed with their mother. When Kitty was ten, a woman the children called Aunt Melanie moved in and helped take care of them. But even eyes that couldn't see could see that Aunt Melanie, with her square body and cowboy swagger, was not her mother's sister.

Craig and Kitty fell in love.

Hazelle let his son use the car almost every weekend. Craig would drive Kitty to the McKinley Marina Park down at the lakefront, a mile up from Juneau Park on Lake Drive. He'd park the silver '84 Ford LTD Crown Victoria station wagon as many spaces as he could from the other lovers' cars. After he'd collapsed the back seat flat, Craig and Kitty would stretch out and get lost in deep conversations that led to petal-sweet kisses in the ride he called the Love Boat. Craig would knead, gently, her breasts, lush pillows he'd rest his head upon after the breathtaking ballet of foreplay. He'd run his hot hands up her thighs and explore between her legs with one finger, then two, her back arching, her neck agape, her belly wide to the moon. She'd eat his neck between the nape and the back of the ear like someone eating her first meal after fasting. They'd commune for hours serenaded by syrupy love songs from the evening program where the deejay spoke in a voice slow and low as a moan. Craig would keep her curfew every time.

Except once.

That night, the sky was clear, the stars bright. The scent of fresh water and fish skipped away on a breeze that was just right. Holding hands, Craig and Kitty walked along the pier. "Have you ever thought about your biological mother," Kitty asked.

"I think about who she is and where she might be," said Craig. "Mostly, I think about why."

"Why she did it, you mean?"

Craig nodded.

"Me too," Kitty agreed. "I don't suppose she had a choice. That's what I think about mine."

"Everyone always has a choice. No exceptions. I just wanna know why she made the one she made."

"I was born in India and my birth mother couldn't feed me is what Mom said. So many babies are still starving over there."

"Mama told me that my birth mother was in college when she had me.

She thinks my name was Jody or Bernard, she can't remember which, but she saw my name on a piece of paper and she's pretty sure she heard the foster family call me Jody when they said goodbye to me."

"Do you think you'll ever look for her one day? I wouldn't know where to begin."

"My sister got all this information not too long ago from the agency that handled her case. It was a two-page story about her biological parents. Her father was black and her mother was a German woman who'd an affair with him while her husband was out of the country. Her father was shot dead in Montana, or somewhere out west, and her mother has other children from her husband. While I was reading it, I wondered if I could ever be ready to read all of that stuff about myself. I just don't know."

"I really wanna know where this nose came from," said Kitty. They both laughed. They stopped walking and looked out over the water, which was now a black tarpaulin. Beneath it was another whole world, full of mysterious incarnations Craig would probably never meet.

"Right now," said Craig, wistfully, "I just wish I could see a picture of her. Of him, too, I guess. Just to see who I looked like. It's funny how everybody says I look like my mother..."

"You do."

"...but I'd... yeah—I guess so. They feed you long enough you start looking like'm. But, I don't know, I've always wanted to know who I really looked like."

"I was in kindergarten when my mom told me I was adopted. I wasn't surprised since I could see that I didn't look like my parents the way other kids looked like theirs. My parents always made us feel so special."

"My parents did with us, too. They told us that we were lucky because they chose us. No way would we ever have to wonder whether or not we were wanted because they picked us out. Same as I picked out Chico from all the other puppies."

"Oh, Craig. You can't compare the two. Picking out a dog is totally different from picking out a baby."

"Is it? Really?"

"Well, of course it is. You can't compare a dog to a child."

"Why not?"

"It's not right. A puppy is a pet. A child is a person, someone you're gonna take care of until they get old enough to take care of themselves."

"A pet never gets old enough to take care of itself."

"You're not saying you think a pet is superior to a child, are you?"

"Am I?"

"Stop that. I hate when you do that."

"When I do what?" Kitty pushed her shoulder playfully into his chest.

Craig held on, his right arm around her waist. "I just wonder," he said, "if the feeling of picking out a child is anything like the feeling I had when I picked out Chico. It's a living thing, a helpless little living thing that didn't come out of you, that you didn't have anything to do with creating, something somebody else didn't want or couldn't keep, and you're bringing it into your life, into your home, and calling it your own." Craig shrugged his shoulders and sighed. "I wonder how they do it."

Kitty looked at her watch. "Oh, my God, look at the time," her voice painted with panic. "I'm gonna miss my curfew. You gotta get me home."

Her mother was sitting on the couch when Craig ushered Kitty into the foyer. Kitty didn't give her a chance to utter a word. "Mom, please don't be mad, it wasn't his fault, really it wasn't. It was a perfect night, Mom. Everything was perfect. And after the movie we took a walk down by the pier near the marina. I don't know if you remember or not, but Craig and his sister are also adopted. Anyway, we got into this, like, long conversation about, you know: *that*. We just, like, lost track of time and got home as soon as we could. So, mom, please don't be mad. It won't happen again."

And it didn't.

Kitty's mother invited Craig to stay for hot chocolate and cookies before he went home. When he got there, his father was asleep in bed, his mother snoring on the couch. She woke up when he walked into the living room.

"Look at me layin up here, TV watchin me," she muttered in her just-woke-up voice. "You have a good time tonight, son?"

"Best night ever."

"That's good, son. That's good. There some mashed potatoes on the stove, some chicken in the oven if you're still hungry." Mary grabbed her pillow and dragged her blanket to the bedroom. "Good night, son. When you talk to Kitty to tell her you got home safely, tell her I said hi."

Craig did just that and then fixed himself a plate. He was always hungry for his mother's food.

4 By senior year, Joseph was thoroughly confused. Craig went out with Kitty almost every weekend and went over to Roy's after swim practice once or twice during the week. "Hey, van den Landeberg, walk me home after practice." He assumed it was one of the nights Craig would visit Roy. "I gotta figure something out with you."

"No can do. I'm going back to school on the bus today."

"Then skip the shower so we can talk before the bus leaves."

Craig obliged. The first out of the locker room, they stood in the parking lot and talked. The sun had just disappeared. The whipping wind made it feel colder than it was. Joseph was chomping at the bit. Allergic to chlorine, Craig kept sneezing. "So what's the big emergency?"

"I need to know what's going on with you. You say you are so in love with Kitty but what about Roy?"

"What about Roy?"

"I thought you said you loved him, too."

"I do."

"How can you love Kitty and Roy at the same time?"

"Do you love both your parents? Do your parents love both you and your sister?"

"That's different."

"How so? Love is love. Why should a person only be able to love one person at a time? Doesn't that limit love too much?"

"Where do you get this stuff from? Nobody thinks that way."

"The last time I checked, I was somebody. I don't care what anybody else thinks."

"Craig van den Landenberger Hickman, you just make it up as you go, don't you?"

"If you say so, Joseph the Jew. But I'd rather make up my own rules than follow the ones somebody else made up for me. Then at least I live my own life. That way I've only got myself to blame if I don't like the life I'm living. Wouldn't you get tired of living the life somebody else wanted you to live?"

"I've never looked at it like that."

"Then it's about time you get some new glasses. Wait a minute." Craig frowned and then sneezed three times. "Is this what's so important? Is my love life the subject of your urgency, or is there something else going on?" Craig paused and then looked squarely in Joseph's eyes. "Do you think you're like I am?"

"No. Yes. *No*. Well, I mean, of course, I'm like you, Craig, I'm a lot like you, but not like *that*. Sometimes I feel like we're the same person, nobody likes to talk to me about the kinds of things we talk about, but then you're so different from me, too. I'm Jewish, you're black. I'm... Well, I have to say, Landeberg, only the ladies can get me off. Men just don't get me hard. "

"Me neither."

"Wait." Joseph wrinkled his brow. "You mean you and Roy don't—?"

"What I mean is men just don't get me hard. If men *just* got me hard, I wouldn't bother with'm. It's about so much more than getting hard or getting off. Something I can't explain. But you'd know it if you felt it, Joe. That much I can guarantee." Craig sneezed, obliterating, momentarily, the clapping sound of the stars and stripes on the gymnasium's flagpole whipped by the wind. "You'd know it if you felt it."

"Do you think Kitty knows about you?"

"I don't know. No. Well, she hasn't acted like it anyway. But, I mean, really, how could she not? You heard what someone blurted out when Lise and I were announced for homecoming court, didn't you?"

"Yeah. I remember. 'Look at the two princesses' or something like that. I thought it was kind of funny."

"Me too. Made me wish I'd worn a dress."

"That would've made me so mad. But you gotta admit, it was still kind of funny."

"It would've made you mad if I'd worn a dress?"

"No, silly. If somebody called me a princess."

"Joe, I doubt anybody would ever call *you* a princess." Craig punched Joseph on the shoulder in jest. Like a girl playing hopscotch Joseph squeaked; like an actress on a soap opera, he slapped Craig's face. They laughed and pushed each other. Then Craig said, "But yeah, it was funny. I didn't really care though. Our class elected *me* junior prince, not the fool who said it. He was probably just jealous cuz he wasn't walking down the red carpet with such a beautiful girl on his arm."

"It must be nice having it both ways."

"It is what it is. I don't think about it that much. Bottom line: Sarah loves me; I love her. Roy loves me; I love him. I'm not gonna spend the rest of my life with either one of them, but I sure am enjoying myself right now."

"Who're you gonna spend the rest of your life with?"

"I don't know." Craig watched the fog funneling from Joe's mouth disappear in a hurry. "I haven't met him yet."

"You're too much," Joseph said, laughing. A small group of teammates came out of the building.

"I'd rather be too much than not enough," said Craig, walking toward the bus. "See you tomorrow. And get your own love life, will ya?" Craig climbed into the bus. Joseph waited till the bus filled up with the last teammate and pulled away. He waved to Craig as the bus turned west onto Locust Avenue. Craig waved back. He saw Joseph pull his hat down over his ears, adjust his backpack, and start walking east toward home.

ROOSEVELT

1 After he told her about Sarah and Joseph, Jennifer wanted to go and see Roosevelt's gravesite. May as well, thought Craig. I've told her about everything else, may as well go on and tell her about Roosevelt. Ain't much more of the story left anyhow. I'll tell her about one more thing, and that's it. If she don't get a clear picture about my life by then, well, then, that's her problem. Even still, she better tell me what she made me wait till we got to Milwaukee to tell me. And if she doesn't—swear to God—I'm gone have to slap her. Ain't never thought about hitting another woman in my whole entire life, and here I am thinking about slapping the one who brought me here. Lord have mercy. Must be channeling *her* again. Cuz Lord knows, by now, she must really wanna slap the one who brought her here. But anyway....

They arrived at Evergreen Cemetery, which was only a few minutes away from Rufus King.

2 Roosevelt looked like no other boy Craig had ever seen. On the first day of kindergarten, they faced each other, two curious little boys in the middle of the classroom looking for a way to bridge the barrier between them. "Hey, you," asked Craig, "why are your teeth so big?"

Roosevelt looked back through bubble eyes bulging from a head way too big for his skinny body and replied, "I don't know. Why are your arms so long? You look like a monkey."

They became immediate friends, sharing among many things, a zeal for football. In the realm of their fantasies, they were sports broadcasters who followed every season of the NFL. They documented their predictions for each season in a comic strip complete with dialogue, outrageous detail, and catchy cartoon figures. Whenever they couldn't agree on the dialogue or on who would draw what team's figures, they'd have a fight. Whoever won the fight won the right to write or draw whatever he wanted. Their fights were always physical, but they rarely hurt each other. The one who was hit too hard or pinned to the ground during a wrestling match would only have to say, "Stop," and that was that. Once, during a slapfest over which one would draw the Miami Dolphins, Roosevelt slapped Craig so hard, his face stung for hours. In response, Craig slapped Roosevelt with the back of his hand, but his knuckle connected in just the right way with Roosevelt's large front teeth that they cut through the skin, drawing blood. "That's what you get for trying that backhand," Roosevelt taunted, laughing. "God don't like ugly. You know the backhand isn't allowed." With a stinging cheek and a drawing hand in need of first aid, Craig surrendered. Roosevelt drew the best Miami Dolphins strip ever.

Roosevelt was the brother Craig never had. As brothers, Roosevelt never made Craig feel he needed to be anything other than who he was. As brothers, Roosevelt accepted all of Craig's faults, including his blunt and sarcastic mouth. And though some of their classmates found it necessary to call Craig "sissy," "faggot," "punk," "mama's boy," or "little girl," Roosevelt only called him by his name. They knew each other's favorite things. Salami was Craig's preferred lunchmeat; bologna, Roosevelt's. Craig ate his salami with a dollop of Miracle Whip; Roosevelt couldn't spread enough mustard on his Oscar Mayer. Craig loved the crunch of chunky peanut butter, Roosevelt preferred creamy. Craig couldn't choose a favorite flower, while Roosevelt adored red roses. Appropriate since his name was from the Dutch for "field of roses." Craig's world was blessed. Brilliantly blessed. Hansel had his gingerbread rooftop; Gretel, her candy-caned windowpanes. But Craig had his Roosevelt. What more could a little boy want?

3 And it came to pass on the thirtieth day of March, in the nineteen hundred and seventy-seventh year, that Roosevelt didn't come to school.

That evening, Craig was eating dinner with his sister and his father when the phone rang. Gina Louise went to the hallway just off the kitchen and picked up the phone. The call was brief.

"Who was it?" Hazelle asked his daughter.

"Lena Triplett. Roosevelt died today."

"Oh, my God. What happened?"

"All she said was that he was in the hospital and his lungs collapsed.

Craig, did you know he was in the hospital?"

Craig couldn't answer. He ran down the back stairs and out the door into the backyard where he threw up under the Mountain Ashe tree and slumped onto the grass. A few minutes later, he heard his mother thank the woman who gave her a ride home from her church meeting. He ran to the front of the house crying out, "Roosevelt died, Mama, Roosevelt *died*, Mama, and it's all my fault."

Mary picked her son up from the ground and carried him into the house, laying him on the mustard-colored couch in the living room.

"Why?" was the only question Craig could ask in the days that followed.

"I don't know why, son, but Roosevelt has gone on to a better place. It was meant to be this way. We don't always know what the good Lord has in store for us."

"But, Daddy, why did He have to take my friend? We said we would be best friends forever. I'll never have a friend like him again, Daddy. He just disappeared. He didn't even say goodbye. Where did he go? Why did he have to go?"

No one could give him an answer that made any sense because, in his mind, it *was* his fault.

4 The AmerIndians called it Milwaukee, the place "where the rivers meet." Settled in the eighteen thirties by French fur traders who benefited from the three rivers that flow into Lake Michigan, Milwaukee became home to many German, Irish, Scandinavian, and Polish settlers. By the eighteen forties, German immigrants became the largest group. They lived together in enclaves and wanted their language and culture to take a strong foothold in Milwaukee.

By the eighteen sixties, Brew City boasted nineteen German breweries; the smallest of these housed taverns. The largest had beer gardens outside where extended families came together for embellished chatter, for society, for the soul soothing delight of freshly cased bratwurst boiled in vats of beer over flaming cauldrons. Thousands of men, women, and children would gather every Sunday at Schlitz Garden, the biggest one in the Middle West.

These convivial, working-class immigrants also brought to Milwaukee the tradition of forming and joining associations. The church became the main meeting place of many of these Vereine. German Catholics, Jews, and Lutherans built churches and temples on almost every street corner in every neighborhood. Here they worshipped and thanked their gods for deliverance through danger on their journeys across the ocean to an unknown land. This ethic influenced the culture of every immigrant group that came to Milwaukee, including the thousands of Southern blacks who migrated north in the Great Diaspora after World War I. Milwaukee became a city of segregated neighborhoods where deep ethnic pride and the guarding of staked-out territory created enemy lines that caused decades of conflict and unrest. During the sixties, Milwaukee was called the Selma of the North when a throng of Negroes marched against Jim Crow and violence.

The children of Siloah Lutheran Evangelical Church and School were the children of these activists—wrought, cast, and molded in the same smelting furnaces from the same sturdy iron. The strongest ones turned to steel, able to withstand anything. Most of them worked hard. All of them played hard. On their playground, you could play their games only if you followed their strict and competitive rules. If you wouldn't, couldn't, or did not want to, you automatically forfeited the game and lost. It was that simple. Cheaters had no allies. Those wanting to change the rules—no jurors. Whether it was doubledutch, basketball, hopscotch, or kickball, the majority favorite, you had to play by the rules if you wanted to win and didn't everybody *love* to win?

Roosevelt and Craig were always on the same kickball team. A few days after the Miami Dolphins Backhand, as they both immediately came to call it, their team played a nailbiter. Their opponents had a better record of wins and losses, and if they were to make the kickball playoffs, they needed to win. Roosevelt seemed more tired than usual, but he decided to play anyway because the stakes were so high. At the bottom of the last inning—last because recess was about to end and no game was ever extended into the next recess—Roosevelt was up to kick. He looked at his best friend and said, "I can't do it."

Craig had never heard these words from him. "Yes you can. You have to. You know we can't skip your turn or let somebody kick in your place."

"I know, Craig, but I just can't. I'm too tired."

"Just one last kick. C'mon, Roosevelt. Please. We gotta get the runners on second and third home just to tie this game."

Roosevelt corralled himself, shored up his energy, and kicked a home run over the playground's back fence. Jumping about like they'd just won the pennant, his teammates cheered as the runners crossed home plate. Roosevelt's crossing gave them the one-point victory just as the bell rang for the end of recess.

The next day, Roosevelt didn't come to school.

5 It was April, the season of storms. Sinister clouds the color of coal dust billowed swiftly above. The atmosphere, still as meditation, held a hue of yellowish-green and the glorified scent of freshly cut grass.

The funeral was held at New Hope Baptist, the church Roosevelt's mother belonged to, which stood on the corner of Atkinson Avenue and Roosevelt Drive, five blocks away from the Hickmans' house. The whole event played like a dream from which Craig couldn't wake up. About halfway through the service, the Reverend Roy Wilkins asked for a moment of stillness. What little afternoon light there was leaking into the church through the stained glass windows darkened to the color of night. Soon, the stillness was shaken by torrents of rain beating so hard against the roof it seemed as if the whole church might tumble in on itself. Minutes later, a tornado passed over, howling as it moved from the balcony choir loft to the altar and then whistled away into the distance. In unison, the congregation exhaled.

When the service resumed, it was time to view the body. Roosevelt's mother said one last goodbye, kissing her son's eight-year-old body on the forehead.

Craig would become her surrogate son. Soon, she would bring him all of Roosevelt's clothes. He would wear them with equal parts pride and despair to school everyday for the rest of third grade. She would be moved by the engraved crucifix memorial Craig would choose with their teacher to hang on the cement-block wall just above their favorite reading area. She would attend his high school graduation nineteen years later and hear his unconventional valedictory address. She would pray for him as he departed east for oceans and leagues of ivy. But Craig could never replace her Roosevelt, and she would have to find strength in her Lord, in her*self*, to get through the heart-shattering stupidity of burying a child.

For the funeral, she designated Craig an honorary pallbearer because he wasn't strong enough to carry the weight of Roosevelt's casket. After the procession, Roosevelt's mother also allowed Craig to ride in the family limousine in the mile-long procession to the graveyard. Evergreen Cemetery, which abutted Lincoln Park, the inner city's largest public park, was where she chose to lay her son's body down. There, on every thirtieth of March, every one of his birthdays, and every Memorial Day, she would turn the area around Roosevelt's flat-on-the-ground headstone into a field of red roses.

Craig sat in the back seat listening to the wipers whoosh across the windshield, to Rufus and Chaka's EVERLASTING LOVE on the radio, not realizing how strange it was for the radio to be on at all. On the way to Roosevelt's earth, the tombstones blurred by as Craig absentmindedly picked on the scab that had crusted over the knuckle on his right hand. But it was too soon.

Much. Too. Soon.

He raised his hand to his mouth and licked away the blood that dripped from his wound.

CHURCH

✎

1 Sunbeams pierced the humid air and melted wads of gum glistened on the sidewalk in front of the church. It was Sabbath morning and Jennifer and Craig went to Sharon SDA Church for worship service. Jennifer hadn't planned on stepping foot in her old church while she was in Milwaukee but when Craig told her he wanted to go there, she said, "If that's what you really want, son, then I'll do it. Just for you, son." The service was boring, the stinging sermon another rehash of the first commandment—thou shalt have no other gods before me—a thin veil for: every religion in the whole entire world is wrong, except for this one. Following the sermon, a trio of men with voices higher than pre-pubescent boys tightly harmonized a few songs. The benediction sent the congregation on their way, but a crowd remained and swarmed around Jennifer as though she owed all of them money. Of course, Jennifer hadn't been in their midst in a number of years. Because of her gregariousness (not to mention her family name), many of the congregants knew who she was. Another crowd of people, all of them women, gathered around Craig and got so close up in his face, he felt like he'd just given a performance. Questions popped from the small crowd like champagne corks.

"Aren't you Joshua's son?"

"*Must* be. Which one are you? Little Josh or Christian?"

"Doesn't he look like *all* of them?"

"Well, I didn't know *Jennifer* had a son. Doesn't she just have three girls?"

"When *exactly* were you born?"

"*Where* exactly were you born?"

"Exactly how old were you when you were adopted?"

"Do you live here in Milwaukee?"

"Doesn't it feel just wonderful—just *wonderful*—to find your mother after all these years?"

"I'm gonna run to my car and get my camera. Will you take a picture with me so I can show my daughter? She's not gonna *believe* this."

"Are you an Adventist?"

"Are you married?"

He answered the ones they asked and a few they didn't. If they wanted to make something up in the re-telling at least they had all the facts to work with. When they retreated, a black man who looked no older than Craig and carrying a baby girl walked up to him. As the man got closer, Craig recognized him as the pianist who sang with and accompanied the singers earlier. "Did I hear you say that you went to Siloah?" the man asked.

"Sure did."

"My good cousins, Kenyatta and Roxanne Dixon, go there."

"Of course. I went to school with them. I used to usher in church with your uncle."

"That's my mother's brother."

"Adrian, this is my son, Joseph," said Jennifer, walking over from her group of women. "Joseph, this is Adrian. Remember when I told you my mother was like a mother to a few of the children from a big family? Well, this is one of those children. She literally helped raise him."

Adrian freed one of his arms from the baby and hugged Jennifer. "Good to see you, Missus Plain, good to see you. How is Sister White?"

"She's fine. We were just down in Georgia visiting my mother last week." Jennifer shook the baby's foot. "And who is *this* little angel?"

"This is my daughter, Kamika. That's my wife over there." Adrian, pointed to a round woman standing near the piano.

Same story, different decade, thought Craig. How many men had Craig seen (danced with, even) throughout his life—femme men, butch men, many of them married-with-children men—who, on their knees, worshipped the Lord every Sunday (or Saturday) morning after worshipping cock on the same knees and dancing naked with men on blankets or beneath trees the night before? It's the new millennium for heaven's sake. Isn't it time, at last, for people to release themselves from the duplicity terror requires? "How old is little miss adorable Kamika?" Kamika smiled at Craig.

"Sixteen months," said Adrian.

"She's absolutely beautiful," said Jennifer. "Congratulations." She tickled Kamika in that kootchie-kootchie-coo place, making Kamika giggle, her smile opening to a yawn. "Tomorrow, we're going to Siloah with Joseph's family where hopefully I'll get to meet your cousins if they're there."

"You probably know some of my other brothers," Adrian said to Craig. He recited a small list of names of brothers who played organ or piano or directed the choir at area churches, and a few other names of brothers, believed to be of his father but not his mother, who did the same.

"Your father sounds like my birth father. Had more sons with more different women than an Old Testament king. Biggest difference between yours and mine: only *one* of his is actually *known* to have had anything to do with the *choir*." They both winked a knowing eye and laughed a knowing laugh. Adrian gave Craig his phone number and told him to call if he wanted to go out some night while he was in town.

Craig and Jennifer gathered their belongings and left the church. On the way to the parking lot Jennifer said, "One of his brothers died of AIDS a few years ago."

"Was he gay?"

"Yes."

"Then I guess it runs in the family." They got in the car. When he pulled out of the parking lot, Craig said, "Tomorrow when we go to my church, we'll get there early and I'll show you around the school section. Remind me to show you the classroom and tell you the story of how I got caught."

"Got caught with what?"

"I'll tell you tomorrow."

2 "You better sit down," she told them. When Mary Juanita and Hazelle arrived at Siloah Lutheran School that bitter-cold afternoon, their son's first-grade teacher, Carol Kado, simply handed Hazelle the three-page letter and said in her trademark monotone, "I found this on the floor near your son's desk after school yesterday."

As Craig watched his father read, Craig's heart leapt out of his chest and landed on the floor right where Miss Kado had picked up the letter. "What the *hell* is this," yelled Hazelle, "about you and Dante doin up each other in the bathroom?" The anger in Hazelle's eyes and the pitch of his voice, like some fire-and-brimstone preacher, told Craig that his father already knew the answer. Craig kept his mouth shut. "What's wrong, boy? Cat got your tongue?" Hazelle persisted, pulling on his son's left ear. "Now stop your crying and answer me, you little faggot." Still, his son said nothing. Craig had already left the afterschool meeting and flown to a place where everything was as good as it gets.

And it came to pass on the eighth day of December, in the nineteen hundred and sixty-seventh year, that Craig's libido came out of the womb long before the rest of him. At the age of two, he couldn't have told anyone his favorite foods, sights, sounds, or colors. But he knew some things he liked, and how to get them: boys, boys, boys, and more boys. Growing up on Twenty-Fourth Street in Milwaukee, Wisconsin—home of "Laverne and Shirley," "Happy Days," beer, bratwurst, chocolate, frozen custard, and serial killers—Stanley was the only other boy on the block and he, too, was a sensually enlightened tot.

Their favorite game was simple. Stanley was older than Craig, but smaller, a bit shier. Craig played the heroic mother, melting her boy's pains away. Stanley would take off his clothes. Fueled by the sensation of soft skin over lithe muscle, Craig would rub Stanley's chest or stomach to calm Stanley's pretend cough or bellyache. Sometimes, Craig would lay Stanley on his stomach and rub Vaseline all over his back, his little booty, down his skinny legs, imagining the thick, unctuous jelly the camphorated oil Craig's mother rubbed on him when he caught cold. They never switched roles because Stanley enjoyed Craig's hot hands too much; Craig, the sweet Play-Doh Stanley's body became under his sure touch. Craig loved not only Stanley with his egghead and teensy ears, but the vital thing he'd become in their rooms behind closed doors. They knew better than to tell it. Not out of guilt or shame—they knew not the language of guilt, weren't yet attuned to the frequencies of shame—but because any telling might taint the pure grace of their sacred game.

When Craig was old enough to attend parochial school, he could choose from so many boys. Most of the boys were just experimenting with Craig because he was always eager to rub their backs. But Dante was his steady, his mainstay. Craig and Dante had a thing going on from the first week of kindergarten. The first time they played, they hid in the coat closet while the rest of the class assembled for recess. Dante's palms started on Craig's chest and slid, slowly, down his stomach till they paused just below his belt buckle. Dante took back his hands, unzipped his own pants, and pushed the door ajar to let in a little light. "Show me yours," said Dante, "and I'll show you mine." Without hesitation, Craig unzipped his pants. But this first time, Dante only wanted to look, not touch. Dante leaned toward Craig and pressed, softly, his bee-stung lips against Craig's.

That first tender kiss gave Craig something new to crave. As surely as catching a whiff of the oven's delights, simply looking at Dante stirred Craig's hunger. Dante had skin the color of molasses and a nose that spread across his face like batter, overtaking the corners of his croissant smile in a race for ear-to-ear. At five, they couldn't know what pleasures awaited a restless pair of precocious little boys, couldn't know all the things their bodies could do, before their bodies could do much. In their eyes, however, lived the knowledge that only they could offer one another such pleasure.

By second grade, Craig and Dante were love-stricken fools. During Dr. Seuss reading hour, they would sit up under each other and surreptitiously hold hands. When they were supposed to be memorizing their multiplication tables, they would pass notes to each other. The shortest ones said: *Meet me in the church basement bathroom before the end of lunch. How we get away? Ask Miss Kado to go to the bathroom.*

On the day before Valentine's, Craig wrote Dante a three-page letter pronouncing his love and reminiscing the intimate moments they stole during school hours. He created it in cursive, perfectly executed, on wide-ruled paper with curved corners torn from a Mead black spiral notebook. So proud was he of this letter, so pleased with himself for writing it, in *cursive*, no less, he folded it up all nice and neat, opened his desk to put in inside, but left it sticking out of the front corner just a little bit. Not that he would have, but he didn't want to forget about it. He planned to give it to Dante first thing the next day, before prayer. So caught up in his romance, it never dawned on him that Millicent, the last to leave the classroom that day, would forget something from her desk, which was right in front of his, and knock the letter to the floor with her hip on the way back out.

The next morning when Craig arrived, he rushed to his desk, only to find that his letter wasn't there. Sweat broke over his face like waves. Where was his *magnum opus*, his Hallmark sentiment to his Valentine with a capital *v*? He searched frantically through his desk, looking under his Catechism, his book of Bible stories, his penmanship book. "Did you lose something?" rang Miss Kado's voice over his right shoulder. Startled, he slammed the desk on his left hand. He heard snickers. He couldn't look up. "Go see the nurse to get some ice and I'll talk to you later." Holding his breath, he ran out of the classroom, eyes fixed on the speckled linoleum floor.

In the nurse's office, Craig soaked his hand in a bowl of ice water and his weighty tears poured easily. Even though his teacher didn't come right out and say so, he knew she'd read what he'd lost. Now what? There was no way he could talk himself out of this one—he'd written too much love into the letter. Still pouring when Miss Kado came back, he quickly smeared the tears with his good hand, stopped sniffling, and sat, breathless, while Miss Kado, devoid emotion, spoke deliberately. "I've called your parents. We'll all meet right after school today. You may come back to class now."

When he returned, he couldn't even look at Dante. Or anyone else. He ate no lunch, played no kickball at recess, raised no hand to answer any of Miss Kado's questions during arithmetic, his favorite class. Valentine's Day was ruined and he suspected the worst was yet to come. His punishment, whatever it would be, would be unbearable.

✍

"When we get home, I'll give you something to *really* cry about." Hazelle tore up the letter and threw it in Craig's face. "Then we'll see what you have to say for yourself. *Boy!*"

"So sorry to have caused you this trouble, Carol." Mary Juanita's voice hoarse; her words tumbling like dominoes. She seemed embarrassed less by her son's letter than by her husband's tirade. She didn't need to read the letter anyhow; its contents would only confirm what she already knew, what she had known the day they adopted him, seven years earlier. She'd soon replace the truth with a dream, full of bridesmaids and little grandbabies.

"Let's bow our heads and pray," said the teacher, solemnly. They stood up, joined hands. And so it was that while Hazelle and Mary Juanita, chins tucked snugly against their sternums, pleaded earnestly in Jesus' name for the forgiveness of sins, Craig cried. Quiet as snowfall, he cried.

3   "May the Lord bless you and keep you, may the Lord make His face to shine upon you and be gracious unto you, may the Lord lift up His countenance upon you and give you peace."

"Amen," murmured the congregation after Pastor Westendorf's benediction. It began to scatter around and out of the church then. Mercifully, Siloah's services only lasted a little less than an hour. Craig had almost fallen asleep during the second dry sermon in two days. Mary introduced Jennifer to the pastors, the ushers, the organist, and several families in the congregation. Helen, Alfred, and Kenyatta Dixon were there after all and Jennifer was glad she got a chance to meet them. When Jennifer told Helen, who couldn't stop praising Jennifer's long, straight hair, about England's relationship with Helen's nephew, Adrian, Helen said, "I've always wanted to be a part of the Hickman family, and now you're telling me that we've been a part of it all along." They all laughed. Out on the front steps, the Dixons, the pastors, and a few more of the Hickmans' friends posed with them for pictures. "I sure do wish Job was here," Hazelle said to Craig after the last shutter snapped. Hazelle hadn't seen his son's husband since Easter when he'd driven to Milwaukee with Craig to help him search for the woman with the long, straight hair worthy of Helen Dixon's praise.

On the way back to their cars, Jennifer and Craig walked side by side in front of Mary, Hazelle, and Gina. Jennifer's high-heeled shoes made her appear almost as tall as Craig. "Look at the two of you, looking like brother and sister," said Hazelle. He laughed then. And laughed and laughed.

"What's so funny, Daddy?"

"Everything, son. Everything is too funny."

A MOTHER'S PRAYER

✍

1 Every morning during Jennifer's five-day visit, while Jennifer rested next to Craig on top of Gina's bed, Mary woke up crying and calling out Jennifer's name. Jennifer would arise and go sit with her in the kitchen. The place where Mary studied her Bible and meditated with God each morning before the sun lifted its wings. The place where she might cuss you out at high noon. Mary would ask questions such as, "Why do you think Craig cried so much? Did something happen to Craig in the womb?" Jennifer would give answers such as, "No, I took very good care of myself during my pregnancy. I didn't even eat any salt. Joseph gets that from my father, who cried if the wind changed directions." Mary had cleaned up her son's vomit, changed his diapers, calmed his fears, and encouraged him to share his whole life with her. Still, Mary wanted to better understand her son. She sought this understanding from the woman who bore him, a woman who met him not three months ago.

Perhaps that's why she woke up every morning a rooster crowing "Jennifer, Jennifer, Jennifer," as if her sanity depended on it. Sometimes Mary came right into the room, unable to wait until Jennifer arose. Craig had never seen his mother cry so freely, so profusely; never heard her talk so much about her childhood, her father, her mother, her stepmother, her grandmother, her ancestors; talk so much about her *life*. Some of her stories he'd heard before; most of them he hadn't. All of them he gulped, like milk.

Jennifer's presence was the TNT that blew Mary's stubborn dam wide open. Still, Mary would keep some things to herself. She winced every time Jennifer called him Joseph—his name was CRAIG, Lord have mercy—but she never said a word about *that*. She just kept spilling, like the flooding river that washed away her Ohio childhood town.

To Mary, Jennifer repeatedly expressed her gratitude (Thank the *Lord*!) for taking such good care of their son while she was away. But there was always some indeterminable thing, something tasting of rind, loitering behind her thank-yous that made Craig alert as wild whitetails in November.

One night, he sat with Jennifer on the bed in Gina's room, a room where he'd shared a bunk bed with his sister till he got too old and Mary made him sleep in the den on the pullout couch.

"I promised that I wouldn't have anything bad to say, son,"—her voice was soft, soothing, mechanical, like a flight attendant's—"and so I won't say anything bad. But you *know* I don't believe in homosexuality. I understand why you chose your lifestyle, son, because I wasn't there for you, son. I understand that, son, and I have to accept your choice and take it up with the Lord. But from reading some of your writings, knowing that you had girlfriends, hearing all that you've told me, it seems like you struggled, son. You struggled so much with yourself, with your choice. Did you seek any counseling?"

"Is this the big topic you waited to talk about after you saw my life in Milwaukee?" Craig's stomach started to hurt.

"Yes, son. But I promise I don't have anything bad to say."

A pause. "I know you believe what you believe and think what you think, but know *this*: it wouldn't have mattered if you kept me or not. I would still love men."

"We don't know that, son. Only the Lord knows that..."

"I don't claim to know what the Lord knows, but I know it."

"What I do know is that if you had been with me, you *definitely* wouldna been going to no Juneau Park."

What would you have done? Locked me in the basement? thought Craig. Juneau Park was his sanctuary, one of his houses of worship, and no one could have stopped him from going there and dancing naked with the men in the trees on the side of that hill.

With her proclamation, Jennifer had in her half-closed eyes, eyes that stayed half-closed even when they were wide open, the same look she had when she said with the same conviction on that day back in April shortly after Craig showed up with her brother James on her doorstep, "You weren't born on no December the eighth. You were born on December the third. That I *definitely* know. Because I would always fast on the third, and wonder where you were in your life, if you were married yet, how many children you had. It was the third, not the eighth. I fasted on the third. Every third of December, I fasted. *I'm* the mother. I don't care what your birth certificate or any of those other papers you got say. They can change those things you know. I'm the one who gave birth to you. If anybody should know, I'm the one. I'm the mother. I should know. You were born on the third, son, not the eighth. I *know*."

She didn't. Her Madison General Hospital records, which Craig later insisted she get a copy of, came from the hospital archives just before they left Atlanta for Milwaukee, confirming what he always knew, revealing what she didn't. Later, she conceded she must have blocked it out. All of it, including her labor and delivery. "I don't know, son, I guess I was so traumatized that I can't remember anything about the hospital. Except for naming you. That, I remember." And for the umpteenth time, she told the story:

"It was like being on death row, son, and I had one last request before they took you away. They weren't supposed to let me, but I demanded that I have a moment with you in the room with no doctors, no nurses, no brothers, no parents, no technicians, no one. But the laws in the state of Wisconsin forbade such a request. Birth mothers couldn't see, much less hold, their children after delivery if they had already consented to give them up. But I told them rules were meant to be broken and who would find out about it anyway? So I held you in my arms and looked you in your eyes and said, 'You look just like your father. Someday you will grow up to be a handsome and smart man, son. But I may not get to see any of it because Mommy has to go away now. I have no choice. But I remember the story of Joseph from the Bible. How his brothers sold him into slavery and how he was lost from his brothers and his father for all those years. And then he became the ruler of Egypt. And during the great famine when his brothers came to him to get food, he recognized them, but he didn't let them know who he was. When he finally let them know, he told them to go and get Jacob because he wanted to be reunited with his father before his father died. And they were. And so I name you Joseph, because I know that someday you'll come back to me. Someday you'll find me. I don't know if I'll be living or dead, but I know you'll find me. Just as Joseph in the Bible was reunited with his family, so shall you also be reunited with me. I just know it. Someday.'

"And here you are, son, so my prayer was answered. But I blocked out everything else. I don't remember going into labor or giving birth to you. I've prayed and prayed, but I guess the Lord doesn't want me to remember any of that right now. I really thought you were born on the third."

The first time she told it, Craig fell in love with her story. She told it to him often. She told it to anyone who asked her why she named him Joseph and even to some who didn't. The more he heard it, the more he asked himself, How could she remember all of that and forget everything else?

Whatever the answer, Craig knew something about himself that she didn't know, what her single-minded devotion couldn't allow her to know.

Although she would concede his birthday—she had the documents to prove it—she wouldn't concede something she didn't "believe in" and the flesh and blood before her eyes, the evidence of things seen, apparently wasn't evidence enough.

"Not that any of it matters, but you can believe whatever you wanna believe about Juneau Park," said Craig at last. He gritted his teeth, took a deep breath, and slid his hips back, moving himself farther away from her on the bed. "A boy who loved men found Juneau Park; Juneau Park didn't make a boy love men. I woulda still loved men if you'd kept me, I woulda loved men if someone else adopted me, I woulda loved men no matter how I was raised. The only *choice* I ever made is to live my life in the open."

"It matters to me, son. Your pain is my pain. I never imagined there woulda been so much pain in your life. You struggled, son, I know it. I can see that you still struggle."

She was crossing his border, and he was letting her go—no, *encouraging* her to go—as far as she could. It was the only way for him to see.

"I've loved many women, I've loved many men. I knew, in a place you can't now or ever will see, I knew as a child the same thing that I know now: I belong with a man."

"Mama Mary didn't notice you struggling, didn't see to it that you got any counseling, didn't take you to see your pastor? There are many—I've known some in my own church—who've been healed."

She was crossing his border, just as she let herself—no, felt entitled to—cross anyone's borders. That's what borders were for, after all. No one could have stopped her for it was the only way she knew how to be.

Mama Mary, who, through closed doors, overhears everything but claims to remember nothing, was sitting in the kitchen. Sitting exactly where she sat when she used to tell her high-school-aged children, "If you're gonna experiment with any drugs, or anything you feel desperate to have, do it at home so at least I'll be here if some harm should befall you." The kitchen was next to the bedroom. The bedroom door was open.

"My mother didn't have anything to do with—"

"Did she even *pray* for you, son? You know, the Lord hears a mother's prayers before he hears anyone else's. When a mother is really in tune with her children, she can see things about them. She knows things about them even before they know them about themselves. The Lord answers a mother's prayer, son. You needed prayer. I woulda got you some counseling. I woulda prayed. I *know* you woulda made an excellent husband and father. With your brains and your talent, with our great Turner-White genes, I know you woulda made a great lawyer and provided well for your family."

Her fantasy swelled in the room like dread. They were in a horror movie where the shadows of evil seeped up the walls and spread across the ceiling, covering it in darkness, changing the whole room into a suffocating cave with no way to escape. He sat right in front of her, but, in the dark, she could not see him, did not hear him, would not stop herself from doing what she was doing. And she knew exactly what she was doing. She had mastered it. Her mastery, safe to say, had gone far enough.

"When you were seventeen and fucking Frank down at Oakwood College against her orders, think your mother wasn't praying every day, begging the Lord on bended knee *every single day* for your purity, hoping you'd be unspoiled before marriage, like she *wasn't?*"

He rose from the bed and lunged across the hall, his breathing short, fast. He closed the bathroom door behind him. He lowered the toilet seat, sat down, and began to cry. It's a good thing we're out of here in a few days, he thought. Mama needs some sleep.

He cradled his head in his burning palms, his stomach twisting in pain. Deliberately, he slowed his breathing until it was deep, rhythmic, calming. He thought of his parents. In their house, Jennifer had the nerve to try to take his mother and, by extension, his father, out of the picture of his life. If she could've seen them for the kind of people they really were, she would've known exactly how grave was her blind, blind mistake. What was she thinking? How could she dishonor these people, *his* people, with such desperate, calculating arrogance?

✍

On his way back to Boston, Craig would fly to Atlanta with Jennifer. He would tell her a story of the people she had never even bothered to ask about, the people who had made room for her flesh and blood in their home—in their hearts—because she had no room for him in her own.

HAZELLE

1 And it came to pass in those days that Hitler committed suicide in his Berlin bunker. One week later, during the second week of May in the nineteen hundred and forty-fifth year, Nazi Germany surrendered unconditionally and the war in Europe ended.

In the first weeks of August, the United States dropped the atomic bomb on Nagasaki and Hiroshima and the Soviet Union declared war on Japan and invaded Manchuria. On the fourteenth day of the month, Japan announced its surrender—so long as it could keep its emperor—and World War II, a most devastating war in terms of material destruction, global scale, and lives lost, ended.

Hazelle returned from the Philippines, where he had been stationed since the nineteen hundred and forty-second year, and found that the country he'd left behind wasn't too kind to Negro servicemen returning from war.

Hazelle came back through California with a few of the others he'd attended Tuskegee with in the nineteen hundred and thirty-ninth year. After hanging out in the Arizona desert, he returned to Tennessee, to the city of Beale Street and barbeque, basement slow dances and jazz, three years before Elvis moved in from Tupelo, Mississippi.

Still, Hazelle couldn't find work. And so it was on the fifteenth day of January in the nineteen hundred and forty-sixth year that he went up from Memphis, Tennessee, to Milwaukee, Wisconsin, on a Greyhound bus. "Mighty nice day for a bus ride," said Hazelle looking up at the driver from the curb. "What's your name, sir?"

"Frankie," the driver responded.

"My name is Hazelle, but you can call me Mister Charlie." His tone was respectful with a hint of sarcasm. Hazelle tipped his hat to Frankie, flashed his gold tooth and moved to the back of the bus. And so he went up on a Greyhound Bus to the beer capital of America where his one-and-only brother Willie Lee said it was easier for a Negro man to find work.

2 Hazelle the second son was born by a midwife to Lee and Emma Ball Hickman in Inverness, Mississippi, sometime in the second month of the year.

Apparently, on the day he was born, no one glanced at the calendar. If someone had, they failed to record what day it was.

It wouldn't become clear until the nineteen eighties exactly when Hazelle was born (and even then, his wife would ferociously debate the date or attempt to conceal the obvious), but throughout most of his life, Hazelle observed his birth on the twentieth day of February, in the nineteen hundred and twenty-fourth year.

Whenever he was born, one thing was clear without refute—Hazelle was jazz's fraternal twin. Hazelle may not have been born in New Orleans, but he and jazz grew up together in the nineteen twenties, matured in the thirties, and took to the world in the forties. Hazelle claimed to have met Bessie Smith, heard Louis Armstrong play live, and auditioned for one of Billie Holiday's back-up singers in Harlem—all before entering the service at the age of sixteen.

Believing himself sixteen-years-old in nineteen hundred and forty, he had to lie to gain entrance into the service, which only admitted young men of eighteen. Hazelle was blessed with a full head of gray hair at the ripe age of twelve (or sixteen, as the case may be). The service had no difficulty believing him to be nineteen.

3 And so it was that Hazelle entered the Army Air Force and concerned himself with the taking off and landing of airplanes. During the Second World War, he became a plotter. When he got to Milwaukee, Hazelle pursued his desire to work at a civilian airport.

Dressed up sharp, Army Air Force papers in hand, Hazelle took the long trolley ride from Sixth and Vine streets, where he lived with his brother, through the south side to General Mitchell Field, Milwaukee's municipal airport.

He had called ahead for the interview, and over the phone, the hiring manager thought that Hazelle's military plotting experience made him a very good candidate for the job of air traffic controller.

"Hazelle Hickman to see Mister Black about the plotter job."

The eyes of the bifocaled receptionist with the fire-engine pompadour and pale, freckled skin scanned his tweed pants, his matching jacket, his rust and brown tie with the gold slanted stripes, his silver hair, and his colored skin and replied, "You can have a seat there and he'll be right with you."

Hazelle did what he was told, as he had for at least the last six years. Outside the window, he could see the two-engine prop planes rising and landing. Even though an emergency crash landing he'd endured during the war rendered him unwilling and unable to ever get inside those winged steel vessels again, airplanes would always deserve his wonder with their miraculous ability to defy the maw of gravity and take flight.

More than a dozen planes had come and gone while Hazelle waited patiently for Mister Black to be right with him. Finally, the pale-skinned woman emerged from behind a windowed door on the other side of the waiting area. "I'm so sorry that you've waited so long and that no one was able to call you before you came all this way. I'm so sorry, really I am. I wish I was able to help you, but the position was filled just today." Her face flushed red as her mountain of hair. "You know what? Maybe I can help," she continued, raising the pitch of her voice as though she'd made a remarkable discovery. "Consider this your lucky day. If you check downstairs in personnel, I know for a fact that there are *several* openings for second- and third-shift janitors."

"Thank you, ma'am. You tell Mister Black there that I sure hope God blesses him." He tipped his hat as he walked out the door. "You have yourself a real nice afternoon, ya hear?"

And so Hazelle became an interior decorator, a waiter, a cook, a chef, a house painter, and even pondered a career as a nightclub singer and a recording artist—oh, how that tenor voice could croon!—before he began his thirty-plus year tenure in office services at the Pabst Blue Ribbon Company. But before he met Pabst, he met the woman with whom he'd spend the rest of his life.

4 "I met her almost as soon as I got to Milwaukee. It was forty-six and I couldna been here for more than a month. I went to a USO dance at the Pfister Hotel. They had these events for veterans every so often. They were social gatherings where all the beautiful young ladies might come and give us handsome gentlemen a bit of their time and attention. It was one of the few events back in the day where black and white folk could mingle. They even had a big band. Live. You better believe couples were cuttin a rug, jitterbuggin all over the dance floor.

"I hadn't yet picked out any beauties to test my toe and get my heart a-jumpin. Then my buddy, Smitty, stopped in the middle of our conversation and raised his eyebrows. He motioned for me to turn and look at the little bit of heaven standin just behind me with a smile on her face bright as a Mississippi morning. I walked right over to her.

"'Well, hello sunshine,' I kinda half sung in my best Nat King Cole impersonation. If a colored girl could blush, her face woulda glowed hot as the Arizona desert.

"I reached for her hand. 'Before you try kissing it,' she said, pulling her hand gently away from the path to my lips, 'why don't you take me on the dance floor and introduce yourself properly.'

"How can a man with a heartbeat resist that? They say it only happens in fairy tales. At the first sight of her, the very first sight, I knew it was love. So I guess you could say our fairy tale started on the dance floor that very night."

MARY JUANITA

I am the mother of sorrows,
I am the ender of grief.

—Paul Laurence Dunbar
THE PARADOX

How often I have longed to gather your
children together, as a hen gathers her
chicks under her wings...

—LUKE 12:34

1 "I don't know what Hazelle is talking about. You'd be better off listening to a fool. Pay him no never mind, you hear what I say to you? He's always talking and don't know what he's even talkin bout. I did *not* ask him to dance. I did no such thing, I say to you. No such thing. I was sitting with my girlfriends on this long wooden bench, and your father came over and said something to me, but I wasn't studying him one bit.

"But he wouldn't leave me alone. Yeah, he was handsome and all, dressed up nice and sharp—think he was wearing a navy-blue suit—but I wasn't really trying to be bothered. I only went because my girlfriend, Mattie, asked me to go with her. You know, she didn't want to be alone.

"But he persisted and persisted, I say to you, and he just wouldn't give up. Finally, we danced.

"Yeah, he's a good dancer. Real good. He danced me right into marrying him."

2 And it came to pass in those days, that the decade roared and roared. Flappers decked out in beaded chiffon spaghetti-strapped tubes and cloche hats cut up the dance floors to the music of Duke Ellington's big band. Bessie Smith, empress of the blues, stunned her crowds with great singing and something more. George Gershwin and Al Jolson became legends in their own time using colored people's music. Langston Hughes published his first book of poetry and the Harlem Renaissance was born in salons around Manhattan. Al Capone and other back-alley, speakeasy

gangsters raked in the cash from moonshine and violence. Nicolo Sacco and Bartolomeo Vanzetti suffered electrocution at the hands of the state. Henry Ford gave the driving kind its beloved jalopies. Those with a spirit of adventure—and money—took to the skies in the Wright brothers' invention. Radio was all the rage and Herbert Hoover made a catastrophe of the economy.

The second daughter in a family of three children, Mary Juanita was born just before the Great Depression in Wish, a little township in eastern Ohio. When she was seven, Wish was wiped away by a flood. After raining nonstop for several days, the Ohio River spilled out of its basin.

And kept on spilling.

"From our front stoop, you could actually see stoves and tables, even a few bodies, floating in the river down what was left of the street," she used to tell her children while she dropped dumplings in pot liquor and built heaven. "It was crazy, I say to you, some kind of crazy rain. It didn't stop for twenty days and nights. I ain't seen nothing like it since, and hope to Christ I never do. We were lucky, though. As the good Lord would have it, we only lost the outhouse in the woods out back. It was a miracle, I say to you, a miracle.

"Imagine working as hard as you could most of your natural life for your family and then have it all washed away in the blink of an eye. The trials of Job, I say to you, the trials of Job. And there wasn't no such thing as flood relief back then like they got now. I don't think that came along till Roosevelt. He did so much for the poor and downtrodden, you know.

"I don't know what we would've done if we'd lost everything. Like Mister and Missus Warren did. And they had seven sons, God bless'm. Seven sons. Can you imagine? I wonder what ever came of them. I think your grandmother told us that Mister Warren had some family up near this way himself so I think they all ended up here in Milwaukee. Or maybe it was Chicago. Or was it St. Louis? Detroit? The devil if I know. Wherever they are, I sure hope they was able to get back on their feet.

"Seven sons. Have mercy.

"The Lord works in mysterious ways, I say to you, mysterious ways, yes He does. We were some of the lucky ones. We didn't lose much ourselves. No, we didn't. That outhouse out back and a lot of your Grandma Magnolia's antiques and sentimental things that she kept down in the basement from her time in Arkansas and Alabama before the Great War. Ours was about the only house that hadn't been rocked right out of its foundation from the force of the rushing river. After the basement drained and we cleaned it out, we might've been able to stay put. But since the rest of the town was gone, we had to get up and go too. Just as well. If it wasn't for the flood, I might've been stuck in Wish right today and never met your father.

"I think back on those days sometimes, missing my home. Sitting on your front stoop in a town no bigger than a bird's nest and knowing everybody from the slaughterhouse butcher to the sheriff by their first names. There's nothing like it, I say to you, nothing like it.

"Citified folk. That's the way of the world now. Everybody aching for these citified ways. I can't let myself dwell on Wish and the past for too long. Just have to fold up that memory like a quilt and put it away. Ain't no going back now even if I wanted to. My hometown is gone. Wish's washed away. It ain't even on the map no more. Imagine that."

To hear her tell it, it was hard sometimes to determine if she was happy to have left Wish or full of regret. But she moved on, just like the Warrens had to.

Her father Timothy, who'd been a railway porter most of his working life, had some relatives nearby. So he took his wife Magnolia, Mary Juanita, her younger brother, Timothy Junior, and older sister, Juniper Belle, just across the Pennsylvania border to the township of Washington.

For the next four years, Mary and her siblings watched the Depression ruin their parent's marriage; they divorced when she was eleven. Magnolia stayed in Pennsylvania, remarried and had seven more children: Perceval, Celestial, Mitzi, Wellington, Priest, Minneola, and Sela. Their father, James Marshall, who was of African and Shawnee Nation descent, had the surname of a small fruit, so Magnolia Price, née Coleman, became Magnolia Littleberry, a name belonging to no other.

And so it was that Timothy moved his children to Milwaukee where he searched for a new life. He'd heard about all the factories and breweries there and he hoped the Depression increased a man's thirst for beer. But the breweries were brewing with a short list of employees, and most of them were immigrants from western Europe. Still, Timothy was never one to let circumstances get the best of him. He always had a little something up his sleeve—coveted, efficient, unpredicted. He connected with the right players in the right places and put food on the table running the numbers. After a few months, he settled into his job as a chauffeur and drove the likes of Joe Louis, Louis Armstrong, and Jack Johnson when they had business or pleasure in the Brew City.

Timothy also found a new wife in Alma Leigh, a young woman with a flair for fantasy. And she was quite young—barely older than Juniper Belle, his oldest child, who was thirteen.

Now Alma Leigh wanted to be a jazz singer. Only problem was: she couldn't carry a note in a handbag. But that minor detail didn't do a damn thing to keep her from wishing on big bands and a bigger sea of faces, all blues and mystery. Despite being laughed out of the church choir behind her back, thank you very much, Alma Leigh prayed that someday Count Basie himself would discover her in some no-name smoky jazz club.

"Alma would get all dolled up, stand in front of this full-length mirror we had in the front hallway. Hair pressed and set just so with some Madame C.J. Walker, lips red as Scarlett O'Hara's, she would put an Ella Fitzgerald or Lena Horne seventy-eight on the victrola and begin her mirror act, mouthing the words to STORMY WEATHER or a TISKET, A TASKET." Craig loved his mother's monologues, many of which she'd relate without even being asked anything. They came out of nowhere, verbal reflexes to a stimuli only she could feel.

"I'm telling you she would slink and shimmy all sultry-like in her hip-hugging red dress and swing her mink stole round her neck for dramatic effect whenever a song changed keys. She musta thought she was one fine jazz singer, the cat's meow, singing to the big old audience of herself. Only thing is, I could never understand why she always wore that same red dress every time she served up her show."

Mary Juanita was a little wary of Alma at first, but at least she tolerated her enough to talk to her. Juniper Belle thought Alma was surely touched, and not by an angel. But Alma Leigh never gave up on her wish to be a jazz singer. It just had to mean something to birth, nurture, and hold on to a wish, no matter how thin the prospects for fulfillment. Especially since she couldn't birth any real babies. That's right: Alma Leigh was barren. This mattered none to Timothy—he already had his mouths to feed.

Alma Leigh loved her husband for his Hollywood good looks and tender ways. But she adored Timothy precisely because he wanted no more children. Now she had the chance to help raise his kids as if they were her own, fulfilling her desire to be a mother. But what young woman could wrap her whole heart around the belief that she could raise children only five years her junior, especially if she didn't *have* to? If anything, Alma Leigh was more like a big sister than a mother, and the trio of mouths made it clear they didn't want one of those. Alma Leigh never talked about any of this, but she wore the conflict on her face like makeup she could never remove.

Juniper resented her stepmother simply for being there. For occupying space in a place where absence had been easier to take. Throughout their remaining lives, Juniper said nary a word to Alma Leigh, but that's a whole other story, full of rolled eyes and padlocked lips and no one is searching for the key. Not even Mary Juanita, who was able to unveil mysteries.

For Mary Juanita, concerns of the supernatural were no mystery at all.

At some point in her life, Mary was a devout Methodist. No. Actually, she was a Baptist churchgoing woman. Almost everyone she called a friend came from some church.

"This here is Clyde and Laverne from Mount Zion, and this is Kozelle and Shirlene from Garden of Gethsemane, and, oh, now *here*—here go Buford and Mary Alice from St. Phillip and the Redeemer," she'd tell Craig, pointing over his shoulder as they looked through her photo albums. "Hickman, you remember me playing Bid Whist with them on Tuesday nights when we lived over on Thirteenth Street?"

Nobody loves the Lord more than she does, but that love has been tested time and time again. Mary Juanita wanted to give Hazelle several children from her womb and raise them up in the ways of her Lord and Savior Jesus Christ. But her Lord had other plans. She would conceive several times, but never bear fruit.

She pondered these things in her heart. And so she prayed. Not being able to bear fruit became the genesis of her sorrow. Like a disease with no cure, her sorrow would remain the rest of her life, defying her effort to fold it away. And so she prayed.

She would begin to see that the Lord meant for her to raise children, not bear them. This was her purpose and she knew it with the conviction of saints, for concerns of the supernatural where no mystery to Mary at all.

But Mary Juanita kept all these things, and pondered them in her heart.

Hazelle thought it was *his* fault. And so he drank. Perhaps this was the Lord's way of teaching him a lesson regarding all the Filipino women he'd loved during his time on the islands during the war. Who did he think he was anyway, Lot's wife, his seed turned to salt for having looked with favor upon so many women? Mary would've told him how ludicrous that was had he ever confided in her. But he hadn't. Never could. And so he drank. Had he ever confided in her, it wouldn't have mattered anyway.

Mary *knew* her purpose, and it had nothing to do with her husband's made-up earthly punishment.

And so she would encourage her children to find the women who gave birth to them when they were ready to find them. For what woman in her right mind and true heart could carry a child for nine months, move this child out of her womb in excruciating pain, hear its first cry, maybe even see its face, name it, give it away, and never desire to see it again?

Mary could not fathom there was a single woman dead, alive, or yet to be born who would never desire to see her child again. See how she smiles, or whose nose he has. Does he walk like his father, talk like me? Will she have the temperament of her grandfather, the creativity of her second cousin? Suffer these little babies to come unto me, Mary prayed. She would prepare a way for them to go to the mothers whom they chose to come through.

Ten years after they married, Mary Juanita's prayers were answered and she and Hazelle helped raise three foster children, Freddie, Reggie, and Arnold, the sons of a woman having a difficult time in life.

Ten years after that, her prayers were answered again and they adopted their first child, a beautiful ten-month-old girl, and named her Gina Louise. Daddy had *his* little girl, and there wasn't anything you could say to him in those early days to wipe that ever-present smile off his face. His high cheekbones, inherited from Blackfoot Indian ancestors, rose even higher.

Gina Louise, who, at age three, won her first kiddy contest at Alma Leigh's church, was the pride and joy of the family that lived on the second floor of the brown house with yellow trim on Thirteenth Street, near the corner of Finn Place. The Hickmans rented from the Davidsons, a black couple that lived downstairs. The Davidsons had adopted their two daughters, Debbie Rae and Donna Mae, and offered encouragement and support for the Hickmans in their quest to extend their family.

The Davidsons also introduced the Hickmans to their camping group. Once Gina came along, Hazelle and Mary wanted to expose their dearest daughter to more than the inner-city neighborhoods. No way would they deny their offspring a life with varied scenes and experiences, even if they couldn't afford to travel very far.

But the Hickmans were brilliantly blessed in every way. They purchased a tan and white Volkswagen van and took their first camping trip with the Davidsons and their camping group in the summer of nineteen hundred and sixty seven, the summer Jennifer was pregnant—and under house arrest.

3 A brief record of the genealogy of Joseph Craig the son of James, the son of Timothy:

James was the father of James,
James was the father of Jennifer Minnie, whose mother was England
Jennifer Minnie, of whom was born Joseph, who is called Craig

Timothy was the father of Timothy
Timothy was the father of Mary Juanita, whose mother was Magnolia
Mary Juanita, who adopted Joseph, whom she named Craig

4 And it came to pass in those days, that the Supreme Court had yet to issue its decree, and abortion was illegal throughout the land. So Jennifer Minnie went up from the city of Milwaukee, in Milwaukee County, in the state of Wisconsin, to Madison, in Dane County, in the state of Wisconsin, because she was with child, unwed, and in college. Her mother England was caught up in a terror-filled spinning. England did not want to

bring public disgrace and shame on herself, on the good White name, and so she secretly sent her daughter away.

And so it was, that, while she was there, the days were accomplished that she should be delivered.

And so she brought forth her firstborn son, and wrapped him in her arms, and named him Joseph, and gave him up for adoption because there was no room for him in the White house.

5 And there was in the same neighborhood where she lived in Milwaukee, a family awaiting the birth of their second child, a son.

And in April of the nineteen hundred and sixty-ninth year, the family went to Children's Services Society of Wisconsin and the social worker said unto them: "I have good news for your entire family. We have found your son in a white foster home in DeForest, Wisconsin. You will meet him next Saturday, and take him home with you the Sunday after that."

And so it was that on Sunday, the twenty-seventh of April, Craig went permanently to the home of Hazelle and Mary Juanita Hickman on Thirteenth Street in Milwaukee, Wisconsin, right around the corner from the White house.

Book III

LEAVES

One must say Yes to life, and embrace it wherever it is found—and it is found in terrible places... For nothing is fixed, forever and forever, it is not fixed; the earth is always shifting, the light is always changing, the sea does not cease to grind down rock. Generations do not cease to be born, and we are responsible to them because we are the only witnesses they have. The sea rises, the light fails, lovers cling to each other, and children cling to us. The moment we cease to hold each other, the moment we break faith with one another, the sea engulfs us and the light goes out.

—James Baldwin
NOTHING PERSONAL

SHADOW

1 It was just before sundown on Friday, July 20, 2001, when Craig noticed the photophobia. When he left the house to walk the dogs that early but eerily bright evening, he immediately became dizzy. Eyes closed, he saw speckles of orange light swirling in front of him like a hoard of fireflies. He opened his eyes. Much. Too. Bright. "C'mon boys," he said, beckoning the dogs back inside. They'd have to wait till the other daddy came home before they had their evening walk.

Hammers began to bang beneath his skull. He took a nap. Job woke him up for a late dinner, but he didn't feel like eating. Picking over his plate, Craig said, "I think something is seriously wrong."

"What is it?"

"I can't eat, I'm dizzy, and I feel weird. *Really* weird."

"You've been through quite a bit lately. Yeah, it's been wonderful, but it's also been extremely exhausting. Get a good night's sleep. You'll feel better in the morning." That was Job's favorite response whenever Craig fell ill, which didn't happen often. Craig hardly ever caught a cold and never came down with the flu. Except for seasonal allergies and a connective tissue disorder called Marfan's Syndrome, he was in great health. But once every two or three years, as far back in his life as he could remember, he would be taken down by some bizarre ailment that required a short hospital visit. Just after his birthday in 1999, he'd developed a fever and a red patch formed on his inner thigh. When he awoke after a night of mediocre sleep, the fever held, the patch spread down to his knee. Job took him to the emergency room. He stayed in the hospital for three days on an IV antibiotic drip. He was diagnosed with cellulitis, a general but acute inflammation of cells caused by an unspecified bacterium.

Whatever was coming now was much worse and Craig knew it but he couldn't go to the hospital on intuition alone. He went back to bed but he couldn't sleep. Later, Job joined him. "How're you feeling?"

"No better. I think we should...well...let's see what happens by morning, like you said."

"You'll be fine," Job said and fell asleep.

In the middle of the night, revolt ravaged Craig's alimentary canal. Nausea fired the upper dilatation; cramps sliced through the lower. He was unable to lie still, shifting positions to try to outsmart the pain. He moved into the guestroom bed so his fumbling wouldn't disturb Job. Later, he stumbled to the bathroom and slumped onto the cold tile floor in front of the toilet.

He cradled his stomach. He waited. He knew it would come. And then he opened up and began to purge. He hoisted his chest against the front of the toilet and leaned his mouth over the opening not quite in time. His belly contracted. He purged. Breathing hurt. Contraction. Purge. Even after his stomach had nothing left to expel, his belly refused to stop. He gagged and grunted and screamed. His neck stiffened, and he couldn't move his head from side to side. He lugged himself back to the guest bed.

The sun began to scour the sky. Job awoke and found Craig groaning and trembling and muttering nonsense on the floor. Job held him. "Oh, my God, you're on fire." He ran back to the bedroom and shuffled through the nightstand drawers searching for the thermometer. "I coulda sworn I put that thing in here," he said, uncovering nothing. He walked quickly out of the bedroom. He jerked still in the middle of the hallway. "The closet." There it was, in a basket on the black shelves in the bathroom linen closet. He ran back into the guestroom to take Craig's temperature.

One hundred four point eight degrees Fahrenheit.

Job ran back to the nightstand and picked up the phone. "I need an ambulance at Twenty Two Ridge Street in Roslindale right now. Dangerously high fever and delirium. Please, get here fast." While they waited for the ambulance, Job corralled his wits and rubbed his husband down with wet-towel-covered ice packs. "How bad does it feel?"

"Like death."

On the stretcher in the ambulance, Craig thrashed and bucked. He couldn't hold his arms down; he reached up and out, flailing them all around as though swatting a plague of gnats. He could feel his eyes rolling back in his head but he couldn't control them. When he finally got onto a bed in the emergency room, his bowels opened up and poured forth faster than Job could clean up. Yelling in vain for help, Job filled up five bedpans with Craig's subterranean mire. He carried one of them over to the central nurse's station and left it on the counter. As he walked away, a nurse shouted, "You can't leave that there."

"If my husband has to lie around in his own shit for half an hour like an animal, you can deal with a dirty bed pan under your nose," Job snapped back. He returned to his husband's side. Finally a nurse came to change the soiled bedding and remove the pans from the room.

Craig's fever showed no signs of breaking. "We need ice in here," Job shouted toward the nursing station. "I can't believe they haven't put you in a bath of alcohol by now." The fear in his voice louder than the disbelief.

The admitting physician ordered an array of blood work and a CAT scan. "Do your best to keep him awake," the doctor told Job before he left the room. "With this high a fever, we can't risk him falling unconscious."

A sweet-smelling black woman who introduced herself as Sierra Washington interviewed him once again about the details surrounding the onset of his symptoms the prior evening. But this woman, a Harvard medical student, pushed further than any of the four interviewers who came before her. "Craig, have you been around any young children lately?"

He shook his head. "No. Wait."

Job could see that his husband's labored breathing made it difficult to speak. "What is it? Just breathe. Take your time."

"The... air... play..."

"Airplane?"

Craig nodded.

"You mean there were young children on the airplane?"

He nodded again.

"A few weeks ago, he traveled from Atlanta to Milwaukee to Boston. Musta been the stress of the trip. He took his birth mother, who he just found, to meet his parents in Milwaukee."

"Stress can cause any number of problems but there *is* a serious infection somewhere and I'm gonna find it. I'm recommending that his doctor order a spinal tap," Sierra explained, looking at his chart. "We have to rule out encephalitis, West Nile virus, or any other infections of the nervous system." She put the chart down and looked intently at Craig. "That musta been special. I was adopted too."

"Absolutely amazing. It seems like everyone he meets lately is adopted. The photographer who just took their family portrait in Milwaukee was also adopted. Have you ever thought about searching?"

"I've thought about it. But I'll be a doctor. When will I have time?"

"Tell me about it. He was so determined he devoted the better part of six years to finding her. But this last trip was too much, too fast. I told both of them they were going too fast, but neither one of them would listen. I went to Atlanta with him in April when he found her and I'm glad I went because I needed to experience it with him, be right there, not hear about it after the fact." Job wrung out a cold cloth and wiped the sweat from his husband's head. "He wanted me there with him this time, too, but I had to stay here in Boston and work. It just seemed like something he should do by himself. When he got back, he didn't talk much about it and he's the kind of person who'll talk about almost anything. I could tell it was stressful, though; he was exhausted. He's been sleeping a lot ever since. Please, tell me this is from all the stress."

Craig barely heard them. He was falling.

"C'mon, honey," Job pleaded, blowing hard on Craig's face and slapping his cheeks. "C'mon. You *have* to stay awake."

But he was falling. Fast.

✍

Someone comes to wheel him to radiology. Just above his head, the ceiling becomes a deep mist, the kind that forms at dusk or dawn. Which one it is, he does not know.

The air is warm. Still. He smells honeysuckle. And copper. He is naked. His skin weeps. The tallest pines he's ever seen push through the silver mist and brush the indigo sky.

He walks through the shoulder-high mist, slowly, his feet crumpling fronds that sound dried by autumn. Through a coppice of purple and gold raspberries, the path gives way to a large clearing. The chicory- and chamomile-covered meadow dives into a valley. In its middle pools a small pond lined on the east by a dozen honeysuckles.

He steps down the hill. The pond bubbles like a hot alpine spring. Platinum vapor rises from the water, like prayer.

He steps closer. His skin dries.

The pond evaporates, slowly, revealing three figures sitting in a triangle on the gentle slope of the pond basin.

Closer.

The figures are his husband, his husband's oldest sister, Nelleke, and his husband's mother, Betsy. His husband wears linen; his mother, sackcloth; his sister, nothing at all. All three are crying. Sobbing.

Three of the twelve honeysuckles turn into three men: Johannes called Hans, his husband's brother, Johannes called Han, his husband's father, and Johannes called Johan, his husband's mother's father. The three men, the dearly departed, who'd left the trinity of mourners inconsolable and sitting on the earth of an evaporating pond, gather round. They stretch out their arms, join hands, and dance in a circle round the wailing triangle.

The triangle cannot see the circle, cannot feel the circle, cannot be consoled.

Craig sees himself step between Hans and Han, joining the circle of dancers, dancing to an everlasting symphony of lamentations.

He feels hot. Blisteringly hot. He feels his surface begin to swell.

His father-in-law stops the dance. Johannes the father grabs his son-in-law's hot hands and lays them on the third eye of his third son sitting in the triangle. Before his son-in-law can look up, look out, look *over*, Han, his second son, and his wife's father turn back to honeysuckle on the eastern bank of the pond.

The sagging mist condenses on Craig's skin quicker than sweat.

2 On the third day, Craig had healed quickly enough to leave the hospital. By the time his fever broke, he'd had lab work revealing nothing, a CAT scan revealing nothing, and a crossing-over visitation revealing everything. By the time his fever broke, Job had called Mary and Jennifer. By the time his fever broke, Jennifer had decided to fly to Boston.

After Craig's fever broke, a spinal tap revealed the viral meningitis that threatened to keep him in the hospital for at least two weeks. For three days, potassium and magnesium flowed into his veins through an IV. Percocet tablets relieved the pain emanating from his lumbar spine where a student and then a doctor had punctured it, not once, not twice, but three times with the biggest needle he'd ever seen attached to a syringe the size of a taper. After the doctor delivered the diagnosis to them, Craig looked at Job, eyes pooled with fear.

Help came in the middle of the night. Job picked up Jennifer at Logan Airport and brought her unannounced to Craig's bedside. Craig wasn't sure he wanted her to be there.

"It hasn't been three months and I've already made my son deathly ill," said Jennifer as she sashayed into Craig's hospital room, dropping her coat on the chair by the foot of his bed.

With one deceptively seamless motion, she checked his forehead, his fluids, and the name of his nurse scribbled on the whiteboard on the wall next to the bathroom. She meant business and if she had her way, her presence alone would render the nurses unnecessary. She didn't have her way, but by the time he left, the nurses considered Craig's healing nothing short of a miracle.

She, too, believed his recovery miraculous. She considered it the second birth. The second time she got to push him into the world. This time, she wouldn't let him go. This time, she would be there for him and make it *all* right. Right all the wrongs that overcame him in her absence. She would stay for three weeks, cooking brown rice and lentils, kale and carrots, overseeing his diet, his gait, his every move. "Son, I know Job is glad I'm here because now he doesn't have to worry about you while he's out working. He knows mother's here taking good care of you. He hasn't said anything, son, but I know." She knew everything, understood everything, and nothing made her flinch.

Just like she didn't flinch on that day back in April when her son looked her in the eye and said, "I'm truly blessed and I'm glad that I've come all this way and looked at you face-to-face. Earlier, when I was on the phone talking to my mother, I heard you ask if my wife was in the car outside waiting for me to come and get her. Well, Job here is my husband."

"Ooooooh. Okaaaaaaaaay," she said, half singing, the pitch of her voice rising as she stretched each note.

"Nice to meet you, Jennifer. What should I call you?" Job peeked from behind the camera.

"Call me Mom, just like so many others. I'm mother to many, you know."

Now, she was in her son's home, close enough to try to make her firstborn see that she was the only mother he needed.

3 Craig was startled awake by the ringing and thunderous sound of jackhammers cutting up pavement. He slowly unfolded himself and rose from the bed. On the way to the kitchen, he stepped out the front door to greet the late-morning sun and see what all the commotion was about. The dial on the window thermometer was already nearing a hundred degrees and the foul odor of melted tar hung in the humid air. Sweat glistened on the tar-smeared chests of the shirtless men repaving the street at the side of the house. Craig closed the door and went into the kitchen where Jennifer was already baking cinnamon rolls. He poured a cup of coffee, sat down at the kitchen table, and watched Jennifer knead dough.

August, the month Craig and Job got married, was just around the corner. All Jennifer's offspring had ceremonies in August, her youngest, first; her eldest, last.

"Does Mama Mary do anything special for you and Job's anniversary, son?" Jennifer asked.

Mama Mary had attended Craig and Job's backyard wedding, joining one hundred family and friends. Hazelle sang EBB TIDE, Craig's favorite love song, to honor their union. On their first anniversary, Mama had sent them a card. On their second, she'd sent a card and a check, which was *just enough*, she'd written, *for a nice dinner*. "I can't say she does anything special. I don't even remember her sending us a card," Craig replied at last, surprised by his lie, more surprised that he didn't correct it.

Jennifer dropped a pan on the floor. She picked it up, set it forcefully on the counter, and leaned over it, shaking her head.

"What's wrong?"

"I was gonna—Nothing, son. Nothing."

"You were gonna what? Just say it."

"I was gonna arrange a dinner for all my children and their husbands down in Georgia since you all got married in August. I can't believe she never even sent you a card, son, I just can't believe it. It's too bad you're just getting over being sick because you need your rest and don't need to be traveling and alla that so I'm not gonna be able to do it, and I'm just so upset right now, son, that's all." She sighed and looked up. "Lord, what do you want from me?"

"Where were you intending to have this dinner?"

"I wasn't sure. Probably at my friend Irma's who you met. I hadn't planned the whole thing out yet."

"Why wouldn't you have it at Uncle Josh's. They have that huge kitchen and dining room and he said I could use it anytime. So much in the family has happened in August, so many birthdays and deaths, why not have it be a bigger celebration, not just for your children's anniversaries, but it could be a big reunion, a family celebration, and my family could meet your family and wouldn't that just be a wonderful time for everyone? That is, you know, if you still wanna do something for all your children." He called her bluff, although he wasn't exactly sure she was bluffing.

She backed up and leaned on the sink, her shoulders slumping with resignation. "You really wanna have it there?"

"Sure, why not?"

"Nana'll probably cause some problems, but nothing you'll have to deal with, son. You know she didn't come to your sister Tanzania's wedding."

"But didn't she get married at Uncle Josh's house, which may as well be Nana's house since she lives there?"

"Yes, but she didn't come because Soldier is not an Adventist."

"What did she do during the ceremony?"

"Her and Granddad stayed in their apartment. My father wanted to come, I just know he did, but he always went along with what she wanted. They eventually came out for the reception."

"She wouldn't show her face at the wedding, but she joined them at the reception." He couldn't believe what he was hearing. Jennifer had told him that Tanzania and Soldier were actually joined by a justice of the peace at a secret marriage in June, which she and Rwanda, Tanzania's sister, attended. Their August wedding at Uncle Josh's was a show for family and friends, even though only three other people knew the truth. "I wonder how Nana would react if she knew her boycott was all for naught, but I don't suppose we'll ever know since Tanzania's actual anniversary passes in secret."

"We'll never know because she'll *never* find out. Son, I've told you a lot of things about my family, by which I mean my immediate family, me and my daughters and now you, that no one else in the family knows, and I trust that you'll keep it that way."

"I'm just trying to get to know all of you."

"As far as the event is concerned, if you want it at Uncle Josh's, then that's where we'll have it. We need to talk to Aunt Crystal and work out the details. We need to move fast because we have to get the invitations out. As for Nana, I can guarantee she'll be a problem, but I'll deal with whatever I have to deal with, just for you, son. If this is what you really want."

Absolutely. And nothing could have kept him from it. Nothing at all. Not even a walk through the shadow of the valley of death.

LOVE: A LETTER

1 Hello family. As a part of what you all call the *koude kant*—the cold side—of the family, I would like to address the women from what I'll call the warm side. My reasons for writing this letter are motivated by a desire for the nearness that openness can create.

First of all, I want to thank you all for your thoughts and prayers during my hospital stay and illness last weekend. I believe that your well-wishes contributed to my speedy recovery. I was expected to be in the hospital for at least two weeks, but I was out in only three days.

I wish my Dutch were much better than it is but, unfortunately, I will have to write this letter in English because it is so close to my heart and using my first language is the only way I have a chance to express myself correctly. Since some of you understand English better than others, you may have to talk to each other about this letter in order to fully understand it. This could be a good thing and the reason why I didn't want Job to translate it before I sent it.

When I was in the hospital on Saturday morning, I can tell you for certain that I was close to death. My fever was high and I was drifting in and out of consciousness. During one of these out-of-conscious moments, Pa came to me. This isn't the first time Pa has come to me and it probably won't be the last.

Ma, do you remember the very first time I came to Holland? I stood in your living room and looked out over the canal toward the trees beyond it and I was overtaken with emotion. I said something in Dutch, which I couldn't understand and can't remember, and asked what was beyond the trees. Job said that his father was buried in a cemetery there. Later that day, in Dutch that I could understand, I told you that Pa wanted to be let go. "*Laat mij gaan,*" was his mantra. We went to visit his grave the next day.

When Job and I returned from Paris after our engagement, you'd brought so much energy into the apartment I was hit with it as soon as I crossed the threshold. You'd dug out a box of old pictures of your father and of Hans, pictures Job hadn't seen in years. You'd even brought out pictures of Pa. In fact, you'd hung a picture of Pa on the wall right next to the window where I stood days earlier. It was then that I realized how strange it was, to me anyway, that you didn't have a single picture of Pa on display anywhere in your home prior to that. I wonder if you do now.

Ma, family is the most important thing to me, more important than money and power and houses and other possessions. You are a strong woman. When you came to our wedding, I was so grateful. Thank you for that. Thank you for being here for Job's graduation. Because of language, I know that it is not always easy for us to understand each other but I have love for you. I hope you also know how much I love your son. You have buried your husband and two of your three sons. The bond you have with Job is even more special now that he is the only son you have left. And he lives far away from you, across that big old ocean that takes a whole day of travel and lag to overcome. I understand that you want him to be happy. I want you to understand that I only want for him to be happy too.

Job is in a great deal of pain about his life. No one is to blame for this—it's just how it is. I know his pain because I live with it everyday. Job shares this pain with me sometimes in ways that hurt me, sometimes in ways that let both of us heal, but he is my husband and I will be with him to help him through his pain until death do us part.

I know sometimes when you come to visit us, it may look like Job is doing too much, or doing more than I, or that I am taking advantage of him in some way. But things are not always as they appear. Job and I have gone through things that only we know about and the fact that we've been able to get through them and stay together is nothing short of a miracle of love. I love your son more than I have ever loved another man, and no matter what, I will always be there for him and be good to him, even though we argue and fuss and fight. I come from a background that argues and fusses and fights in order to get out our feelings. I know that Job is not used to that and sometimes it frustrates him, but we are learning how to deal with each other better and that is because of the miracle. So please, Ma, I hope you understand how much your son means to me. I will continue to learn to love him better.

Nelleke, during parts of Job's childhood, you had to be like a parent to Job. When I first met you, you asked me questions that only a big sister would ask of the man who would eventually become her little brother's life mate. I appreciated the way you took your time to get to know me in order to feel sure your brother wasn't choosing someone who'd hurt him again. You have been and, I suspect, always will be the protector of your mother and father regarding the way they brought you all up. My sister Gina is the older of us and she's the same way. I respect her and love her for it. But, children need to be able to feel the pain from some of the mistakes their parents made so that they can release it all and let go of it. When I wrote the poem STOLEN MARBLES a few years ago that Job shared with you and Wilma, I wasn't trying to blame Pa for anything or to suggest that he didn't love all of you the best way he knew how. When Job first read the poem, he cried and cried and cried.

Job will heal, I have no doubt. But his healing will be challenged if he feels like he has no right to feel his pain. As often as I can, I reassure him that he has a right to all of his feelings, no matter what they are. Pa did everything he could to make sure Ma and you all were taken care of. But as with many fathers, he had his limitations, especially when it came to letting his young children mourn the tragedy of brother Hans' death. No one could say his name or talk about him, none of his daughters could even date guys with the same name. Again, that was the way it was. It was the only way he thought to handle the loss, but that doesn't mean that it didn't cause his children even more pain.

Thank you for coming for his 40th birthday party. I will continue to love your little Bol the best I can.

Wilma, sister of compassion, thank you for being there for us through thick and thin. I know that Sjaak has shared the most about our relationship with you and what you know is very little. I wish he would share even more, but that's up to him. You have been a bedrock of support to him when he is at his most vulnerable, and I want to thank you for always listening to his pain and giving him sound and wise advice. You have helped me so much by helping him so much, and I wish I could see you—all of you—more than I do. But the ocean is wide and money doesn't grow on trees. I know that family is also the most important thing to you. I will continue to love.

Els, it saddened me that we did not get to see you for Job's 40th or at his graduation. I don't feel that I know you as well as I would like to, so I am not exactly sure why you decided not to come to either of these important events in your youngest brother's life. I know you and Sjaak were very close as children, and then something changed. That's only for you and Job to explore. But I want to know you better and see you more. I don't know how

Job felt about your absence because he didn't comment. But I was sad because I knew that the "plan" for his 40th birthday was that all the family would come to America and share it with him. I know how much you appreciated us being there for your 40th.

I am grateful for your prayers and wishes and cards and thoughts over these four-plus years. I look forward to the time when I see you again.

Family, your son-brother and I will be celebrating our third wedding anniversary this year in Dalton, Georgia. Because of everything we've been through together, especially this past year, our anniversary is very important to us.

This anniversary is special for another reason.

Next month, at the big house of Mother Jennifer's brother, Uncle Josh, we are having a family celebration/banquet/reunion. You will all be getting an invitation in the mail in the next few weeks. I would imagine that there isn't much of a chance that any of you can come. It's short notice, some of you are probably already on holiday, finances may be tight, etc. But if there is any way whatsoever for any of you to throw caution to the wind and get on a plane and fly to Atlanta that weekend for what could be a once in our lifetime event.... Well, I would just not know how to contain my happiness. My heart would burst a good burst. No one is getting any younger, and none of us are guaranteed another birthday or holiday or anniversary. Please consider.

You are my family.

Your son-brother,

Craig

THE FEAST OF FAMILIES

1 On August 25, 2001, they observed the Feast of Families. Members of the clan came to the house on Ella Lane from across the country: Jennifer and Craig drove down a week earlier from Boston to prepare; Mary, Hazelle, and Gina came from Milwaukee; uncles and cousins arrived from California and Alabama; Aunt Crystal's people came from Texas, Ohio, and Alabama; and all Jennifer's children attended with their spouses.

The Feast, as the invitation outlined, would observe three memorials, four birthdays, and four wedding anniversaries. It was the last of these that generated the most pre-event buzz. The Sabbath could not be kept holy by honoring the unholy union of homosexual men. Burundi, twin sister of Rwanda, had tried to avoid such blasphemy. "I think maybe, um, we should just not, um, like, just not really focus, um, on the wedding anniversaries," she'd mumbled under her breath to Craig over the phone. "It's probably just better to just, um, call the whole event a, like, um, family reunion and not, um, single out any birthdays or anniversaries or memorials on the invitation."

Oblivious at the time to Burundi's attempt at cover-up, Craig stood his ground. "Why would I do that? Besides, it was your mother who wanted to do something special for all our anniversaries. Why not let the families know how this event was conceived?" Burundi had no answer. She mumbled some other words he couldn't decipher. Their conversation ended.

Also ending was the possibility that her husband's parents would attend the Feast. Burundi's father-in-law, Deacon Peacock, an Elder at his congregation in Huntsville, Alabama, was a retired Adventist minister, and he couldn't show his face at such an event. Gossip, safe to say, that he condoned such brazen ungodliness might circle like hawks. What a scandal might ensue; what quarry he might become. Never mind that he'd already, only a month before, invited the heathens into his home, sat them down at his supper table, and broke bread with them. (Perhaps ravenous vultures were already picking at carrion.) Craig enjoyed meeting his sister's husband's parents. Save the incessant Ellen G. White quotes and his expressed desire to remain trapped forever in his earthly body, elder Deacon, a small man with a big personality and bigger sense of humor, reminded Craig of Hazelle. Shirley Peacock, a stout woman not known for her talkativeness, was chattier than a gossipmonger at a class reunion.

That her in-laws would not attend the Feast gave Burundi, who ordinarily got what she wanted, all kinds of stomach stress. Burundi wanted so badly for her in-laws to meet her brother's parents from Milwaukee that she desperately tried to convince them to come for part of the day, if only to attend Sabbath morning worship services at the church right around the corner. They refused.

The show went on without them.

And oh, what a show went on. Jennifer, who battled a war backstage with England, ran the kitchen like a commander in chief. She kept close account of the preparation and timing of all stages of the food to ensure completion before Sabbath sundown. The ambitious menu she put together with Craig and Burundi took three days to prepare. Her brother James often referred to her as The Cook. Six years prior, she had catered her daughter Tanzania's wedding out of the same gourmet kitchen, replete with Corian counters, two sinks, two dishwashers, an eight-burner, commercial-grade cook top and stove, three microwaves, and an island big enough for a dozen grown people to stand round.

This time Jennifer monitored the creation of her popular but tedious-to-prepare barbequed gluten strips; filo dough stuffed with wild mushrooms; rice salad with sun-dried tomatoes and balsamic vinaigrette; roasted new potatoes with garlic and mint; beefsteak tomatoes stuffed with red cabbage, cornbread, and beet greens; chilled string bean and onion salad; vegetarian tuna and chicken salad; and an assortment of mini-breads, remoulades, gourmet cheeses, crudités and fresh fruits. And these were just the hors d'oeuvres.

After church, the family gathered for the memorial where James remembered shopping with his father for the suit and tie he was wearing. He told his polite but inattentive family that that was the last time he had seen his father, who passed on three years and one day ago, alive. Job memorialized his brothers, Hans and Gerrit, who'd departed life thirty-two years apart, Hans on the first of the month, Gerrit on the twenty-second, exactly one year to the day after Job married Craig.

After prayer, Jennifer, her son, and her three daughters served the luncheon of hors d'oeuvres on Aunt Crystal's freshly polished silver platters. "Look at how beautiful this food is," said Netta, one of Crystal's sisters. Jennifer and Craig stood behind her. She turned to them. "My, my, I see he's got your good cooking genes, too. You two oughtta start a catering business together."

Jennifer eyed Craig and smiled. "Well, my son and I have talked about just that, and when we get back to Boston, that's exactly what we're gonna do."

"So you're going back to Boston. I didn't know that. How long're you gonna stay, you think?"

"Long as he'll have me." They laughed.

"Well, I wish you all the best." Netta went to get her camera. She and several members of the hungry family quickly snapped pictures of the colorful display before piling their plates.

Charles, the godfather of Tanzania's son, Quincy, and Rwanda's first love, questioned The Cook about who prepared what. He refused to eat anything the homosexual created.

The afternoon went by without drama. At least none that anyone could see from the front of the house. Some folks toured the nearby Seventh-Day Adventist college, which Uncle Josh's son, Little Josh, and his new fiancée, April Marie, attended. Others went back to their hotel rooms and took naps. The day-trippers, most from neighboring Alabama, hung around the house, trying to confirm rumors about the circumstances thirty-three years earlier that had laid the foundation for the event they'd come to see. Mary didn't like such nosiness. When Sister Meeks, Aunt Crystal's mother and England's historical nemesis, asked Mary, who sat tense as a dental patient on the other end of the couch opposite the kitchen, questions such as, "So when and where did Jennifer have Joseph Craig? How did your son find her?"

Mary responded with answers such as, "Those are private matters which I couldn't disclose because of adoption law. You would have to ask Jennifer and Craig yourself." She promptly changed the subject. "Craig, what did you and Job do for your anniversary on Wednesday?"

"I'll tell you about it later, Mama," said Craig, returning to food preparations.

Jennifer knew Craig had planned to make a statement regarding the anniversaries to the gathering after dinner. But she didn't know exactly what he'd planned to state and she couldn't risk it. So she pre-empted his remarks before dinner by asking everyone with August birthdays and anniversaries to stand up and be counted. Aunt Crystal's brother D.L. and his partner Greg stood up and told the family that they had met ten years ago on the first of the month. After the rest of the standing stated their events, Jennifer ordered the gathering to the doublewide, palatial front staircase for photographs. Job and Joshua took black-and-white and color prints of the honored group. Costumed in summer dresses or floor-length gowns of purple, black, and silver; three-piece suits with bowties or dark jackets with shirt and tie, the family members looked as though they were on their way to a New Year's Eve party. Or a debutante ball.

Around seven o'clock, dinner was served buffet style. Craig's award-winning macaroni and cheese with six cheeses and a puree of secrets stole the show. Charles even helped himself three times when he thought no one was looking. It amazes how some people are caught, in secret, doing exactly what they protest in public. It amazes more how others do in public exactly what they protest in private. England, who spoke loudly and often to her granddaughters about the disaster of cheese as nutrition, ate heaps of Craig's golden ambrosia. There were also roasting pans of Egyptian-style stuffed red and green bell peppers; honey-glazed vegetarian dinner loaf; vegetarian Fri Chik; bread stuffing; wild rice with fresh herbs; and candied yams. All of it accompanied by a pot of steamed broccoli, a huge vat of collard and mustard greens, and corn muffins and dinner rolls Burundi had made from scratch.

In the main dining room, Craig and his father sat on opposite ends of a forty-thousand-dollar mahogany dining-room table adorned with two-foot-tall twin glass vases overflowing with fresh-cut purple and gold flowers and Aunt Crystal's best china and Waterford. Oiled by the light of the hundred-pound Maria Theresa crystal chandelier trimmed in twenty-four karat gold, Craig witnessed a union of family and relatives right out of a fairy tale. Uncle Josh and Aunt Crystal's twenty-two-room house on Ella Lane was his castle in the sky, and the people gathered round his welcoming table, every one of them, brought their own fantasies to the spread. Craig's family acted as if they enjoyed bell peppers stuffed with fake meat. Hazelle would've given a hefty donation for some slow-basted pork ribs and a six-pack of Pabst. Mary would've given up her faith to sit on his left hand instead of looking down the table at the woman who birthed her son sit there instead. Job wanted his father *present* and in his earthly absence, his mother or Wilhelmina called Wilma, his closest sister, who were asleep in their homes across the world in the Netherlands. Gina, Craig's only *real* sister, for, in his world, real meant the one who shared his history, was so overwhelmed by the mendacity she smelled in the castle, she disappeared immediately after dinner (besides, her brother hadn't baked the sweet potato pie) and retired to her hotel room. And the rest: Jennifer; England; Tanzania and her husband Soldier; Burundi and her husband Zion; Rwanda and her husband

Lovelace, stayed in the dream they'd always dreamed; wondering how, if at all, they could include in it the brother, son, grandson—the *stranger*—who sat the head of the table.

The twenty other relatives who sat round rented fold-up tables and chairs in the living room-cum-banquet hall that opened off the dining room were the first to slice into dessert. Other than the gluten hors d'oeuvre—which had to be mixed, set overnight, rinsed out, set overnight, stretched and twisted into eye-pleasing braids, boiled in heavily seasoned water, set once more, then grilled in doctored-up, store-bought barbeque sauce—dessert had been prepared first. Jennifer insisted on this to avoid the pastries stealing even a hue of flavor from the chopped fresh garlic or the simmering celery and onions. With the efficiency of a beaver, she'd prepared a huge apple pie, so good it was the only apple pie her nephew Christian (who didn't show up) would eat, three cheesecakes, and four sweet potato pies on the Wednesday morning before the event. Her cheesecake, a modified recipe off a graham cracker crumbs box, was a family favorite. Her daughters sang Hallelujah! for her desserts as if Christ himself had prepared them.

By now, Craig had tasted enough of Jennifer's cooking to admit her abundant talent. She could alchemize the most ordinary ingredients into savory gems without the need to taste them during the entire process. It was the only way she knew how to serve her love without testing it first. But all recipes, including his own, could be improved.

He'd come into the kitchen that morning and scanned the cooling pastries on the island counter top. His eyes rested on the four sweet potato pies. He wrinkled his brow and pushed his bottom lip forward a bit further than it naturally protruded. Jennifer was busy near the sink. Her daughters stood round the island.

"My goodness, how long you been up?"

"Since six o'clock. I had to get these desserts outta the way. You gonna get started on that cake pretty soon, son?"

"I see. I thought we agreed that I was gonna make sweet potato pecan pie to honor my father and a—"

"Have you tasted Mom's sweet potato pie?" Rwanda interrupted.

"Yeah. But mine's better."

Jennifer dropped a mixing bowl on the floor. She didn't turn around. Rwanda rolled her eyes. Burundi and Tanzania looked at each other as though stunned by the news that someone close to them had died. None of them spoke.

What Craig didn't know was that he had just cursed their mother. He'd never before met a mother, no matter how good a cook, who didn't mind her children finding a way to do *anything* better. But Jennifer had trained her daughters like house pets: she could say no wrong, do no wrong, and nobody could touch her. They could hardly wipe their behinds without consulting her for the best brand of bathroom tissue to use.

What the four women didn't know was that "mine's" referred to the potato pies his late Granny Alma, his mother's stepmother, and his daddy, both of them proud Negroes from Mississippi, made. Jennifer's pie of sweet potatoes, butter, eggs, sugar, evaporated milk, cinnamon, and pure vanilla extract just didn't satisfy his soul. Those ingredients, save the butter and milk, were fine. But he needed his grandmother's heavy cream and ginger, his daddy's nutmeg and a hint of cloves, too. Unlike his grandmother, he would cut the sugar by half and include a dollop of pure maple syrup. Unlike his daddy, he would add a smidgen of his own orange extract, a pinch of cardamom and just enough salt to make the flavors fly. When he wanted more decadence, he would take his daddy's pecans, glazed with Karo, molasses, and melted brown sugar, and add them to the top before baking. The result was a marriage of southern desserts that would make the thickhearted break down, and cry. "Mine's" wasn't so much his as it was *theirs*. Jennifer, unmistakably, despite their understanding, wanted to make hers.

And so it was that Craig baked only his burnt sugar caramel cake, his mama's favorite pastry, instead. He hadn't baked one in years, but he thought the family celebration was the perfect opportunity to prepare one for her. She used to come home from work every afternoon and wonder what her son was trying to make out of the original Betty Crocker cookbook. Other than watching his parents, both of them great creators in the kitchen, Betty Crocker taught him how to *burn,* as Mary was wont to say. Before her diabetes diagnosis round the time Craig was ten, she would request his burnt sugar caramel cake with his hand-churned homemade caramel ice cream on the side even more than she requested his ice-box cheesecake, which became her second favorite. After her diagnosis, a "sliver" of any dessert was all she'd allow herself.

At the Feast of Families, Mary takes an extra dose of insulin. She slices herself a mighty big wedge. She sits herself down, digs her fork, prongs down, through three layers of what she has missed for more than twenty years. She opens her mouth and closes her eyes. She slides, slowly, the moist, bitter-tinged cake and the rich brown-sugar frosting sprinkled with crushed pecans across her taste buds. She swallows his love. She is reunited with a place deep inside herself where her son is all hers.

2 Craig called him Unc. He was the man who flew the day after a five-hour phone conversation from Murrieta, California, to Milwaukee, Wisconsin on April 18, 2001 to meet his nephew. The man who, two

stormy mornings later, drove with Craig and Job the eight hundred miles down through Illinois, Indiana, Kentucky, Tennessee, Alabama, back through Tennessee, past the Dalton Exit on interstate 75 in Georgia, to Roswell to introduce his nephew to his sister for the first time. James hadn't seen Jennifer for almost a year. Their last encounter had left him dissatisfied; she wouldn't listen to any of his Jewish theology and he rejected outright her claims that if he took his medication as prescribed and kept his manic depression in check, he'd come to his senses and come back to the Adventist faith. But he no longer had any use for the counterfeit Jews, as he called Seventh-Day Adventists, even though their mother England, who called them the same thing, still had plenty use for them.

Presenting his nephew to his sister was poetic justice. Having none of his own, James considered Craig more a son than a nephew. After all, it was James who shouted from the back of the courtroom on that Monday morning, December 18, 1967, "I'll take him. Let *me* take him." But England wouldn't listen to him; the judge, bound by archaic laws, couldn't. The Honorable Ervin M. Bruner presided only to declare the parental rights of the mother Jennifer Minnie White over her baby, the illegitimate Joseph Bernard White, a minor, permanently terminated. Uncle James wanted him; England wouldn't hear of it.

Her daughter's open sin, as designated by Adventists, had to be covered up. And so it was that the boy had to go. England sent Jennifer to a boarding house in Madison, seventy-five miles west of Milwaukee, so no one would know she was pregnant. Shortly after her son's birth and his immediate, pre-arranged placement with a white foster family just outside of Madison, Jennifer was re-baptized, a rite necessary for her to rejoin the faith and belong to the true Israel of God, as the strictest followers of Ellen G. White considered themselves.

When Uncle James left the following at the age of thirty-three, he also had to go. England turned her back on her firstborn. Shortly thereafter, James experienced the first of many aggressive and frightening episodes that ended his marriage and career. He was also cast aside by his brother, his sister, one of his daughters, his nieces and nephews.

For the next twenty years, his sister and mother would compete with each other over who was better able to handle his illness. Jennifer would claim she faced down knives; England, with her daughter's support, would arrange more than once to have him committed. But by their own admission, Uncle James proved too brilliant for all of that. He knew exactly what to say before any judge; he escaped commitment with the ease of a great magician. One time, he ran out of tricks. He traveled by bus to Portland, Maine on his way to Lubec, the easternmost port in the United States. He wanted to be among the first in the country one morning to witness the sun seep into the horizon, be among the first to feel its rays anoint his mahogany-brown skin. He never got to his final destination. He was arrested in Portland for setting a small fire in a hotel room and babbling nonsense about numbers to the front desk clerk. He went to jail and remained there for most of '97 and part of '98. The district attorney hadn't officially charged him with anything; the eighteen months a random sentence that finally ended because a judge's clerk inadvertently pulled the file for her boss from the archives. Moved by something unknown, the judge reviewed the file he hadn't requested and set free James Eathel White III. The only ones to see him while imprisoned were his parents. Not even his wife came to visit. England and her husband James II had driven twice the eleven hundred miles from Dalton to Portland, the first time to visit, the last, to pick him up and take him back to Georgia. It was this trip, the final journey he took with his father still alive, that James III had reminisced about during the memorial service after church on the Sabbath.

Later that afternoon, he had cornered his nephew in the laundry room, which was next to the door of his mother's apartment at the back of the house. James closed the door and stood in front of it. Sweat dripped from his face and drenched his shirt down to his stomach; his father's tie hung loosened from his neck.

"Unc, please, let me by. I've got to get this food out," Craig had pleaded gently. The laundry room had two extra refrigerators and a large freezer where they'd stored completed dinner items and leftovers from afternoon hors d'oeuvres.

"I have to show you something from the Old Testament. I hold the proof, man. Right here. Let me show you where the Bible tells you that I *am* Israel."

"I'll read it later, Unc. I promise. But first I have to get this dressing into the oven so it's heated in time for dinner tonight." Craig tried to move past him but James could not be sidetracked. "Unc, if you don't let me out of here, I'm gonna have to drop this tray and move you myself. I don't wanna do that."

"Alright. I'm Israel, man. I'm *Israel*."

"Then you need to let this Israelite go."

His episode had begun the night before at the nearby Day's Inn. He'd become so agitated, Sonja feared him, and Aunt Grace, his father's sister, who shared their room, mustered all the energy her eighty-three-year-old, ninety-three-pound frame could and had thrown his six-foot, two-hundred-pound body down on the floor, holding her walking cane cross his neck till he calmed down.

Now, here in the laundry room, Craig was thankful that no such aggression was necessary. Uncle James capitulated and moved away from the door. Craig found Jennifer and asked her to handle the oncoming storm. Jennifer, remembering that Uncle Herman, her mother's brother, used to walk for miles when *his* illness flared up, quickly changed her slippers into sneakers and took her brother on a long walk. England wanted to give her son barley green powder mixed with freshly pressed carrot juice, but Jennifer insisted they walk first.

When they returned, both of them sopping wet with sweat, James was calm; he told his mother to drink the concoction herself. He lay on his mother's bed where sleep captured him faster than Jennifer could close the bedroom door.

Just before she left the apartment, Jennifer knifed her eyes right through her mother.

Neither one of them spoke.

3   Four days later, Craig, Jennifer, James, Sonja, and Aunt Crystal's sister, Raven, were the only people left who didn't live in the house on Ella Lane. That *any* guests remained gave England pleasure. After her husband had succumbed to a massive heart attack while helping build a house with the Habitat for Humanity Jimmy Carter Work Project in Georgia, England didn't have much company in the apartment at the back of the house. Joshua had designed the apartment for his parents, who moved there after they sold the house on Sixteenth Street in Milwaukee. Crystal's father built the house, just as he had for another of his daughters in Huntsville, Alabama. A few youngsters from the congregation stayed with England every once in a while, and the grandchildren who didn't live in the front of the house visited her less than that. England was rarely included in the infrequent gatherings of the main house, a cold house where no love lived, as she often said. Not long after James II passed, Aunt Crystal wanted England out. England refused to leave. Where would she go? What would people think? In the time it took for a weather front to move across the nation, word would get out in every black Adventist church in California, Missouri, Wisconsin, Alabama, Georgia, Tennessee and Florida—everywhere she'd ever been a member and even where she hadn't—that her very own son had kicked her out. When her husband surrendered to his mother's refusals, Crystal locked him out of her heart, leaving cold in the place where warm used to live.

In a few days, after the last guests finally depart, England will be back in the apartment, starving for company. Starving for the company of someone like Mary who had sat in England's kitchen during much of her five-day visit. At the kitchen table, England had spread out all her special books, teaching Mary which foods naturally stimulated the pancreas, which nutrients facilitated circulation the best. At the kitchen table, England, so adept at covering up her own, had pried open the vault of Mary's insecurity. At the kitchen table, England and Mary had clung to each other like long lost sisters, testifying the Lord's blessings and whining life's disappointments. The disappointments of a teenaged daughter who'd gone astray, of a son who'd gone and turned gay. Of a daughter who'd shown no respect when she thought she needed it most, of a grown son who'd cursed in her face when she thought she deserved it least. How could the Lord have delivered them such tribulation? No different than anyone's children, England's only daughter and Mary's only son were riddles that couldn't be solved. England Martanna and Mary Juanita, born ten days and five hundred miles apart, were more identical than either would see and as dissimilar as fraternal twins could be.

"Take this fructose and give it to your mother for her diabetes. I could never thank that woman enough," England had said to Mary's son the second time he'd come to her home back in June. "Please, son, give this to her from me and tell her that I could never thank her enough, praise the Lord."

"Call her up and tell her yourself."

And so she did what he told her. Her call installed a lifeline each would cling to for her reasons, all of them mysterious. Craig could hardly believe how swiftly, how wholly, his mother made England her authority. During her visit, Mary had pranced around the house murmuring, to no one in particular, such things as, "Think I better try some beet juice after I take my morning insulin. Nana's gonna get me. I better not let her see me have any more dessert. Don't tell Nana, but I didn't like that barley green stuff too much." This angered him. His mother had allowed England so deep inside her vault she couldn't even eat in peace. How was it that these women, first Jennifer in Milwaukee, and then England, gotten her so? What possessed her such that she would splay her viscera before them like some slaughtered animal? What debt was she trying to pay?

But Mary was still Mary and when she'd said, "Take these pictures of Craig and Gina and put them right there in that frame with the rest of your grandchildren," Nana did what she told her. And when Mary had said, "Those pictures I gave you better stay right where you put them," Nana assured her they would. And so they did.

Now, Sister Mary had gone back to Milwaukee and the son England couldn't thank Mary enough for mothering, her own flesh and blood, kept refusing to sit with England and look at all the dusty books and worn documents and sepia photographs and yellowed newsprint and family memorabilia she wanted to show him. Eventually, he would give in. But right now, Craig finished talking on the phone to Job in Boston and joined Crystal and Raven at the kitchen table in the main house for some leftovers. Jennifer, James, Sonja, and England were standing in England's apartment. The door was open. "What could you *possibly* know about all the things I've been through because of James?" England was shouting at Jennifer.

"Mother, I'm tired of hearing you say that. I was the one who walked with him last Saturday and calmed him down."

"So what so what so *what*. That doesn't make you some kind of expert psychiatrist. Sonja has had to put up with more than any of us, and she takes care of my son and stands by him better than anybody, praise the Lord."

"I've done better than Brenda has," Sonja chimed in with a timid self-righteousness. "Been through more than Brenda went through with him, that's for sure."

Jennifer rung back, "You still going on and on about Brenda? They been divorced for more than twenty years..."

"This woman has been a blessing sent from heaven to take care of my boy." England's face began to harden. "Who knows *where* James would be without her."

"This *woman* didn't even have the sense to tell anybody the police were coming." Three days earlier, while Craig was loading his parents' and his husband's luggage into the car, the police had arrived. Early that Sunday morning, Sonja had once again feared her husband in their hotel room and, telling no one (no one except England who excused her from everything), she'd called the police. Called them not to come to the hotel, but to the front of the house on Ella Lane. She'd brought James to his mother's apartment and, with England's collusion, had kept him settled there till the police arrived. As soon as they arrived, Aunt Sonja disappeared. With the alacrity and conviction of a preacher, Uncle Josh, who, during most of the Feast, had to care for sick children at his pediatric clinic down the street, assured the police that everything in his house, including his brother, was under control. The police left. "If she takes such good care of him," Jennifer continued, "why did she have them come here instead of the hotel? She always does this mess. Pushing him off on his family and then leaving the scene. She did the same thing at Tanzania's house back when Joseph first found me."

England's mouth twisted. Her caramel-colored skin flushed red. She bristled like a horned lizard with narrowed eyes about to spew blood at her undeterred predator. She pushed her big-boned body right up on her daughter's big-boned body and flashed her gritted teeth. Within seconds, Vesuvius roared: "What in hell do *you* know? You gonna stand here and talk foul of this woman? You get out. *Get* out. Get *out*. Get. Out. My. House!"

Jennifer fought back tears and moved into the kitchen where the three were watching in awe. Craig fixed her a plate of leftovers and set it on the table. "Here. Sit down and eat something." Jennifer sat down. But England wasn't finished. She marched into the main kitchen without limping, without the cane she'd used all week as a sympathy prop. Craig stood between her and Jennifer, who remained seated. Soon as England opened her mouth again, he began riffing, "Please, let my mother eat in peace."

"You think I have to listen to what *you* say?"

"Please, let my mother eat in peace."

"You think just because you keep saying that that I'm gonna what? Back off and go home like some child?"

"Please, let my mother eat in *peace*."

"You don't know me."

"*Please*, let my mother eat in peace."

"You don't know how we do things around here."

"You made sure of that didn't you?"

"Joseph," Jennifer began her overlapping mantra, her voice a cutting whisper.

"What? I made sure of what?"

"Joseph."

"You made *sure* I didn't get to know how you do things round here, didn't you?"

"Joseph."

"You coulda been *dead?*"

"Joseph."

"I *woulda* been dead, just like the rest of you, if you had kept me in this hell you call a life."

"*Joseph.*"

"Eat your food," he snapped at Jennifer. "And stop calling me that." He turned his attention back to England. "For the last time, let my mother eat in peace and get outta my face."

"You don't know me."

"You don't know *me.*" Craig stretched up his spine ramrod straight. He seared his eyes right into hers. "I don't roll over for anybody, especially not the likes of you. And since you don't know me, you have no idea what you're walking into. I would advise you for the *very* last time to step back, step down, and get *out* of my face. You don't believe fat meat is greazy—try me."

England harrumphed and went back to her apartment. During a moment that hung over the room like thick cobwebs, no one spoke. Jennifer stared absentmindedly at her plate. Aunt Crystal, softly smiling, stared at the strange-familiar man standing in her kitchen. Finally, Crystal said, "Nana, meet Nana."

Aunt Raven looked over at Jennifer, who began to pick slowly through her food. "There's nothing like having a son's protection," said Raven, trying to clean the air. "A son by your side is so much different than a daughter. Jennifer, you must be so happy that he found you."

England came back into the kitchen and slammed a pile of books on the table. Jennifer took her plate and walked with her son up the stairs off the kitchen and away from her mother to Joshua's playroom.

That England could so easily, so thoroughly, shame Jennifer into a seventeen-year-old girl made Craig feel scorn and sadness for both of them, especially as he watched Jennifer, an escaped convict, completely avoid her mother in her brother's den for the next three days.

Just as well, Craig thought, that I hadn't bothered to tell Job about Milwaukee. If I had, Job mighta never asked Jennifer before we drove down here to bring back enough of her own things to make the guest room more like home.

"You're gonna stay awhile," Job had said, surprising Craig, who wasn't sure if he wanted Jennifer in their home for another minute. But after thirty-three years, why not examine at close, close range the intriguing woman who couldn't remember pushing him into the world?

And so it was that three days after Vesuvius erupted, Jennifer packed most of her belongings in the back of her son's black Jeep Grand Cherokee and began the thousand-mile drive back to Boston.

ANOTHER COUNTRY

1 Nelleke, I hope you have the patience to "listen" and at least a modicum of respect for my thoughts and feelings. I hope this time I can write a letter that you don't circulate to your accomplice and informant here in America. This time, I will address you and only you. I'd prefer that if you need to respond to anything I say here, please direct it only to me. It's time to take others, especially Job, out of the middle of this.

It's unfortunate that my letter was such a "bomb" in your life and that you failed to see any love in it. But I did not write the letter as a bomb to drop on you or anyone else. I did not write it because I was feeling emotional about finding my birth family. The letter was overdue. I sensed a negative dynamic going on in the family regarding me, a dynamic no one opened their mouth to say anything to me about. The dynamic was affecting my marriage and you better believe I will do whatever it takes to extract from my marriage any poison, no matter the source.

When the angel of death visits, you realize that tomorrow is a fantasy guaranteed to no one. I'm sure you watched those twin towers tumble over and over again on the news. I can't stand the news but I couldn't take my eyes off those recurring images of the World Trade Center mushrooming into the air like the clouds from the atomic bombs dropped on Nagasaki and Hiroshima more than half a century ago. Because of my letter, Ma expresses her love for Job more than she ever has, even though Job says it's not typical for the Dutch to say "*Ik hou van jou*" to each other very often. He says you all think we Americans have taken the meaning out of "I love you" by saying it so much. True or false, the words are rarely used to hurt the person for whom they are intended. They could never be used to manipulate those who love themselves.

I do not define love as you do. But as you define it, you do not appear to love me at all. Love, as you say, is about taking an interest in the concerns of someone else's life. You do not seem interested whatsoever in the concerns of my life. Not that you've ever claimed to love me, mind you. I wonder, however, if the way in which you have taken such an interest in the concerns of your brother's life comes from a place of love or control.

Control is not love. Love is not control.

Some time before or after you were here for Job's 40th birthday, you decided that he would be better off without me. Some time after your decision, you began scheming with Gwynne, who'd decided the very same thing, to get me out of your brother's life. I had no idea such a trans-Atlantic soap opera was brewing. Gwynne would tell you some bad news, which usually meant Job and I had a fight about who was more afraid of whatever it was that made us both afraid, you would call Job out of the clear blue and ask him if everything was okay with us because you just had a *feeling*. Whatever you'd say to comfort him seemed only to feed his fear. He'd hang up the phone and become more distant, more irritable and agitated with me than he was before you called.

But we remain. Your scheme hasn't yielded the intended result.

You might consider finding a way to accept me as your brother's husband, like it or lump it.

2   Now, about your visit here for Job's birthday. Job was not at all upset, as you've suggested, because of the rituals that I established to honor the spirits of your brothers and father, your ancestors. Job's been with me long enough to have seen many a ritual that I enact for the ancestors. The rituals may not be his cup of tea, he may not even understand why I do what I do, but he is unmoved. Nelleke, you were the one who was upset. Because you felt so suffocated, as you claimed in your letter to us, you found it necessary to take the pictures of your father and brother off our cocktail table and put them face down on a side table in the living room. What were you thinking? This is our house, not yours. Those were his pictures, not yours. If seeing your ancestors in the center of our living room during your visit made you uncomfortable, perhaps you might consider looking closely at what their images provoke inside you. Nevertheless, you remove the stimuli and then claim—a whole year later, mind you—that I ruined your visit (like mother, like daughter) because Job came home from work upset about seeing pictures of his family on display in the living room. I repeat: I ruined your visit because you thought Job was upset when he came home from work to see pictures of his family on display in the living room. How

does this make any sense? I'm shaking my head in disbelief.

Job and I go through hell with each other but we always find our way back to Paradise. I have empathy for him. I sense his pain in places that make it feel like my own. For you it seems that your family pain is the only pain that matters. You have even implied that your family's tragedies and the way your family has dealt with them are sacred—not to be commented upon by anyone else, simply because they were not *there*. But you don't even allow your brother, who *was* there, to be honest with you about how those tragedies have affected him. He sacrifices so much that he cannot risk expressing something that may hurt you, or, more accurately, remind you of how much you are already hurting. He'd rather choke on his own pain and keep his mouth shut. Job has been firmer with your mother about all of this than he has been with you. That's how strong your control is, Nelleke. Or maybe he feels he owes you something for all that you did for him when he was young. Or maybe he doesn't want to worry you. But you worry anyway; worry that I must be taking advantage of him; worry that I will control him the way you do. Whatever the case, you don't seem to respect his feelings. And he knows that you don't. And you know that you don't. So he talks himself out of his feelings so he won't hurt you or face your rejection.

From whom or where could he have possibly learned how to talk himself out of his feelings, Nelleke? When Job sent you the poem STOLEN MARBLES, which he sent without even asking me, so needful he was for you to read it, to get something out of it that you hadn't gotten from anywhere else in all the years, you took offense. Told him that he hadn't remembered everything correctly. That Pa was actually very proud of him, that Pa could not possibly have felt scorn for him. Based on his apparently faulty memory (you said he was too *young* to remember) his feelings were, therefore, unfounded. After talking to you, he once again tried to convince himself that his feelings were wrong. He didn't succeed. His true feelings came out anyway, with urgency and destruction.

That seems to be the family way. Telling someone that they were too young to understand or remember something is a delusion. After you shared the poem with Ma (Job didn't ask you to share it with her), she called Job and suggested the same thing. Perhaps what you mean is that if people can *think* themselves through a situation, they wouldn't feel whatever they feel. Feelings don't respond to brainwashing. You know this. You either feel your feelings, your feelings change, or you try to shut them out before they change. And sometimes you need help shutting them out. You smoked at least two packs of cigarettes a day the entire time you were here.

It seems clear to me now that it was the poem—a poem I never intended for you to read in the first place—that made you and Ma decide that it was time for me to go.

I have a take-charge personality. Quiet as it's kept, it's one of the things about me that attracted Job. You seem to hold Job in your heart as if he is a small child, the little boy you used to call Bol, who still, after all these years, needs your protection. You want to protect him from me. And so you have used your energies to work with Gwynne and Ma behind our backs to see if you can achieve your goal.

You have stepped way out of line. You betrayed your brother, your sisters, your mother, and yourself by forwarding my letter to Gwynne. You found my letter unconscionable because "it became a family email in which the 4 women in our family were labeled for all the others to see." If that's what hurt you so deeply, then why share it with Gwynne? Using Gwynne as a weapon to try to come between us has backfired, Nelleke, and Gwynne was too blind and foolish to realize what you were doing. You are Job's sister, his eldest sister, whom he loves and respects, despite everything. You are not his protector, even if you once were. You treat him as if he is still a child and take advantage of his insecurities when you communicate with him. When he tells you how this makes him feel, you promptly convince him he's being ludicrous. You might want to stop that.

I have already asked you not to, but if you send this letter to Gwynne it won't accomplish anything constructive. It really is none of her business. Gwynne has become a cold, heartless, lonely, bitter woman who has used Job to fulfill her desire to have a mate. She can go out into the world and have sex with all the black men who desire her and sometimes get pregnant by them and sometimes have their children, but she could never marry any of them; they are all beneath her, only to be used for their mythic cocks and sexual prowess. And so she needs Job. He cannot have sex with her, but he provides her a sense of partnership because of the superficial things they have in common. Gwynne didn't even allow Job the honor of witnessing the birth of her son, something he had hoped for, something he unfortunately came to expect based on their "friendship." But she denied him this and it hurt him. Do I call you, Nelleke, and report on Gwynne to you in an attempt to get Gwynne out of his life? No. Friends don't conspire to punish their friends. Her intentions were malicious and completely self-serving. She was angry that Job chose not to attend her birthday dinner a month ago after she invited all of us and then, at the last minute, told Job she didn't want Jennifer to come, hoping that I wouldn't show up either. She was angry that Job has neither the time nor energy to continue to be used by her in the same way. She remains angry with me because in her eyes, I took Job away from her. As if he was her private possession. Job is no one's possession, but he chose to become one with me. Gwynne can't accept that, and neither can you, it seems. She was so desperate, she called Job's friends behind his back to try to get them involved in something that was none of their business, but they refused, as true friends do. True friends don't get involved in other people's marriages unless they are specifically requested to do so.

When that didn't work, she decided to address me directly through an email full of lies, distortions, and her fantasies of what a no-good, low-down, lazy person I am. (If she'd just come right out and called me a lazy nigger, I might've respected her more. Sometimes I wonder if that rancid sentiment loiters in the back of your mind, too.) Gwynne had no concern for Job or his feelings when she wrote that venom to me. She didn't even bother to talk to Job about it before she did it. She sent that mess to me and copied it to you and Job with the email addresses you had given her. (Did you ever stop to ask yourself why Job hadn't even bothered to give his "best friend" his new email address?) But no matter: I've no doubt you enjoyed seeing that someone had finally put me "in my place." You must've laughed with vindication as you forwarded her email to your mother and sisters.

All of this would be too hard to believe if it hadn't really happened. And orchestrated by *grown* people no less.

Nelleke, you can believe what you need to believe about Gwynne, but I have firsthand experience of how she meddles in our affairs. That you could even think that my family letter was ill intentioned, and that hers came from her burning love for Job strikes me as the height of incredulity and seems to represent something about you that I cannot even put into words right now.

Right now, I'm blinded by my anger and it's hard for me to see all the good in you. The love in you. However, I hope and pray that my vision will clear up with time. You are my beloved's sister. I first thought you were evil to do what you did, but now I have come to realize that you were just misguided and desperate—for what, I'm not exactly sure—but desperate nonetheless. If you applied half the energy you spent trying to get me out of Job's life to understanding us and supporting our marriage, perhaps you'd feel better.

Love begets love.

I can only pray that you will one day be able to look yourself in the mirror and see yourself for the divine spirit you are. Perhaps you might stop smoking, too. It keeps your pain at bay. Clouds the view. Perhaps you might stop trying to talk people out of their feelings. Perhaps you might stop considering me the enemy and accept me as the man with whom your brother has chosen to live out his life. Perhaps you might stop trying to manipulate your brother with your well-rehearsed tactics. Perhaps you might accept that your little brother is a grown man capable of making his own decisions. Perhaps you might simply mind your own business.

And perhaps you might respond to me directly and not deflect your thoughts in Dutch through emails to Job because you want to keep Job in the middle of something, a place where he doesn't belong. Gwynne doesn't speak a lick of Dutch, and I know firsthand that you can put your feelings into English quite well. If, however, you must use Dutch, I will get out my dictionary and translate it for myself. Although I don't speak it or write it very well, I understand more Dutch than you probably realize. From this point forward, if you have a problem with something I do or say, address it directly to me. Don't go behind my or your brother's back and try to use his so-called friends to get your points across.

Something very real has happened in the world, something that we had no control over, and it has shaken our lives, made many of us more terrified than we already were. You saw the twin towers disintegrate into clouds of ash on your television screen, your computer screen, in your newspapers. I looked squarely into the eyes of a former boss whose best friend boarded in Boston one of the planes that became a missile. Let us walk with more care and love and respect for one another.

That we can control.

STOLEN MARBLES

1 "That's fine," said Job, matter-of-factly, after turning over the last page of the letter. "I'm sure she'll still have a problem with it, but thanks for taking my suggestions and cutting out some of the overkill. When are you gonna send it?"

"I'll email it to her later tonight." Craig also thought Nelleke was going to have a problem with it. But that's because he knew by now that Nelleke had a problem with anything he said or did or wrote, no matter how it was worded. In the hearts and minds of two of the three other women on Job's side, the first letter Craig had written bordered on sacrilege. Els responded quickly and succinctly, directly to him, stating in no uncertain terms that he knew nothing whatsoever about her relationship with her brother, that her father was not a strong man, and how dare he try to stir up trouble within the family. Wilma responded in installments. First, she said that he saw the family relations clearly, but wanted to re-read the letter to give a more thoughtful response. After a few days, she admitted that she was at first taken aback, but came to see that his deep love for her brother made such a communication necessary. When Betsy finally responded after two weeks, she expressed an anger that sickened her, reiterated her assertion that he ruined her last visit to America, and made her overall position clear: he had no right at all to comment on any of her daughters' actions, no right at all to claim any connection to her dead husband, and no right at all to try to create a rift between her (family) and her son, which was the only reason why he would write such a terrible letter, do such a terrible thing in the first place. How convenient, thought Craig. How convenient.

Job tried to smooth it over. Perhaps, he said, something was lost in translation. So he translated the entire letter into Dutch hoping they would see that their reactions were overblown and based upon things Craig hadn't even written. Over the next few months, after several conversations with his mother, Job came to realize that Betsy was resentful that he never returned to Holland from Zaire, as he'd said he would more than twenty years ago. How could she be happy with her (only) son so far away from her? She also revealed that she couldn't understand why her husband's spirit would visit Craig and not her. If she looked at it long enough, thought Craig, she'd understand why. But she wasn't about to look.

✑

October marched on and the chrysanthemums in Job and Craig's rock garden burst with flowers the color of blood and saffron. In the backyard, tiny tornadoes swirled fallen leaves turning brown on ground covered with pine needles.

When Job received word that Nelleke had a breakdown in the center of her town the day after reading Craig's recent letter, he too became convinced that Craig had done a terrible thing. Over dinner that evening, Jennifer felt the tension at the table and said, "What's going on, sons?" She'd started working at a hospital a few weeks ago. Home less, surely she missed more than she wanted to, thought Craig.

Job broke out in tears and taunted his husband. "How do you feel now, huh? Huh, Craig? Now that you know what your letter has caused?"

Craig felt no pity for Job or his sister. "When people do nasty, nasty things, you know, nothing major, honey, just little things"—his voice was thick with sarcasm—"like trying to destroy other peoples' lives, if they have *any* conscience whatsoever, when they get caught, you know, when, surprise, surprise, they're found out, and their ill-advised actions, their tricks and deceptions and lies are revealed to themselves, they usually have a crisis. You really wanna know how I feel, Job? I'm *glad* Nelleke broke down. Maybe now she can put herself back together again. But I doubt it. That would be too much like right. Nelleke broke down in a public place because she wanted everyone's pity. She wanted to make a spectacle of herself. So all of you could say, 'Poor, poor, poor Nelleke. Look what that bad, bad Craig did to her.' And look at you—it worked. But that don't fly with me. *Nobody* made her do what she did. Now she's all *hurt*. Humph. She brought it on herself. She shoulda thought about her heart *before* she tried to tear us apart." Job's tears dried up quicker than they came. He knew better than to try to solicit a retraction from Craig, but he had to try. "And as for you," Craig continued, standing up, "I bet you wish you woulda thought twice before sending Nelleke that poem I wrote. Take some responsibility, if you dare, for the way things have changed between your family and me. I shared that poem with *you*, Job. Right here at this very table, I shared that poem with you and you cried more than I've ever seen you cry, before or since. I *never* asked you to send it to Nelleke *or* Wilma. But you did, without even asking me. For whatever reason, you did. And now look where we are. Perhaps you ought to re-read the poem and remind yourself what it was you wanted them to see about you. I'm going for a walk."

"You want me to come with you, son?" Craig shook his head. "I'm not the one who needs to talk." He left his full plate on the table and took the dogs to the park.

While Craig was out, Job found a copy of the poem and read it again, right in front of Jennifer. "Do you mind if I take a look?" she asked. He slid it across the table and she read it.

Stolen Marbles

The sky is crying and there's a little boy playing marbles,
playing marbles under the weight of his father's gaze,
his father's gaze grown heavy with scorn and praise
                                    but mostly scorn.

The sky is crying and there's a little boy playing marbles and
falling in, falling into himself under the weight of
his father's gaze grown heavy with scorn and praise
                                    but mostly scorn.

The sky is crying and the little boy can't hide his raining eyes,
won't hide his raining eyes that his father
can't see, that his father can't see, that his father won't see.
No, son, you can't talk about your brother, son,
can't talk about Hans, son, don't talk about Hans.

The sky is crying and the little boy wants his brother back,
wants his brother back, wants his father back.
But the riverbed can't give him his brother back, can't give him his
brother back, wont give back his brother alive.

The sky is crying and the little boy wishes for Hans,
the little boy wishes for Hans, but even more than that,
he wishes he could talk about Hans, and where is Hans,
and what exactly happened to Hans,
and how did it happen and why, Pa, why, Pa, and,

please, Pa, I can't even say his name?
I want my marbles, Pa, I want my marbles, Pa, no,
Pa, Hans played softball, not me, Hans played softball, not me,
Pa, I don't want softballs, I want my marbles, Pa, my marbles,
and no, Pa, I can't take his place, Pa, I can't take his place,
please, Pa, don't make me take his place, and, Pa,
where is the rainbow?

The sky is crying and his pa can't tell him, his pa won't tell him
where the rainbow is. Now, the little boy imagines playing marbles,
and every time he hits one marble with another, the clouds crack open,
not like clouds, but like brick walls, the clouds crack open like brick walls
and in comes the sunshine, let the sun shine in.

And in between the cracks there looms a rainbow the
color of marbles, the color of marbles, a rainbow the color of
stolen marbles. And under that marbled-colored rainbow
Hans appears, as ordinary as a big brother should be.
He puts down his mitt and plays marbles with his little brother.

The sky is crying and the little boy is falling, is falling in,
is falling away, is falling down, but his father can't see,
but his father won't see, and the little boy can't dry his raining eyes,
can't dry his raining eyes, can't be Hans, won't ever be Hans, can't
take his brother's place.

The sky is crying and the little boy wants his brother back,
the little boy wants his father back,
but most of all, the little boy—
sitting under the weight of scorn and praise,
but mostly scorn, and crying skies—

most of all, the little boy wants back his marbles.

When Craig came back from the park a few hours later, Job and Jennifer were still talking at the table. Whatever they shared seemed to help, for Job appeared less constipated. Craig kissed Job, gave Jennifer a hug before she demanded one, and went to bed.

A month later, just after Thanksgiving, Job went to Holland to see his family face-to-face. He would try, once and for all, to make them see his life, including his marriage, for what it was.

NATALIS

1 On the morning of December 8, 2001, Craig walked through Harvard Yard with Jennifer, Burundi, Rwanda, Tanzania, and Quincy. Uncle James, whom Craig had sent for, and Aunt Sonja were back at his house helping Job prepare for the party he would throw for Craig later that night. Sonja had put James out and he was staying at a roach infested motel in San Diego, but when Sonja heard about the party, she wasn't about to miss it, so she flew to Boston for the weekend. It was Craig's birthday and he found it hard to believe that he was sharing it with members of his birth family. Mary, Hazelle, and Gina had called him earlier. He wished they could have joined in the celebration, but he was giddy enough already. For the party, Craig was planning to wear his black tuxedo so he could also wear, for the first time, his grandfather's cummerbund and bowtie that England had given to him in the days following her eruption in Georgia. Walking through the Yard, while Jennifer recited for her daughters some of the stories about Harvard that Craig had told her, Craig recalled the conversation he'd finally had with England in the back of the house on Ella Lane.

"Why did you do it?" Craig is sitting on the couch in England's small apartment.

"It was the best thing for an eighteen-year-old girl." England is sitting on a chair next to the couch.

"Uncle James said he wanted to keep me."

"He was getting ready to go to medical school, he couldn't raise a child.

We had to pay for his medical school. And we still had Jennifer and Joshua's educations to provide for. We couldn't afford to raise another child."

"But you could afford the room where you put Jennifer away."

"We just didn't have the money."

"That's a lie."

"I couldn't do it."

"Why not? You praise my mother so much. Thank her so much for what she did for me. You're both the same age and she did it. You had more money, too. Why didn't you raise me yourself?"

"I made an agreement with the Lord." England pauses and closes her eyes. When she opens them, she says, "I know you met Adrian when you and Jennifer went to our old church in Milwaukee."

"I did."

"That boy is one talented musician. Such a beautiful voice and he can play the piano and organ with the highest praise. Adrian was a very sick baby. He had some rare, mysterious illness that threatened his young life. I had done so much for his mother and her family I felt like they were my own. I prayed for his deliverance, told the Lord that if he healed that baby, I would pay for his schooling for the rest of his life. The Lord answered my prayer. I kept my end of the bargain and put him through Oakwood Academy and Oakwood College so he could get a good Seventh-Day Adventist education."

"So instead of raising your own daughter's child, you supported another woman's child simply because you made a bargain with God?"

"I didn't say I was perfect. I'm just trying live the way Jesus told me to."

"Jesus told you to give me away?"

"I didn't say I was there yet. I told you I had mixed emotions."

"So if I understand you correctly, the reason you couldn't keep me was because your son was going to medical school, and because you had to pay for Adrian's education? Is that it?"

"That's right."

"That's all?"

"That's right."

"I think you're lying."

"Think what you wanna think."

"You want me to believe that your good name had *nothing* to do with your decision to hide your daughter away and get rid of me?"

"Believe what you wanna believe."

"We all believe what we wanna believe, Nana. Stop evading the issue."

"I told you I had mixed emotions about what happened in 1967." She pauses. "Maybe James' illness is my punishment for what I did to you. He had a brilliant career until his illness set in. He was a wonderful doctor. One of the top obstetrician-gynecologists in the whole country. So many women went to him. He's still recognized by women he's forgotten all about because he treated them so well when they were his patients. Some of their children even know who he is. Everything was taken from him after his bipolar disorder set in. It runs in my family so he gets it from me. I guess that's my punishment."

"You don't like yourself very much."

"I hate myself."

England moans, rises slowly from the chair, and trudges into her bedroom. She's using her cane again. "I have a few things in here, I think you might like," she says from a place Craig can't see. When she returns to the living room, she has a pile of papers, three long boxes, and what looks like a small wall plaque with a bust superimposed on it. She sits back down.

"You figured you'd take your secret to your grave, didn't you? Expected everybody to keep their mouths shut, take your secret to *their* grave, isn't that right? You never thought you'd see me again, did you?"

"It sure made Jennifer happy to see you again. All she ever wanted was to see you again. I guess her prayers were answered."

"Jennifer's happiness means something to you?"

"Sure it does."

"Then why do you torture her? Still?"

"What are you talking about?"

"Nana, look at me. Look at me closely."

Craig waits for her to finally look him in his eyes.

"What do you see, England?"

"I see you."

"Who am I?"

"My grandson."

"Then why did you tell her that I wasn't? Why did you claim that I might have been Frank's child but that I must've come out of some other woman?"

"I said no such thing."

"Liar." Craig spits out the word as though it is a rotten berry in his mouth. "Why did you tell her that if I *was* her child that my perverted ass was exactly what she deserved for spreading her legs before wedlock?"

England doesn't answer.

"Put your hand in my hair."

England raises her eyebrow.

"Just do it."

England leans forward, stretches out her arm, and puts her hand, gently, on his head.

"Now feel my hair. Pull on it if you have to, but feel it. I don't have coodies. C'mon, feel it. Feel its texture, its oiliness, its wiry thickness."

England pulls her timid fingers through his hair.

"What's it feel like?"

"Hair."

"Whose hair?"

"Your hair."

"Josh's hair. Your son and I have the same hair, and you can feel it, Nana, even though you denied it when I told you last week. 'You don't have hair like Josh. No, no. Josh is the one in our family with the good hair.' That's what you said. Good hair, bad hair, whatever difference *that* makes to you, he rubbed his hands in my hair, I rubbed my hands in his, and we acknowledged the truth of what our hands felt. Can't you feel it? It's easier to deny what you see than what you feel. And you just felt my hair. You've felt your son's hair, haven't you?"

Craig waits for a reply that doesn't come.

"Deny what you will," he continues, "but I'm a part of you, England. A perversion, an abomination in the eyes of your God, the God of Moses, I'm a part of you. Just like you, I see things. And you see that I see and you don't like it that I see you. But you can't fool me, England. I see right into you. You torture your daughter to make you feel better about your hateful self. She's right where she was when she was a little, little girl, even before she worshipped desire and became pregnant, and that's right where you want her to be, right where you keep her. Your cruelty has not gone unnoticed by any of your children, and if you see me as one of your children, then see that I won't ever play your games and deny what I see in front of me just because it's ugly."

"What makes you think that what you say is right?"

"You can still feel my hair on your hands, can't you?"

England doesn't answer.

"What do you want for your daughter?"

"I don't wanna have to worry about her."

"That's what you want for yourself. What do you want for *her*?"

"You weren't around when she had her hysterectomy. She had no one to care for her, so I did. I took her to the hospital, sat with her through the night. I worry. And I wish I didn't have to."

"You never have to worry, England. That's your choice. Where's your faith? Your professed belief in God is at odds with your need to worry. If you pray, if you believe that what you pray for will come to pass, then why waste energy on worry?"

"You have an answer for everything."

"I have a question for everything. What would make you not worry so much?"

"If Jennifer would find herself a good husband, somebody to take care of her, then I wouldn't have to worry so much. She needs a good Christian man in her life. If she would finally finish her degree and go back into dietetics, something like that would make her happy, I'm sure of it. But she'd rather run around Georgia selling vacuum cleaners instead of trying to reach her full potential by getting her degree." There is a moment of silence. "Open those boxes. They belonged to my husband, your grandfather."

Craig does what she tells him. Inside the three boxes are three cummerbunds and matching bow ties. Craig picks up the most colorful set, the one with bright green, canary yellow, fuchsia, red, and violet in it.

"That's the one your grandfather wore on our fiftieth anniversary down in the Cayman Islands."

"I wish I could've met him before he died, but I found you too late." Craig smells the tie, rubs the cummerbund on his face. "I wonder what his prayers were for me."

"My prayers were answered, too, thank the Lord. Your mother is a lady I could never thank enough."

"You don't have to thank her. She didn't do anything for you. What she did for me had nothing to do with you. Why haven't you said anything about my father?"

"The woman is responsible for rearing children."

"I see. Well, my father is the one who gave me the confidence to be able to do whatever I put my mind to. That was his biggest contribution to the content of my character. 'Nothing is impossible.' That's what he said. 'Don't ever settle for second-best.' He said that, too. I honor my father for that and much, much more." Craig puts the cummerbunds and ties back in their boxes. "Are you giving these to me?"

"None of my boys want them, not my sons or my other grandsons, so you can have them."

"Are you kidding me?"

"Here's your great grandmother's bust from her sorority. You can have this as well." Under the bust there is a small gold nameplate with the inscription:

MADREE PENN WHITE
1892 – 1967
FOUNDER
DELTA SIGMA THETA SORORITY, INC.

"You want some of her papers and publications too?"

Craig can't answer. He licks salty water from the corner of his mouth.

"Your Aunt Grace, my husband's sister, has all of her mother's effects."

England sorts through a stack of the ones she has. "You can have these, here. And take these pictures of her and your great great grandfather, Samuel. Make yourself some copies and bring them back before you go, son. I got a book of poems by Paul Laurence Dunbar I think you'd like." She sits back in her chair and sighs. "You're just like Madree, you know that? Just like her. Just like her. You're a poet, just like she was, an author, just like she was, and you have an answer for everything, just like she did. She was born the twenty-first of November and you the eighth of December, one day after my wedding anniversary."

"Then both of us are Sagittarians, too. So are you. So is my mother."

"But it's more than that, son. You're just like Madree. It's almost like you're..." England doesn't finish her thought.

"What? It's almost like I'm what?"

"I see why you came back to us, son."

"I'm glad that you see."

"Your birthday this year really oughtta be something else." England stares into a space just above her head in the center of the room. As though caught up in a reverie.

"Why do you say that?" Craig looks at her and then at the place where she stares.

"Because that's what I see."

✍

When they get back from Harvard, Jennifer and her daughters take their time getting out of the car. Craig walks into the house first, down the hallway, through the mask room, and into the kitchen. When he sees the man in the bright yellow shirt, brandy snifter in hand, sitting on the counter next to Job, Craig's knees buckle, he hunches over, his tears run fast.

"Happy Birthday, son," Frank says.

"Surprise!" Job sings, and then laughs. "Happy Birthday, darling."

Craig crosses to hug Job. "How did you do this?"

"I arranged everything from Holland with Frank's wife. We just got back from the airport."

"Now I see why everyone was so eager to go shopping in Harvard Square this morning." Craig hugs Frank. "I can't believe you're here." He holds on.

✍

The party was a dream. The front doors—1867 original, mahogany Victorian double entry doors with tall, narrow arched windows—were wide open. The atmosphere—electric, colorful, festive—pulled you right into the house. Craig had strung more lights than ever before on the trees and shrubs in the front yard, along the eaves of the front porch, round and round the garland twisted up the banister of the main staircase just inside the entrance. The gigantic Christmas tree almost touched the ten-foot-high ceiling. Trimmed in purple, gold, and white ornaments, it sparkled dramatically against the pumpkin-colored walls of the mask room in the center of the house. The flames from long tapers glowed in every room.

More than fifty of Craig and Job's closest friends, many of them dressed in bright red, green, or purple sweaters, attended. Although Job had told a few of his friends, none of Craig's friends knew that both Jennifer and Frank would be there. When Gail and Tara walked in and Craig introduced them to Frank, they both sat on the foot of the staircase for a few minutes with their hands on their chests. Throughout the evening, many guests let their emotions about the significance of the event flow effusively.

Earlier, Job, denying anyone's offers to help, prepared platter after platter of hors d'oeuvres, including stuffed mushrooms, shrimp cocktail, mini-quiches, pancetta-wrapped cantaloupe, crab cakes, jerk chicken wings, and crudités. Jennifer baked an Italian lasagna with imitation ground beef. Rwanda, Burundi, and Tanzania arranged a platter of romaine and baby spinach with berries and nuts. Many of the guests brought bottles of wine and champagne.

Job ran around greeting guests, piling gifts under the tree, refilling drinks, clearing plates, snapping pictures. Jennifer had a conversation with almost every single person at the party. Her daughters sat up under each other all night on the same chair and studied everybody with confused glances. Frank and James drank Budweiser and brandy and reminisced about their college-day adventures.

At 8:50 p.m., twelve hours after the hour of his birth, Craig and Tanzania blow out the candles on the birthday cake. (At Jennifer's urging, Craig had agreed to have the bakery put Tanzania's name on the cake beneath Joseph Craig. Her birthday is tomorrow.) The crowd sings HAPPY BIRTHDAY for Craig and then again for Tanzania.

Shortly after ten o'clock, the first snowfall of the season comes. Fat, wet flakes fall fast and cling to the earth. Several guests move to the porch or outside to "Ooh" and "Aah" the marvel and magic of the first snow. Craig joins James and Frank, who are playing in the snow like young brothers, throwing snowballs at each other and laughing, laughing, laughing.

Tanzania and Quincy will sleep in the main guest room with Jennifer. The twins will share a bed in the other guestroom. Frank will sleep in Craig and Job's bed. Craig and Job will leave and go to the after party at their friend Phyllis' nearby house, play cards till all hours, and sleep in one of Phyllis' many guest rooms. There, Craig will say to Job, "I cannot believe that the two people who came together and started my life are sleeping together—at the same time, anyway—on my *birthday*, no less, in our house. Be sure to pinch me when I wake up in the morning."

✍

The next morning, Craig will open his gifts: two writing journals; an expensive Williams & Sonoma gift certificate a group of friends pitched in for; stationery inscribed with the initial j; a collection of votives; and several books. The present that will move him the most is a GUINNESS WORLD RECORDS 2002 book with these words written on the inside front cover:

December 8, 2001

To a very special son who I see has the capacity to love many, I say love those many, but only trust a very few. I'm happy you found me and I've truly enjoyed the time spent this weekend. I hope there are more times like this betwixt and between us. For all of us this is a new beginning; let's make the best of it. Remember, I'll always love you.

> *With all my love,*
> *Your dear young*
> *Dad,*
> > *Frank*

✍

That evening, after she has a chance to reflect on all the happenings of the night before, their friend, Terutha, will call to congratulate Craig once more for his courageous endeavor and to thank Job for such an overwhelmingly spectacular experience where love's glory was exhilarating, abundant, and all over the place.

WHITE CHRISTMAS

1 "JOSEPH'S 1ST CHRISTMAS" was engraved on the heart-shaped tag dangling from the hood of the satin-finished, silver-plated baby carriage keepsake ornament. Beneath the hood, a baby teddy bear's head peeked over the blanket. Craig handed it to Job to look at and opened his next gift: a mahogany-finished book from Things Remembered that opened, on the right, to a quartz clock; on the left, to a gold plate engraved with his birth name and the current date. From the gold plate, he wiped the droplets of water falling from his eyes and gave it to Job to look at. Jennifer shook her head while she looked at the gold-framed and matted eight-by-ten portrait of her, Craig, Gina, Mary, and Hazelle taken in Milwaukee; the matching eight-by-ten portrait of her, Craig, and Quincy taken in Boston; the matching five-by-seven of Craig and Job; and the three matching five-by-seven frames and mattes for portraits of her own choosing. Job and Craig exchanged gifts next, followed by Craig and Rwanda. Other than reading their cards aloud, they could not speak.

Later, after their voices returned, they shared Christmas dinner with the man from Milwaukee who pulled up to the curb out front in a silver 2002 Mercedes Benz S430 at noon. He'd driven from Manhattan where he was home on Christmas vacation from medical school in Barbados, which is where Rwanda lived with her husband, a registered nurse, who attended the same school. Now, Rwanda was in Boston, staying with Job and Craig while she looked at area medical schools and continued her own nursing career, beginning in cardiology at Boston Medical Center. Finally, she had found someone who really understood her, who was kind and loving and made her feel better than she'd ever felt before in her whole entire life. Which is what she told Craig the first time she called him from Barbados to tell him how happy she was because of this really terrific guy she was seeing. He wasn't an Adventist but happened to be a brilliant chemist and had, along with several business partners, real estate ventures all over the world. Craig wondered why on earth *she* was the one paying the rent for the small apartment they leased on the island for their clandestine fucks while her husband was in class. And if her husband was so busy studying that he didn't have any time for her, how was this man able to give her so much of his? "The funny part," she said to Craig, who wasn't laughing, "is that he's your age and he's also from Milwaukee. I can't believe a man so sweet and so nice has never been married." Whatever discomfort she had once expressed for seeing a guy while she was still married was a far-away sentiment.

Over a plate of Cornish hens and wild rice, collard greens and candied yams, Craig eyed, closely, the man from Milwaukee who had a young face, old eyes, and no respect for marriage. Or so Craig thought. "Can either of you," began the man, looking at Craig and Job, "tell me what the secret of a good marriage is?"

"We've only been married three years," said Job. "We're practically newlyweds."

"Check back in ten years, and we might be able to tell you," said Craig. "I take it you've never been married?"

"No," the man replied, looking up and to the left a bit.

"And you went to Milwaukee Tech for high school?"

"Yes."

"What year did you graduate?"

"Rwanda told me you went to Rufus King."

"She told you the truth."

"What year did you graduate?"

"I asked you first."

The man from Milwaukee had no answer. Craig shot Rwanda a glance. She didn't look up from her plate. Jennifer ate her food slowly, deliberately. Job went to the bathroom. The hush that hovered till the end of Christmas dinner was mighty, mighty loud.

WEEKEND IN MAINE

1 A soaring lion ushered in 2002 bearing deliverance on its wings. In the first week of January, Rwanda and Lovelace met in Huntsville, Alabama, which is where they lived before moving to Barbados, and got a quick divorce. Jennifer was so upset she spent a string of days in the guestroom with the door closed. Whenever she came out, Craig was the recipient of her endless litany of complaints: "Rwanda has always been my most difficult child and she needs to take some time and be alone and get to know herself instead of running from man to man and she's being completely selfish hasn't thought one bit about Lovelace down there studying to be a doctor and having to go through a painful divorce in the middle of it and who knows what's gonna happen to his immigrant status now that he's divorced from an American citizen if he has to go back to Chad then I *know* Rwanda will wish she would've given them another chance and things at work are getting really really tough son nobody knows how to do anything right and my manager is incompetent and I just don't know how much more of it I can take."

Neither did Craig. When Rwanda returned, she and her mother fought a war of attrition that seemed to have begun in another life—so exacting, so devastating was their artillery. The battlefield his home became quickly rattled his center. His couldn't-possibly-have-even-dreamed birthday party already felt long, long ago.

Job wasn't feeling any more at ease. In the inevitable post-holiday letdowns, he was able to contemplate his November trip to Holland and his failure to make his mother and sister see his life with Craig for what it was. It wasn't helping that every single time he had spoken with Betsy since he returned or read one of the emails she'd sent, she told her son that she couldn't get out of bed because she was in too much pain, or she had fallen *again* and wasn't able to get up for an hour and was never close enough to a phone to call her daughters or her boyfriend, who lived nearby, to come and help her up. The pity Job felt for her and the guilt he felt for himself he tried to smoke away. But not even a pack a day was powerful enough to slay those parasites. So when Craig, shortly after sundown on January 4, suggested that Betsy was exaggerating her woes, at best, or flat-out faking them, at worst, Job became so enraged he went right over to Gwynneth's house to vent about Craig and hear what she had to say. Which would be exactly what he wanted to hear.

Now Craig was mad. Not two months ago, Job promised Craig that before he re-established a relationship with Gwynneth, the three of them would sit down together to talk about moving past the drama she had set in motion with her scheming. But Craig had no energy for battle. He simply packed his journal, his laptop, the portrait of his family, a few pairs of underwear, climbed into his Jeep, and drove out of town, heading north on interstate 95.

2 For the whole weekend, the sun shone—penetrating, intense, and absolutely glorious. Other than the weekend Craig and Job had spent in Portland in November 2001, when they first looked for vacation property in Maine, Craig hadn't been to Portland since 1997 when he performed, for the last time, his solo theater piece, SKIN & ORNAMENTS, at the Oak Street Theater. Focused on the logistics of his performance, he was unable to spend any time enjoying the light. The first time Craig visited Portland—back in 1990—he sat on a dock in the Old Port waiting for the ferry that would sail over Casco Bay and take him to the Peaks Island summer cottage a former boyfriend owned. Where the morning after, the sunrise was so enchanting, Craig was inspired to make, from scratch, sour cream flapjacks with blueberries, bananas, and a hint of cinnamon so good his former boyfriend's boyfriend said, "Someday, you're gonna make some man a good husband." As he looked out over the bay, waiting for the ferry and staring at a lighthouse, the rays of light burst and he could see their colorful particles again. He hadn't seen this since Juneau Park. I'll come here again, someday, thought Craig. Maybe to stay.

The serenity Craig feels now that he's sitting on the ocean shore again under a Portland sun deserves the highest praise. Too cold outside to stay for too long, Craig gets back in his car, which is parked in the lot of the East End Beach Boat-Launch and Trail at the hem of the Eastern Promenade. There, he opens his journal and writes, writes, writes.

Hours pass.

Each day, for three days, he leaves the Inn at St. John, drives to the Eastern Promenade at sunrise and writes. Each day, for three days, he walks to the Western Promenade at sundown and writes.

The time has come.

✍

On Monday, January 7, 2002, Craig signs a one-year lease on a tiny, one-bedroom apartment in the West End. Job tells Craig that this must be the beginning of the end. Craig tells Job that it is the beginning of the end of living in madness. Jennifer tells Craig that she cannot understand why he would leave without telling her first. She also tells him that she doesn't know what to do or what to say to him anymore. Craig tells Jennifer to pray. Later, Craig calls his mother Mary in a moment of despair and she imparts the wisdom needed for him to pull through it.

For the next two months, Craig spends four days a week in Portland. He reflects, meditates, and writes. The three days he spends in Boston are strained days, made heavier by Jennifer's see-through attempts to expand the wedge between him and his husband. "Job must be on drugs," and: "Son, you have no idea what your time away has allowed Job to get away with around here," and: "I didn't wanna tell you this, but I think you need to stay home more because Job might be stepping out on you again." Jennifer offers such observations without hesitation, studying Craig closely to see how he might react. Craig thinks Jennifer's tactics are desperately ordinary. Surely, she can do better than that, can't she? Guess not. Her days in his house are numbered anyhow. His neutral reactions give her nothing more to work with.

She doesn't realize that, by now, Craig doesn't care if what she says is true or not. Job can drug or step out or get away with whatever his heart desires, whenever his heart desires it. Craig's heart beats in Portland, the place where he can reflect, meditate, write. The more he reflects and meditates and writes, the clearer it all becomes.

In a moment of clarity, Craig decides that there is something he must do. When he tells Job of his decision, Job expresses worry and fear. When Craig tells Jennifer of his decision, she is relieved and thanks the Lord for bringing her son back to do the things for her family the Lord knows she doesn't have the time to do herself. How romantic, thinks Craig. How convenient.

PILGRIMAGE

In a murderous time
the heart breaks and breaks
and lives by breaking.

—Stanley Kunitz

1 The first week of March 2002. He could hardly wrap his mind around what he was about to do. The plan seemed simple enough. Craig's flight itinerary would take him to Ontario, California, with an hour layover in Salt Lake City. Craig would get his uncle and drive him across the country to Boston, stopping on the way in St. Louis to meet one of Craig's sisters from Frank's side, and in Dayton, Ohio, to meet two of his brothers from Frank's side. In Ontario, Uncle James would pick up Craig at the airport. That evening, they would have dinner just outside Riverside at the Olive Garden with Uncle Josh and Aunt Crystal, who just happened to be in California on business, and James' daughter, Trisha, who lived in Riverside. Craig hadn't seen them since the Feast. Later, Craig would meet Trisha's mother Brenda, Uncle James' first wife, at a separate meeting, also at the Olive Garden. Ever since their divorce, Brenda was unable to occupy the same space at the same time as her ex-husband. She would pull up in a grand car that Craig thought only a preacher should be driving. Brenda, sporting a bigger version of the same Supremes hairstyle she wore in her 1967 year-book picture, would wonder how he was able, if at all, to fit into a family with so many secrets. He would tell her he wasn't interested in keeping any of their secrets. She would say, "How refreshing to hear. I hope you get along okay with them, Joseph—or is it Craig? Shouldn't I be calling you Craig?"—Craig would nod—"That's what I thought. Well, Craig, I hope you get along. That side of the family is very troubled, very difficult. I just don't understand all the secrets. England taught Jennifer to keep secrets, and Jennifer taught all her daughters to keep secrets, and they don't seem to be the better for it. It made no sense to me that I had to find out

about Rwanda and Lovelace's divorce from somebody at my church all the way out here in California. I didn't even know their marriage was in trouble. But, Lord only knows, you might be just what they need. And be careful with James. I don't know if you know what he's capable of. That man has many personalities and any one of them'll turn on you without notice. May the Lord be with you on your journey. I do hope you know what you're doing."

"I'm not afraid," Craig would say and wish her farewell.

Craig and James would spend the night at a Motel 6 down the street from the restaurant. They would rise with the sun and begin the first stretch to Salt Lake City where they would stay at another Motel 6. Agitated and growing more anxious with each passing hour, James wouldn't be able to sleep that night. Craig would relax his uncle by giving him a middle-of-the-night bath, a back massage, and reading to him from the book of Isaiah.

The next afternoon, James would see John Dixon, the best man from his first wedding, for the first time since then. He would also see the Mormon Tabernacle close up, something he'd always wanted to see.

Craig had dreamed of driving across the country, and there seemed no better opportunity than this.

2   Since early last December, James had moved from roach-infested motel to rat-infested motel living on his disability income. In three months, he'd been robbed and beaten twice, once when he tried to score cocaine. Sonja had put James out, and other than seeing James at Craig's birthday party, she wanted nothing whatsoever to do with him. During a recent encounter, when Sonja allowed James back into the house for a few nights, they'd fought and James threw a hammer. She'd immediately put the word out around the family that he'd bludgeoned her with it, although she had no bruises on her body. At least none that Craig could see when he went to their house in Murrieta sometime between his arrival in California and dinner at the Olive Garden.

"Joseph, I had to take out a restraining order against James this time. He hit me with a hammer. Right in my head," said Sonja, pointing to her head. She stood on the landing outside her front door. The sunlight oiled her silver-gray hair and her girlish, siditty face. She wore a white tank top and light purple shorts. Her feet, bare. "I'm not gonna put up with that," Sonja continued. "He won't take his medicine, Joseph. He's not allowed here. Where is he, by the way?"

"He knows not to come here," said Craig, assuredly. "He wanted me to see his house."

"You mean he wanted you to see *my* house."

"I mean he wanted me to see where he lives, Aunt Sonja. Where you live. If this is a bad time, believe me, I don't have—"

"Come in. I have some people visiting, but I can show you around."

She stepped aside, allowing Craig to enter. He followed her into the kitchen where she introduced him to her guests, a retired reverend and his wife who had just moved to southern California from Florida. They knew the family well. The reverend mentioned that he used to baby-sit for Jennifer's twins when he lived in Arizona. He'd heard through the circle that Jennifer had a son who recently found her, so when Craig told him that he was that son, and that, in fact, Jennifer was living at his house back in Boston, Clive and Viola, who, eyes bulging, turned from the sink where she was rinsing lettuce, nearly fell out.

"Who's your father?" asked Clive.

"Frank East."

Now, Craig thought Clive was going to have a heart attack. Clive and Viola knew Frank quite well from Oakwood and marveled at the incredulity of Craig's presence in Sonja's kitchen. After Clive and Viola regrouped, Craig told them that he had to get going, that Uncle James was around the corner, waiting.

Sonja walked Craig swiftly around the light and airy cream-colored rooms with mint green and pastel-purple furnishings and decorations and to the front door. Craig was simply going to say goodbye, but his mouth had other plans.

"I didn't wanna come here to see you, Aunt Sonja, but Unc insisted that I see where he lived, so here I am. Meeting your friends is just another coincidence that makes me see my decision to come and get James was right on time. Sonja, only you and Unc know what's going on between you two, but I have a sneaking suspicion it isn't at bad as you let on."

"How can you say that? You don't know what he's capable of, Joseph. You don't know what he did to me."

"What I know is that you married James at the apex of his illness. That you knew all about Brenda and how verbally abusive he was to her. That no matter how quote-unquote crazy he got that he never laid a hand on a woman or physically harmed one in any other way. What I know, Sonja, is that you knew exactly what you signed up for when you took James as your husband."

"I put up with a lot more than Brenda did, that's for sure," she said defensively.

"So what? You want a cookie?" Craig asked, growing more perturbed. He struggled to keep his neck still, his voice, low. "I don't have a cookie for you, and I sure don't have any pity for you. If everything between you two is as terrible as you say it is, you'd have left him a long time ago. And if it is, perhaps you ought to. But, as always, you'll get over being mad at him for being sick or not sleeping at night or not taking his medication and the two of you will get back together. But don't front, Sonja. You didn't have to completely cut James off. The least you could've done is allowed him to continue using your flight privileges so he could've gotten himself to friends or family. You kicked him out of his house. Where did you suppose he would go?"

"He found a place to stay."

"Mere shelter, which may be more than many have, but you know how important being around family is to him."

"If Trisha wasn't scared of him, he could go be with her."

"But she is, so he can't. The only family he could possibly stay with is on the other side of the country. Don't you even care about his welfare?"

"He's got you to rescue him," she said with a hint of contrition, or sarcasm, in her voice.

"I didn't come out here to rescue him, Sonja. I came because I love him and I'd rather have him be in a safer place than where he is. Like I said, you'll get over it and both of you will be back together. Until then, you know how to reach me." Craig turned and walked away.

"He doesn't have any of his medication with him." The concern in her voice was real. "Be careful."

Craig turned back while walking and said, "Don't be afraid. We'll be alright."

3 "Do you know who Matthew Shepard is?" Craig asked his uncle. They were driving west from Red Desert, Wyoming, on interstate 80, where they'd just passed the Continental Divide for the second time in twenty-five miles.

"No."

"You consider yourself an informed man and you don't know who Matthew Shepard is?"

"No."

"Matthew Shepard was a twenty-one-year-old shepherd named Matthew, a shepherd of hearts. He was crucified—literally, upside down on a wooden buck fence—by two hateful little rednecks, simply because he loved men."

"I think I might've heard something about that."

"When we get to Laramie, I'm gonna try and find the site where it happened. May as well. Can't say I'll ever be by this way again." Craig took in the sand-smoothed, rainbow-colored plateaus rimming the fiery horizon as far as his eyes could see. "If it weren't for you, I wouldn't be here, right now, in awe of this breathtaking landscape. This has to be the most beautiful stretch of the trip so far, including the mountains in Utah. Absolutely breathtaking."

Before they got to Laramie, a truck driver tried to run them off the road, not once, not twice, but three times. Each time Craig tried to pass the truck on the left, the driver waited till the last minute and switched lanes, forcing Craig to slam on the brakes and veer off the road into the ditch that divided the highway. One time, Craig had to swerve abruptly to avoid driving directly into a mile marker post. Before they got to Laramie, a little red car pulled up beside their little red rental car and escorted them for twenty miles or so. Four white boys who looked no older than twelve derided them through the windows. One of the boys in the back seat, his right hand formed in the point of a gun, kept pulling the trigger. The other back-seat boy mimed tying a rope around his neck, tilted his head to the side, widened his mouth, bulged his eyes. The boy on the passenger side leaned forward and gestured like a monkey. All the driver could do was flip them the bird, repeatedly. They laughed and laughed and laughed. When the boys finally sped ahead of them, Craig saw the bumper sticker that bore the emblem on the Confederate flag.

When they got to Laramie, they pulled up in front of a small convenience store on the town's main street. The cover of the LARAMIE DAILY BOOMERANG caught Craig's attention before he could ask the girl behind the counter if she knew where the murder happened. It had been about three-and-a-half years, but Craig figured that the event still resonated in the small, impoverished ranching town. As it turned out, the town paper's headline article told him that THE MATTHEW SHEPARD STORY, a made-for-television movie, was being screened for the first time at Laramie's lone theater that very weekend.

"You'll wanna go out just past the Wal-Mart," said the cashier girl with native America in her face. "There's a housing subdivision across the street. The place is in the fields set way back off the road behind the houses. There'll probably still be stones and memorials left behind. Where you guys from anyway?"

"I'm from Boston. He's from California." James squinted his eyes to see if there was any tobacco on the shelves behind the cashier. "We're driving cross country."

"Stay a while," said the girl. "I wouldn't want you to think Laramie is full of terrible people because of what happened to that poor soul. You'll see that we're a pretty friendly town."

Craig and James drove to the fields behind the subdivision. A dirt road wound through the field in the direction of a hill ridge. The tall sagebrush waved in the wind. The late-afternoon sun spread over the flat horizon, like blood. Craig drove toward the ridge until the car's wheels could no longer navigate the mud the dirt became.

※

Uncle James waits near the car while Craig begins walking. Craig has no idea which way to go. He simply walks in a direction that feels right. A shelf of clouds hangs in the sky, a blue ceiling stretching over the high, vast plains that seems close enough to reach up and touch. From a distance of a hundred yards or so, Craig sees the wooden buck fence he remembers from photographs in the media years before. He's already weeping by the time he's close enough to see the flowers and tokens stuck in the fence, the collection of stones laid out in the form of a cross on the dirt in front of it. Craig sits down near the cross, cradles his pulled up knees and buries his head between them. For minutes, he weeps and heaves, his tears and snot puddling on the dirt underneath. Surely, all this crying can't be for Matthew Shepard alone, a young man whose senseless death moved millions all over the world but whom Craig did not even know. If not for him, then for whom is this lament? For himself? For James? For Jennifer? For Job? His mother? His many, many dead friends? For a planet of people gripped by terror and gone completely mad?

Craig gathers himself, searches for, finds, and adds another small stone to the top of the cross. He returns to the car, which is stuck in the mud and isn't going anywhere. Craig calls AAA. While he and his uncle wait for the tow truck to pull them back on solid ground, they listen to the sound of the wind licking the tall, bitter-smelling sagebrush and say nothing at all—two black men under a bleeding Wyoming sky close enough to touch.

4 After stopping for dinner in Denver, they begin the seven-hundred-fifty-mile drive to St. Louis. James sleeps through most of this stretch and even Craig decides to lie back in the front seat and sleep for a few hours at a rest stop just before dawn. Shortly after the car is moving along interstate 70 again, James wakes up and mutters, "Do you think Jesus had homosexual relations?" as though he were dreaming about it seconds earlier.

"I believe Jesus was a sexual being," replies Craig. "Who he had sex with, I couldn't tell you. The Bible—well, the version we have anyway—is silent on the matter."

"I bet Jesus fucked around with Mary *and* Martha and all of his disciples. And if not all of them then definitely John," says James who is already wide-awake and fidgety. "I wanna fuck two sisters or a mother and a daughter. Bible says you're not supposed to, but I sure would like to. Maybe I'm homosexual too because God fucked me."

"Unc, were you just having a dream or are you getting ready to have an episode right out here in the middle of this Aryan nation?"

"I think Sonja fucks around with other women." James is suddenly subdued. "I think my wife is a lesbian."

Craig almost runs off the road.

"I also think the only reason she won't leave me or keeps trying to have me committed is because she needs my disability income."

"One thing at a time." Craig has regained control of the wheel. "What makes you think Aunt Sonja is a dyke?"

"She ain't been fucking me, that's for sure, so she gotta be fucking somebody."

"And no other men come to mind?"

"She's got this girlfriend named Sylvia. They're real close. Matter of fact, she been staying over at the house a lot since I've been gone." He pauses, then smiles. "Can't you see it? Sonja and Sylvia. Instead of S and M, they make S and S." James is cracking himself up.

"You sure you're not just fantasizing?"

"Hell no." James is serious. "I'm not one of these guys that wants to get off watching women play around. Yeah, I said I wanna have my way with two sisters, but not at the same time. But I do think S and S got something more than friendship going on between them."

"I see. And why does Aunt Sonja need your money?"

"Because she can't afford her lifestyle on her own salary. She doesn't make enough money at the airline to afford the mortgage and all of her shopping sprees. She's never gonna give up shopping. It's in her blood, man. She spends all our money shopping and she likes expensive things." James pauses for a moment. "I don't know, man. I'm glad you came to get me. I'll have some time when we get to Boston to do some thinking. I might wanna move back to Tennessee. The only reason we moved to California to begin with was because of Sonja's job. But I didn't wanna go. I've had more episodes in California in the two years we've been there than I did the entire five years we lived in Chattanooga."

Craig considers this for a moment. "Are you feeling like you want out of your marriage?"

"I don't know, man. I don't know. I love my wife, I don't care if she's a lesbian or not. But I have a lot of thinking to do out in Boston. But I promise, man, I'm not gonna stay in your house for more than a few weeks and wear out my welcome like my sister has. You and Job need your house back all to yourselves. As soon as I open a bank account there, I'm gonna get my checks deposited right into it. I'm gonna let you handle all my finances so I don't screw up." James sounds like a child who's just been punished. "My father handled my finances for me before he died. Speaking of which, how much money do I have left?" James voluntarily gave Craig all of his cash back in California.

"Enough to help get us where we're going."

5 When they get to St. Louis, James gives Craig a tour of the neighborhood where his family lived. James even tries to show him inside their first house, but the who-you-say-you-looking-for? woman who lives there with a flock of mimicking birds won't allow it. They stay overnight at a Super 8 Motel and the next night, they meet Sonetta, Craig's sister on his birth father's side. The first time he spoke to her was on his birthday, when Frank had called her to introduce them. A social worker for the past six years, Sonetta is exactly like her voice sounded over the phone—calm, even, and deep. A splitting image of her father, she could have emerged fully formed out of his head. She has three children, Jared, who's five, Joshua, who's two, and Justin, who's seven months. All J's. Her day has been long, for a few of her clients presented complications that caused her to drive all over town. After a take-out, fast-food dinner and a brief visit with her husband Jerome, a big man with a big smile and puppy-dog eyes, Craig snaps a few pictures of his new family and he and James leave them to ready their children for bed.

From there, they head to Dayton, Ohio, where they meet Frank Junior commonly called Butch. Craig spoke with Butch once in the weeks following his finding. More annoyed than surprised that another one of Frank's kids "dropped out of the sky on him," Butch, nevertheless, said he couldn't wait to meet his new brother someday. At his home, Butch introduces them to his girlfriend, Aneeka, who is pregnant with their third child together, and although she's actually seven months pregnant, James tells her she must see a doctor to have the fetus checked because she only looks about four months pregnant. Nine months ago, she gave birth to Micah, whose overgrown afro and infectious smile make Craig laugh; two years ago, she gave birth to Savion, the boisterous spirit with the big, round head who reminded Craig of himself at that age. Six years ago, when she was with another man, Aneeka gave birth to Selena who "I thought was gonna be my only child," she says, laughing and taking another hit from her joint. "This stuff right here"—she raises the joint in the air—"is what keeps me going. I love this stuff right here. So this one I got in here now"—she rubs her belly—"I was trying to be in denial about, you know what I'm sayin? I just got through with Micah and I wasn't bout ready to have no more. But this stuff right *here*"—she waves the joint and takes another hit—"this is my life. I guess I'm bout to have me a marijuana baby, and that's about the size of it."

Craig is speechless—the rarest of rarities.

Later, Butch takes Craig and James to his mother Verita's house where they eat a fried-chicken dinner she has prepared for them. They meet two of Butch's other children, Paula and Chablis (each have different mothers), who are visiting their grandmother. Also visiting is Jamelle, a too-smart-for-her-age eight-year-old who calls Craig Superman and looks exactly like Gina when she was eight. Bright face, long, jet-black hair parted down the middle and braided in two. Jamelle is one of the daughters of Greg, Verita's youngest son, who's in jail for three more weeks. Greg's son, Darnell, who's ten, comes over from his mother's house around the corner and down the street, while James and Verita catch up on the whereabouts of their classmates at Oakwood. Craig meets four-year-old Solomon, Greg's youngest and only son from his wife Trisha, who is living three doors down with her mother and contemplating divorce because Greg, before this latest jail sentence, has been shacked up across town with a woman who's about to have another one of his babies.

Butch, whose left arm was smashed in a freight-elevator door three years ago, has been unemployed ever since. Butch has also been diagnosed with bipolar disorder and he and James stay up all night the first night, drinking Budweiser and talking about medications and episodes and stupid judges who can be fooled easier than gullible children. For two nights, Craig and James sleep on couches in Butch and Aneeka's first-floor apartment in a house suffering from what a social worker would call environmental neglect. The smell of urine permeates the air, marijuana plants grow under blue lamps in the corner of Butch's bedroom closet, the toilet doesn't flush (Savion stuffed a T-shirt in it days earlier), the refrigerator, where baby formula sits uncovered on filthy shelves, doesn't work, the kitchen is piled high with dirty dishes, and too-full garbage bags, which attract fat southern Ohio flies, are strewn about the kitchen floor. Despair all over the place. When Craig asks Butch what on earth is going on, Butch replies, "I'm just trying to make it, dawg. My girl is crazy, she's fucked up all the time on pot and pills, and she's driving me crazy, dawg, and my worker's comp ain't coming in cause I got caught selling stolen car parts out my garage out back. But I'm gone get it together, dawg. I should have some money coming in soon from a few thangs I been workin on with some of m'boys."

"If she's fucked up all the time, what's she doing pregnant again?" Right now, Craig wants to take Savion and Micah home with him. Wants the unborn baby, too. But even though they share his blood—his genes—they aren't his.

"C'mon dawg, don't lay it on me, bro. It was a accident, aiight. I didn't expect her to be able to get pregnant so fast after Micah, but she is and I'm just hoping everything'll be aiight with the next one, you know what I mean, bro?"

"God takes care of fools and babies."

The next afternoon, Craig and Butch drive in his '85 Ford pickup with the counterfeit plates to a regional chain department store and Craig buys a mini-refrigerator. After they drop it back at the house and set it up, Butch takes Craig and James on a drive around the city.

※

Dayton is a depressing place with littered, abandoned lots, boarded-up buildings, and burnt front lawns. There are more police cars on the streets than in any place Craig has ever been, including Paris. Butch, who rattles off facts and trivia and whole philosophies with the convincing authority of a college professor, claims the city is the biggest crossroads of the drug trade in North America. A few miles north of Dayton, interstate 70 (which runs from Baltimore, Maryland, to Cove Fort, Utah, where it connects with interstate 15, which runs from San Diego to Sweetgrass, Montana) and interstate 75 (which runs from Miami, Florida, to the Canadian border at the Upper Peninsula of Michigan) intersect.

Dayton is also full of Frank Senior's offspring. Like door-to-door salesmen—or Jehovah's Witnesses—Butch and Craig walk or drive around Butch's childhood neighborhood and he introduces his brother to at least four others and one sister who is ill and can't take the visit.

On the morning of their last day in Dayton, Butch takes them to meet Greg at the Dayton Correctional Institution. In the middle of the gymnasium where they sit round a table, James nods off, Butch and Greg catch up on life inside, life outside, and then Craig and Greg talk about family reunions in Florida. During their conversations, Craig notices that the three brothers have the same noses, the same-sized heads covered with the same short afros, the same patches of curly, uneven stubble around the jaw and chin.

"When I get out of here," Greg says at the end of their allowable time, "I'm coming to the east coast to visit my big brother, the professor." Despite his orange garments and the bars he'll return to for another few weeks, Greg's jovial eyes accent his optimism about where his life will take him.

"Oh, I'm no professor," says Craig. "You've already confused me with Butch."

"If it looks like a professor and talks like a professor, it's a professor." Greg laughs. They embrace. "Yo, bro," Greg yells back to Craig just before disappearing through the door, "and don't forget: you ain't prettier than me. I'm still the prettiest of all."

※

On the way back to Boston, James wants to stop in New York to see the ashen remains of the World Trade Center. But Ground Zero shall remain a mystery. Sleep deprived and getting a sore throat, Craig wants to go straight home. While James snores on the flattened-out passenger seat for most of the remainder of their journey, Craig makes the eight-hundred-mile haul from Dayton to Boston in just less than fifteen hours.

MERCURY IN RETROGRADE

✑

1 When they walked into Grace Church of All Nations, the choir was singing a moving rendition of I LOVE THE LORD. Neither one of them had stepped foot in a church, solely for themselves, in a long, long time. Before Jennifer, Craig had attended the First Unitarian Church in Brookline during the holidays in 1999 to hear Job sing in the choir he'd joined a few months earlier. But the choir Craig heard that day sounded nothing like the choir he now heard singing one of his favorite songs in a church that Job had often said he wanted to return to someday. This choir seemed to sing for the duration of the service and Craig couldn't have been more pleased.

Church was about music, lively and dance inspiring, about singing from the soles of the feet up through the bone of the pelvis. Church was about music that made you raise your head, stretch your arms up, up, up. Made you roll your backbone back and forth and forth and back and stomp your feet and bend and bounce. Made you jump in circles like a rain calling native of New Zealand or New Mexico; a warrior, victorious, in Mongolia or Mozambique. Church was about music that split open your heart.

When they walked into Grace Church of All Nations, Craig felt compelled to dance, show out, and then some, but they sat down instead.

After the sermon, an uplifting delivery about the potential of the human spirit, it was time for the altar call. A big woman from the choir came and stood in the aisle at the entrance of their row. She had a hairstyle that reminded Craig of the pictures of Mahalia Jackson he saw in JET magazine as a youngster. In her face he saw Africa, Europe, and the America of the AmerIndians. When she motioned for them to come into the aisle and down to the altar, they were both on their way before Craig realized it.

A crowd of supplicants, bereft and full of agony, gathers round. Down at the cross, in the center of the storm, the rays of fluorescent light above filtered and blurred by his copious tears, Craig feels the trembling anguish, feels it take hold and enter, moving through him like shockwaves, its synapses tingling his limbs and chilling his spine. Down at the cross, in the center of the storm, is where they bring their pain, fear, and terror; their anguish, guilt, and torment. He cannot tell what comes from whom, but he can feel a spirit caught between the Scylla and Charibdis of loss and longing; another desperately trying to wake up, wake up, wake *up*; another torn asunder by a shame so deep, it might never mend. But it doesn't matter. For down at the cross, salvation is as easy as a fat wet snowflake.

When they got home from church, Craig and Job were so moved by what they felt that they decided to return to Grace together. For the next several Sundays, they rose earlier than usual and drove to church. The reverend continued his inspirational sermons, variations of the one they heard the first time. Most of the congregants were welcoming, supportive, and genuinely *nice*. Eventually, Craig even joined the choir. After one of their rehearsals, several members of the choir said a prayer for Craig the Wednesday before he left for California.

2 Spring was just around the corner and the crocuses were beginning to poke their fingers through the ground. The branches of the smoke tree in the front yard spit out buds the color of fresh pea pods. The tree's roots that grew out of the ground and snaked along the retaining wall already sprouted tiny leaves.

A week after Craig returned from his cross-country passage with Uncle James, Burundi came to Boston to visit Rwanda. To talk to her about the relationship Rwanda had begun in her island hideaway with the man from Milwaukee who attended medical school with her husband in Barbados. To convince her that anything borne from adultery could only lead to disaster. To talk her out of her ongoing sin (as far as Burundi was concerned, that is), as if she could talk her twin out of anything. Rwanda was like Gina—once she made up her mind, it would be easier to change the order of seasons than it would be to change her mind. And her mind was made up. The man from Milwaukee belonged to her and she would do anything to keep him. But more than that, she would do anything for him to keep her. Even if it meant ignoring her mother's control, which she'd hardly ever ignored; her sister's collusion, which she wouldn't ever question; her brother's foresight, which she'd never seen before; and her man's big, big lies, which she never saw coming. In fact, it was Jennifer who had convinced Burundi to fly to

Boston and talk to her twin sister in the first place. And if that didn't work, then, as Jennifer would eventually admit to Craig, "I need to break them up, and if it takes getting her father—who's talked to him over the phone several times and who I know can't stand him either—out here from Oakland to do what's necessary, then that's what I'm gonna do." None of it worked. The seasons changed as usual. The following spring, Rwanda would elope to Hawaii with the man from Milwaukee.

Meantime Burundi was visiting her mother at Craig's house wondering when her brother would get out of bed or, at the very least, let her come into his room and talk to her. Congested and more ornery than a feverish child, Craig had been laid up for days now. Jennifer had demanded hugs, complained about how awful her job was, left middle-of-the-night messages on Craig's cell phone, arrived from Rwanda's at six in the morning the prior Sunday and started to clean the bathroom. She must have begun to smell the impending putout but wasn't about to make it easy. Yesterday, Craig had heard her through the window as she spoke to Job on the terrace below: "If Joseph wants me to leave, I have no problem with that. All he has to do is ask."

James told her she shouldn't wait to be asked. That she had overstayed her welcome. That nobody should be up under her children that long for any reason, a thirty-three year separation notwithstanding. Matter of fact, she shouldn't have lived with Tanzania for so long, despite her husband's six-month assignment in Bosnia. Today, stretched out to his full length on the bed, listening to the rain beat against the roof, Craig pondered these things. How was it that he had allowed Jennifer to live in his home for nine months without asking her to contribute a single thing? Why had he become her caretaker?

The knock on the door interrupted Craig's self-interrogation. Uncle James was sitting in a chair near the foot of the bed and Job was putting a pair of pants on a hanger in the closet. Job closed the closet and opened the door. Burundi stood, shoulders slumped, looking like the dejected girl on the playground who wasn't chosen for the kickball team.

"I just want—please," Burundi whined, "can I see my brother." She twisted her perfunctory face and managed to force out a few tears.

"C'mon in," said Job as though he were beckoning a sick puppy. He and Uncle James left the room quicker than smoke through an open window. Craig rolled his eyes. Burundi crossed the threshold.

"Come over here and sit down," said Craig, mustering up as much love as he could. Burundi climbed onto the bed.

"This is a really nice bed," she mumbled. "Very comfortable. What kind of mattress is this?"

"I don't know. What's going on, Burundi?"

"Well, uh, um, I came all the way out here to see my brother, but we haven't, um, uh, been able to do anything together."

"As I'm sure you already know, I haven't been feeling well since before you came to town and don't seem to be getting any better right about now. Your trip was a surprise to me, and as far as I understood, you came all the way out here to talk to Rwanda about what was going on in her sinful life."

"We already had our talk." After a short stretch of silence, she continued, "Um, uh, I just wish I knew why you haven't even been able to talk to Mom. I mean, um, uh, if you think that she wouldn't understand, um, uh, that you need some space from her, then you don't know Mom. All you'd have to do is tell her that. I mean, um, of course, I don't live here so maybe it's not so easy, but, um, uh, Mom understands. If you thought she wouldn't understand, um, uh, well, um, uh, then you don't know Mom."

"Burundi, if you came up here as your mother's ambassador in order to get information from me to take back to her, let me say to you right now that your efforts will bear no fruit. Why I will or won't talk to her is none of your business. I hope you have a safe trip back home and tell Zion I said hello. Please close the door on your way out." Stunned, Burundi rose from the bed to leave. "Oh," said Craig when she got to the door, "and can you please ask Job to bring me a cup of tea?"

"I can get it for you." Her voice meek and high-pitched, like a little girl's.

"Thank you, but that's okay. Please ask Job to bring it."

Minutes later, Job returned with the tea and a face stoned by frustration. He placed the tea on the night table and Craig asked him what caused such a hard look. "The kitchen faucet broke off in Burundi's hand. Now I have to go get another one. I don't know how much more of this I can take, Craig."

"There'll be no need for us to find out." Craig sat up in the bed. "Last week, when Jennifer came in here to talk to you in the middle of the night while I was out walking with Unc after she agitated him, I was too through. Up till then, she had never come into our bedroom."

Job sat down on the bed. "I told you she seemed like she was trying to defend herself against whatever it was she had done to Uncle James."

"I wish you'd told her you needed to sleep, but accommodating as you are, you obliged. Either way, she probably wouldn't have taken no for an answer. On our walk, Unc tried to tell me what she did to make him so upset but I told him I didn't wanna hear it. I didn't need anything else to add to my distaste."

"For a whole year, our lives have been controlled by your birth family. I know the planets in our universe have realigned, but it feels like we're in another solar system and it's completely taken us over. All we've been doing is taking care of them and living their drama. Where are *we* in all of this?"

Job shook his head. "It's all too much, Craig, it's just too much."

The relatives were wearing Job down. All the times Job said Yes when he meant No; all the times he offered to pick Jennifer up from work when he really wanted to do nothing more than put up his feet and read the newspaper. Where were they, indeed?

"You're right, even more so now that Unc is here. As I told you when I got back from California, Unc can take his disability check and rent a furnished room nearby. But Jennifer—her time is up. I've tried to make it clear to her that I can't deal with her anymore, but she doesn't wanna take the hint. I even gave her that sermon I wrote, which included that vision I had years ago of that Zairian woman walking down the street in Paris."

"Ah, yes. I remember. I don't know where that came from. It had your beatitudes in it, too, didn't it?"

"Yes."

"Why did you give it to her?"

"Because it reminds me of her, and I'm not really sure why. When Uncle James first read it, he thought it was about his whole family. It came out of me almost as soon as I started searching for them. So I gave it to her because maybe she would see in it whatever her brother saw that made him think of his family." Craig leaned forward and coughed. Job rubbed Craig's back and adjusted the pillows behind him. "All my hints aren't working, honey." Craig slumped back into the pillows. "This Sunday, after church, I'm gonna ask her to leave." Craig paused. "I have a sneaking suspicion she's gonna try and make it complicated, though."

"She said all you had to do is ask."

"I know. But I don't believe her anymore."

GO TELL IT ON THE MOUNTAIN

I wish that all the Lord's people were prophets and that the Lord would put his Spirit on them!

—NUMBERS 11:29

Mankind was one single nation. And Allah sent Messengers with glad tidings and warnings; and with them he sent the book in truth...

—SURAH 2:213

1 People are so afraid. So afraid to end one cycle and begin another, full of newness and love, pregnant with the possibility of transcendence. Fear begets fear. And with hardly any nurturing whatsoever, fear matures to thieving terror.

People caught up in the terror-filled spinning: as common as spirit-dead people breathing. It becomes so difficult for anyone to *choose* the real when fear lurks wherever one turns: In a neighbor's eyes. On the preacher's face. In the backyard mingling with the grass roots. In line at the grocery store. Near the shower under the toiletry basket. Between the azaleas and rhododendrons. Over the hill, behind the projects. On television before, during, and after the weather report. In the mirror. When a person is caught up in the terror-filled spinning, trying to turn toward clarity is an impossible illusion. Like seeing the face of God in a burning bush.

Illusions by nature may sometimes be sweet, but behind the shroud of lies, lies a bitter treat. Or, heaven is the place where terror turns to autumn leaves and drifts away...

All of it can be passed on, you know, but many people don't realize it. And I mean *all* of it. This seeing. This hearing. This knowing. It was there all along: from the very end, middle, beginning. And we all know it, as clearly as we know our own breath. But so many have forgotten it—a forgetting that's completely understandable with so much terror spinning round. See, even though you can't see them with your physical eyes or touch them with your physical hands, you can hear them if you let yourself. And sometimes see them with your soul vision. Your rhythm vision. At the river, they watch over you when you don't even know it, can't even hear it, won't even see it, passing on gifts from generation to generation.

Can't you feel it? Feel it. Feel the water of life pulse into you, pulse through you. Flow from you. Blood flows in the river, I say to you. Blood flows. Infuse yourself with the water of life and join in the fullest experience of all there is to know and see. And hear. Get it?

When things get too tough for you to face, when they start stirring up the feelings that line your gut like ulcers, you don't want to talk about them. You won't talk about them. You honor not your innermost but revel so in the external, caring so much what others have to say about you. Your life. Your life choices. You can talk about everybody else's story, so well, sometimes, you'd think you had firsthand knowledge of what you were telling. But when push comes to shove, you can't seem to get a grip on your own life. Can't hush your soul's sobbing. Won't rock the madness out then cradle it back to sleep again. Instead, you tell a joke, snap out a wisecrack, or, in your insistent reading of the dozens, render some universal truth (you do have it, after all) nearly unseen. Unheard. Unknown.

Some things never change. Or, the leaves turn their colors just as one looks away from them...

2 Indeed, I say to you, it will all be revealed. In time. Completely clear. In time. Sooner than later the blind will see. In time. But, till then, in times like these, you would want to remember what someone wise once said: patience is a virtue. *Know* it.

Brilliantly blessed are those who *know*.

Brilliantly blessed are those who forgive themselves, for they will be able to forgive all others their greatest wrongdoings.

Brilliantly blessed are those who walk with courage through the depths of their own sorrow, for they will walk also through the greatest joy and their Spirits will grow exponentially; for them, a healing will come.

Brilliantly blessed are those who share what they have with those who have not, for their generosity will be rewarded with even more to share.

Brilliantly blessed are those who seek perfection not in people or things, but in the process of Loving itself, for they shall possess clarity of insight.

Brilliantly blessed are those who walk with courage through the depths of their own fear, for they will Love from the bottom of their hearts.

Brilliantly blessed are those who belong to the trees and the animals, for their voices will grow plants like the sun and their kindness will kill the anger of strangers.

Brilliantly blessed are those who strive to create unity out of vast diversity, for they will experience Heaven on earth.

3 *Stop.* No, you are no bad luck children. You are not terrible people. *Look.*

Nor are you deceitful and manipulative. Your flaws are like those of the chaff. *Listen to your heart, hear what its saying?*

There are as many chaffed straws in the bale of hay as there are snowflakes in the winter storm.

Swallow the mystery life. Blood flows in the river, I say to you, it flows. Taste the current of minerals in the wind. Bathe in the light of loves lost and gained and lost again.

Stop. Look. Now, see the Parisian woman with the pale face walking down the street. She ushers a small child into a small food store, but she does not see him go inside when his hand slips from hers and the door closes in front of him.

Stop. Look. Instead, her attention rests on the Zairian woman, encircled with an aura of gold, walking up the boulevard de Strasbourg against the rush of oncoming traffic. Caught up in the rapture of this Zairian woman who, right before her eyes, defies those reckless, ruthless French drivers, the Parisian woman does not see her little boy with the dark brown curls climb atop the window display shelf and stare out onto the street. Still transfixed by the sight of the Zairian woman, now parting traffic at high noon, the Parisian woman with the pale face cannot see what her little boy sees through the engraved picture window of the little French salon:

Two blocks up the street, a little Haitian girl with three pigtails sits on the sidewalk in front of a beauty store.

It rains on her.

Only on her, it rains; everywhere else, the sun shines brightly, fiercely, at high noon. The little Haitian girl sits still in her rain, does not try to cover herself, does not melt.

The little Haitian girl with three pigtails sits also, despite her rain, in a beam of purple-pink light that emanates from above and behind her, away from her, and out onto the street, down the block.

The Zairian woman parting the traffic now walks down the middle of the boulevard as if drawn directly to the child's light, which does not come from the sun in the sky above at high noon. She sees nothing else. No traffic, no flailing arms waving at her to move onto the sidewalk. She hears no car horns.

See now that the little boy sees all this.

Listen. He bangs feverishly on the window trying to get his mother's attention. But he can't get what's not there to be gotten. Still, her attention rests on the Zairian woman, encircled with an aura of gold, walking down the boulevard de Strasbourg parting the oncoming traffic. There, the Parisian woman with the pale face savors a desire for disaster. But while waiting, mouth agape, to witness a disaster that will never happen, she does not, cannot, will not see what her little boy sees:

The little Haitian girl with the three pigtails who sits in rain and purple-pink light draws the Zairian woman to her with the force and mystery of miracles. And later, when the woman arrives, the little pigtailed Haitian girl will lead the Zairian woman inside the building and up the stairs to a room with walls the color of death where her mother eagerly awaits the woman's arrival. And for the little girl's mother, the radiant Zairian woman will perform a miracle. And the little curly haired boy beating feverishly against the inside of the storefront window knows this. He knows the power of the Zairian miracle worker. And he wants to show this to his mother, who does not know. Flesh of her flesh, fruit of her womb, he embodies his mother's hopes and dreams for the future, her highest imagination of what is possible in the realm of the mortal. But more than that, the child, still untainted by too much expecting, knows more about mystery and magic than the adults he looks to for guidance.

This his mother knows. In the recesses of her mind, the well of her spirit, the marrow of her bones, she knows this secret all too well, for she, too, was once a child. But she cannot call forth this knowledge from the darkness of its chamber, the silence of its hiding place: she has grown too distracted by the scent of chaos, the copper taste of disaster.

And so, as if pounding on a wall of cotton while blindfolded, the brown-haired boy's beating on the inside of the storefront window remains unheard; his vision, unseen. And the pale-faced Parisian woman, now accompanied in her desire by the swarming multitude of onlookers and a bevy of paralyzed Parisian police, blindly awaits a disaster that will never happen.

THE BENEDICTION

✍

1 The next Sunday, Job and Craig go to church. Near the end of another one of his stirring sermons, the Preacher Reverend A. Livingston Foxworth tells the congregation, "Go home and get the devil outta your house. I *saaaaid*-uh... you better go *hooooome*-uh... and get the devil-uh... ouch yo house."

Later that afternoon Craig asks Jennifer to meet him in his basement healing room. She sits down on the couch, holding on to a copy of GO TELL IT IN THE MOUNTAIN, the manuscript he gave her to read last week. Craig sits on top of the massage table.

"Son, come over here and sit next to your mother. I need you to be close to your mother, son."

"I'd rather stay over here. I'm ready to tell you what's going on."

"I already know what's going on, son. When I read this,"—she waves the stack of paper in her hand—"I felt the Lord had answered my prayers. He allowed me to see what was going on with you, why you have been so distant lately. You know I don't believe in spirits, son."

"You claim not to believe in homosexuality either despite the flesh and blood—*your* flesh and blood—sitting right in front of you. You believe in spirits, Jennifer. Evil and otherwise. You believe your mother has the power to keep me from writing my book. Said she was the reason why I had writer's block. And her evil spirit is still trapped in her hateful body. I can only imagine what you'd believe her spirit could do if she were already dead."

"Spirits are machinations of the devil, son. Yes, there are good spirits and evil spirits, but I doubt that you can tell the difference. The devil is the greatest trickster, the master of disguise. He can make evil spirits appear as good ones. You're an artist, son, and artists write about themselves. You said that some of this here in my hands was about me, but I don't see it like that, son. I see that what you have written here is all about you. You're the one who's afraid, son. You're the one spinning round and round, not sure of which way to go."

"I'm sure, positively certain, that it's time for you to go."

"Oh." Jennifer looks around the small room at the unlit candles on the shelves to her left, the large quilt Job's mother quilted hanging on the wall to her right. At the large white pieces of paper Job had pinned to the wall behind Craig bearing her name and the names of her brother and mother with the word FOUND and the corresponding dates written beneath them. Her eyes end up in her lap. Finally, she looks up and asks, "Where will I go? Where do you suppose I should go, son?"

"Back where you came from, I guess. Back to the only thing you believe. Jennifer, you are fifty-two-years-old. I wanna believe that someday you'll figure it out. Figure out how to live your own life, figure out how to make some friends, figure out how to date again, figure out how to stay *out* of your daughters' hair and let them live."

"God is my husband, son. I don't have time for a man. My daughters are my whole life. God is first, my children are second, and I'm third. Those are the sacrifices I've made in my life. You won't ever understand, son, what a mother has to do for her children. Unless you're a mother, you'll never understand. Only a mother knows, son. Only a mother knows."

"Jennifer, look me in my eyes." Craig waits for her eyes to find his. "Do you think you know what's best for me?"

She can't hold them there. "No. I don't think so. I don't think I know what's best for you."

"You can't even look at me and say that?"

"I looked at you, son. What are you trying to get at?"

"If you look at me, open your eyes and really look, maybe you'll see. It might take me a while to discover what's best for me, but I can assure you that you don't have even the slightest inkling about such things. And by the way, I've *been* a mother. Grandmother, too. In ways you can't see or won't allow yourself to see or believe. But just because you don't see something, doesn't mean it's not there and just because you don't believe something doesn't mean it's not truth. There's a reason why so many people call me Grandma. Even Aunt Crystal saw it down at the family celebration. And though I haven't yet lived long enough to be a great grandmother, I've been a great mother. We both know you don't need to push a child out of your womb to become a mother. Quite frankly, you don't even need to *have* a womb. At this very moment, neither one of us has one and still—we've both been mothers. So don't inflate yourself. I know much more than you think I know about being a mother. And as a mother, Mother, I'm telling you to just stop it."

"Stop what?"

"Stop using your mother role as an excuse to control, as an excuse to oversee, as an excuse to avoid having your own friends, your own loves, your own life, as an excuse for putting up with unacceptable behavior from your mother. All of it has less to do with being a mother than it does with being afraid."

"I'm not afraid of anything."

"Then let your daughters go."

"My daughters need me."

"Precisely because you need them so much. You're too afraid of living your own life."

"I'm not afraid of anything."

"You've nurtured in your daughters such a dependence on you, they can't do anything without seeking your approval. They see you as the infallible mother with a capital m whose all-knowing ways have kept them from finding out who they really are with their own eyes. Their eyes aren't watching God, they're watching the images you project onto the big screens of their minds. Screens so big, they can't see anything else. You're more like your mother than you think, Jennifer."

"I'm nothing like my mother, son. You can't say that."

"Take a closer look at the narrative in my adoption agency papers. I'm sure you still have them. Re-read them closely when you get a chance. The intake notes the social worker transcribed almost thirty-five years ago about you and your mother say the same thing: that you're both rigid and controlling. Nothing has changed. You still can't stand up to her, you still won't stand up to her, and she's the excuse you hide behind for all of the mistakes you've made in your whole life. But she's not the problem, Jennifer. You are."

"I'm not afraid, son. A person who's afraid doesn't do the things I've done, moved all over the country, doing whatever I could do to make sure my daughters got the best life."

"Why'd you really move to Huntsville when the twins went to college?"

"I told you, son, because I wasn't able to afford college housing for them, and it was much better that way. All my daughters have told me how grateful they are because I was there with them. A mother's job doesn't end just because her children go away to school."

"Certainly not if she thinks her job is to prevent her perfect little Seventh-Day Adventist daughters from making the same mistakes she made. Your parents would've paid for their housing if you couldn't afford it, and you know it."

"Son, what are you trying to say? That I went down there just to keep them from getting pregnant?"

He lets that one fall for a moment. "Did you?"

"I did what I had to do."

"I have no doubt about that. But what exactly did you *have* to do, Mother? Keep a close watch? Make sure they didn't worship desire, even for a moment? Not let them out of your sight? Like you claim you would've done with me if you'd had the courage to keep me? Then you wouldn't have had to blame anyone for me loving men the way I love men. If you'd had the courage to keep me, you would have ensured I turned out straight, right, Mother?"

Jennifer doesn't answer.

"We've lived out some of your fantasy to try and make up for the time you gave up with little baby Joseph, but enough is enough. Little baby Joseph is all grown up now, his name has changed, and he's married to a man. This is my life, the life I love and live with no apologies, and I want my life back. It's time for you to go."

"Why won't you go to Texas and visit your sister, Burundi, son?"

"That's between her and me. Tell her that—since you tell each other everything, all the time—tell Burundi that if she wants to know, she needs to ask me. I'll have no problem telling her. But don't change the subject. Why I will or won't visit Burundi has nothing whatsoever to do with any of this."

"So just like *that*, you wanna get rid of the woman who gave you life?"

"God gave me life. You were simply the vessel I came through. My mother and father helped shape the life God gave me, and don't you ever forget it. You didn't have the courage. And frankly, I'm glad you didn't. For the last few months, even though it's become very clear that you've worn out your welcome, even though your own brother told you to get out of here and get your own life and don't wait to be asked, and even though you've said more than once to Job that you'd gladly leave, that all I had to do was ask, here I am asking you, *telling* you, and you're trying to guilt trip me into taking responsibility for your life."

"Your uncle told me the only reason why you found me is to get retribution for what my mother made me do to you. I see that he must've been right."

Craig fights back a screeching scream. He imagines himself lying on the massage table, beneath his own hands, following his own guidance: Take in a deep breath. When you exhale, imagine that you are letting out a deep sigh or blowing out a candle, slowly, across the room.

"I see that you are blinder than I thought you were."

"If Rwanda wasn't here you wouldn't be doing this. Son, isn't this all because your sister's in Boston now?"

"Consider yourself lucky that she *is* here because it's time for you to go, whether she was here or in Australia or Timbuktu. You've worn out your welcome and you know it. That's why you've been extra full of pity lately, talking about how bad your job is, how stressful. That's why last week you called me up on my cell phone from your cell phone in the middle of the night and left a message telling me how I needed to drink that nasty tea you made for my congestion. You're right down the hall in the guest room and you called me on my cell phone from your cell phone to tell me that the know-all, see-all mother with a capital *m* had the cure. Talk about control. No concoction of yours is gonna heal me, Jennifer. I'm congested with *you*. When you go, I'll be able to sing again."

"You accuse me of being controlling and competing with you. You're the one who's controlling and competing with me, son. You're the one who's competing with me, son."

"What in hell are you talking about?"

"Like with my brother, James. You knew that I was planning to go out to California to see what was going on with him, but before I could arrange anything, you just hopped on the plane and flew out there."

"Remember what you said to me when I called you from Portland to tell you I was gonna get Unc from California?"

Jennifer searches her memory but comes up with nothing.

"Let me remind you then. You said, 'Now I know why the Lord brought you back to me, son, because he just knew I couldn't do everything I needed to do, he just *knew* I needed my son to help me with my family.' You must've *conveniently* forgotten, but that's what you said. Now you tell me that *you* were planning to go see about your brother? How? And on whose dime? You've been living here for nine months for free; you just started working not too long ago; what little extra money you claim you have, you send to Tanzania because her husband is too lazy, too depressed, too *whatever* to find a job and take care of his own kids; and *now* you say that you were gonna *arrange* to go to California? You don't *arrange* anything. All you do is complain. And you don't do a damn thing to change whatever it is you're complaining about."

"Take the catering business, son. You kept it as a sole proprietorship and I wasn't able to deduct any of the expenses on my taxes. The business was a loss for me too, son, and I don't get to deduct it. I wanted to just sell desserts, get a good client base built up starting with just desserts. But you had to compete with that idea, so you totally took over and did it your way, son, and that wasn't at all fair to me. I haven't even seen any of the money we've made."

Take in a deep breath. When you exhale, imagine that you're letting out a deep sigh or blowing out a candle, slowly, across the room.

"Job and I put one-hundred percent of our money into the business, Mother. You contributed zero, Mother. Zilch. Nada. Every single client we served came from our group of friends or the marketing I did when I was running around town walking other people's dogs for peanuts. You brought in no business, not one single client, Mother. Zero. Zilch. *Nada*. Still, you ate here for free, lived here for free, and ran up humongous phone bills to Barbados talking to Rwanda, telling her things no mother needs to be telling a grown woman. You spent an hour telling her how to fix her split ends! I never asked you to pay for anything and you sure as hell never offered to contribute. How dare you sit there and whine, Mother, *whine* about your cut of what little business we did? We haven't even earned enough money to cover the initial investment. I don't know whether I'll continue the business or not. However, if I do, your services won't be necessary."

Jennifer can't speak.

"I'm gonna get back to my life," he continues. "I suggest you get one. Do whatever you need to do. Jennifer, you pushed me into the world, even if you can't remember it. For that, you will always hold a special place in my heart. I will always think of you, I will always be able to see your face, thank God, in my memory's eye. But I have one mother, one father, and one sister. I've already been raised and I don't need you to try and make up for lost time because you are overwhelmed, still, after thirty-four years, by the guilt and shame lodged inside that rusted-shut tin box you call a heart." He begins to cry. "Jennifer, may the Lord bless you and keep you. May the Lord make his face shine upon you and be gracious unto you. Be blessed, Jennifer, be brilliantly blessed in every which way. Be at peace. At *peace*.

"Be out of my house as soon as possible."

The next day, Jennifer packs up her belongings and moves into Rwanda's condo across town. She leaves just enough behind—her stereo, half a closet of clothes—to have an excuse to come back.

Job and Craig never go back to Grace Church of All Nations. It gave them exactly what they needed exactly when they needed it.

Now, they can move on.

Book IV

LIGHT

*I believe in growing things,
and in the things
which have grown and died
magnificently.*

*I believe in people
and in the simple aspects
of human life,
and in the relation of man
to nature.*

*I believe man
must be free,
both in spirit and society,
that he must
build strength into himself,
affirming the
enormous beauty of the world
and acquiring
the confidence to see
and to
express his vision.*

—Ansel Adams

YOUR MOTHER

Your children are not your children.
They are the sons and daughters of Life's longing for itself.
They come through you, but not from you...
You may house their bodies but not their souls,
For their souls dwell in the house of tomorrow,
Which you cannot visit, not even in your dreams...
[S]eek not to make them like you.
For life goes not backward nor tarries with yesterday.

–Kahlil Gibran
THE PROPHET

1 You wouldn't know Jesus Christ if he Entered you. He tried. But you wouldn't let him inside. Jesus Christ Entered me. And I knew it. I felt it. His Entrance was so forceful, so consuming, just like you, I tried to push him out at first. But my body wouldn't let me. You see, don't you? The spirit is willing, and the flesh is strong. Jesus Christ Entered me so good, so long, so hard, I was finally able to feel Him for who He truly is.

So I left, the hollow rituals, the false virgin prophets, the visionary impersonators, the closeted homophobes, the pedophile preachers, the fools who refused to let Jesus go all the way. I left the prison of dogma alone. Now, when I praise His holy name my whole body trembles with His first divine Entrance. And I let Him Enter me again and again and it gets better and better every single time.

Heaven is found here. So is hell. Why wait till your body dies to enjoy your salvation? Christ has already come again. If you are so excited about the promise of His second coming, just wait till you experience His third, His fourth, His fifth... If you believe that Jesus would only come, could only come twice, you underestimate Him in all His power and glory, forever and ever. Amen.

2 There are so many cocks crowing up in God's house, so many hens settle for the preacher's, not realizing Jesus has a bigger one, a better one, castrated though He is in your sanctified imagination.

Of all the cocks crowing up in God's house, you let Frank East, a man with freedom in his name and strength in his seed, enter you again and again. The same way he entered so many other women again and again. Women who wouldn't let Jesus Enter them the way they should have.

(Your father not her only lover, hypocrite that she is, was envy the reason your mother disapproved so strongly of your sex?)

Of all the cocks crowing up in God's house, you let the man with freedom in his name and strength in his seed enter you, even though your Father, Son, and Holy Ghost forbade such an entrance.

Of all the cocks crowing up in God's house, you let the man with freedom in his name and strength in his seed enter you, even though your mother, that three-dollar bill, who thinks she is holier than that other three-dollar bill, Ellen G. White, forbade such an entrance.

(Even though your father entered her *before* marrying her—hypocrite she'll forever be—was envy the reason your mother disapproved so strongly of your sex?)

3 I am the god of you, the afterbirth lived after you gave up the ghost. My body is the temple where the god of you lives, true to Frank's name, true to Frank's seed, true to the name Mama gave me, strong enough to be as free as you wish in secret you could be.

You have kept so many secrets; spread so many lies. That which is concealed will always be brought to light. If only you would let go. If only you would let loose the secrets and let lay the lies. If only you would release the guilt and relinquish the shame. If only you would rise up from the dead just like your Lord and Savior Jesus Christ told you that you could, told you that you would. If only you could put aside your pity, denounce your delusion and feel Him for what He truly is. If only you would let go and let Him Enter you. Finally.

4 Before I met you physically, I knew you psychically, I knew you spiritually and you were so much better for me then—Hallelujah! —there—Hallelujah!—in that intangible realm where children of a lesser God fear to tread.

In that intangible realm, you were always with me, giving voice to my creativity. You helped me become what I never thought I could be. All substance and pure fire, you spoke plain language through me, and gave me poetry.

That voice inside was always female; the artistry within was always yours. Putting it all together in RITUALS, you gave me SKIN & ORNAMENTS, THE

LANGUAGE OF MIRRORS, and PORTRAITS OF A BLACK QUEEN gone THROUGH THE FIRE.

That voice inside was always female; the artistry within was always yours. You gave me Chaniqua B. Meek, Dessa Rose Flowers, Dolores Jeffers Price, and Vanna Black, troubled women, wise women, powerful women, all of them unafraid to tell the unadulterated unpleasant truth.

But most of all you gave me you. As April Marie Lynette Jones, who weaved stories better than she weaved hair, you spoke volumes to me, volumes through me, helping me become what I never thought I could be. You saved me with poetry.

5   I did not seek you out in order to be raised again, reared right, or guided down the paths of unrighteousness as your namesake. I did not seek you out to quake in the iniquity of your hypocrisy. I did not find you to fall into the den of your shame. I did not come back to sit on your right hand, or your left. I am *of* you, but not *from* you. I chose to come through you, but I do not belong to you. I am not yours; you are not mine.

Mama raised me, reared me, and guided me, pulled me out of prison, and with Daddy's help, led me onward to freedom.

I did not seek you out to go back into bondage.

I found you to see whom I look like, to see how it happened, to see where I came from, to see who you are, to see why. Was blind but now, I see.

6   You believe yourself to be the Mother of Mothers, the best of the rest, the kind of mother who knows where all other mothers fail. Oh, how you wish *you* were there to keep Dante out of my bed, to keep me out of Juneau Park, to pray me straight. No prayers of *any* mother can be that powerful, for I am exactly who I am created to be.

You believe yourself to be the Mother of Mothers, the best of the rest, the kind of mother who looks down her nose where all other mothers fail. But you are the Mother of Sorrows, the Beginner of Grief, undone by your own machinations.

Like mother, like daughter.

The enemy is within you and it doesn't have horns, breathe fire, or live under the ground. The enemy is in front of you when you look in the mirror, *if* you look in the mirror, you will see.

The daughters you raised, that beautiful trinity of daughters you raised, is destroyed: all three of them, destroyed, each in their own way, destroyed, all the same, suffocated in the bosom of damnation by what their mother taught them, by what their preachers told them, by what their minds cling to.

What is evil spelled backwards? Turn yourself around and see.

7 I am the god of you, the afterbirth lived after you gave up the ghost. I am the god of you, the part of you that's free, the part you let go, let out into the world to be without constraint, to be without delusion, to be without the burden of a mind imprisoned by dogma.

I am the god of you, the man(child) that got away, the psychic and spiritual part of you that you couldn't allow yourself to embrace, won't allow yourself to be, trapped as you are in the bosom of damnation by what your mother taught you, by what your preachers told you, by what your mind clings to.

In your physical state, controlled by your mental state, you cannot, will not allow yourself to believe that who I am is exactly who I am created to be.

But your psychic state, your spiritual state, unencumbered by your mental state, believes what can only by contradicted by the blind: I am exactly who I should be, *precisely* because you let me go. Thank you, therefore, for letting me go, letting me be, leaving me physically alone.

8 You are exactly who you limit yourself to be. So long as you turn your back on your God (and you turned your back long ago), so long as you limit yourself (and you've limited yourself for *so long*), I have no need for you. What do you need me for? To limit me in the throes of family madness? You already delivered me from the iniquity of that hypocrisy, already saved me from your original sin.

For you so loved me that you gave away your only begotten son and insofar as I believed in myself, my soul would not perish, but have everlasting peace. Therefore, let me go, let me be. Leave me physically, alone. Again.

Without you, I am free.

Without you, I can be *with* you.

Without you, I remain the god of you, able to be.

Just as I am.

SORORITAS

Do not think that I have come to bring peace on earth; I have not come to bring peace, but a sword. For I have come to set a man against his father, and a daughter against her mother...

—MATTHEW 10:34-35

For whatever is hidden is meant to be disclosed,
and whatever is concealed is meant to be brought out into the open.

—MARK 4:22

1 Mothers do some pretty outrageous things for their children. At their best, they make the impossible possible. Blindfolded, they simultaneously pull two different rabbits out of two different hats in two different rooms, all the while making lunch and dinner *and* trying to teach you a lesson they know you can only learn the hard way.

At their worst, they make grave and damaging mistakes from which their children may never recover.

Your mother did things for you, good, bad, wise, foolish, I can never know. My mother did things for me, good, bad, wise, foolish, you can never know.

It is one of the most difficult things in the world to criticize your mother to her face.

It is one of the most difficult things in the world to see that the image your mother has sold you of herself is not at all who she really is.

Of course, what they sell you is often well intentioned, motivated by a loving desire to mother better.

Mother better than their mothers mothered them, better than their mothers' mothers mothered *them*, presuming any of these mothers did any mothering whatsoever after their child left their womb.

Always trying to mother better, sometimes they succeed, primarily when they mature, emotionally. But sometimes, too much trying and not enough maturing cracks their mask, revealing a worse mother than the one who tried too hard to mother better in the first place.

I have dealt directly with this with my mother. There has been pain, separation, tears, and misunderstandings. But most of all there has been the development of a more mature relationship between us because we have to challenge ourselves to be *different* in our relationship with each other, and that challenge is constant.

I am now dealing directly with the very same reality with your mother.

It comes with pain and sadness, therefore, that I must tell you, if you already do not know, that for complicated reasons, which perhaps, someday, I am able to explain to you, I am unable to continue to relate with your mother right now.

Because you are all so terribly close to her, I know that this situation is also troubling for you. I don't know, therefore, what kind of a relationship I can have with any one of you, assuming you want to continue to have one with me.

I tried.

I tried to be a good brother to you even though I didn't really know how because I was not a part of your lives for so long. I didn't even know you existed. I don't know, therefore, if I can really be any part of your lives now, especially since I can't have a relationship with your mother.

I tried.

I tried to deny my anger for all of you. But denial cannot ever dismantle the reality of its object. I am angry with all of you. It does not consume me for I am angry for one reason, and one reason only: you did not try to find me even after you knew I existed because you didn't want to upset your grandmother. Even though you (or at least two of you) have claimed that you always wanted a big brother. Well, when you found out you had one, you did nothing about it.

You didn't even try.

In time, the sting of pain ebbs. I will get past this. I love you all as much as a brother could love his sisters in a situation like ours.

Take *nothing* for granted.

I have wholeheartedly enjoyed meeting each one of you. This did not have to be so. Such special treasures of complexity and angst, getting to know you over the last year has assisted me greatly in my own healing. I have been able to fit more pieces into the puzzle of my soul, and have gained a far greater understanding of my purpose here in this life. I pray the same for you.

So startled I was, so overwhelming it was, to meet each of you, in person or by telephone, all in the same evening, within a single hour of walking across the threshold of your life's door. So startled I was, so overwhelming it was, my vision slipped slightly out of focus, blurred by wonder and joy, by excitement and curiosity.

But, blurred vision, no matter the cause, causes a person to see things differently than they really are.

Over recent months, my vision has refocused. I now see things clearly and the truth of this vision has advanced my healing threefold. I pray that your healing advances as well.

I shall take the role of many a man in a family controlled by controlling women: my absence will influence you more than my presence. I might come around from time to time—if you allow it, that is—to share my love with you. I might be complained about for not coming around enough; you might not be able to wait to see me go.

It will all be revealed in time.

Therefore, perhaps having failed as a big brother, right now, I shall be the best big brother I know how to be, and I shall give you love the only way I know how. I shall tell the truth. I cannot know everything. I know only what I know. I do not see everything. I see only what I see.

It will all be revealed in time.

I seek only to share with you the gift of insight as it has been given to me. Share it, I must, in order to keep it. If I do not share it, it will drive me mad.

Some of what has been revealed to me concerns what might be considered the subconscious, so I certainly will understand your initial rejection of much of what is written here.

But please return to it later, if you can. We must walk through grueling places, for we won't really know ourselves until we face the ugliness of it all.

I know the language of Judeo-Christianity, of high art, of academia. Although I have had much compassion in my life, I have yet to master its language.

I have a lot of work to do.

I will understand it if you feel that I am arrogant, condescending, or self-righteous; I am fluent in the languages of Judeo-Christianity, high art, academia. Please see through that veil and know that a man who has compassion for you and who loves you as much as a brother can love his sisters in a situation such as ours is also speaking to you from the bottom of his heart.

If you consider this blasphemous, remember that Christ was considered a blasphemer during his life.

I am only trying to live my life the way Christ lived his, according to what I was taught, according to how I have interpreted that teaching and accepted it into my life.

I am, therefore, an emulator of Christ, a Christian. I belong to Grace Church of God in All of Us, Mosque 12867, Berea Eighth-Day Adventist Church, St. Joseph's Universal Catholic, House of Prayer and Deliverance from Madness, Kingdom's Hall of Bearing Witness, the Tabernacle of Peace and Love, the Synagogue of Faith and Truth.

My life is a metaphor for Christ's. Christ's life is a metaphor for mine.

I'm here to live the purpose God has revealed to me in this life. That is all I'm here to do. I am grateful for that knowledge. But sometimes, I doubt that I can fulfill my purpose, sometimes I have excruciating pain, sometimes I simply do not wish to do it.

Just like Christ, I am human.

I press onward, a Christian soldier.

If you believe this to be motivated by anger alone, then, sadly, you will hear none of it.

Know, instead, that my love for you motivates me foremost.

My desire for healing motivates me most.

I invite you to tell me to my face what you see in me or about me, if you see anything at all.

I give it much better than I take it, but I can take it from someone strong enough to give it.

I also invite you to read some of my explorations of my mind's mysteries in some of my other work. It might help you to see that I am not perfect, do not pretend to be, and do not think that I am morally better than any of you are simply because I have clearer vision.

If you don't like what I see, then paint a different picture.

This is my prayer.

2   When Cain slew Abel, did evil conquer good, or did good conquer evil?

Rwanda, first daughter, twin sister, you are my sister of hiding. A person who loves a woman knows when she's a virgin. That very same person knows when she's *not*. Your first husband is one such person. When he said what he said on your wedding night, he told the truth. How insulted you were that he did not deny the truth of what he sensed, like everybody else has done before and since. Until now.

How dare he? I can almost hear the chorus of your voices wail. I dare to because it's in my nature to dare.

Your grandmother has said that her female offspring are hot women. She may as well have said her female offspring are sex fiends, because that is what she meant. Your uncle has said that we have all had trouble with sex. Some have it worse than others.

I got it pretty bad. I get it from both sides of the genetic family tree. So does your mother, both your uncles, and your grandmother.

You got it pretty bad, too, and that is why seeing you having sex with one of your mates before the one you first married was no surprise to me.

Neither was your denial of the same when you called to talk to me about this for the first time over the phone. I asked you if you were a virgin when you married him. "Of course, I was," you remarked. *Too afraid to tell anyone I wasn't*, whispered the water during the silence that followed.

I was taking a bath.

What have you to gain by allowing your self, your sisters, your mother, your father, this folly? What have you to lose? Your sisters have only their respect for you to lose, if they haven't already lost it. They will find it again. Your mother has only her pride to lose, so proud she is in believing that all three of her daughters were virgins when they married.

That was the very first thing she told me about you all. Imagine that. On the night her only begotten son walked back into her life after thirty-three years, the first thing she wanted me to believe about her daughters was that she delivered them to their first husbands, unsoiled. As if I cared. But, when she said it, she looked up and to the right a bit. Then, I cared. In the same look up and to the right a bit, she also said that she understood why I *chose* to be gay, that she understood why I *chose* my lifestyle, simply because she wasn't there for me. All this within three hours of my arrival on her doorstep.

Anyone who tells you something while looking up and to the right a bit (or even to the left) is lying.

Pay attention.

Deep inside, she knows the truth about you, about herself, about me, too, and that is only one of many reasons why she wanted you to remain married so long after you knew your marriage was over, which was actually before it began. She couldn't possibly want you to become the damaged goods a divorced woman becomes as portrayed in the Bible, the damaged goods she became when she divorced your father. We know how much she worships the Bible. I understand her not wanting you to become as she was. I understand her not wanting you to endure the very same pain she endures.

But the ends don't justify the means.

Might you be even a little angry that she pushed so hard for you to stay married, *convinced* you even, even when you knew you shouldn't be?

She has also said that if she had truly known that you never loved your husband, and that, as you claimed, you only married him to have sex, then she would have preferred that you had had sex with him without marrying him.

But we all know that's a lie, or you wouldn't have to lie about your premarital virginity. Still.

I understand, therefore, your pain, having to hold on to so many lies. I don't know how many times growing up I chose not to tell the whole truth about who I was because I thought those closest to me might reject me for not living up to the image they had of me. Lying is so easy under those circumstances. The hard choice is telling yourself, and everybody else, the truth about you.

As hard as that choice is, liberation is your ultimate reward. You don't have to remain dishonest because you feel you need to lie to survive.

The trouble with your reproductive system is inherited, but it is not genetic. Your grandmother had trouble with her womb, and so, too, with her children. Your mother had trouble with her children, and so, too, with her womb. Your mother's womb almost killed her, so it was removed. Your grandmother's will more than likely kill her, too, if she doesn't let it be removed. Yours will not kill you, nor will it need to be removed.

There, in your womb, all your anger, your pain, your stress, your worry, your shame, your guilt is locked away. What you hold in it may kill you, after all, if you let it, but, without an intervention, your womb will never house children.

From your very beginning, in your mother's womb, you had something to hide. Sensing that your mother hid your brother there, you hid your sister in the very same place. It wasn't until your mother gave birth to you that you revealed your secret to her.

While you had only nine months to keep your secret, she kept hers for twenty-eight years.

You must have known that when you got out of there, your brother wouldn't be at home, waiting. How angry you must have been, how sad. Growing up, no wonder that you must have said to your mother a thousand times how you wish you had a brother.

In a place somewhere beneath your navel, in a place you couldn't even name, you knew you already had a brother, and you've tried to punish her ever since for rendering you a brotherless girl.

Under your circumstances, you have done a great job.

It hurt me to see the way you and your mother relate to each other. Having you both in our home at the same time gave me much more insight into what was going on between the two of you. I know you must understand this, given that, if you paid attention, you probably have some insight into what's going on between my husband and me.

The tone of voice, the sarcasm, the pettiness of the gripes the two of you expressed to each other was disheartening. That quiet riot was everywhere, in the post office when you were filling out your Massachusetts nursing licensure verification requests, in the furniture store when you were ordering the furniture for your new condo, walking down the street, getting in and out of the car, over the telephone, figuring out which one of you was going to take you back to your condo from my house. It was like witnessing sisters, both jealous for thinking their daddy likes the other one better, fight like kittens. It reached the summit of surrealism during the time just before, during, and after visits from the man from Milwaukee. Surreal also became my relationship with you, with your mother, with our uncle, and with my husband. I will not detail any of that madness here. But it was sheer madness, pure hell, self-professed "grown" people acting like spoiled, selfish little brats, standing, waving, pontificating, pouting, acting like idiots, doing whatever we could to get the attention none of us were able to give to ourselves, and all five of us know it.

Ever since the first stages of puberty, you have gone from man to man to man perhaps looking for the big brother who should have been at home, waiting for you. After I walked into your life, in spite of your mother's protest and projected pity, you divorced your husband, the husband you claim you never loved, marrying him only to have sex.

Your father was wise to suggest you annul your marriage right away, but not because your husband told you the truth about yourself.

Now, you believe yourself to be in love with a man from Milwaukee who claimed to be the same age as your brother, to never have been married, and to have no children.

Three lies.

Three strikes, he should have been out, so skilled he is at hiding his true self from you. But you keep letting him in, and he won't let you go. You may be in love with him, Rwanda, you certainly are in *need* of him, the same way you have needed all the others, band-aids on your bullet wounds of sorrow. Shortly after you so quickly forgave him the three strikes, he threatened to have someone murder your first love—perhaps your true love, your first nephew's godfather—if you continued to refuse to break off all contact with him. He threatened this right in front of me, right in front of our laid-up-in-the-hospital-with-congestive-heart-failure uncle, right in front of your mother. With that strike, he really *was* out—out of his mind—but you keep letting him in, and he won't let you go. That you brought him into our home on the first Christmas you would spend with your long lost brother, the one you always wished for, struck me. Hard.

No longer able to hide your sister, now you hide your self. Killing yourself softly with the songs of a string of men, unavailable to you precisely because you remain unavailable to them, so skilled you are at hiding.

I have already told you what I see regarding you and the man from Milwaukee. I cannot allow myself to sketch that vision here in black and white.

I make no presumption that you do, but, if you want a deep, abiding, and loving relationship with a man, a man who supports your living and not your dying, you first have to be real with yourself and reveal that realness to a man.

Your first-and-only brother, let me be the first of many men who revels in the revelation of your true self. If you allow this, you really might get out of there. Finally.

My prayer for you is that you don't become a woman, alone at death, eyes closed long before she draws her last labored breath.

3 Burundi, second daughter, twin sister, you are my sister in hiding. She who chooses to hide craves freedom the most. She is also most afraid of the freedom she craves. If she walks with courage through that fear, she will become the freest of the free.

Sister in hiding, you sensed your mother's surprise—her shock—when you showed up unannounced just outside the threshold of her womb. You became your mother's protector. By telling her exactly what she needs to hear, whether or not what she needs to hear is true, you have defended her most against her mother's arrows, against her own.

Under your circumstances you have done a great job.

I am trying to help you. Trying to save her life in return for saving mine. Put another way, I am trying to help her save herself here in this life, without having to wait for someone to save us in the after life, and take us to some infinite kingdom high in the sky. Why wait for all that drama? The drama unfolding here is much more interesting and we have it right now. We don't have to wait for anything.

Life is to be enjoyed, not filled with so much misery, so much misery we perpetuate ourselves because that's all we think we deserve, here and now, until we are delivered out of the here and now into everlasting life. But there is no deliverance from the here and now. Here and now is all we will ever have, forever and ever, it will always be here, always be now.

Tomorrow is fantasy.

Within a few weeks of meeting me, your mother said that of all her daughters, I was the most like you. We both chose to come through a womb where we could hide. There, the similarity ends. When I got out of her womb, I got away. You are still there, hiding. Hiding away in shopping malls, hiding out in dogma, hiding in food, hiding from your self, so skilled you are at being hidden.

I used to hide out in sex, hide away in alcohol, hide away in pity, hideout in anger, escape into fantasy. Sometimes, I still do. None of us can deal well with all of life's turns all the time. But I had to leave indoctrination completely alone because it was killing me. It looks like it's killing you too and I pray to get to know your true self someday.

You will have at least one daughter, if a soul chooses to come through you. Should more than one chose you, the one I see here will be your first daughter. Even though she will go along, on the surface, with all that you try to teach her, she will, at the same time, rebel with passion against the very same. If you try to make her like yourself, she will run away from you, even if she stays with you. She will be the contradiction of contradictions, and your relationship with her will be riddled with discord. You will always consider her your most troublesome child. You will resent her because of it. She will always seek your approval, but you will never give it to her, keeping it hidden behind a thick veil of control. She will drink your resentment more greedily than she drank your milk. Unless she breaks free, her spirit will die, and in this life, she will keep an ever abiding, deep and abiding sorrow. She will always remind you, mostly in deed, but sometimes in word, just how much trouble for you she really can be. Even though she rebels so much, you will never let her go. If you let her go, encourage her to go her own way, let her out from under your reins, she will come back to you and try to help you live a better life. If you don't let her out, you will continue to confuse control and destruction with love.

When I first returned, you were unable to join the surprise reunion in Georgia. You were undone. But there is Reason for everything. When I finally met you for the first time a few months later, you were the sister most interested in my adoption papers. You skimmed, perused, read them, and took as much as you could take, piecing together bits and pieces of a story that you had never been told. Unfortunately, you still don't know the whole story, because you have too much difficulty skimming, perusing, reading the books I've composed about my own life, so sure you are, deep down within you, that my being is a result of your devil's handiwork. I sense that contempt every time we speak, Burundi, every time you look at my friends, sometimes even when you look at my husband, who is not my husband, according to what you believe. Which is why you didn't want anyone to know that the Feast of Families began as a wedding anniversary celebration for all of your mother's offspring.

If you wonder why I haven't come to visit you yet, wonder no more. I have already been where you are and I don't want to go back, if I can help it. And I can help it. That same contempt I see in your face I used to see in my own as I looked in the mirror, as I looked at my friends, as I looked at strangers who looked like me. You and I were raised separately, but we were both taught to believe that who I am is perverse, an abomination, created only by the devil you worship. Imagine believing that who you are, your very essence, is the result of evil. Imagine having that reinforced in everything you saw, read, and heard. Everyday. Everywhere. This could make anyone full of pity. And I was. Full. And I didn't need anyone else to make me feel that way. I took care of that all by myself. So, take it personally that I have not wanted to visit you, but don't take it personally. I still have work to do. I don't like having to revisit those pitiful faces, but sometimes someone close to me takes me near that abyss again, and I have to work to get back from it. Your presence in my life has taken me near that abyss. So has your mother's. I can only pray that you do your work. The next time I see your face, I pray that there is less contempt in your eyes.

Before we went to your grandmother's house together for the first time, you scanned over my suitcase, informing me that, of anything I might choose, choose something conservative for the sake of your grandmother's eyes. "That's Burundi," your mother said to me after she caught a glimpse of my eyes rolling back in my head. "That's Burundi." That is, Burundi, why I could see that you also wanted me to choose something conservative for the sake of your own eyes. Anyone in my life who has ever suggested what I ought to wear without my solicitation has always been met with my apprehension. Someone so concerned about what I wear on the outside is oftentimes completely unable to deal with what I wear on the inside, and I don't bother, therefore, to open myself up to them without a great deal of effort.

I do not presume that you do, but, if you want us to have a mutually satisfying and meaningful relationship, you must first be able to see me for who I really am. In order to see me, you must first lay down your heavy armor. All of it. If you lay it down, you will be able to fully open your mouth when you speak. Before you lay down your heavy armor—all of it—you must first see yourself for who you really are. Otherwise you will remain more concerned with the appearance of people and things than who and what they really are.

How could you have possibly known that it might have mattered to me to see your mother fix a plate for Frank at my 34th birthday party? My husband created a reality that I had never even dreamed possible. There, in our house, on my birthday, were the two people who facilitated my re-creation. I had my cake, and I was eating it, too. But you denied me the icing. You knew Frank was attending my party several weeks before I did. Perhaps you might have used that time to express your expectations to your mother regarding her behavior toward Frank. Why was it so important for you that your mother didn't fix a plate for Frank? Isn't it entirely possible that your mother might fix a plate for your father at *your* birthday party? Do you think I would object, tell your mother that she need not do that, because, after all, it's not like she's *married* to him or anything? Indeed, it was funny when your mother, submitting to your control, informed me that I needed to fix his plate because you wouldn't let her do it for the above reasons. Imagine that. At my party, I needed to fix a plate for Frank because you told your mother that she shouldn't, that she couldn't. I say *your* mother because when she decided on this issue, so small, so big, she certainly didn't act like any mother of mine. It was my party and I could have cried if I wanted to, so sensitive I am, but I chose to laugh first. Frank fixed his own plate. You got exactly what you wanted.

My prayer for you is that you don't become an elderly woman, alone by death, so tormented by her shame that she becomes a bitter, frigid, vindictive, rigid, and overly controlling matriarch whose Machiavellian machinations seek only to insidiously destroy generations of her offspring.

4 Tanzania, third daughter, mother sister, you are the other side of me. Your mother was so convinced I was born on the 3rd of December, she delivered her 3rd daughter 3 x 3 days into December, almost 8 years to the day after she delivered your brother, who was really born on the 8th of December. I am the first; you are the last. No surprise, therefore, that I would meet my last sister first.

Under her life circumstances, we are both your mother's accidents. We chose, however, to come through her on purpose. We were conceived just as she was ending her relationship with our fathers. We are the bookends, supporting twin books from either side. No wonder it has taken you so long to relate to them; no one realized you were so busy holding them up. Under your circumstances, you did a great job. One bookend can hold up two books if both books lean on the bookend. In case I am not allowed to support them from the other side, keep standing upright, and never slide so far away that they fall down.

If you are my other side, then Antoine Evan, your latest, is my grand other side. I now know why I was so excited when you first became pregnant. As my grand other side, Antoine will, therefore, become a grander version of me. Your mother was so convinced I was born on the 3rd day, Antoine came into your world on the 3rd day after the first anniversary of the day in April when I came back into your mother's world. Antoine will become a grander version of me. In every single way. And you won't be able to do anything to change that.

Yours is the choice between devastation and peace. You can encourage him to live his life as who he is, no matter what. Or, you can try to make him live his life the way you want him to live it, no matter what. Choose the first, you get the last. Chose the last, you get the first. I presume not to know which one you want.

As I write this, my husband has just called to inform me that you, unannounced, brought Antoine with you to the house of a friend of ours who was throwing a party. You saw his car and thought I might be there with him, but I am in Portland enjoying the light. You saw Job's car, left your mother in your sister's car, and walked right on up. I had already made it clear that during this time, I had no interest in picking you up at the airport or spending any time with you or Antoine or your mother. Just because I didn't return your calls doesn't mean that I wouldn't have a problem with you showing up at my doorstep or somewhere you think I am without picking up your cell phone and calling me first.

Yes, I showed up on your doorstep unannounced last April, but that was different, and you know it. Had you turned me away, I would have gone. If you would have told me that you didn't want to see me again, I would not try to impose myself on you. You disregarded my boundaries and showed up anyway, and not even at my own house. Did you or your mother think I wouldn't have refused such an intrusion at a party in the presence of my friends? Clearly, you don't see me. Understandable given that we haven't spent any time at all getting to know each other without your mother being in the middle of it. My husband, the closest thing to me of anyone in life (just as he ought to be) saw Antoine, as he wished, and I didn't see him, as I wished.

I accept your anger at me for not wanting to visit with you, but let's be real: I did not tell you to come to Boston, Tanzania, as you told my husband. You told me *when* you were coming to Boston and gave me the dates of your arrival and departure. What I told you was that, as far as I could see, I could make time to see you when you were here. But between that conversation and your arrival last week, my vision cleared up. Life happens while you're making plans. You cannot make me see something that I don't want to see until I am ready to see it for myself. You may bring it to my attention, but I still won't see it until I am ready.

Isn't that the point of *all* of this?

I pray Antoine is granted the strength and the wisdom to live his life as who he is. I pray that his older brother Quincy does not slay him because of it. My prayer for you is that you do not become a middle-aged woman, alone by divorce, so afraid to live her own life, she must live *through* her children, live *with* her children, with or without their spouses, in their homes.

5 My prayer for all of you is that you stop keeping so many secrets. I was born in secret. One of you married in secret. One of you divorced in secret. One of us will die in secret.

Live your life in the open. You have less to remember.

Separate yourselves. You are so intertwined, it is difficult sometimes to see where one of you ends and the other begins, so fluent you are in the language of guilt, constraint, shame.

Often, obligation motivates you more than love, and even though you owe no one anything, you are obligated to your mothers thus:

You are obligated to both praise and criticize them, to their faces.

You are obligated to tell them how they have harmed you, to their faces.

You are obligated to tell your grandmother, to her face, how she has harmed you by harming your mother so much.

You are obligated to tell your mother, to her face, if you are angry, sad, or disappointed that she gave your brother away or waited so long to tell you about him or never tried to find him herself.

You are obligated to encourage your mother to live her own life.

You are obligated, as such, to disentangle your life from hers, to make your own decisions, mistakes, and missteps without the need for her approval or advice.

You are obligated to love your mothers more than you need them, and if you achieve this, your burden will be lighter, lifted, free.

You are obligated to do these things whether or not you have done them before, whether or not it is in your personality to do so, whether or not you are afraid of the consequences.

Peace is yours for the taking. Love is yours for the giving. Be blessed. Brilliantly blessed in every way.

Your one and only brother,
Craig

WHITE LIES

Woe to those who call evil good and good evil,
who put darkness for light and light for darkness...

—ISAIAH 5:20

In their hearts is a disease; and Allah has increased
their disease: and grievous is the chastisement they
incur, because they lied to themselves.

—SURAH 2:10

1 When I first found all of you, you sent me a typed letter on stationery that had a beautiful one-inch, left-hand-side gold border. There, in the gold border, was a relief of doves. The stationery was an exact match to the wedding invitations I designed four years prior for my marriage to my husband.

How connected we are needs no proof.

In the letter you told me that you had mixed emotions about what happened in 1967, that your family was extremely complex and in constant need of prayer, and as only a matriarch could do, you welcomed me back into the family from which you expelled me. While it took me almost a year to confirm my initial feelings—feelings I had to suppress in order to hang around long enough to confirm them—I find that your family is not complex at all. Rather, the simple truth is simply this: Your family is totally destroyed by the dogma you introduced to them in 1951. A religious conversion that your very own husband resisted for as long as he could, until you browbeat him into it. And that is what you do to everyone, England. You whip them into your way of doing things, and if they don't do things your way, they spend the rest of their lives keeping secrets from you, just as you taught them to do, and lying to your face, just as you do to other people. Because of your terrorism, your last-born son, who obviously wants you to get out of his house, hates you with almost every fiber of his being. (Where would you go? What would the Adventist circle think? How could you possibly show your face?) A man who cannot stand secrets, he has made no secret of his contempt for you, in both word and deed. Your firstborn son has been driven mad by your dogma and your control, and even though he has tried again and again to tell you that you have driven him and the rest of the family into madness, you refuse to hear him or do anything to make amends for your harm. (Shortly after we spoke in your home after the Feast, after most of the guests went home, during the three-day cold war you negotiated with your daughter who avoided you like an infection, I began a poem that I only was able to finish a few weeks ago. It follows on the pages after this letter.) When you say you have a long way to go before you live like Jesus lived...

Your daughter is so destroyed by you—*to this day*—that she can't live her own life free from your dominion. Every single Sabbath shortly after sundown, you called my house to make sure Jennifer was home, praying, meditating, worshipping, doing holy things on your holy day. Making sure her heathen son wasn't distracting her from her holiness. She still needs your approval, and since you won't give it, keeping it hidden behind a thick veil of control and shame and fear, she poisons herself and her children with everything that you taught her, believing herself to be a better mother than you are, when, in fact, she's become just like you in spite of herself. Your firstborn son, who nobody made you give up, even though you conceived him before *you* got married, such a hypocrite you are, told me in the very first conversation we had over the phone that I had returned to the family in order to help all of you heal.

What a dream. But even if it's truth, nobody in your family desires healing. Jesus got all yall by the coattails, and as restrictive as that is, it must be comfortable. All of you are so comfortable in your suffering, so comfortable playing judge and victim with one another, with yourselves, that the freedom you would get from healing is too scary a proposition for any of you to dare.

So you wait and you hope and you pray. You wait and you hope and you pray that the blood of Jesus really has washed you clean of your suffering and sins and someday, when He returns, He raises you up from physical death, reunites you with your eternal soul, and takes you all to some mythological mansion in the sky where you will be reunited with your loved ones, those died-in-the-wool Adventists who lived and died for such a dream, and you will all live the rest of your days, together, without misery, in perfect union with the Almighty. If you say so.

You have almost single-handedly destroyed the integrity of two generations of your offspring. Now, cancer is killing the place where you housed your children and it may kill you, too, if you don't have your womb removed. Poetry. Or, to put it another way, you reap what you sow.

The devil lives all up in you and you live in hell. Everyday of your life has been pure hell. There is no place for Christ in your life, no acceptance of the truth of his teachings, and so you judge your family members, telling them that they must live a life based on your dream and that they must must *must* follow the Bible as interpreted by a woman you believe yourself to be the reincarnation of. I didn't realize Adventists believed in reincarnation. And what's really twisted: deep down in your heart you know all these things that I'm telling you are true but you don't allow anyone else to know who you really are.

Thank you.

Thank you for banishing me from your life. Thank you for giving me back bits and pieces of mine so I could complete the puzzle of my soul, knowing, in the end, that I lacked nothing, never needed any of you to be happy and fulfilled. Thank you for giving me the peace in understanding that my immediate family, Mama and Daddy and Gina, and now Job, are all I ever needed.

You said you could never thank my mother enough for what she did for me. Not only can you never thank her enough, England, you can't really thank her at all because what she did for me had nothing to do with you. And you know it. Which is why at the Feast of Families, like a vulture, you preyed upon her insecurities. So insecure she was on some level about not being able to raise children she brought into the world, but more than that, about having raised a son who loves men. You sensed this and you dug deeper. But she got over you, England, because she's like you, except that she is not utterly terrified of showing herself to others. She knew what you were doing. She still knows what you're doing, but wise woman that she is, she accepts you for who you are, both to your face *and* behind your back. You could learn a lot from her, England. And so could I. If you want to thank my mother for anything, thank her for being a good mother, a wise woman, who trusts that the people in her life will be able to find a way of life that allows them to be who they really are, allows them to be free. It's no mistake she named me after a rock and my sister after royalty. Thank her for being such a wise person that she raised a son who is strong, and when he is at his best, he doesn't need anyone's approval, not even hers.

If only you would be able to think for yourself, create your own moral and ethical universe, and not be so concerned with what others in the Adventist circle—that toxic, poisonous ring that manifests the devil you worship in its purest form—think about you or your failures or your successes. But you don't want the responsibility of thinking for yourself.

You have behaved miserably and you know it. You have succeeded in breaking the integrity of your children and you know it. You have left a trail of destruction in your wake more intense than the scorched earth policy of Sherman who burned through Georgia during the Civil War and you *know* it. That war wasn't civil, and neither is the war you have waged on your family since 1951.

I'm a man who loves men, a faggot, a perversion, and an abomination before *your* God, which, to you, means the devil is all up in me. We see each other similarly. You don't accept me for who I am, and I don't accept you for who you pretend to be. Thank you, therefore, for convincing your daughter to get rid of me. You obviously knew that she needed you more than she needed me. Like a fretting woman jealous of her lover's spouse, you made her choose between the two of us. She chose you. And you have kept her exactly where you want her: suckling your venom after all these years.

It has to be hard work working so hard to make people believe you're something that you're not. I worked too hard this past year trying to be a part of your family, but I am not a part of your family and never will be. Yes, your blood courses through my veins. Yes, your DNA is written all over my face. But I am not a part of your terrorized family, England. Even though I gave into some fantasy of what might have been and tried to be something I wasn't, I failed miserably. And so have you, England. You cannot fool me.

How connected we are needs no proof.

I see you for who you really are, but I despise the ugly, ugly masks you wear. That is why you knew I had to go. You didn't want anyone in your family to tell you to your face that you are a fraud. No wonder why you can't sleep at night. And you could have enjoyed so much heaven on earth, but you chose to live in hell instead. Your ultimate sin was to pass that hell onto your offspring, and you punish yourself for it every single day. As long as you continue to draw breath, you still have a chance to find some salvation before you close your eyes. Try it. Because after your eyes close, you will find out that heaven is as imaginary as you imagined it to be, based upon what your book of law told you it is. And all this suffering you endured, all this suffering you perpetuated on this earth, waiting to get a piece of the pie in the sky, waiting for the manifestation of the "earth made new," all this suffering was all for nothing. There is no pie in the sky. Heaven is found here. And so is hell. If you want to do your small part in contributing to the "earth made new," then tell everyone that you've ever hurt, but most of all, tell your children, James and Jennifer and Joshua, tell your husband when you lie awake at night, tell your grandchildren, tell them *all* that you messed up, that you shattered their integrity, and that you are very sorry because you only did what you knew how to do, you only did what you were taught by the adults in your life, you only did what you thought was best for them, even though you were and are unable to let them go, let them live their own lives, free from your dominion.

Tell them that. Tell them that you are sorry, *before* your body dies. If you do, you may find heaven, after all. If you do, that part of you that is loving, and gracious and generous and eternal and of God will light up your eyes, and that is what will make people eulogize you more honestly, even though, right now, you don't care about honesty. If you don't, hell for you will continue, eternally, and people will continue to lie about you, forever and ever, in this life and the next and the next and the next.... If you don't, hell for your offspring will almost certainly continue, eternally. If you do, you might make heaven possible for those you leave behind. The choice is yours, England. Eternal heaven or eternal hell. Which one, England, will you choose?

Blinded

You said it was the best thing
for your eighteen-year-old girl.
You spoke of promises you made God
promises to put someone else's son
through college if he was spared
a premature death
that imminent snatching of
life that loomed over his
four-year-old head
like a dove
carrying an olive branch.
Promises kept after you expelled your
own daughter's firstborn and only son
putting her to death
instead.

You said I coulda been dead.
Perhaps I woulda been dead
had you not put me out,
put me away, with her, in that unholy
place where no one could see.

Under the dominion of your
matriarchy, I might have died several
deaths, never to be resurrected,
just like all your children,
that troubled trinity.

Under the dominion of your
matriarchy, I might have died
several deaths, never again resurrected

just like your own firstborn son,
so close he came to
living again.

He calls himself JEW
due to the initials he
inherited from
his father, from his
father's father.
James the Third.

The third time should
be the charm.
Indeed, it was.
But your family
could not see
would not see
behind their
Jericho's Wall of
shame.

The third time is the charm.
In your firstborn son, the third
James E. White, God blessed you
with the first manchild
brought to you
come through you
offering your face salvation.

But you turned your face more eagerly
to the false white light of Ellen G.

While you turned away
he turned his face to
a light so bright,
it burned through his
eyes and melted his
mind.

So close he came to
breathing again,
he broke, instead,

*and no religion,
no food, clean or
unclean, no
medicine or men
can put him
back together again.*

*You said his breaking
was your punishment
for kicking me out.
After you banished me
he said his entire life
every major event of
his life had every thing
to do with me.*

*And so he eventually left the church
but he never left the Jews.
A group of people who
made a tradition that you told
him was real, unlike
the counterfeit version
evangelized by the
counterfeit Ellen G.
whose illusory light blinded
you to your own salvation.*

*I see your heavy gaze,
I hear your weary voice and
In your presence,
I cannot expel my age-old anger,
will not express my rage,
boiling up,
not over.
In your presence,
I am too constipated by what
I won't let myself know,
can't let myself feel.*

*But I see it, still. No, it was
the very best thing for a
thirty-nine-year-old woman.*

the Mother of Secrets
the Matriarch of Lies.

Hardly about your daughter,
it was all about you.
how could your child,
flesh of your flesh,
fruit of your womb
be not perfect?
What Adventist mother
would not ask this with a frown
her nose pointed up toward
some false god?
which one would require your
answer more readily than Him?

The gray haze of shame
a face in need of saving
a will unwilling to bend
compelled your Secret
necessitated your Lie—
to yourself,
to your daughter,
to your God.
Unbent still,
you utter the same
false tale
to me.

I see your shame,
I see your pain.

I am your ultimate Secret,
I am your biggest Lie
I am your boomerang
come back to
offer your face
salvation.

REFLECTIONS

1 The pen freezes after scrawling the last word. "There," Craig says out loud to himself. "It is finished." Finished at last. Finished with all the games and maneuvers and lies and assumptions that threaten to keep his heart in solitary confinement. He will tarry no longer in a place with no doors. Three letters to five women are the ways back, back into a world he knows, a world he understands, a world where he is comfortable. Sitting in the Western Promenade, a park high atop a hill, Craig closes his journal and watches the early-May sun fall over Portland. Although, at times, he felt as though he was, he cannot let himself believe he is the master of his destiny. He would need to rely on too much self-deception to go on believing that lie. Yes, he can master the *way* he lives. But he masters his destiny no more or less than a deciduous tree sheds its painted foliage in autumn and grows green again come spring. Here, to this place atop this hill, destiny has carried him, exasperated but acquiescent. Sitting on the grass in a bound angle pose and gazing at the horizon swallow up that huge copper ball of light, Craig finds himself in a contemptuous place. But the disdain he felt for the five women (and for himself for allowing it all to go as far as it went) dies away like falling leaves in the time it has taken for his pen to blacken the white pages.

2 "You crossed over the line a bit, I think," said Gina, after reading the letters Craig shared with her a few weeks later. It was the weekend before Memorial Day and he was visiting his family in Milwaukee. Gina had re-arranged her room in the back of the house since the last time he was

there. They were sitting on her bed. "How can you sit in judgment of them like this?" While she spoke, Gina flipped through the pages as though she wanted to make sure that what she'd read was really there. "You may be your own god, but you are not theirs, no matter what you might think, no matter *how* you might feel. What gives you the right to judge them?"

Her words stung him like true words can. As with a mosquito bite or the sting of bee, a good prick now and then can wake you up; remind you that you really *are* alive. "What gives anybody," Craig finally replied, "the right to say or do anything, Gina?"

"You know what I mean, Craig."

"And you know what I mean. They wanted to know what was going on with me, why I stopped talking to them, so I told them. I bet it's not what they wanna hear, but it's what they wanna know." Craig paused. "I don't suppose you read anything that you could connect with." His voice impatient, half-questioning.

"Of course I did, Craig. That's what makes you so exasperating sometimes. Your judgments can be annoying as all hell, but nine times out of ten, you hit the nail right on the head." Gina paused, put the letters down on the bed, and then said, "I told Jennifer to chill out."

"You actually talked to her?"

"Yes. She called Mom on Mother's Day and after she spoke to her, she wanted to talk to me. She asked me for my advice. I told her the pendulum would swing, and when it did, watch out because it would slice deep. I told her to be patient, to wait, to sit tight and do nothing, say nothing, try nothing. But it's hard for people who don't have a sense of themselves to be still and wait. Every time I said something, she'd say 'Oh, I know *that*.' But if she really knew, she wouldn't be calling me up trying to get me to tell her how I saw things and to find out what I thought was going on with you."

"It got theatrical and tragic and downright ugly, girl." Craig smiled. "It was actually kind of funny, too."

"Knowing you and sensing her, I can only imagine what went on between the lines. I'm sure your letters, even as long as they are, only scratched the surface of the tensions and dynamics between you all."

"If only you knew."

"Maybe I will someday. But *you* know, and don't you ever forget it."

"Not till all the stars fall from the sky."

"So are you gonna send them or did you just write them for yourself?"

He wasn't sure what he was going to do with them. The last time he wrote and sent a family letter, a letter he thought was much less confrontational than these three, all hell broke loose. But that's because hell was there for the breaking. This time, he didn't know what would happen. He thought that Jennifer and England would read them, but his sisters would not. Perhaps he'd send all the letters to all of them. Or maybe, accidentally on purpose, he'd send Jennifer's letter to England, England's to Jennifer, and send his sisters' letter to them both. Whichever way, it would save them time when gossiping with each other about what he had written, and none of them would be able to take his words out of context. Perhaps he'd truly written them only for himself. That's what Gina asked and maybe—just *maybe*—that's what she was actually telling him. "I don't know, sis," Craig finally answered. "But one thing I know for sure: whether I send them or not, I certainly feel better."

They were quiet for a few moments then Gina said, "I'm not sure if I have to search anymore."

"Excuse me?"

"I don't know, Craig. I don't wanna hurt Daddy. Plus, seeing what you went through, it almost feels like I went through it, too. I'm not sure if I'm ready to have my whole life opened up before me quite like you did."

"Oh, sistergirl," said Craig, sighing. "Two things. First, Daddy hasn't dropped dead of a heart attack since I found my relatives. Yes, I know he might feel closer to you than me, but over the last ten years, Daddy and I have become very close. And he has always said that we're *his*, no matter what. Nobody can take us away from him, or make him feel any less like our father. And second, there is nothing written anywhere that says the experience you'll have if you find your relatives will be anything like mine has been, for you or for them. For heaven's sake, your mother was a white woman who had an affair with a black man while her husband was off in Vietnam. Who knows *what* situation you'd find her in?"

"I just think it would be better, if I do search, to wait until at least Daddy dies."

"Honey, there's no guarantee, even as old as he is, that you're gonna outlive him. Mama either. Stubborn as they are, both of them might live past a hundred, and that's almost twenty years from now. You and I could be long gone by then."

"That's true, but I don't know, Craig. I just don't know. The back-and-forth searches I've done in the past have taken so much out of me emotionally. I think I'm just satisfied knowing that you did it, that you found what you were looking for."

"You don't have to decide anything right now. Follow your heart, Gina. That's all you can do. And know that I'll be here to help you should you decide to give it another try."

Gina pulled a Kleenex from the box on the nightstand. "Allow me," said Craig. Craig took the tissue from her hand and wiped the tears streaking both her cheeks. "No matter what, you'll always be my little big sister. Always."

"And you'll always be my big little brother."

They hugged each other, giggling like five-year-old kids opening their eyes on Christmas morning.

3 Hazelle was sitting at the picnic table in the backyard, drinking a Pabst and bopping his head to the be-bop of Charlie Parker blaring from his boom box when Craig walked over and sat across from him. The strong aroma of hickory scented the air. "What're you smoking, Daddy?"

"I got me a nice piece of salmon from Sendik's."

"Did you cure it first this time?"

"In Kosher salt. Just two days, though." The last time he smoked a salmon filet, he didn't cure it and he thought it lacked flavor. He walked over to the orange upright smoker and checked on the fish. "Son, I've been meaning to ask you. How's Uncle James doing?"

Just before Mother's Day, Uncle James had suffered a heart attack that triggered another episode and he spent a few days in Brigham and Women's Hospital. England had come to Boston to visit him then. Just after Mother's Day, he had an episode that triggered a stroke and since then was staying in a psychiatric unit at Beth Israel Deaconess. Since then, Sonja came to visit, tried once more to have him committed (no such luck), and they later reconciled. US Airways relocated her to Charlotte, North Carolina, and when the doctors decided James could be safely released, James would go to Charlotte and be with his wife.

"I talked to him briefly before I drove out here," said Craig. "He sounded pretty good. The stroke didn't mess with his speech too, too much. He's looking forward to getting out of there and getting back together with Sonja."

"Too bad he's had such a hard time of it," said Hazelle in a sad sounding voice. He sat back down. "You wanna know something, son? He was about the only one of them who had anything to say to me. He talks more than your mother and is crazier than a loon, but he's a good man, son. Your birth mom, your grandmother either, I didn't care for them too much. Jennifer sat in this house, right in front of me, and thanked your mother for everything and said not a word to me. Your grandmother did the same thing when we were down in Georgia for the reunion. They're the kind of women who don't think a man has anything to do with how a child turns out. They think he's only supposed to stand upright to the Lord and pay the water bill. But my father always said, 'A man who doesn't shape the character of his child is no man at all.' Your uncle and my dad would've gotten along fine."

"Remember what Unc said to you when he first met you, when we were getting ready to leave and go meet Jennifer?"

"Sure do, son. I'll never forget it."

"Well, he was right. I couldn't have been in a better place than with you and Mama, Daddy. And I'm truly grateful."

"We didn't have much, but we always made the best of it. I never told you, son, but when you were having trouble with Job and Jennifer, and you called your mother from Portland a few months ago, crying and not knowing which way to go, you made her so very happy, son."

"Really?"

"Yes, you did, son. You sure did. She was so afraid that she had lost you, that you didn't need her anymore now that you were with your birth mother. She never came right out and said so, but I could tell. It was much harder than she let on. But when you called her, all of a sudden she seemed more alive because you gave her something she thought she was never gonna have again."

"I never thought of it that way," said Craig. He stares into the air, remembering the moment his father just spoke about. He is sitting on the floor of his bare Portland apartment, scrunched in a corner, phone in hand, sobbing, sobbing, sobbing, holding tight to his lifeline. "You know what Mama told me?" said Craig, returning to the present. "Of course she told me many things, but out of all the things she told me, you wanna know what stuck, Daddy? She said, 'Craig, you need to go sit down somewhere and be quiet.' And let me tell you, that's exactly what I needed to hear. And that's why Portland is so important to me. That is where I am able to be quiet, where I can really listen to what I need to hear inside of me."

"Your mother is wiser than Solomon, son. That's why I married her." He took a swig of beer. "Oh, yeah," he continued, "and so I could have somebody to nag me to death. And, son, that's about the size of it."

They shared a good laugh and for the next hour, not another word. Craig joined his father in a few beers. They sat together and waved a neck or stomped a heel or drummed the table to the rhythms of the jazz mingling with the hickory smoke and rising, rising, rising into the air like an offering.

4 "Craig, I got me some Brussels sprouts from the store yesterday, and I wanna know what to do with'em." Mary was sitting at the kitchen table when Craig came back into the house. "Now how should I cook them?

"I don't like Brussels sprouts too much, Mama, but steam them till they turn bright green, toss them in a little balsamic vinegar, and season them however you like. Or you could toss them in lemon juice and butter, but be sure to add a sprinkle of sugar to whatever seasoning you use. If you wanna be fancy, I'm sure Daddy has some nuts around here. Take some pecans or walnuts, even cashews, toast them, crush them up, and mix them in."

"I don't need to be fancy. But if you want to, son, go right ahead."

"Oh, I see. So you want me to cook them."

"Well, I don't wanna mess them up."

"What else are you planning to have with them?"

"I'm not really that hungry, tell you the truth. But I gotta eat after I take my insulin. Seems like all I do is eat. Your father's been sitting out there with his salmon all day. I made some potato salad earlier and I might make up some salmon croquettes."

"Ooh, yeah." Craig was excited. He couldn't remember the last time he'd eaten her croquettes, one of his favorite meals. "You make salmon croquettes and I'll cook the Brussels sprouts for you. Do we have anything for a salad?" Craig moved toward the refrigerator.

"You better wash your hands before you go fumbling around in my refrigerator, m'dear," said Mary, authoritatively.

"Yeah, yeah, yeah," sighed Craig, heading to the bathroom. He returned with clean hands and found what he wanted for the salad: romaine, tomatoes, a cucumber, a red bell pepper, a few scallions, a bag of carrots, and a jar of Bac-Os.

"I don't know if I should ask or not, but I'm going to anyway," said Mary in a don't-even-try-to-stop-me tone. "Have you spoken with your mother?"

"I'm speaking with her right now, Mama."

"You know what I mean. I'm talking about Jennifer."

"Then call her who she is. And no, I haven't spoken to her in a while now, nor do I intend to."

"You just need to go to your corner and she can go to her corner and then the two of you can get along again."

"What do you think we are, Mama? Prizefighters? I don't know that we'll ever get along again."

"I talk to her sometimes. Talk to your grandmother, too. She always asks me if you ask about them."

"And what do you say?"

"I tell her that you do."

"So you lie to her?"

"Well, I wouldn't call it lying."

"Oh, really? Well then what would you call it since I don't ask about them at all?"

"I just tell her that to make her feel better."

"I'd bet my life that England, of all people, can hear the lie in your voice when you tell it. But, hey, if that's what you need to do to make your*self* feel better, Mama, then go right ahead. I can almost assure you, you can't make England feel better about anything."

"I did promise your mother, I mean Jennifer, that I would tell her if you ever got sick or something."

"Why?"

"Because she asked me to."

"What if I didn't want her to know if I ever got sick or something?"

"Well, I promised her I would tell her and I would keep my promise."

"Then I suppose if I ever got sick or something and didn't want her to know, I'd have to make sure not to tell you, too."

"Oh, Craig, don't say that."

"You made your promise and you've just made it clear that you intend to keep it. It's only a hypothetical anyway. What else do you and Jennifer talk about?"

"Nothing too much. I talk to your grandmother mostly. Sometimes your sisters call and say hello. For the life of me I can't get their names straight. But I don't say anything about you, if that's what you wanna know. I did wanna ask you something, though. Jennifer asked me one time why I didn't ask to talk to her whenever I called you."

"She asked you *what?*"

"She said since I knew she was there living with you, why was it that I didn't ask to talk to her when I called you."

"I hope you cussed her out."

"I wasn't trying to make her feel bad. If I had known it would've made her feel bad, I guess I could've talked to her when I called. But I wanted to ask you if Job feels that way when I call you?"

"She really knows how to work the guilt factor, doesn't she?"

"I don't feel guilty."

"If you say so, Mama. And no, Job doesn't care when you call me and don't ask to talk to him. He's got more sense than that. I'm just about finished with this salad. You want me to do anything else before you start the croquettes?"

"Uh uh, no, son, I don't feel no guilt. Not me, son. And no, I'll wait till you sit down before I get started so you're not in my way. This kitchen ain't but big enough for a fly."

Craig sat down. Mary got up. "I can tell you this now, son, but when you and Jennifer were here last summer, I was standing right here looking out the window at you and your father outside and I didn't remember why I came into the kitchen, and so I asked myself out loud. Well, Jennifer was right behind me, and you know what she said? She said that I was just being nosy. She told me I was being nosy in my own house. She sure did."

"Why didn't you tell me that before?" Craig was beginning to feel like he would send Jennifer the letter after all.

"Because I couldn't, son. I just couldn't."

"Why are you telling me now?"

Mary gathered the ingredients she needed for the croquettes: two cans of salmon, two eggs, a bell pepper, a stalk of celery, a few small onions, cayenne pepper, garlic powder, Old Bay, cornmeal, and vegetable oil.

"I just am," Mary answered at last. "She sure had some nerve. Made me kinda mad. But nobody's perfect, son, nobody. Only God is perfect, I say to you. I'm praying each and every day that there's healing in the family and that someday you and her can be reconciled. Now I know I don't know the whole story, son. But whatever happened, happened. Neither one of you can take anything back."

"It got pretty intense, Mama. Among other things, Jennifer is overly controlling, thinks she knows what's best for me, and, contrary to what she says about herself, she doesn't listen, and she's not a very nice person. But more than that, I didn't like myself when I was around her. I never lied so much in my life, Mama."

"What do you mean? What did you lie about?"

"Seems like a lied about everything. Told her what she wanted to hear, told her things about myself that weren't true just to see what kind of reaction I'd get. Lying is never okay, under any circumstances. Yes, I suppose if this were the Underground Railroad and the slave catchers were at the door, it would be okay to lie. Or maybe if the cops were looking for me to take me down for a crime you know I didn't commit, it would be fine to say that you hadn't seen me in weeks. Lying to save someone you care for from a fatal injustice is probably okay. But other than that, lies are the source of evil. The bigger the lie, the bigger the evil. And the biggest lie of all is lying to yourself because you're too afraid to deal with who you really are. Jennifer is a liar, Mama. And I was lying right along with her. It made me sick. But I wanna heal, Mama. I will always hold a special place for her in my heart. She gave birth to me, after all. She will always be the woman who pushed me into the world. I don't despise her, and I wish her no harm, but if I never see her again—"

"Don't say that. How can you say that?"

"The same way I can say this. Can you please stop what you're doing for one second and look at me?" Mary finished chopping the celery and put it in the bowl with the seasoned flakes of salmon. She wiped her hands and turned to look at her son. "I'm not gonna wait until you get sick or something, or worse, die, before I say this to you. Mama, you're my mother. You've been there for me when I've needed you, you've given me great advice, and you've loved me without condition. Sure, I grew up, grew away, and became something more mysterious than the little boy who used to sit and watch soap operas with you all day. You're the only mother I've ever had, the only mother I'll ever have, and the only mother I've ever wanted.

But what's most special to me, Mama, is that through thick and thin, we have remained friends and our friendship has grown stronger. Thank you, Mama, for being my friend." Craig licked the salt from his upper lip. He rose from the table, walked over and kissed his mother on her forehead. They embraced. After they let go, he patted her, gently, on the top of her head like she was *his* child. She smiled and said, "Now go tell your sister and your father that we can eat in twenty minutes. The Brussels sprouts don't take that long do they?"

"No, Mama. Mama?" Mary didn't answer. "Mama."

"Then get on out of here and let me finish what I'm doing," said Mary, finally, her voice wavering.

Craig walked away but turned and peeked at Mary from behind the hallway wall before going outside. Mary hadn't cut the onions yet so the tears she wiped away with a napkin had to have come from somewhere else.

THE CHOSEN ONES

✍

1 "Okay, okay, Craig," says Gina, her voice brimming with enthusiasm. "I have to get this gumbo I'm making for Dennis just right." Dennis, a Milwaukee County sheriff who went to Rufus King High the same time as Craig, is Gina's new beau. Dennis has helped Craig's parents with so much, from taking Hazelle to and from the doctor who removed his cataracts, to helping them purchase a new (used) car without being robbed blind. Whenever they talk, Craig hears more passion in Gina's voice in the short time she's been seeing Dennis than he heard the entire time she struggled with her last man. Craig feels relieved that Gina has finally ended it with the head coach of the Portland Trailblazers, who jerked her around for too many years. Craig prays that Dennis will make Gina see that it's about time she tear down the citadel she has fortified at the entrance of her heart.

"Well, girl," Craig says, turning on his preacher's voice, "you gotsta get the roux right. You hear me talkin? The roux is the base, the bottom. It binds it, lifts it, gives the gumbo depth and body and character, can I get a amen? If you mess that up, you may as well *give* it up. Now, you got some folk so scared of burning the roux, they don't cook it long enough. But a undercooked roux'll ruin the gumbo quick as a burnt one. Who you know? C'mon. *Tell* me. I *saaaaid*-uh, who *you* know want gumbo thin as chicken soup? I'll tell you who: *nobody*. That's who." He turns down the flame under the rice and, like a man inhabited by Spirit, adds jumps and gestures to go along with the voice. "So git you a good old cast-iron skillet seasoned at least five hours. And when you cook that roux, cook it slow. I said, cook it slow, and don't stop the stirring. You hear what I'm telling you, people? Don't stop the stirring. Pull up a stool, keep a glass of ambrosia for yourself within reach and have a seat cuz you gotsta be patient. Cook it for an hour, if need be, but don't turn off that heat till that roux turns the color of an old, old penny and it smells like nuts toasting in the oven. If patience is a virtue, then gumbo is shaw nuff a virtuous dish. Can I get a amen? I *saaaaid*-uh, can I get a amen?"

Gina cackles. "Craig, you are too many things."

"But seriously though," he says, minus the performance, "don't mess up the roux, girl. I don't care how good the recipe is or how many different kinds of crustaceans or sausage you throw in—Don't. Mess up. The roux. Now let me get off this phone so I can get back to my own cooking. We got company coming over."

Darlin is in town for Memorial Day weekend, as he has been every Memorial Day since he left Boston for San Francisco. Darlin has remained an active member of a twelve-step program and he celebrates his anniversary with his home Boston meeting group every year. He also calls Boston home because Craig and Gail live here and no matter how much time passes, he still misses the time when the three of them lived together in their Cambridge apartment. Craig and Job arrange a last-minute backyard barbeque and invite Darlin, Gail, Tara, and Joseph, who, though he lives next door, has not come over to visit in months.

All of them come.

After the hamburgers, barbequed ribs, curried chicken kabobs, sweet potato salad, jambalaya, coleslaw, and greens dwindle in their serving containers, and when the mosquitoes (outlasting the Citronella-fueled torches that are supposed to repel them) become unbearable, the six humans move from the backyard terrace into the house. Craig serves the cheesecake in the mask room.

2 Almost all of them come from a kingdom of tribes in the heart of Africa. According to Ladislas Segy, whose book MASKS OF BLACK AFRICA sits on a shelf near the foot of the altar, the masks are figures, things done, created with direct, spontaneous gestures, containers containing energy, an essence beyond form, tangible and visible points of concentration for something sensed but unseen, toward which its creators, artists of the Bakuba people of Zaire, wanted to reach with fervor, beyond all known knowledge, till their faces met the stars. These artists, like all artists, function like magnifying glasses, reducing the complexities of the human spirit condition to their essence, and clarifying them. The masks—helmets, face coverings, headdresses, and crowns—assembled from carved wood or ivory, cloth, raffia, cowrie shells, beads, pieces of metal, vegetable fibers, teeth, and hair, with their repetitive patterns and features both animal and

human, are structures of expressive form, artful and authentic, and like all things authentic and artful, they were born in a style completely unaware of itself. For centuries, Africans all over the continent have worn them in rituals of abundance, agricultural festivities, funerary ceremonies, and ancestral devotions. The energy they contain is everlasting and ever-alive. You can feel it when you walk into the room. Whether or not you can hear them, they are always speaking to you, telling you something, asking you something, showing you something. Whether or not you can hear them, you will listen to what they tell, answer what they ask, see what they show.

Twelve of them hang from the walls or are suspended on the points of music-stand poles in a small sitting room in the heart of Job and Craig's home. The hand-carved wooden altar that stands amidst the trio of suspended masks is covered by small statues of African and Asian deities and warriors; an Aztec truth stick their friend and healer, Charlotte, gave them; photographs of deceased family members; two wine glasses filled with fresh water; hand-made candles; a purple heart made of crystal; a Tibetan incense holder where a stick of Indonesian incense burns; a small arrangement of cactus; a stone goblet, the common cup from which they drink sweet libation when they partake in their sacred communion; and their wedding basket, also from Charlotte, full of thoughts, prayers, and well-wishes that many of their wedding guests had written on cards during the ceremony and dropped inside as an offering for unity.

> **WHEREAS** we are of sound mind, body and spirit; and
> **WHEREAS** we have been living and loving together for nearly two years; and
> **WHEREAS** we have made, in the presence of our families, friends, ancestors and all that is holy, a public pronouncement of our intent to enter this union, we
>
> *Jacobus Dirk Blom & Craig Von Hickman*
>
> the undersigned, on this 22nd day of August 1998, as witnessed by those closest to us,
>
> **PROMISE** to have and to hold each other, in sickness and in health, in joy and in sorrow, in prosperity and in destitution, all the days of our lives on this earth. We further
>
> **PROMISE** to recognize this union as sacred and unbreakable and will, in times of trouble or weakness, turn to God and to all those who have witnessed this declaration to support us on our lifelong journey together

reads their DECLARATION OF LIFELONG COMMITMENT, situated between the Order of Service and their Wedding Song in the purple-and-gold-matted and framed triptych on the wall above the altar.

Before the altar, the six humans sit on chairs arranged in a circle in the center of the room. In the middle, a small cocktail table holds their beverages. The masks bear witness—unobtrusive but *present*.

"I'm gonna have to get up and slap you," Darlin says, getting up and slapping Craig playfully on the face. He fingers his long brown hair back behind his ear as he sits back down. "This cheesecake is too fierce, sister."

"I swear I just bit into a toenail," says Gail. Her dreadlocks are gathered on top of her head. She looks like a pineapple. "You put your foot all up in this." They all laugh. "What in heaven is in this crust, man?"

"I'll never tell," says Craig, still laughing. But then he does, whispering, "Molasses."

"I'm lactose intolerant, people," says Joseph, "I'm not even supposed to be eating any. I'll probably pay for it later, but right now, it's pure heaven."

"Heaven's cheesecake," says Tara. And then, as though stumbling upon enlightenment in some unexpected place, she says with conviction: "*That's* what heaven is: everlasting cheesecake."

"Which reminds me," says Gail, rising and walking into the kitchen. She returns with a bread plate on which she has placed a small slice of cheesecake and sets it on the altar. "Can't forget about the ancestors."

"Alright, now," Darlin says. "Let's keep the spirit moving up in here. Sister, *where* did you come up with this recipe?"

"I got it from Jennifer. She found it years ago on a box of graham cracker crumbs and modified it. I modified the modified."

"Yes," says Job, "and they sold a good many of them through their catering business."

"How is Jennifer anyway?"

By now, everyone knows what has happened except Darlin. There is silence while they wait for Craig's answer. After a few moments, Gail speaks first. "Craig, go on and get you a copy of that letter you wrote to Jennifer and let Darlin read it for the people. Better yet, let *me* read it." Craig rises and goes upstairs to his office to get the letter. When he returns he gives it to Gail, who reads it to the rapt audience.

"Well alright, now," Darlin exclaims when Gail finishes. "Sister, why did you have to crack her face like *that?*"

"Because she's pure evil," Tara blurts out.

"When did you know?" Job asks.

"I saw it as soon as she walked in the house," Tara says, vehemently. "She was pure evil. It was in her eyes. Ugly as sin."

"I saw it too," says Joseph.

"How could you not?" Tara continues, looking at Joseph. "You were here with us right in this room the night Craig and Job brought her back from Atlanta. She sure surprised the hell out of me. After dinner, Gail and I gave Craig that purple heart and a card. Gail was crying, Job was crying, Craig was crying, you were crying, and what was Jennifer doing? Looking at all of us like we were the ones with horns growing out of our heads. When we left out of here, I told Gail to keep her away from Craig."

"She sure did," Gail says, "but how was I supposed to do that?"

"Then, when we almost lost you," Tara says to Craig, "when you got meningitis and almost died, I told Gail that *that's* what I was afraid of. All that ugly-ass evil damn near killed you." She slumps back in her chair, grabbing the straps of her overalls with her thumbs.

"I always got my money on you," Gail says, turning to Craig. "You were the one who sought her out and brought her here. She thanked me for taking such good care of you while she was away, as if she had just gotten home from work and I was the baby-sitter. The tone of her voice was so dismissive. It was almost like she said, Thank you, but I'm here now, so you won't be needed anymore."

"I missed all of that," says Craig.

"Of course you did, and why wouldn't you? You weren't supposed to see it. Or hear it. You were supposed to experience everything that you experienced. As my mother used to say, you had to go on and see the end of it."

"I think that's why I invited her to live here," Job adds. "Although I have to say, the only thing I could see, especially in the beginning, was just how happy Craig was when he found her. Like something fell off his face and he was glowing."

"That's how he looked when yall got back," says Joseph.

"I thought they got to a point where they were going too fast," Job continues, "trying to get to know each other too fast, deal with too much, too fast. But I think deep inside, a part of me figured that as long as they were going so fast, they may as well get it over with, whatever it was, you know what I mean? Forget the long conversations over the phone every single day; I figured she may as well be here so they could do whatever they had to do to get to know each other and get it over with."

"Well, when I saw," says Joseph, "how she just came in here and took over, I was *too* through. I couldn't believe how she acted like the kitchen was hers, rearranging all the cupboards and whatnot. And then, when yall showed the video of when yall first met her down in Atlanta, I rolled my eyes to myself. I couldn't believe what I was watching. Craig was overflowing with emotion and Jennifer seemed so cold. I'm sure she was shocked and all, that her son just showed up on her doorstep totally out of the blue and all, thirty-three years after she put him up for adoption and all, but I still thought it was bizarre that she didn't shed a single tear. She immediately got on the phone and started calling her daughters and her mother before she spent any time with you." He looked at Craig so intensely, his big eyes seemed even bigger.

"That surprised me, too," says Job. "But how could I know how she was feeling?"

"Didn't look like she felt anything," Joseph continues, "as if her heart had turned to stone. But what really got me was one night not too long after she moved in, I was over and yall had gone to bed, and me and her were sitting in here talking. Jennifer always had some advice to give; no matter what you told her, she always offered her advice, whether you asked for it or not. I have to say, though, some of it was good. And so I felt like I could share with her how I was struggling with my break-up from Carlos, and how I felt so betrayed, and that I wasn't feeling particularly interested in putting my heart back on the line with another man, even though all yall and my other friends were telling me to get out there, date a little, have some fun. Well, she took my reticence as an opportunity to do a little proselytizing, and I was completely turned off."

"Proselytizing?"

"How so?"

"What you mean, child."

"Go on. Say it."

"You know I'm from a Jehovah's Witness background, so I'm an expert at sensing when I'm being worked, *okay*." Joseph leans back, stretches out his right arm and snaps an exclamation point in the center of the circle. "She suggested that perhaps God was sending me a sign of some kind, that since I was feeling so down on men, that just maybe He was trying to tell me that my lifestyle might not be the best thing for me."

"Are you kidding me?"

"Uh, uh, Joseph, why you telling that tale?"

"Evil bitch."

"Naw, child, no she didn't."

"Oh, yes she did. And I had to kinda sit back and make sure my face wasn't twisting up too much for her to see." He's performing now. "So I said, 'Well, you know, Craig is Craig and his lifestyle is no different from mine, and he's not gonna change, and him and Job got married right in front of this altar in their backyard four years ago and I was the emcee, thank you very much, and they seem destined to be together forever, so how are you gonna deal with that?' And she said, 'I'll just have to take that up with the Lord.' And that's when I knew. I knew exactly what that meant. Heard many a lady in my mother's church say the same kinda shit. My mother said it too. It meant that she was gonna pray day in and day out for me to go straight. I wouldn't be surprised if Jennifer was on her knees morning, noon, and night, Craig, right upstairs in your own house praying for the day you would renounce your homosexuality and get right with the Lord. I don't understand how a person who claims to accept you and says she loves you unconditionally can all the while be praying behind your back for you to change." His performance ends. He is subdued once again. His big eyes sparkle. "That's when I stopped coming over here, Craig. I just couldn't be around her anymore. It seemed to me like you were sensing something was off, too, so I left you alone. I wasn't gonna meddle. The situation was too delicate. But I'm with Gail. I was never worried about it. I knew at some point you would stop and say, 'Wait a minute. What am I doing?' What the *hell* is going on?' I knew you'd come around."

"And aren't we so glad you weren't gone too long!" says Gail.

"Right on."

"*Okay.*"

"I didn't wanna have to come over here and hurt nobody." Tara is dead serious. She rises. "Lemme get me another piece of cake. Anybody?" Nobody.

"I had no idea about any of this," says Darlin, regretfully. "So how is all of it for you now, sister? I remember me, you, and Gail were over in 351 Harvard Street, Apartment 2E looking through your papers and trying to figure out what her name was. When I first talked to her on the phone, her voice sounded like yours. To hear all of this now is astounding to me."

"It's hard, Darlin, but I believe it's for the best. It was hard to watch the terrified little girl whose hateful mother made her give away her baby, which is exactly who Jennifer remains. As hard as it's been for me, it's been just as hard, perhaps even harder in some ways, for my mother, whom Jennifer actually tried to blame for me loving men. But my mother's already past all of that. Now, she just wishes Jennifer and I would reconcile."

"How *are* your parents?"

"They're doing really well, thanks. My mother asks me about you from time to time. Gina's doing well, too. She finally found her a good man, and I hope he's for keeps. I spent some good quality time with them in Milwaukee last week, and after I told them what I decided, they all took it upon themselves to share similar sentiments with me about Jennifer," Craig says, looking at Joseph and Gail. Tara has returned, her wedge of cheesecake already near the crust. "I'm surprised no one bothered to say anything to me beforehand, though."

"How could we?" Gail says in a don't-be-foolish tone. "Craig, your people truly love you and have faith in you. And by your people, I mean Miss Mary, Mister Hazelle, and Gina. Shit, I feel like they're *my* people. I don't think any of us would've let anything get too far out of hand, but at the same time, we just had to step aside and let you take your journey. Despite my instincts or how I felt about her, I didn't *know* Jennifer. I wasn't gonna risk telling you something that might put a wedge between us. None of us know what it was like for you. You searched for Jennifer for five or six years, and when you found her, you were overjoyed. You had to see her for yourself. None of us could know what was going on with you except you." She pauses and looks at Job. "And maybe your husband."

"I only knew what he shared with me," says Job. "As it turns out, he kept quite a bit to himself, especially towards the last few months she was in our house."

"I bet he did. I bet he had to. But I'll say it again: I always got my money on you, Craig. I've *been* there with you, Craig. I've seen what you can handle."

Gail is right. She *has* been there with Craig. Seeing what he can handle. For a decade, in fact. She was there during the early years, when Craig married his art and launched his career in solo performance. There in the falling years, when three of his artistic mentors and three of his closest friends, two from AIDS and one from suicide so he wouldn't have to from AIDS, died—all that falling within sixth months. In the lean years, when his roommates where stealing from him, his agent was mishandling his affairs, and he had to file for bankruptcy just to keep a roof over his head. In the boy years, when all the men he dated acted all the time like frightened little boys and Craig couldn't be bothered. In the book years, when he felt so lonely he read the same book over and over so the characters he'd come to know would keep him company round midnight. She was there for the audition year, when Craig announced he was ready for a mate, *finally*, said he was going to "audition for a husband," and a month or so later Job showed up on the Internet. For the marriage year, when they married in their backyard right before the altar that sits in this room. And before this altar—four summers ago—after she signed their DECLARATION OF LIFELONG COMMITMENT, she stood, opened her journal to her poem, WHO DO LOVE, and read: "I heard your love wears high-draped pants with stripes that are really yellow, love wears high-draped pants with stripes that are really yellow, and like Billie's man, your love is fine and mellow…" She was there when Craig began walking on his journey to find his people, picking him up off the floor and holding him when it didn't look like he was going to get there. And she is right here, right now, seeing what he can handle.

"Craig, let's talk about family," Tara begins in her same serious tone. "Let me tell you something about family. Wait a minute. Allow me to put it"—she stands, sticks out her chest, and raises her voice—"*another* way: let me tell you about the difference between your *relatives* and your *family*. You can't choose your relatives, but you *can* choose your family. Why? Because your family is the people you connect with right here"—she cups her chest with her hands and pats it three times—"in your *heart*. It might include your relatives; it might not. How many distant relatives do we *all* have that we don't ever even think of?"

"*Too* many, child."

"Since I never think of em, I don't even know."

"Ain't that the truth."

"You better say that."

"But your family is *always* close because they live in your heart. You *choose* who lives in your heart and you think of them most of the time. And most of the time you're thinking about them, at the *same* time, they're thinking about you, too. Your mother, your father, your sister: they're your family, Craig. They chose you. You chose them. You continue to choose one another"—she opens her arms to the room—"and we're your family because we've chosen each other, you know what I'm talkin bout? We're choosing each other right now. Now *tell* me you know what I'm talkin bout."

"Alrighty now, don't start no *preaching* up in here, girl."

"Yes, yes, yeeaaaah!"

"Tell it!"

"You better *say* that!"

"Amen belongs right there!"

"Can I get a witness?"

Tara's sermon started right on time. Job rises and clears the dishes into the kitchen. For those who drink, he pours brandy or wine or pops open a beer. For those who don't, he refills coffee and boils more water for herbal tea.

"Time to get this party started." Darlin chooses a Kirk Franklin CD from the tower in the stereo closet that opens off the room behind him. He puts it in the player and turns the music up so loud, the bass so high, that the masks turn their faces round and round the poles on which they are suspended.

"We bout to get our groove on now," says Gail, clapping her hands just above her head and shaking her ass to the music. "C'mon, Craig. Gimme some." Craig closes his eyes, raises his arms, throws back his head, and rotates his waist. Gail pushes back on him. Their gyrations fuse. "Aaaaaah, yeah." Darlin joins them. Job falls in step behind him. Tara and Joseph slide the chairs into the dining room, push the table against the wall, and take their places. Now they all have room enough to *worship*. It's time. For church.

THICKER THAN BLOOD

✍

1 192 was tranquil. Full of spirits and magic and peace. Built in 1811, the two-story, post-and-beam cape with three bedrooms was one of the first farmhouses in Winthrop, a small town in a watery region of central Maine. Annabessacook Farm was named for the lake on which a piece of its forty acres bordered. According to local legend, Lake Annabessacook was named after a sea captain's mistress called Anna, who was the best cook around.

Even before Job and Craig stepped foot in 192, they knew it was theirs. When they pulled up to the farm, they were drawn like mallards to the pond behind the house. "We're actually gonna start outside," Craig told Sharon, the real estate agent with the voice of a kindergarten teacher.

"Go right ahead, I'll wait for you inside."

They went right ahead and sat down next to the pond on a bench made out of a carved tree trunk. From there, they surveyed the place and took in its splendor. On the left, tall cattails and pond reeds sprang up out of the water. White birches, crab apple trees, and flowering perennials lined its banks all around. To the right, a giant weeping willow stretched up, up and out, its branches bent down to the ground. Straight across, reflected in the pond, was the big red barn with the big white door. Job got up and ran beyond the pond, past the barn, into the small grove of apple trees, and back. "Let's make an offer," said Craig.

"But we haven't even seen the inside."

"Doesn't matter. Whatever we don't like inside, we can change. But this out here—I've never felt anything like it. Look at you—you can't even stop smiling. On your way back over here, I thought you were gonna start turning cartwheels."

They walked through the farmer's porch on the side of the house where Sharon had entered and finally went inside. The expansive country kitchen with open, mustard-colored cupboards featured a huge antique wood-burning cook stove. "This is *definitely* it," said Craig, eyeing the stove with wonder. On the front of it, he ran his fingers over the embossed lettering that spelled OUR MAINE. The kitchen opened to the first of two front parlors, which had a square-paneled drop ceiling and a fireplace with a wooden mantle and brick hearth. The second parlor, with its original wood paneling and three exposed tree-trunk beams stretching west to east above them, was just through a small foyer, the original front entrance to the house. A huge brick mantle, remarkably masoned, with a beehive oven, an alcove for storing wood, and a cast-iron woodstove inserted in its triangular hollow intensified the rustic feel of the room. A single solid slab of granite formed the hearth. "This is gonna be the mask room," said Job. Original pine boards at least a foot wide—the widest looked about two feet—covered both parlors' floors. The rustic parlor opened into a small birthing room, which had become an office. This room, which was also where—back in the day—the sick convalesced and bodies lay down to die, was wide awake. Craig could feel their energy, could hear their voices. "This house is haunted," he said to Job.

"You think?"

"Can't you feel it?"

"No."

"When we get here, you'll see. It's all good, though. It's all good. You'll see."

Right then the floor started to tremble. But the spirits weren't welcoming them into the house—yet. Across the meadow on the other side of the road, a long freight train was moving slowly down the track shaking 192 as it went by.

They walked back through the first parlor and the kitchen and through a French door on the northwest corner. The owners had turned the country porch—with its eight, six-over-six windows overlooking the riding ring—into a dining area for bed-and-breakfast guests.

Opposite the porch's French door, on the other side of the kitchen was a narrow staircase with thin but steep stairs. Upstairs, two of the three guest rooms had dormers wide enough to accommodate queen-sized beds. All of the rooms showcased painted pine floors and loud wallpaper. "This will have to go," said Job looking at the bold stripes and the horns of plenty stenciled around all the walls near the ceiling. Craig smiled when he saw the antique claw foot tub in the guest bathroom. It was painted gold. Sharon took them back downstairs, back through the kitchen, past the main side entrance, and into the back of the house where the owners lived. "This part was added in nineteen ninety-four," she said as she walked them through the living room. "This used to be the carriage house, but the current owners tore it off and built this."

"How big would you say the foundation is over here?" asked Job.

"Thirty by thirty. There's a lot of space."

On one side, the living room opened onto a short hallway that led to the bathroom with a shower and laundry; on the opposite, a master bedroom and recreation room. The master bedroom had a long bathroom with a huge green-and-white tiled shower, but no closet. The closet was behind the built-in entertainment center across the living room next to the bathroom hallway. The recreation room, which had a mural of the countryside painted on all four walls above dark-blue, waist-high wainscoting, opened onto a three-season porch that overlooked the pond. Craig thought the Crayola-colored landscape was so wrong for the room—for any room, mind you—that it was hard for him to keep his mouth shut. Somehow, he managed.

They climbed a staircase with two turns that led upstairs where three spacious bedrooms and another bathroom were situated. "All these walls are coming down," said Craig. He looked out one of the small windows on the back wall of one of the two rooms that overlooked the pond. "Job, c'mere. Quick." Job came. A large crane, which had just soared from beyond the trees behind the tree-trunk bench and circled round the pond, was wading in the water, bending for the tiny catfish that lived there. "After we tear down the walls, this is where we're gonna live," said Craig. "We'll put in huge picture windows and get a much better view of the pond. I bet that crane comes here everyday."

Forest-green carpeting covered the staircase and floors throughout the entire addition, except the bathrooms. "This might be the ugliest carpet I've ever seen," Job whispered so the realtor couldn't hear him.

"Sharon, do you know what's under this carpet?" asked Craig.

"Just plywood, I think."

"Besides being ugly, I have too many allergies to have carpeting," Craig whispered. "How about we rip this up and lay more wide pine floors?"

"Sounds good to me," said Job.

"It's gonna take a lot of work to get this the way we want it, but nothing in here has made me change my mind."

"So," said Sharon, walking toward the stairwell, "are you ready to see your lake?"

On their way, they walked through the big white door of their big red barn big enough for seven horses or other livestock. They walked down Henry Lane, their private road, past the two lakefront cottages and the two year-round houses, which had been built on single-acre plots siphoned from the farm twenty years earlier, to their wooded lot on the lake. They hiked along the trail through the trees. "Over there," said Sharon, pointing to part of the area bordering the brook that flowed into the lake, "wild raspberries and blueberries grow in season." A small sandy beach slid into the lake, which looked more like a wide river that stretched north to south out of view. A tire was attached to the end of a thick, knotted rope hanging from a tree that had grown out over the lake about twenty feet. Someone had nailed slats of wood up the trunk of the tree every foot or so for easy access to the rope. Craig visualized himself swinging on the tire and flying into the lake. South, down the lake to their right, too far for either one of them to swim to, a tree-covered island reached up out of the lake. As they took it all in, neither of them spoke.

When they got back to the house, Job and Craig made their offer. The next day, the deal was done.

Four weeks later, on October 11, 2002, Craig and Job moved from Boston to heaven. Since 1811, 192 had changed hands three times.

2

On March 11, 2003, Craig was grilling farm-raised lamb chops on the Viking in their newly renovated kitchen when his cell phone rang. "Craig, this is Craig Bailey."

"Oh, my word. To what do I owe this surprise?" Craig Bailey was a friend from Boston and Craig's primary photographer throughout his performing career. Craig hadn't seen or talked to him since he collected the pictures that Craig Bailey had taken of him, Jennifer, and Quincy during their visit for Job's graduation last May.

"Are you sitting down?"

"No, child. I'm up in my dream-come-true kitchen cooking up a storm. You know we moved to Maine."

"You need to sit down?"

"Craig, what is it?"

"Are you sitting down?"

"Just tell me, for heaven's sake. What's going on?"

"It's Thomas."

✍

Back in 1991, on his twenty-fourth birthday, Craig went to the Boston Center for the Arts to see the Pomo Afro Homos (Postmodern African-American Homosexuals) perform their acclaimed show FIERCE LOVE. The next day, Brian Freeman, one of the performance trio, conducted a writing and performance workshop. There, Craig met Jeffrey Armstead and Thomas

Grimes and the three of them became Brothers du Jour. They considered themselves a biblical trinity. Thomas, the father; Jeff, the son; Craig, the holy ghost.

Brothers du Jour wrote the choredrama THROUGH THE FIRE and burned up Boston, Cambridge, New York, Louisville, and a Kentucky state correctional facility. In 1993, Thomas urged Craig to do his own thing. "If you take the two monologues you wrote for THROUGH THE FIRE," Thomas opined, "and add a few other pieces, you've definitely got yourself a one-man show. As much as the critics praised your pieces in our show, it makes sense for you to expand them into a solo show. Brother, I wouldn't tell you this if it wasn't meant to be. None of these performance artists out there right now are baring body and soul the way you are, Craig. You've got something really special going on."

"But what about THROUGH THE FIRE? I didn't think we were done with that already. Or do you know something I don't?"

On February 24, 1994, Craig's show SKIN & ORNAMENTS debuted at the Institute of Contemporary Art in Boston to a standing ovation. The critics' raves followed.

On March 16, Jeff died. Alienated from his father, and his mother already gone, Jeff had Thomas and Craig, along with Robin and Lois, two of Jeff's spiritual sisters, to care for him during his last days. To be at his side round the clock, Thomas and Craig had to tell the hospital staff they were Jeff's brothers. Not a lie, for as Thomas often said, "Spirit is thicker than blood." During Jeff's last week, he allowed only his spiritual family to wash him, to administer his medication, to change his IV. After he spit out his last breath and smiled, Thomas and Craig rolled their brother into the morgue. They memorialized Jeff through poetry at his funeral and a few weeks later at a memorial service.

Over the next three years, together, Thomas and Craig, along with their friend Philip, would memorialize too many friends and mentors at World AIDS Day observances and community events around Boston. Thomas and Craig would talk often about co-writing another theater piece as Brothers du Jour, but without Jeff, they couldn't bring themselves to walk that talk. Instead, Craig would publish two of Thomas' books of poetry.

Their brotherhood was characterized by quality, not quantity. Thomas and Craig might not talk or see each other for months, but when they spoke, their three-, four-, and five-hour conversations—full of testifying and signifying and upright divining—were downright cathartic. As Lois would testify less than a week later, Craig also felt that Thomas could give him back the pieces of himself he'd forgotten.

In 1998, Thomas stood up as a person of honor at Craig and Job's wedding. In his mellifluous baritone, he read two selections about marriage during the service. "I don't have to worry about you anymore," he said to Craig, and to Job, "Welcome to the family, brother-in-law."

In August of 2002, a few months before he moved to heaven, Craig visited Thomas at his apartment in Boston's Lower Roxbury, a few blocks from Dudley Station. They discussed Thomas' new play, the benefits of leaving Boston versus staying, their families, Craig's recent, difficult decision. "Are you still not speaking to your birth mom?" Thomas was sitting in the living room in his favorite chair. Behind him, his cluttered office looked like that of a playwright in high demand. Posters from his produced plays and pictures of entire casts hung from every wall.

"Brother, I've already been raised," said Craig, facing Thomas from the couch. "She's so desperate to make up for lost time, she keeps forgetting that."

"When I first met her at your house, I could sense a heaviness all around her. Craig, I'm sure your choice was and still is very tough, but I'm also sure it's for the best. You know, I ran into her at Mass General Hospital a few months ago." Craig's face asked, What were you doing there? "Tina was there for some tests," Thomas continued, answering Craig's face. Craig didn't buy it. Thomas' face was thin; his jeans too big. Craig didn't question or interrupt. "As soon as I saw Jennifer, I remembered when you told me she'd gotten a job in food service over there. Sure enough when I got in the elevator and saw her standing next to one of those tall food carts, I recognized her immediately. She didn't recognize me so I just said, 'Jennifer, right? Aren't you Craig's mother?' She looked at me kind of puzzled. Finally she said, 'You're Joseph's friend, right?' And I said, 'I'm Craig's brother. We met at his house.' She seemed to remember me, but I'm not sure if she did. Brother, she didn't look good at all. That is one deeply unhappy woman. Her eyes are closed and her aura is dim. It's too bad."

"It's painful to see. Sure, she was suffocating and all of that. Lord knows, when I'm at my best, I can deal with suffocating people. But, Brother Father, when all was said and done, it hurt too much to watch her suffer so willingly."

"All she had to do," said Thomas, "was be still and listen and love you enough to learn how to forgive herself."

After Craig moved, he would call Thomas often and tell him all about his new house, his new life. About the chickens and goats and sheep and pigs and alpacas and white horses he would get. About the seedlings of thyme, coriander, mint, parsley, and much, much more germinating in peat moss on the breakfast porch. About Maine's enthralling beauty and idyllic settings. Its spellbinding light. He would call Thomas and tell him how much he wanted his brother to come up—for a weekend, a week, a lifetime—and get away from it all. But Craig always had to leave a message because Thomas wasn't picking up and he wasn't calling back. Craig knew Thomas could go underground, as Thomas would call it, for months at a time. When Thomas would come up from under, a call to Craig was one of the first he'd make.

Now, the man who shared his name was calling to tell Craig that Thomas Grimes, his beloved brother-father-friend, wasn't coming up again, that his twin sister, Tina, had found him in his bathtub this morning. Dead. Craig immediately thought of his friend who—back in 1994—took his own life so AIDS wouldn't and wondered if such a thing had come to pass again. Now, Craig knew why Thomas had been on his mind all day yesterday. Now, Craig knew why he woke up today with a neck so stiff and sore, he knew something in his universe was misaligned.

Craig hangs up the phone, turns off the stove and walks to his shore of the lake. There, he sits down, at last. In the wind rush and tree creek, Craig listens for the unmistakable sound of Thomas' voice. There. He hears it. No. Feels it. Cloaking his shoulders like a quilt. Craig looks toward the island, a dark mound of earth that sits, all alone, in the middle of icy water. His tears flow. He smiles.

The sun hung high in the sky-blue sky. The bright, bright light was more intense than it had been in weeks. The days were getting longer.

SWEET HOME

1 From the stereo, Ella serenades them through the wide-open, second-floor picture windows at the back of the house with her rendition of SPRING CAN REALLY HANG YOU UP THE MOST. Job and Craig are raking into piles all the brush from the perennial flowerbeds around the house and pond. They will burn it later tonight in a bonfire next to the pond. March is rapidly coming to a close and it's time to open the earth, to begin preparing it for this year's crop. "Do you think your parents will come this spring?"

"They said they wanted to, but I don't know if they'll be able to," Craig replies. "They're planning a vacation to New Orleans this fall."

This past Christmas, Craig's parents came to the farm to see their sons' new home. Mary and Hazelle took the twenty-four-hour Amtrak ride from Milwaukee to Boston, where Craig picked them up at South Station and drove them to Winthrop. A few days later, Gina flew in and Gail drove up from Boston. Craig and Job had completed the renovations in the kitchen and the guestrooms in time for Christmas, and the family enjoyed a quiet week together, warmed by the heat from the kitchen's antique wood-burning cook stove. Only once during the week did they venture out to Freeport, Maine, for some shopping at L.L. Bean. Mary wanted a non-traditional Christmas dinner. Gina suggested something Maine, something southern; Craig obliged. The vat of seafood gumbo, which took Craig three days to prepare—featuring Maine lobster and shrimp, as well as scallops, shrimp, oysters, chicken, and chorizo—disappeared in five hours.

Three weeks ago, right before Thomas died, Job's sister, Wilma, and her husband Frans traveled from Holland and visited the farm for six days. Craig was happy that someone from Job's family came to see their home.

Job and Wilma sat awake at the kitchen table talking about their family till all hours every night of her visit. Each morning they furrowed their brows at the three or four empty wine bottles on the table, swearing that the ghosts must've drunk all the wine because they certainly couldn't have. Wilma sensed a brooding unhappiness beneath Job's surface. Despite everything that had happened, he missed his mother terribly and wished his father were able to see his new life.

✍

Job carries a pile of straw to the copper cauldron next to the pond where Craig has just laid a pile. "Wilma can't stop talking about how much fun she had," says Job. "She can't wait to come back when the weather breaks and experience Maine without snow. She's still going on and on about what a great time she had when you drove her around to all the antique stores." Job sits down on the bench next to the pond and stares, wistfully, into the water. "I really wish Ma would come."

Oh, she'll come. It'll take a little over a year, but she'll come toward the middle of next April. By the time she comes, the pigs will've been slaughtered and one of the old white mares will've been buried behind the barn. When she comes, Wilma will come with her, not only to see Maine without snow, but also to see firsthand what happens while her mother is here. That way, Betsy won't be able to make up anything about her visit and spread the poison throughout the family in Holland. When she comes, Job will cry all night the first night of her visit because he didn't believe (nor did Craig) that she was ever going to be in their home, so afraid was she that Craig would "ruin" her visit again. But when she comes, Craig will cook for her, laugh with her, play cards with her. She'll laugh and take pictures when her daughter climbs, for the first time, on top of a horse—a big, white, sassy old mare, part Appaloosa, part Arabian—named Jesse. She'll sit and watch the pullets roam all over the barnyard each evening; the newborn twin goats, Thomas and Tina, play and climb and dart around their pasture. She'll laugh with Wilma as they watch Craig and Job run around trying to herd the eight Holsteins that have torn through the wired fence and run across the street, stopping what little traffic there is on the country road in front of the house. She'll tell them to plant silver lace vine for the giant bare trellis behind the garage. When she comes, she'll spend every waking hour with her son and they'll talk and cry and laugh and take long walks and pick out the constellations on clear nights and hold on to each other and tell each other the truth at last. When she sleeps, she'll sleep so deeply, snore so loudly, Craig will have to turn up the humidifier to drown out the sound of her satisfaction rising through the floorboards. She'll wake with the chickens and sit on the deck, quilting her beautiful quilts, eating thick slices of Craig's cheesecake for breakfast. For lunch. For dessert. When she returns to Holland, she'll talk about the trip for weeks and weeks, telling her other daughters, Els and Nelleke, what a good time she's had and that she hopes she'll be able to come back, again and again, and maybe—just maybe—bring them with her.

They've begun raking again. The weather is unseasonably warm and both of them are shirtless and sweating, their bodies smeared with dirt. Job takes a break, wipes his brow with the inside of his forearm, and lets out a deep sigh. "You were just getting ready to go in the house and get us drinks, weren't you, darling?" There's a laugh in his voice.

Craig smiles. "Yes, dear."

Craig drops the rake, tosses his work gloves on the ground, and steps out of his clogs before walking into the house. While he washes his hands, the phone rings. He considers letting it ring, but he dries his hands quickly, dashes across the kitchen, and answers it. "Annabessacook Farm."

"Is this Craig or Job?"

"This is Craig." He recognizes the voice straightaway.

"You know why they think you're behaving as you are?"

"Who is *they*, Unc, and how am I behaving as I am?"

"My sister, my brother, Crystal, Rwanda. All of them think that the abrupt way in which you have separated from the family is a manifestation of being bipolar. They think you're sick like me."

Craig laughs and then says, sarcastically, "As far as I'm concerned, everybody's bipolar. But the people who walk around with the weight of an official diagnosis, the insane, can't have legitimate reactions to situations without the so-called normal people dismissing them out of hand as being manic or depressed. If you're crazy, you don't *have* to be taken seriously. How convenient. The *normal* people don't have to look inside themselves to see the ways the co-author every single circumstance of their lives. Unc, I don't know if I'm bipolar or not, and frankly, I don't care. Makes no difference to me. I enjoy my emotions. *All* of them. I simply don't wanna be bothered with any of your people right now, and you know it."

"They're your people too."

"Being related to them isn't enough of a reason to have a relationship with them." Craig changes his tone to sound as though he's just answered the phone. "Well, hello to you, too. Long time. Good to hear your voice, Uncle James. How're you doing these days? Are you taking your heart and blood pressure medication?"

"Tamara's getting married."

Craig swallows. "Wow. Uncle James, that's wonderful. You thought you weren't gonna live long enough to see either of your daughters walk down the aisle."

"Well, I haven't yet. I still got four weeks to go." James cackles. Craig smiles when he hears his uncle laugh his shrill and infectious laugh. It *has* been a long time. Craig tries to remember the last time he spoke to his uncle but can't. His uncle's most recent stroke doesn't seem to have affected his speech as much as Craig had assumed. "How's Maine and how's your book coming along?"

"Maine is heavenly. Hope you can come and see for yourself someday. And the book's coming along just fine, thanks. Where's the wedding gonna be?"

"La Sierra University Seventh-Day Adventist Church in Riverside, California. Tamara actually wants me to give her away."

"That's beautiful. After all you two have been through, that's just beautiful, Unc. I can hardly believe it." The last and only time Craig saw Tamara and her father together was nearly two years ago at the Feast of Families. But they weren't really together. Tamara came with her new boyfriend, Stephen, the man she was about to marry. During the two days they were there, Uncle James spent more time talking to Stephen (as far as James knew, this was Tamara's first serious boyfriend), than to his youngest daughter. Before that weekend, Tamara hadn't spoken many words to her father since she was a child. She was unable to forgive him for the way he treated her mother before and shortly after their divorce.

"I'll call you back later and give you all the information," says James. He pauses. "That is, if you want it."

"Then I'll talk to you when you call back." Craig hangs up the phone, stares at nothing in particular, and shakes his head in disbelief. He wipes away his tears with the back of his hand. He carries the lemonade outside and hands a glass to Job who now sits on the farmer's porch. "Thanks, boo."

"You're welcome." Craig swallows a big gulp, smacks his lips. "Aaaah. What a gorgeous day."

A hummingbird fluttering around the birdhouse at the end of the walkway catches his eye. A blue jay swoops in and perches on a branch of the white birch growing near the birdhouse. It begins to eat from the nearby feeder. A predatory, domineering, aggressive, and greedy bird by nature, Craig is surprised when this one allows a goldfinch to share the sunflower seeds.

He swallows another big gulp. "So, honey," he begins, his voice tentative, "do you wanna go to California next month?"

THE WEDDING

1 April 23, 2003. Craig and Job arrive at the church early. Tamara, stunning in her silk white wedding gown, is being photographed on the front lawn. The sky is clear, the sun bright, the weather perfect. Craig and Job walk into the church, which is still empty except for the five people gathered near the back pew. "Well, well, praise the Lord. You made it after all," says England. She looks them both up and down as though making sure they are dressed appropriately.

"It's Joseph and Job, honey," says Aunt Crystal, whose dress is redder than blood, to Uncle Josh, who's sitting next to her reading the program. He stands to greet them, shakes both their hands, and sits back down.

"Good to see you, Craig, good to see you. And you, too, Job. You, too, Job," says Uncle James. "I didn't know you were coming. How come you didn't tell me, man?"

"He probably wanted to surprise you and if he told you, Lord knows you would've told everybody." Aunt Sonja is trying with a safety pin to adjust her husband's cummerbund, which is sliding down his waist. James's potbelly is gone, his face thinner, its natural angles more apparent.

"I wouldn't have missed this for the world, Unc."

Two years ago to this very day, Craig walked into their lives and already, it's been almost a year since he has seen any of them. During most of the drive from Los Angeles to Riverside, Job sang. "Honey," said Craig, briefly interrupting Job's singing, "I want you to know that all of this was only possible because of you."

"All of what?"

"All of this discovery and rebirth and healing that has come with the fulfillment of my lifelong dream. I found my people, and I couldn't have done it, wouldn't have had the courage to continue on the journey, without you by my side. Thank you for sharing your blessings."

"I love you," said Job. He reached over and took hold of Craig's hand.

"I adore you."

Job returned to his singing. As they got closer to Riverside, Craig began to brood. He wasn't sure how he would handle seeing them all again. Didn't know what he would say to anybody. Wasn't entirely sure he was making the right decision. But, no, he wouldn't have missed it for the world.

Jennifer walks through the door. "She needs to take that awful hat off her head," says England. "I don't know why she'd wear that loud dress with all them colors to a wedding."

"Happy anniversary, son." Jennifer hugs Craig. "I told Rwanda you were coming. I just knew it. She said, 'No *way*,' but I just knew, son, I just knew. Can you believe your cousin got married on our anniversary?" She reaches into her purse and pulls out a small phone book. She opens it to his page and holds it out to him, offering him a pen with her other hand. "Write your contact information down for me, will you?" Hesitant, Craig takes the book and pen and updates his whereabouts. "You know Rwanda is getting married." Her voice is almost a whisper now. She tucks the phone book back in her purse. Her French manicure looks fresh. "They're leaving from here tomorrow and going to Hawaii. Nobody knows, though, except for me and her sisters. I told you before, remember when I told you that she was definitely gonna marry him one day, son? I just knew it." Now Craig knows why Rwanda had been calling him so frequently over the last few months. He wishes he could be hearing this news firsthand from Rwanda. Why couldn't she let her daughter make her own announcement? "Your sisters will be here shortly," Jennifer continues. "You know how slow your sister, Burundi, is getting ready."

Tanzania walks in, holding baby Antoine in her arms, another baby in her belly. When she sees Craig she squeals, "Oh, my God, you're *here*." She gives him a one-armed hug.

Craig kisses Antoine on the forehead. "I thought you were all done with that," he says, eyeing his sister's stomach.

"This one was unexpected. It's gonna be another boy. He's due in August. I'm getting my tubes tied after this." After she greets and hugs Job, she tells Craig, "Soldier stayed home with Quincy. You should call your nephew sometime."

By now, the church is filling up with guests and Job and Craig meet his sisters' father, Ahmad, for the first time. Burundi and Zion also make their way inside just in time for the family of the bride to gather in the mother's room off the lobby. On their way through the lobby, Craig sees Rwanda run up the church stairs and through the door. When she sees Craig, she does a double take, screams, runs over, and throws her arms around him. Then, she covers her mouth with her hand, breaks down, and cries. The man from Milwaukee ushers her into the mother's room, where it takes her several minutes to compose herself and catch her breath. She doesn't let go Craig's hand. The family is stunned into silence by her reaction.

Aunt Brenda, the bride's mother, enters at last and breaks the spell. She instructs the family to line up for the processional. After the bride's "special aunts and uncles" have assembled, Jennifer arranges her brood behind her and Ahmed from oldest to youngest.

As the family walks into the church in pairs, an usher steps in front of Craig and Job. "This is just for the family of the bride," she says. "Are you a member of the family?"

"Look at my face and you tell me." The usher rolls her eyes, Craig rolls his, too, and he and Job continue a few paces behind Jennifer and Ahmad. Craig can feel the sneers in the eyes of some of the guests on both sides of the aisle as they walk by. Craig wishes he'd worn a gown instead of a tan linen suit. He walks, head held high, looking straight ahead and suppressing laughter.

Shortly after the family is seated, the bridesmaids, dazzling in form-fitting, canary-yellow, satin gowns, and the groomsmen, debonair in black tuxedoes, take way too long to process in pairs to their positions on either side of the altar. Rwanda can't let go Craig's hand. Excited and eager, she whispers to him about her upcoming nuptials, which she arranged entirely on the Internet. Craig feigns excitement, but he is not excited. She won't let go his hand. The air is perfumed with the yellow and purple roses adorning the steps in front of the altar and the candelabras on either side of it. Craig turns and makes faces at Antoine, who's bouncing on his mother's lap and gurgling. His sun-colored face breaks into a wide smile, his eyes gleam. Craig hopes for him the best. When Craig turns back, Tamara's sister Trisha, the maid of honor, and the best man finally take their places.

When Tamara and her father appear at the back of the church, the congregation rises. Often mistaken by onlookers as Jennifer's daughter, Tamara looks more like Craig than any of his sisters, except, perhaps, Tanzania. *You're my nephew, but you're more like a son.* Craig hears Uncle James' voice in his head. It almost seems like yesterday that Craig spoke to him on the phone for the first time. Now, two heart attacks and three strokes later, he is walking his youngest daughter down the aisle and into a new life. Sniffles can be heard all around. Rwanda squeezes Craig's hand. The reverend, who happens to be the groom's father, delivers a brief but poignant sermon and bestows the Lord's blessings upon the brand new union.

✍

The reception is held at Azure Hills SDA Church in Grand Terrace, California, a twenty-minute drive away. Jennifer invites herself into the backseat of Craig and Job's rental car and travels there with them.

"So, Joseph—I'm sorry, son, I mean, Craig—when are yall going back to Maine?"

"We leave from San Diego tomorrow. We've been there for most of the week on a much-needed mini vacation. We spent time with some of my friends from high school and college that I hadn't seen in years. The San Diego Zoo was fabulous. The last few nights, we were in Los Angeles where we visited Hollywood for the first time and tried not to do too much shopping on Rodeo Drive."

"And how are you doing, son?" she says to Job.

"Fine. Glad that all the renovations are finally finished."

"Yes, tell me all about the new house."

"It's a beautiful place. Five bedrooms, four for guests. It had seven when we bought it, but we made a master suite out of three of the rooms. Our bathroom is all marble. We put in a whirlpool, a steam room, and a sauna. The house is almost like two houses in one. We re-did almost one whole entire side and installed a gourmet kitchen in the oldest part of the house. It's finally ready to be our B&B."

"That sounds great, sons. I can't wait to see it."

Both of them let that fall.

"How far are you from Portland? And what made you pick Winthrop?"

"We're about an hour north of Portland, and we were both drawn to the house, even from the picture we saw of it on the Internet," says Craig. "Neither of us knew anything about Winthrop, but it's beautiful and perfectly located. We're not more than an hour from mountains or the coast and we're right in the middle of a chain of lakes."

"Sounds gorgeous. I'd love to see it."

There is another moment of silence.

"It sure was a nice wedding," says Craig, finally.

"Yes it was, son. Yes it was. And did you see Trisha?"

"Absolutely ravishing."

"Her makeup was flawless."

"Tamara made a beautiful bride, but I have to tell you, son, I don't think I've ever seen Trisha look so good before."

"How was Little Josh's wedding?" asks Craig. "We had to miss it last

December because my parents were visiting us in Maine for Christmas."

"Very nice, son. April made a beautiful bride, too. But the ceremony was absolutely gorgeous. You know April's pregnant and her baby is due in, guess what?—August, son. Her baby's due in August."

"Guess they didn't waste any time."

"Guess it runs in the family."

✍

At the reception, Jennifer introduces them to as many people as she can, although it's clear to Craig that everyone they meet already knows who they are. Gossip moves quicker in certain circles than in others and the Adventist circle is well greased.

Around the reception hall, on several of the many black faces, pursed lips and furrowed brows are added to the sneers from the ceremony, as Craig and Job fill their plates with bland food at the buffet. This time, Craig allows himself a good out-loud laugh. "What's so funny, honey?" asks Job.

"Everything. Everything is too funny."

Craig recognizes the couple he met back at Uncle James and Aunt Sonja's house in California. He also recognizes John Dixon, the best man from Uncle James' first wedding, whom he met in Salt Lake City. Craig introduces Job to Aunt Brenda and when she realizes who Job is, she gives him a long and welcoming hug. "Congratulations, Aunt Brenda," says Craig, hugging her next, "the wedding was absolutely gorgeous."

"I can't believe you got my invitation that fast. I just sent it a few days ago. I didn't have your address, but I got it from England, who got it from your mother."

"We've been on vacation all last week, so I didn't get it yet." They laughed. "But Unc gave me all the information a while ago and so here we are."

"Good to see you again, Craig. You go by Craig, now, right?" Craig nodded. "And awfully nice to meet you, Job. You have a safe trip home."

"What a genuinely sweet woman," Job whispers as they walk away. "Now I see why she's everybody's favorite aunt."

At the table where the family sits, Burundi, who sits next to England, looks like a replica of her grandmother. Neither of them can manage a smile and they seem to be looking down their noses all the time. In contrast, Zion's eyes always seem to be smiling. Which of their faces, over time, will rub off on the other? Or will his smile increase, her face harden, widening the chasm between them? Uncle Josh and Aunt Crystal are simply glowing. They've been in California on business for more than two weeks and the western sun has worked wonders. Rwanda holds on tight to the man from

Milwaukee, whose deep, expressionless eyes seem to be hiding something. Jennifer talks about her children's accomplishments to a woman she hasn't seen since Oakwood College, while her ex-husband, Ahmad, surveys the room. Earlier, he'd said he wished the punch was spiked. He sits with Chantelle, one of his daughters by another woman, on his lap. She is ten-years-old and looks like she's ready for a nap. Tanzania and Craig and Job are playing, nonstop, with Antoine, whose face can't beam any brighter. Aunt Sonja takes pictures of the maid of honor and the best man as they deliver their remarks from the stage where the wedding party and the parents of the bride and groom have finished their meals. Soon, she'll photograph the bride and groom cut the five-tiered cake with purple and yellow decorations.

And Uncle James cannot be still. He's talking and cackling and cackling and talking and moving from person to person, forgetting whom he told, "Be right back." He's the proud father of the beautiful daughter, Tamara Diane, who just got married. And he's hoping his oldest daughter, Trisha Denise, will fall in love with one of the handsome, single groomsmen right here, right now, so he has a chance to see both of his T.D.'s—his touchdowns—cross the goal line he's painted for them in his heart before he closes his eyes for good.

Winthrop, Maine
April 30, 2004

Appendix I

THE DOCUMENTS
OF HIS GENESIS

The Documents of His Genesis / 327

NOTE:
To be completed by ~rents and/or fa~~ies and worker.

CHILDREN'S SERVICE SOCIETY OF WISCONSIN

OCT 30 1967

Date August 31, 1967

MOTHER OF CHILD

Full Name ███████████ Maiden Name _____

Current Address ███████████ City ███████ State Wisconsin

Home Address ███████████ City ███████ State Wisconsin

Birth Date: Month ███ Day ███ Year 1949 Age: 18

Place of Birth ███████████ Religion Protestant

Occupation Student Employer _____ City _____

Height 5'7-3/4" Usual Weight 140 Build _____

Color: Hair Black & gray Eyes Brown Complexion Light Brown

General Health Good

Physical or Medical Problems None

Education: Highest Grade Completed 13 School ███████ College -

At What Age 17 Grade Average B

Additional Education or Training _____

Interests, Hobbies, Skills or Special Abilities Foods; I want to be a dietitian, sports, homemaking, reading, music

Marital Status Single Marriage: Date _____ Place _____

Divorce: Date _____ Place _____ Verified _____

Children: * Number _____ Ages _____

Paternity: Has court action been started? No In what County? --

Has alleged father admitted paternity in court? --

If yes, on what date? _____

Has there been a Private or Out of Court Settlement? No

Date _____ Terms of Settlement _____

Race: Mother Negro Father Negro

Due Date December 1967

* Describe in Comments Section

	Name	Address City, State	Physical Description				Occupation	Age	Special Abilities	Health * Factors	School Record	If Dead – Age & Cause of Death
			Ht.	Wt.	Eye Color	Hair Color	Complex- ion					
Father			5'9"	160	Brown	Gray-Black	Brown	Linotypist Compositor	44	Printer Youth wrkr	Good	3 yrs. college	
Mother		Same	5'7"	240	"	Black	Light Brown	Housewife	39	Youth wrkr Cook	Good	2 yrs. college	
Brothers & Sisters		Same	6'1"	180	Light Brown	"	Brown	Student	20	Chemistry Sports	Good	3 yrs. college	
		Same	5'4"	100	Brown	"	Light Brown	Student	14	Reading Sports	Good	8 yrs	
			Nationality – Race										
Paternal Grandfather			American Negro					Doctor	76	Civic leader	Good	M.D.	
Paternal Grandmother			498-20-7484					Printer		Civ. Leader		College Graduate	75 yrs. Heart Attack
Maternal Grandfather	MI		"					Minister	70		Good		
Maternal Grandmother	MS		489-20-9593					Matron	62	Cooking Sewing	Good	Grade School	

Remarks:

My father has slight asthma at times.

* Asthma, allergies, diabetes, tuberculosis, mental illness or other medical or hereditary problems.

CHILDREN'S SERVICE SOCIETY OF WISCONSIN

NOTE:
To be completed by parents and/or families and worker.

Joseph. Moore

Date August 31, 1967

FATHER OF CHILD

Full Name _____

Address (City) _____ (State) _____

Birth Date ___, 1947   Age 20

Religion Protestant   Marital Status _____

Occupation Student

Height 5'11"   Weight 160   Build Medium

Color: Hair Black   Eyes Brown   Complexion Light Brown

General Health Good

Physical or Medical Problems   --

Education: Highest Grade Completed 14   School _____ College

At What Age 20   Grade Average C

Additional Education or Training _____

Military: Branch of Service _____   Highest Rating or Rank Achieved _____

Interests, Hobbies and Skills or Special Abilities   Sports

Description of Personality   He gets along with people well.

Children: * Number _____   Ages _____

* Describe in Comments Section

Mother of Child _____

Relatives of Father of Child

| Name | Address City, State | Physical Description ||||| Occupation | Age | Special Abilities | Health* Factors | School Record | If Dead - Age & Cause of Death |
		Ht.	Wt.	Eye Color	Hair Color	Complex-ion						
Father 13 of 12	Dania, Florida	5'9"		Brown	Black	Brown	Minister	—				
Mother 9	"	5'2"		Brown	Black	Light Brown	Housewife	39				
Brothers & Sisters 12 of 13	"	5'5"		Brown	Black	Brown	Student	16				
	Nationality - Race											
Paternal Grandfather	American Negro											
Paternal Grandmother	"											
Maternal Grandfather	"											
Maternal Grandmother	"											

Remarks:

* Asthma, allergies, diabetes, tuberculosis, mental illness or other medical or hereditary problems.

Date 10-25-67

Remarks and Comments:

████ is an 18-year-old Negro girl whose family resides in ████. For the past 3 months ████ has lived in ████ where she has a small apartment in the upstairs of a family residence. Her living arrangements here were worked out by her mother who was most eager to have the girl away from ████ and in a setting where her pregnancy "could not possibly" become known to friends or acquaintances. On the whole, the living situation has worked out well for ████ in that she has made friends with her landlady, spends quite a little time in the latter's home babysitting and visiting.

In appearance, ████ is a fairly large girl, 5'7-3/4" in height and weighs 140 lbs. Since she is large-boned, she carries her weight well and thus gives the impression of being slender. She is a nice-looking young girl, has medium brown skin coloring (tending toward light), very good-quality of hair which is quite thick. Although ████ hair is black, it has a considerable amount of gray sprinkled through it -- not in clusters, but single hairs. Her eyes are brown and features Negroid. According to ████, there is not much variation of coloring in her family. Her mother is medium to light brown, while her father is medium brown (not dark). Siblings and relatives have coloring similar to her parents.

████ is a very pleasant, friendly girl, who tends to respond with warmth and who, when discussing some subjects, can show quite a bit of animation. In spite of this she, like her mother, has a controlling quality in her personality which comes out in little-girl coyness (particularly with her mother) or in direct and determined statements to the effect she does not choose to do this or that. ████ is an intelligent girl and less inhibited than one might expect because of her having been reared by so rigid and controlling a mother and her having been greatly protected by an aura of religion both at home and school. I think of ████ as having the X-factor in her personality, though she has not always used it to the best advantage.

████ family consists of her parents, herself and two brothers. Both parents have had some college training and paternal grandfather was an M.D. At present her older brother is attending medical school in ████ (I think ████). ████ has completed two years of college at Huntsville, Alabama, and was an honor student there. This is a sectarian college supported by the Latter Day Saints, and is inter-racial, although in ████ most of the students are Negro. ████ plans to re-enroll in college this coming semester, but is making application for transfer to a couple other Latter Day Saints' colleges in the west.

The AF is a 20-year-old Negro boy whom ████ met while attending ████ College. He is an only child whose father is in the ministry and whose parents live in ████. ████ did not know whether the AF's father had completed college, but was quite certain he had had some college training.

Indicate who furnished information to complete forms (Check)

Mother of baby x   Grandmother of baby ____
Father of baby ____   Other _____
                      (Specify Relationship)

Worker: ████

▮▮▮▮
P▮▮ory (Continued)

According to ▮▮▮▮, the AF is quite a lively, out-going person, one who is athletically inclined and who was quite popular on the campus. She described him as nice-looking, about 5'11" in height, and weighing about 160 pounds. Although his grade average was C, ▮▮▮▮ thought he could have done better had he studied a little harder. She went with this boy for several months, was very fond of him, but when she learned about her pregnancy, she broke off the relationship and did not tell the boy because her mother thought this best. ▮▮▮▮, too, did not want to risk information getting out because their church group throughout the country is quite a small and congregations in different states are closely linked.

TENTATIVE OUTLINE OF BIRTH REPORT

Name: Joseph Bernard   Agency: Children's Service Society
Foster Home: ▓▓▓   Social Worker: ▓▓▓

A. Mother
   I. Any complications during pregnancy   None
      a. Attempted abortion and type
  II. Behavior before delivery   Normal
 III. History and type of labor
      a. Period of gestation   42 weeks (full term)
      b. Duration of labor   12 hr. 52 min.
         1. First stage   12 hr.
         2. Second stage   50 min.
         3. Third stage   2 min.
      c. Type and description of delivery   obstetric delivery
         1. Presenting part   Head
      d. Type of anesthesia   Xylocaine 1%
  IV. Behavior during labor   Normal
   V. Summary of injuries or probably injury
       to mother and baby   None known
  VI. Laboratory results
      a. Urine
      b. Blood count   Hb. 14.7; Hematocrit 46 (Blood type
      c. V.D. Tests   Negative
      d. R.H. Factor   Positive
      e. Pap smear   Negative

B. Baby
    I. Date of birth   12-8-67
   II. Time   8:50 A.M.
  III. Weight   8 lb. 6 oz.
  IV. Length   22½"
   V. Type of cry   Good - spontaneous
      a. Resuscitation and time before
         spontaneous breathing
  VI. Color at birth
 VII. General condition   "Normal newborn"
         (Dr. C. R. ▓▓▓, Pediatrician
      a. Anomalies or injuries   None known
      b. Any feeding difficulties   None known
      c. Cord serology   Not given
VIII. Temperature   Normal
  IX. Formula   Given to worker at discharge
   X. Weight and condition at time of release   8 lbs. 7 oz.

12-14-67 Dr. ▓▓▓ okayed for guardianship by phone.

BIRTH HISTORY AND MEDICAL INFORMATION

BIRTH

Baby was born on December 8, 1967, in Madison, at 8:50 a.m. He was a full term baby, weighing 8 lbs. 6 oz. and was 22½ inches long. The presenting part was the head.

GROWTH

Date	Weight	Height
12-13-67	8 lbs. 7 oz.	22½ inches
1-26-68	11 lbs. 3 oz.	23½ inches
3-27-68	14 lbs.	24 inches
5-21-68	16 lbs. 8 oz.	26 inches
7-5-68	18 lbs. 1 oz.	28 inches
9-2-68	19 lbs. 7 oz.	28 3/4 inches
1-30-69	20 lbs. 1 oz.	31¼ inches
4-9-69	24 lbs.	31½ inches

ILLNESSES

Baby's health has been good with exception of having an ear infection in January 1969. He was given a shot and penicilin for this and it cleared up within a few days. Baby is bowlegged and was seen by an orthopedic regarding this. He was placed in a brace which he wore at night and remained in the brace from October 1, 1968 until January 31, 1969. He then was put in corrective shoes. The orthopedic felt that he will need to return to the brace but suggested he wear out his orthopedic shoes and then be seen again for an evaluation.

TESTS and INOCULATIONS

DPT - 3-27-68 - 5-21-68 - 7-5-68
STV - 3-27-68 - 5-21-68 - 7-5-68
Measles inoculations 1-30-69

DEVELOPMENT and PERSONALITY

Baby's physical and mental development and progress have been very good. He has always been a very strong baby and responsive. He smiled when a few weeks old. He began cooing and gurgling during the latter part of January 1968. He began walking at 10 months and is now climbing on to furniture, chairs, etc. He is very well coordinated in spite of being bowlegged. He is now beginning to develop a good vocabulary and is able to say about ten words. He has been off his bottle for about 8 months. Baby was placed on 2% milk on 5-21-68 and was put on all table foods on 9-2-68.

▇▇▇, Joseph Bernard

12-13-67 (▇▇▇▇▇▇▇▇)
Joseph Bernard▇▇▇▇ was born at ▇▇▇▇ General Hospital on 12-8-67. He was a full-term baby, weighed 8 lbs. 6 oz. at birth and was 22½ inches in length. His cry at birth was good, spontaneous; color not indicated; his general condition that of a "normal newborn". While in the hospital he was placed on Enfamil formula, at very well, and at time of discharge was taking a full four ounces every four hours. His weight at the time of discharge was 8 lbs. 7 oz.

On 12-13-67, Joseph was placed in the ▇▇▇▇ boarding home. He is a large baby, nicely filled out for his age, but neither the nurse, the boarding mother nor myself thought he seemed unusually long, as indicated by the birth measurement. Joseph, however, comes from a family wherein some members are quite large in both height and build. He is a very handsome Negro baby, with a nicely-shaped head, fair skin (no darker than some Caucasian infants) and even features. The latter do have some negroid characteristics in that his little nose is broad at the base and the lips are full. Baby's eyes are brown and his hair is black but of good texture. On the day of placement he slept quietly on the way to the boarding home but awakened when picked up by the boarding mother. He did not fuss, but yawned and stretched, seemed quite a relaxed infant.

▓▓▓, Joseph Bernard

as are also their married daughters who stop in frequently. Baby is accustomed to having other children in the home and to being taken out when the family goes shopping or to church.

I think Joey should be placed as soon as possible because of his rapid development and the liklihood he will progress faster than the average baby.

1-21-68 (▓▓▓▓▓▓▓▓)
Home visit.
Joey is an exceedingly attractive baby who, as the foster mother says, is so alert and advanced for his age it is difficult to remember he is only six weeks old. He is a fairly large baby, but not overly so; however, the bone structure in his little hands and feet indicate he may grow to be a sizeable person. His skin is medium light brown with bronze undertones, has a soft, velvety texture. His features are very even, his hair is black, fairly long, of good texture and prone to curl when damp. Joey has a nicely shaped head and the only unusual feature is that his ears, which are small and close to his head, seem to be low-set and have a smaller than average rim at the top. One would not notice the small rim, but the foster mother mentioned it to me saying that section of the ear is hard to wash. The foster mother also called my attention to the slightly protruding navel which she thought was probably caused by the cord's not having been cut short enough. (Baby has no indication of naval hernia).

Joey is a very bright and alert baby. For example, I held him through most of the visit, during which time he lay on my lap watching me and seeming to wait for attention. When I played with him he smiled readily and responded with squirming. Mrs. ▓▓▓ states that he began smiling at three weeks. As yet he does not coo, but does make the mouth movements. Physically, Joey is quite strong, likes to be held in a partial sitting position, has a firm finger grip and good strength in his leg muscles.

According to Mrs. ▓▓▓, the baby has presented no problems in care. He gave up his night feeding at 3 weeks and is now on a fairly regular 4-hour feeding schedule. The foster mother really follows demand feedings so baby has set his own schedule. He is a fairly wakeful baby but not fussy beyond the normal expectations for an infant of his age. Joey has not been seen by the doctor since placement, about 5 weeks, but there has been no need for special medical attention. Mrs. ▓▓▓ will arrange for a regular check-up within the coming week.

Both foster parents are giving the baby a great deal of affection and attention,

Joseph Bernard

Extra Copy

6-25-68

Since the last dictation on 1-21-68, Joe has been making excellent progress. Joe was seen by Dr. ▬ on 1-26-68 at which time he weighed 11 lbs. 3 oz. and was 23½ inches in length. On 3-27-68 he was seen by Dr. ▬ again at which time he weighed 14 lbs. and was 24 inches long. On this date he was given his first DPT and STV. On 3-27-68 Joe was placed on cereal and fruit. On 5-21-68 Joe was seen by Dr. ▬ again and weighed 16 lbs. 8 oz. and was 26 inches in length. He was given his second DPT and STV. On this date he was put on 2% milk and all foods. The doctor mentioned that Joe could be given table foods on this date.

Currently Joe is on baby foods, Junior foods and table foods. He drinks water from a glass but still has his milk from his bottle. He takes about 4 oz. of whole milk about four times a day. Joe is given cereal for breakfast, strained vegetables, meat and Junior fruit for lunch, and fruit soup or meat for dinner. Joe doesn't seem particularly fond of cereal.

Joe takes only one nap a day now from about 1:00 p.m. until 3:30 p.m. He retires for the night between 8:30 or 9:00 and sleeps until 8:00 or 8:30 a.m.

Joe is a very alert and exceedingly happy baby. He has been cooing and gurggling since the latter part of January and now is beginning to make sounds. For instance, he can now say "da-da". For several months Joe has been able to turn from his stomach to his back and vice versa. Currently he is able to get up on his feet and hands. He hasn't learned to crawl yet but has been getting up on his knees and hands for some time. He enjoys standing on his feet when helped by someone. Joe is able to sit unpropped for several minutes. During the day time Joe likes to sit in his teeter-babe or in his play-pen. When on the floor, Joe is able to wiggle so that he can move around quite easily even though he is not crawling yet.

Joe is a very responsive baby, smiles and laughs easily and enjoys people talking to him. At times he will goo and gurgle when alone. He is very good natured and likes to be cuddled.

Although Joe doesn't awaken at night he is more or less a restless sleeper as he moves around a great deal in his bed. He startles by loud noises but other than this shows no nervous mannerisms.

Joe is a very attractive baby. He has large brown, expressive eyes and is of a medium brown coloring. Everyone who sees him, falls in love with him because he is such an expressive, happy baby. His hair now is actually quite kinky with tight curls. The foster mother has cut it because it was getting long. He does have the Negroid features such as the flat nose, black curly hair and his lips are average in fullness for a Negro child. The foster mother has been taking Joe to their church with them on Sundays, and he is the baby

Joseph Bernard

that everyone wants to see each Sunday. Even the minister is proud of him and enjoys carrying him around the church.

Joe has been healthy and has had no health problems. He has one good stool a day. He is not a particularly good eater but he is making satisfactory weight gain.

Summary from 6-26-68 to 2-26-69 ()

During this time Joe has been making good progress. He began walking at 10 months and is now climbing onto the davenport, chairs etc. He is very well coordinated in spite of being bow-legged. Because of being bow-legged he was seen in October by an orthopedic and placed in a brace while in bed at night. Recently he was taken out of the brace and now is in corrective shoes. The orthopedic indicated perhaps if this did not correct Joe's feet he might have to go back to that brace again. The foster mother thinks that it is not correcting it and thus is anticipating Joe going back to the brace.

Joe's appetite has greatly increased during the past months. Prior to this, Joe was a very finicky eater and the foster mother was concerned about his eating habits. This was discussed with Dr. who decided Joe needed to be on some additional vitamins. The foster mother happens to sell a vitamin that she feels is excellent and thus asked Dr. if Joe could be put on this. Dr. looked at the ingredients and stated that this would be satisfactory. The vitamin is called "Luqui Lea". Joe is given a teaspoon of this a day. It is a vitamin with iron. Almost immediately after Joe was placed on this vitamin his appetite increased immeasurably. His daily eating habits are now about the following: For breakfast he has a half a bowl of mixed Gerber's Cereal a soft boiled egg, toast and whole milk. For lunch he has either soup or speghetti and some form of fruits. His favorite fruits are banana, apples and apple sauce. In the mid afternoon he is given a treat of usually orange juice. At night he has potatoes, meat and vegetables. He will eat any kind of meat that is soft and can be easily chewed. This includes meat loaf, liver sausage weeners, hamburgers etc. He enjoys carrots and peas if mashed. If the foster family have some vegetable that is not too digestable for a young child, like corn, etc. the foster mother gives him some of Gerber's Junior corn. Joe also likes to nibble on bread, butter and jelly, crackers and soda crackers. He eats some ice cream but he doesn't seem particularly interested in this. Joe is teething and at present has 7 teeth, 4 uppers and three lowers.

Joe's sleeping habits are about the following: He wakes up about 7:30 a.m. He naps from about 1:00 p.m. to 4:00 p.m. He then retires for the night about 8:30 p.m.

Joe plays well with other children. In his foster home there is a $3\frac{1}{2}$ yr. old foster child and a teenage foster daughter. Currently the foster mother is caring for her daughter's twins who are about 9 months old. Joe enjoys playing with the twins and with Kris the $3\frac{1}{2}$ yr. old. He enjoys mimicking Kris and follows him all over the house. Joe's favorite toy is a book, playing cards, trucks, blocks and balloons.

Joe's health has been good with the exception of having an ear infection in January. He had a shot for this and then given penicillin. It cleared up within a few days. During Joe's last physical exam. on 1-30-69, he weighed 20 lbs. 1 oz. and was $31\frac{1}{4}$ in. in length.

Joe is a very handsome child. He has very lovable mannerisms and everyone is automatically taken by him when seeing him. He does have tight curly hair which is very difficult to cut, according to the foster mother and is practically impossible to comb. His nose is broad but his complexion is quite fair and it looks as though he has just a real nice tan. The foster family is aware of the fact that Joe has seen no Negro people, and thus they purposely got involved in an exchange student last summer from ▨. This was a 15 yr. old, very dark blonde girl who visited them for a week. They mentioned that Joe actually looked white compared to this girl who visited. Joe did not seem startled by her and accepted her as anyone else. Thus we anticipate if Joe is placed with a Negro couple, there should not be many problems.

I have prepared Mrs. ▨ for the fact that possibly we might have an adoptive family for Joe. I felt her out about a visit by the adoptive parents to her home, and she felt this was preferable and she would be most happy to cooperate with the agency in any way possible. She Even mentioned that if the couple came before Mrs. ▨'s daughter returned from work to take care of the twins, she knew her daughter could take off work for a day in order to keep the twins home. The ▨'s do live in a large house with a large recreational area in the basement. Mrs. ▨ did mention that she could take the children in the basement recreational area so that the adoptive parents could have the run of the first floor. This is one home where I would feel comfortable in having adoptive parents. The ▨ are very warm people but not needful. They are anxious for Joe to be in his adoptive home as they realize he is getting older. Although the ▨ are very attached to Joe, they want the best for him and certainly are able to control their emotions.

I feel that Joe is ready for placement at this point. Prior to Christmas he was clinging to the foster mother and found it difficult to go to strangers. Since visiting him after Christmas, Joe is coming more readily to me, will sit on my lap etc. Mrs. ▨ mentioned he will go to other adults who come to the home now also.

Joe is beginning to develop a vocabulary. At present he is able to say, bow-wow, dada, mamma, bye-bye, and night-night. He waves his hand when people leave. I also forgot to mention that he has been off his bottle for about 8 months.

4-27-69 (▨)

Transfer Statement:
Joe was seen by his prospective adoptive parents for the first time on Saturday, 4-19-69. The adoptive parents immediately liked him, spent the morning visiting with him. Arrangements were made for the adoptive parents to visit him again on Saturday, take him to with them to their camper, and then to call for him on Sunday morning. Placement went extremely well, the ▨ had Joe prepared for the placement, and Joe laughed at all times, without crying, and went willingly with his new parents.

As Joe is with his new adoptive parents he will be transferred to ▨ at the ▨ Office.

CASE TRANSFERRED.

ASSESSMENT AND SOCIAL SERVICE PLAN - 900

JOSEPH B. ▓▓▓▓
b. 12/8/67

I. **Client Status**

   Child welfare.

II. **Client's Stated Need for Service**

   Adoptive planning, placement and post-placement services. Joseph was born on 12/8/67 to a ▓▓▓▓ County resident UM. The plan to release for adoption was decided upon by his mother prior to his birth. Joseph was placed in a pre-adoptive infant boarding home on 12/13/67 five days after birth. On 12/18/67, TPR hearing was held in ▓▓▓ County Juvenile Court. Judge ▓▓▓▓▓▓▓, presideing and Joseph was placed in the adoptive home of Hazelle and Minnie Hickman on 4/27/70. 69

III. **Health**

   A. Joseph has been in good health since birth. There was a minor orthopedic difficulty initially which has since been corrected by the use of special footwear. Dr. ▓▓▓▓▓, pediatrician, has examined Joseph regularly and verified his present health status.

   B. Joseph's health has caused no concern on the part of his pre-adoptive or his adoptive parents, except for the minor problem mentioned above.

   C. Dr. ▓▓▓ is seeing Joseph once a year since he is now over 18 months of age. He has had all of his regular immunizations and boosters.

IV. **Finances**

   Since Joseph is in an adoptive home, we do not anticipate current or future financial needs either for direct maintenance or ongoing medical expenses.

V. **Living Situations**

   Joseph is a member of the Hickman adoptive family. He has had excellent care in this well kept home. His parents have stimulated him and his development bothe physical and mental has been excellent. He has related well to other relatives and friends of the family.

VI. **Social and Personal Adjustment**

   Joseph has always been a bright, alert happy child. He was ready for adoption when we placed him and adjustment went well in his new adoptive family.

Joseph ▓▓▓ * Continued

VII. Offer of Service

Joseph's mother, a college student, asked adoptive placement services from the agency before his birth and was happy that we would have an adoptive home for him. We believe that this is a good adoptive placement and that this home offers this child an opportunity to develope further. His needs have been and are more than adequately being met by his adoptive parents.

VIII. Impressions and Recommendations.

We believe that the adoptive placement was carried out so well because the very careful pre-placement and post natal planning was of the highest caliber. We feel that decision to place Joseph in adoption was sound and well planned. He has thrived in his adoptive home and that his adoptive parents have been able to meet his physical and emotional needs.

IX. Social Service Plan Development

Children's Service Society of Wisconsin will continue to provide post placement adoptive services for Joseph and the Hickman family and work with them towards furthering his adjustment in this home prior to legal adoption.

X. Appeal Process

We are aware of the details of the appeal procedures.

XI. Fees

None

(10.21.70) ▓▓▓▓

STATE OF WISCONSIN   JUVENILE COURT   ▇▇▇ COUNTY
— — — — — — — — — — — x

Matter of the Termination :
of Parental Rights to
                        :
   JOSEPH BERNARD ▇▇▇,
                        :
a Minor.
                        :
— — — — — — — — — — — x

                 ▇▇▇, Wisconsin, December 18, 1967.

BEFORE: Hon. ▇▇▇, Juvenile Court Judge.

APPEARANCES: ▇▇▇, mother of Joseph Bernard ▇▇▇.

             Mrs. ▇▇▇, mother of ▇▇▇.

             Mr. ▇▇▇, brother of ▇▇▇.

             Miss ▇▇▇, Social Worker, Children's Service Society of Wisconsin.

             Attorney ▇▇▇, guardian ad litem for ▇▇▇.

PROCEEDINGS: A hearing commenced at ▇▇▇ a.m. on a Petition for Termination of Parental Rights, signed ▇▇▇ and dated December 18, 1967.

    THE COURT: Then, this is a proceeding in the ▇▇▇ County Juvenile Court in the matter of the termination of parental rights to Joseph Bernard ▇▇▇.

    And I would now ask that Miss ▇▇▇ and Miss ▇▇▇ please raise their right hands to be sworn.

having been first duly sworn to tell the truth, the whole truth, and nothing but the truth, testified as follows:

EXAMINATION BY THE COURT:

Q   And, Miss ▒▒▒, will you just state your full name for the record please, ma'am?

A   ▒▒▒▒▒▒▒▒▒▒▒▒.

Q   And where do you live, Miss ▒▒▒▒?

A   ▒▒▒▒▒▒▒▒▒▒▒▒▒▒▒▒▒▒, Wisconsin.

Q   Thank you. And how old are you, please?

A   Eighteen.

Q   And, Miss ▒▒▒▒, was there a child born to you on December 8, 1967?

A   Yes.

Q   And is that the child that is designated in your petition as Joseph Bernard ▒▒▒▒?

A   Yes.

Q   And will you tell me where this child was born?

A   ▒▒▒▒▒ General Hospital.

Q   And at the time of the birth of this child were you married?

A   No.

Q   And had you ever been married before that time or since that time?

A   No.

Q   Now, in your petition you state that you are requesting the Court to terminate your parental rights to this child because you feel this would be in the best interest of the child. Is this a fair statement of your feelings?

A   Yes.

Q   Do you understand that you being under 21, that the law provides that the Court appoint an attorney to be your guardian ad litem or legal representative in this proceeding?

A   Yes.

Q   And do you understand that Attorney ▓▓▓ has been so appointed?

A   Yes.

Q   And have you had an opportunity to counsel with Mr. ▓▓▓ this morning?

A   Yes.

THE COURT: Mr. ▓▓▓, I would hand to you from this file two documents, one entitled Waiver of Notice, and one entitled Parental Consent so you could have Miss ▓▓▓ testify as to whether those documents have been explained to her by you, and whether she understands them, and whether she has signed them of her own free will.

MR. ▓▓▓: Thank you, your Honor.

▓▓▓, I am showing you what is entitled Waiver of Notice. And as I explained to you under the law you are entitled to 10-day's notice of this proceeding, is that correct?

4

A Yes.

    MR. ▆▆▆: And I also explained to you that you could waive this 10-day notice so we could go ahead and proceed today?

A Yes.

    MR. ▆▆▆: This document bears a signature. Is that your signature?

A Yes.

    MR. ▆▆▆: And did you sign that freely and voluntarily?

A Yes.

    MR. ▆▆▆: The next document that I will show you is entitled Parental Consent to Termination of Parental Rights, Approval of Guardian ad litem. Now, I discussed this document with you, didn't I?

A Yes.

    MR. ▆▆▆: And I explained to you that based upon your petition to the Court and upon this consent that the Judge could enter an order terminating your rights to the baby?

A Yes.

    MR. ▆▆▆: I explained to you this would be a permanent thing?

A Yes.

    MR. ▆▆▆: It is not something that could be changed in the future. And you understand further, don't you, that the child could be adopted by somebody else?

A Yes.

    MR. ███: And did you sign this freely and voluntarily?

A Yes.

    MR. ███: Is anybody making you sign any of these papers today, or go through this proceeding?

A No.

    MR. ███: All right. And then there is a signature on that document, is that yours?

A Yes.

    THE COURT: Thank you, Mr. ███. Then, if you would make such other report as you feel appropriate as guardian ad litem.

    MR. ███: Your Honor, I have conferred with Miss ███ and also with her mother, who is present in court today. I explained the proceeding involved in termination of parental rights. And we also chatted briefly about adoption.

    I feel it is in the best interest of ███ as well as in the best interest of the baby boy that the Court enter an order terminating her parental rights.

    I feel that ███ is fully aware of the consequen of her actin petitioning the court, in signing the consent. She understands what she is doing. She is doing so freely and voluntarily.

6

I would recommend to the Court that the Court enter an order of termination.

THE COURT: Thank you very much, Mr. ██████.

And, Miss ██████, the petiton states that the infant resides with foster parents in ██████ County and has resided there continuously since December 14, 1967, would this be correct?

MISS ██████: That's correct.

THE COURT: And, if the Court should terminate the parental rights of the mother, would the Children's Service Society of Wisconsin be willing to accept the guardianship of this child?

MISS ██████: Yes, we would.

THE COURT: And you have had an opportunity to counsel with Miss ██████?

MISS GATES: Yes, I have.

THE COURT: Do you know of anything additional that should be called to the Court's attention?

MISS ██████: No.

THE COURT: Miss ██████, I understand that you would prefer to have this child placed in a Protestant foster home?

A Yes.

Q But that you do not make that as a binding provision in that you desire the agency to have some flexibility to find the best home for this child, is that correct?

7

A Yes.

Q Would that be a fair statement of your feelings?

A Yes.

Q And now that you are in court, Miss ▆▆▆, is it still your request that your rights to this child be terminated?

A Yes.

Q And do you have any questions at all about this proceeding?

A No.

THE COURT: Then, the Court finds:

That the minor, Joseph Bernard ▆▆▆, was born on December the 8th, 1967, and is illegitimate.

That the mother of said child is ▆▆▆▆▆▆▆ ▆▆▆, age 18, residing at ▆▆▆▆▆▆▆▆▆▆▆▆▆▆▆▆, ▆▆▆ County, Wisconsin, and she prefers to have the child placed in a Protestant home.

That said minor resides with foster parents in ▆▆▆ County and has resided there continuously since December 14, 1967.

That legal settlement of said minor is in State-at-large.

That grounds exist for termination of parental rights to said child in that the parent has given written consent to the termination of her parental rights because she feels it is in the best interest of the child; and has restated such consent in open court, and this consent has been concurred in, in writing, by her guardian ad litem, Attorney ▓▓▓▓▓▓

    Therefore, it is ordered:

    That all rights of the parent, ▓▓▓▓▓▓▓▓▓▓, to said child are terminated.

    That Children's Service Society of Wisconsin is appointed guardian of said child.

    That a certified copy of this order, a certified copy of the birth certificate of the minor, and a transcript of the testimony in the termination of parental rights hearing be given to the agency appointed guardian.

    And this order is dated December 18, 1967, and effective as of this time.

    That completes the order, Mr. ▓▓▓▓▓, and we are off the record.

    (Thereupon at 9:39 a.m. proceeding ended)

STATE OF WISCONSIN)
) ss.
COUNTY OF ▓▓▓)

    I, ▓▓▓▓▓▓▓▓▓▓, Phonographic Reporter for the ▓▓▓ County Juvenile Court, duly qualified and appointed, hereby certify that the foregoing proceedings were had in the ▓▓▓ County Juvenile Court wherein the matter of the termination of parental rights to Joseph Bernard ▓▓▓, minor, was heard, and all thereof, and is accurately transcribed from my notes.

    Dated January 25, 1968.

Juvenile Court Reporter

Appendix II

THE LAMENTATIONS OF CRAIG

How deserted lies the city, once so full of people!

　　　　　　　　—LAMENTATIONS 1:1

There was no excuse, in this country and in this time, for the spread of a deadly new epidemic.... By the time America paid attention to the disease, it was too late to do anything about it. The virus was already pandemic in the nation, having spread to every corner of the North American continent. The tide of death that would later sweep America could, perhaps, be slowed, but it could not be stopped.

　　　　　　　　—Randy Shilts
　　　　　　　AND THE BAND PLAYED ON

It was poisonous, unnatural to let the dead go with a mere whimpering, a slight murmur, a rose bouquet of good taste. Good taste was out of place in the company of death, death itself was the essence of bad taste. And there must be much rage and saliva in its presence. The body must move and throw itself about, the eyes must roll, the hands should have no peace, and the throat should release all the yearning, despair and outrage that accompany the stupidity of loss.

　　　　　　　　—Toni Morrison
　　　　　　　　SULA

1 James Baldwin, author, holy roller preacher, civil rights activist, and one of the best and most prolific writers about race in America, died on November 30, 1987 in Saint-Paul-de-Vence, France. He was 65.

James Baldwin was born in Harlem on August 2, 1924 to Emma Berdis Jones. His father was unknown, so he took the name of his mother's husband, David Baldwin.

James is best known for his books *The Fire Next Time, Giovanni's Room,* and *Notes of a Native Son.* Like an Old Testament prophet, James carried a message for all, whatever their religion, class, color, or affectional preference. James exiled himself in Europe in his later years and earned himself a 1,700-page FBI file as a suspected communist.

His funeral on December 8, 1987 at New York's Cathedral of St. John the Divine was such a major event, several thousand people attended and Toni Morrison, Maya Angelou and Amiri Baraka gave tributes.

James was mourned all over the world as one of the leading literary figures since World War II.

2 Joseph Fairchild Beam of Philadelphia died on December 27, 1988 due to complications arising from AIDS.

Editor of *In the Life* and the conceiver *of Brother to Brother: New Writings by Black Gay Men,* Joseph began collecting material for *In the Life* after years of frustration with gay literature that had no message for—and little mention of—black gay men. "The bottom line," he wrote, "is this: We are black men who are proudly gay. What we offer is our lives, our love, our visions.... We are coming home with our heads held up high.

After his death, Essex Hemphill picked up the torch and edited *Brother to Brother* with the help and love of Dorothy and Sun Beam, Joseph's parents.

3 Seldon Roy Totsch of Milwaukee, Wisconsin, died on May 14, 1992 due to complications arising from AIDS. He was 40.

4 Melvin Dixon of Stamford, Connecticut, noted gay black author, died on October 26, 1992 due to complications from AIDS. He was 42.

Author of the novels *Red Leaves, Trouble the Water,* and *Vanishing Rooms,* and a volume of poetry, *Change of Territory,* his work appeared in several gay anthologies including *Men on Men2: Best New Gay Fiction; Poets for Life: 76 Poets Respond to AIDS;* and *In the Life.*

He translated *The Collected Poems of Leopold Sedar Senghor,* and received fellowships in poetry and fiction from the National Endowment for the Arts and the New York Arts Foundation.

5 Roy Gonsalves of Boston, Massachusetts, died on July 10, 1993 due to complications arising from AIDS. He was 43.

Roy graduated from English High School and furthered his education at Emerson College. He was a teacher in both the Boston and New York Public Schools.

Roy was also a writer, visual artist, and therapist, and a literary performing artist. Roy's book of three stories and poems, *Perversion*, was published in 1990. It was nominated for the 1991 Gregory Kolovakos Award for AIDS. His other writings and performances have been featured on cable television.

Roy was the recipient of the Bessie Smith Award for Creativity, presented by The Greater Boston Lesbian and Gay Political Alliance.

6 Roberto Colon of Boston, Massachusetts, died at Brigham and Women's Hospital on March 26, 1994 after intentionally ingesting antifreeze. He was 33.

7 Marlon Riggs, professor and filmmaker who won Emmy and Peabody awards for his documentaries on blacks and gays, died of AIDS on April 5, 1994 in Oakland, California. He was 37.

In 1992, presidential candidate Pat Buchanan used a snippet from Marlon's *Tongues Untied*, a documentary about black gay men, as an example of the type of art that conservatives said the government should not fund.

The Buchanan campaign ad accused President George Bush of allowing taxpayer financing of "pornographic and blasphemous art" through the National Endowment for the Arts.

Marlon began making documentaries in 1982 after receiving his master's degree from University of California at Berkeley's journalism school. He later became one of the university's youngest tenured professors.

Riggs' Emmy-winning *Ethnic Notions* and *Color Adjustment*, which won a Peabody, traced the media portrayal of blacks through U.S. history.

Marlon is survived by his family and a large circle of friends.

8 Jeffrey William Armstead, actor, playwright and performing artist, departed this life on May 16, 1994 due to complications arising from AIDS. He was 32.

Born in Boston, Jeffrey was a graduate of English High School and continued his studies at Xavier University in New Orleans. Jeffrey trained theatrically at the Elma Lewis School of Fine Arts under the tutelage of the late Vernon Blackman. A member of the performing arts troupe, Brothers du Jour, Jeff co-wrote and performed in the acclaimed choreodrama *Through the Fire*.

Loved greatly for his sense of humor and wit, Jeffrey is mostly remembered for his ability to make people laugh and assist wherever he found a need. Jeffrey volunteered at the AIDS Action Committee and was associated with the Urban Jesuit Center. In 1993, Jeff was the recipient of a community service award from Christians About AIDS Prevention Education in Louisville, KY.

9 Yves Francois Lubin, also known as Assotto Saint, noted black gay writer, died on June 24, 1994 in New York City from complications arising from AIDS. He was 36.

Founder of Galiens Press, Assotto was the editor of two seminal anthologies of gay black writing: 1991 Lambda Literary Book Award winner, *The Road Before Us: 100 Gay Black Poets* and *Here to Dare: 10 Gay Black Poets*. He was also the author of *Stations*, a book of poetry and such plays as *Risin' to the Love We Need*, *New Love Song*,

Black Fag, and *Nuclear Lovers.*

In 1990, he was both the recipient of a Fellowship in Poetry from the New York Foundation for the Arts and the James Baldwin Award from the Black Gay & Lesbian Leadership forum. Born in Haiti, he lived in New York City with Jan Urban Holmgrem, his life partner and co-founder of Metamorphosis Theater and the art-rock band, Xotika.

10 William Vance Deare of Boston, Massachusetts, died on August 7, 1994 from complications arising from AIDS. He was 41.

William, commonly known as Vance, attended Boston schools. In 1975, Vance graduated from Boston Technical High School and continued his formal education at Tufts University in Boston, graduating with a Bachelor of Science degree.

After travel in Europe, Vance returned to the States, where early on he exhibited a natural talent for marketing, public relations, and producing special events for the entertainment of others. After a successful engagement promoting cultural development and arts in education with the Cultural Education Collaborative in Boston, Vance was recruited to New York to promote and market the New York Philharmonic & Queens Symphony Orchestras.

Vance co-owned Crowd Pleasers, Inc. in New York. Following the untimely death of his business partner, Rodney Thompson, Vance returned to Boston in 1992 to become a senior partner of New Image Associates.

In continuing his commitment to community service, Vance served on committees to produce annual community based events for the AIDS Action Committee, the Bayard Rustin Breakfast, and Men of Color Against AIDS (MOCAA).

11 Steven Corbin, noted gay black writer and ACT UP member, died August 3, 1995 in his native New York City from complications arising from AIDS. He was 41.

Steven was the keynote speaker for the AIDS Action Committee's fourth annual Bayard Rustin Breakfast in 1993. His evoking speech at that time "challenged us to go beyond the red ribbons." He played a major role in re-shaping people's attitudes and their roles in the fight against AIDS. Steven was also a vocal spokesperson in what he perceived to be exclusionary policies in the gay publishing world that kept gay writers from being cultivated.

In 1993, Steven wrote *Fragments That Remain,* the story of an embattled African-American family and its eldest son's interracial gay love affair. His novel *A Hundred Days From Now,* which tells the story of two lovers dealing with AIDS, came out just as Corbin was nominated for a Lambda Literary Award in the category of gay male fiction.

12 Essex Charles Hemphill, a poet and performance artist whose work focused on life as a black gay man, died on November 4, 1995 at the University of Pennsylvania Hospital in Philadelphia. He was 38. The cause was complications arising from AIDS, said Wayson R. Jones, a close friend.

Essex was born in Chicago and grew up in Washington, D.C. He attended the

University of Maryland.

His poetry was published in more than a dozen periodicals and several anthologies. He edited the groundbreaking black gay anthology *Brother to Brother: New Writings by Black Gay Men*, and is the author of the critically acclaimed *Ceremonies*. Of this work, Marlon Riggs said, "Astounding. No voice speaks with more eloquent, insightful, thought provoking clarity about contemporary black gay life in America than that of Essex Hemphill. He offers inspiring testament to all who confront the persecution of difference in life, and find the will and nobility to overcome it."

Essex appeared in Marlon's films, including *Tongues Untied* and *Black Is ... Black Ain't*, in which he recited what Stephen Holden of the *New York Times* described as "spare, intense verses that affirm both his black and gay identities."

Producers included Essex in the "Culture Wars" episode of *The Question of Equality*, broadcast on PBS as a four-part television series.

13

Thomas A. Grimes, playwright, poet, actor, poet, performance artist, and director departed this life on Tuesday, March 11, 2003. He was 45.

"Growing up Black and gay/ In a racist, homophobic society/ Nobody ever said it was gonna be easy./ I've had my share of heartaches, heartbreaks/ My share of being stood up and let down /But I have survived./ I've been abused, misused/ Unappreciated and sometimes/ Simply tolerated/ But I have survived./ I've been invisible, silenced/ Laughed at and scorned/ But I have survived./ I've been tried in the fire/ And I'm comin out pure/ Like black gold." These were the words Thomas penned in 1992, which began the poem that became the title piece of the critically acclaimed choreodrama *Through the Fire*, performed by Brothers du Jour, featuring the late Jeff Armstead, Craig Hickman and himself. With *Through the Fire*, Thomas became the father of black gay and lesbian theater in Boston, paving the way for and inspiring many other gay and lesbian artists of color to share their voices with local and national audiences.

Born in Syracuse, New York, April 29, 1957 at Memorial Hospital along with his twin sister, Tina Marie, Thomas went on to graduate in 1975 from Syracuse Central Technical High School and attended Syracuse University and Westbury College in New York.

At the age of 8, Thomas began writing poetry and writing and directing plays. His first play was performed at Croton Elementary School. His first full production was entitled *Everson's* and was performed at the Regent's Theatre in Syracuse.

Thomas moved to Boston in 1985 and was employed by Boston University until his passing. Thomas starred in and directed many plays in Boston, including *Mattie's Grill, Jesus Made Footprints on Top of the Water, Brother Red*, and *Good Times*. Thomas toured the nation in *Through the Fire* and in the play *The Meeting*, a fictional piece on interactions between Malcolm X, whom he played, and Dr. Martin Luther King, Jr.

His poetry appeared in *Black/Out, The Black Voice, The Boston Herald, The Boston Globe, Roxbury Community News*, and the anthology *Poets on the Horizon*. He read and performed his work at The Dark Room, The Cantab Lounge, The Nuyorican Poets

Café and The Blue Note in Manhattan, The Lizard Lounge, and at the 1993 International Poetry Slam in San Francisco.

Thomas' poetry is also included in the anthology *Milking Black Bull*, edited by the late Assotto Saint for Galiens Press, and in 1993, Parfait de Cocoa Press published Thomas' collection of poems entitled *Deep Talk*. Along with Philip Robinson, Thomas co-founded Writers of Color Workshop and was a founding member of the New African Theater Company. He also wrote songs for many artists, performed voice-overs for commercials, and was featured on several jazz albums, including *Scoop*.

Thomas received many awards for his work, including a Bessie Smith Award for Creativity from the Greater Boston Gay and Lesbian Political Caucus, a 1993 Hometown Video Award for Excellence in Gay and Lesbian Cable Programming, and in 1994, Thomas traveled to Los Angeles to receive a prestigious national award for his independent film, *Allegations*.

As AIDS took its toll on the community of artists locally and nationally, Thomas, along with Craig Hickman and Philip Robinson, co-organized and performed in many memorials, including *When My Brother Fell: A Tribute to Essex Hemphill* at the Institute of Contemporary Art in 1993, and *Celebrating Our Community: Remembering Our Lives* at the Boston Center for the Arts in 1994.

Wake and memorial services celebrating Thomas' life were held on Sunday, March 16 at the Elliot Congregational Church of Roxbury.

Journey
for Brothers du Jour

Holding on to each other,
Love is our grip,
Standing on the solid ground
of self-acceptance,
We live our lives
on the line,
Walking a tightrope
of fear and misunderstanding,
The three of us
found the balance,
Challenged the world
alone and together.

by Thomas Grimes, from *Deep Talk*

Appendix III

THE BOOK OF SONGS

> *"Identity would seem to be the garment with which one covers the nakedness of the self: in which case it is best that the garment be loose, a little like the robes of the desert, through which one's nakedness can always be felt and sometimes discerned. This trust in one's nakedness is all that gives one the power to change robes."*
>
> —James Baldwin

BOOK I
Songs 1 – 3

Song 1

Sonless Mother

A fantasy song for his mothers before he knew the truth.

DENISE mourned the day her
   flowing ceased.
The rape seed sown rooted
deeply on the walls of her womb
weeping blood from her brown baby
   eyes—

eyes which could not eclipse her
   assaulter's scowling face
eyes which could no longer catch
   enough light to sparkle
eyes which could envision her dreams
   aborted.

She wanted not this thing,
this life, this parasite
sucking her own life within.

It was 1967. Only sixteen, she had
no money, no clinic, no doctor, no law
   no choice.

unwilling to risk some back-alley
   mutilation, she
shored up her strength for the struggles
   to come and
moved and moved and moved her love
   out of her womb

down a river in a tightly woven basket.
"Go, go, my child. Be safe."

For sixteen months, lost in rushes and
   reeds
it flowed, flowing into the abyss,
no nurture, no wonder, into that void
   too dark
and lonely, till back over the edge of the
   river basin it fell.

But soon enough,
   it sprouted wings.
"Mama, Mama, please?"

And Mary Juanita heard.
She who had waited and prayed
   and waited.
After six conceptions no child could
cling to her irritable womb,
a womb that bled and bled,
too much too fast
too fast too much
till finally carved out
   it bled no more.

With no hope of seeing a child created
   in her own image,
with no hope of hearing that child cry
   out from new teeth and monsters,
with no hope of tasting her own fruit's
   dreams ripen
she wept.

And she prayed again, not to the gods
whom she blamed for her Dharma,
but for two of her four decades,
she knelt down before
folklore and myth,
in supplication to stork wings
and river reeds.
She waited, and waited, and waited...
"Mama, Mama, please?"

So Mary Juanita took him.
more blessed than Pharaoh's daughter
she relished his majesty
she cradled him in arms warm with love
   and devotion
she counted his fingers with kisses in
   praise they were all there
she breathed her own blood into each
   of his veins.
"You're mine, now. You're mine now."

She strengthened him with the name of
   the rock
of ages of ages of ages of

lost babies
envisioned like this one:
                    her son.

Her *son*. And she, a sonless mother
no more adopted into her home
invited into her life
welcomed into her love
this living

        abortion.

Song 2

The Virtuoso

A song of healing.

My FATHER was a percussionist
a virtuoso, if you will
blessed with
rhythm and soul
and blues and jazz
and oh, could he
play
play play
play play
that drum

when happy or sad
lonely or mad

he beat   and beat   and beat   that
        drum

intoxicated with shot glasses
of despair and pain
disillusioned before mirrors cracked
by the cruelty and deceit
of the Black man's world

he struck the cymbals
and pounded the tom-tom
with sticks or belts
his fist and palms
whatever he chose

he beat   and beat   and beat   that
        drum

sending timbres piercing
and screeching in
pitches so high
they say only dogs
could hear

or low deep droning
moans and groans
some thought came
from the bowels
of the earth

beating and pounding and striking
and
                beating
beating and pounding and striking
        and
                    beating

boom-boom
boom tissssh!

boom-boom
boom tissssh!!

boom-boom
boom tissssh!!!

sometimes I wish
Daddy hadn't played me

so well.

Song 3

Commandments

A song of adolescence.

Honor thy father and thy mother;
that it may be well with thee,
and thou mayest live long
upon the earth.

My father's nurture has always
been sifted through a sieve
of self-hatred, overly salted with
quick fists, generously powdered with
emotional neglect, funneling into

me as unenriched flour falling
heavily upon the meager mounds
of self-esteem in the bowl of my soul.

My mother's intentions are as pure
as a baby's first breath, but her words
are forever piercing, sharp needles
that slide under my skin drawing out
pints of patience from veins clotting
with sweet bitterness.

Honor they father and they mother;
that it may be well with thee,
and thou mayest live long
upon the earth.

Daddy, you say,
I love you.
Please forgive me.
I want you to be happy.
But, Daddy, all you do
is say all of this, and give
nothing whatsoever at all.

You treat me like a prodigal son
who can't find his way.
I'm kneading the dough
of my own life, but
it's too salty for you,
it's too dry for you,
and it just won't rise high enough
for you.

Mama, you say,
I love you.
I miss you.
I want to know you.
But, Mama, you also say,
If you ever get sick and
I have to take care of you,
I'll cut all that hair off your head.

You, meanwhile, cut off the
circulation of our union,
condescending adult to child,
instead of sharing woman to man.

Respect thy sons and thy daughters;
that it may be well with thee,
and thou mayest be honored long
upon the earth.

BOOK II
Songs 4 – 6

Song 4

Lost

In memory of Curtis, an elementary
schoolmate slaughtered by Jeffrey
Dahmer.

*Late nights and desperate hours
teach us to approach loneliness
unarmed, or we risk provoking
it to torture us with endless
living sorrows we believe
only the dead can endure.*[a]

WE MET only once, but
I know you.
Your pain,
your confusion
your lonely, alien existence.

dreaming of men,
touching a man's face
finding peace in his arms,
wanting him
to want you
to love you—
to rescue you.

but mama, teacher
daddy, preacher
say it's all wrong, not natural.
but you know different,
you *feel* different.

down at 219, the YP or Phoenix,
over at La Cage of C'est la Vive,
in backrooms and bathrooms,
behind buildings, over train
tracks beneath bridges,

---

[a] Essex Hemphill, *Ceremonies*.

in front or back seats
on lots abandoned,
luring the company of
insatiable strangers
beneath twilight and trees,
desperate, you find a place,
someplace, any place
where your desires are welcome.

you fear, you trust, you long, you need,
    you explore, you escape, you live?

you Die.

'tis a tragedy Shakespeare could not
    romanticize.

I know you.

Song 5

Deliverance

A song of Jeffrey Dahmer. For all his Isaacs.

THEIR EYES sang the lyrics of
Loverman to me. I could almost
hear Billie's voice when their
eyes stared into mine.
All those young, colored faggots
wore their loneliness as
a wreaking, putrid odor,
and I breathed it in,
let it tingle in my nostrils,
let it ignite the fires in my blood.

I was chosen to offer them
the thing they never had.

Now, *Newsweek, Time, Inside Edition,*
and every newspaper across
this forsaken land features my face,
and they tell the tale that
I'm the Devil himself.
But the Devil would never
have been as kind as I was.

I called my attorney a fool for playing
that plea of insanity,
knowing any number of jurors in their
right minds could ever believe me
    insane.

I knew exactly what I was doing.

No one thought Abraham insane
for preparing to carve up his son
and offer him a burnt,
a burnt! sacrifice,
claiming the voice of God
ordered him so.

Well, I had my voice, and it was
much more powerful than God's.

All my Isaacs came to me
willing, needing, begging
to be delivered
from their empty lives.

It was in their eyes,
    their eyes,
        their eyes—

full of an abject fear
like a child who'd been beaten,
waiting only to be beaten again.

In the bars, on the
abandoned parking lots,
in the bushes, on the streets,
in the bathhouses, they came—
one, after another, after another.

I was chosen to offer them
the thing they never had.

I stroked their fragile egos
with the kindest words.
I promised them a night to remember.
They succumbed to my
nurturing offers.

In the silence of my room,
I made them feel safe.
I laced their drinks with a

touch of bitterness so
they could look deeper,
deeper into me and see
my true calling.
I made them

call out to me.
As their diminishing voices cried,
Jeffrey! over and over, Jeffrey!
I came as I slit their throats
with my blunt-tipped scalpel,
carefully carving their bodies
like an inspired artist.

I wanted their flesh to become my flesh,
so I ate their meat raw.
I bathed in their blood.
    I bathed in their blood.
        I bathed in their blood.
I was baptized in their blood.

I needed to preserve their bodies'
most beautiful parts, so I stored them
in my refrigerator, under my bed,
in my closets. I took pictures—
a constant reminder
of the great work I created.
I could never have burned them.

No one came looking.
No one.
Who wants a colored faggot?

Now, rotting in this frigid, ice-box cell,
I'm the lamb who will sacrifice
his life for their freedom from
want, from AIDS, from rejection,
from fear, from loneliness.

The ultimate deliverance.

Yes,
it was me,
the father they never had.

I did it.

I did it all.

I did them all

a favor.

Song 6

Broken Eardrums

For James Baldwin. For Fatime.[b]

IF BEALE Street could talk, what
would she say?

Would she tell it on the mountain
through the disordered, old-fashioned
revival meetings of men with conked
hair, women with platinum wigs,
tambourines and loud voices
blaring testimony to the brazen,
amen corners of her street
bending back cries of hatred,
misery and love
in noises erupting like the
first rumbles of an earthquake
or the A-Train's growl beneath her
jagged-edged sidewalks?

Would she speak the
tongue-twisting fast-talk
of the numbers runners
who count on recall
like a drunk depends on
cheap whiskey
or the Harlem hipsters,
dealing out their genuine elixir
to all those desperadoes
grasping at ropes frayed and
ready to break?

Would she simply croon the blues,

---

[b]*The song is dedicated to Fatime, another "she who was he as she" who walked the streets of Boston. Like Roxie, he was a young transgender of many talents and dreams who, after being rejected from his family, found home in the streets. Unlike Roxie, Fatime disappeared without notice in September 1993 and never returned.*

those private, vanishing evocations
of a soul dealing with the roars
rising from its inner void,
trying to impose order on
all that noise
as it collides with the airwaves,
or seeps into the dark veils of
dying souls?

Or would she perk up as Roxie,
she who was he as she,
Roxie, her favorite streetwalker
strutted by and shout:
I RAISED HER! Knowing her
cry an unsuitable
recompense for a world that
sent her to the streets
with cuckoo-nested hair
atop a face swollen with bruises
glittering like hot coals?

NOW THAT ROXIE'S A BAD-ASS GIRL.
DON'T TAKE SHIT OFF NOBODY!
Not since the rougher streets
stripped away her hopes
tucked in too-tight clothing,
her heels biting into the concrete
only too eager to bite back and
suck up dreams that disappeared
like her dignity into the murky
corners of Giovanni's room.

I BROUGHT HER HERE FROM
ANOTHER COUNTRY,
HOME WHERE SHE BELONGS,
WHERE THE NOTES OF HER
NATIVE CRIES
WAIL ACROSS MY AVENUE
IN CALL AND RESPONSE TO
SONNY'S BLUES, AND
JIMMY'S BLUES, and other blues, and
other blues...

Gimme that fire baby...
How much for all that sweet
brown ass, pretty Mama?
Repent your wicked ways...

You sick bitch...
Crazy whore...
Jesus saves...

Voices and voices echoing on for so
long, long, long....
in her head, head, head...
it's a wonder she could turn them
off long enough to hear anything
her spiritual eardrums had
long ago been broken.

But girlie girl, she who was he as
she, girlie girl still found work.
Fueled by fire she was the A-Train,
always running on time,
going to meet the men,
carrying blues and ecstasy for
Mister Charlie, never a trick to
apologize for, the price of
the ticket, the ticket, the ticket...
painfully high.

So when men, loitering at
crosswalks or gawking out of
open car windows,
their hair kinky and matted
their bodies so oily the
skin glistened
like wet asphalt
beneath streetlight,
started in with their
jive murphy:
Aw baby, you need to
get your hot ass
on over here and heat
me some up!

Roxie would strike back:
Honey, even Dawn wouldn't
take the grease out your way.
I'll be your fire next time, baby!
And like good looks and
quick money, Roxie was gone...
Now it's dawn, the avenue lay
long and silent, evidence of Roxie
not seen in a while.

But she can never stay gone—
drawn back to the street,
a stray cat
coming home.

Roxie.

Everybody knew her name in the street.
Roxie.

And they blew it up and down
that avenue like some loose whistle.

Roxie.

If everyone in the world could
give her what she wanted,
she wouldn't want for more than she
had, but the street was all she had.

So she returns and rests in one
lonely place before climbing that
narrow stairway to daylight
just above her head.
And Beale Street opens the
rusty pipe of her throat and
screeches with one pained breath:

NOW TELL ME HOW LOOOOOOOOOONG
HAS THIS TRAIN BEEN GONE!

BOOK III
Songs 7 - 9

Song 7

Maestro, If You Please

Now,
part of everything,
belonging to nothing,
I sing of loss.

What becomes of a soul longing
for union, grasping at delusions,
and clutching the edges of mirrors
where stark and murky reflections
linger like debris in melting snow?

What becomes of a soul linked
tenuously to the mind of genius,
wanderlust, reaching toward
frontiers of somewhere and
nowhere at the same time?

What becomes of a soul drained
by futile attempts to mold
a space around it for
others to dance without suffocation?

The lonely linger for brief flashes.
But their incessant going blows
an ill wind which registers a
chill on the heart
like one a restless body knows

when awakened to find
hours of tossing and turning
have dismantled the covers
leaving it susceptible to the
wind rushes rushing in
through half-open windows at bedside.

No one can forever long to
be nourished with
sweet sounds,
wrapping in panting arms,
and held against the
shores of longing by
ropes of I-love-yous
too fragile to secure.

Comes a time
when even the most
desolate lands are covered
with the footfall of settlers.

Comes a time
when the emptiest wells are
cracked open by the
undercurrent of gushing
streams pooling up to wet
the thirsty dirt on the
pit's bottom.

Comes a time

when the time has come.

Shall we?
Let us.
We Must.

Song 8

For Jacobus shortly after they met again.

RACHMANINOFF'S Concerto No. 3 in D minor - Opus 30.
At my side, Darlin plays his Petrof, pouring rivulets of sorrow into each key, each movement, each phrase. Rocked in the cradle of his reckless abandon,

I yearn for your touch, your smile, that downward curl of your lips, that furrowed brow that makes me wonder whether anguish or bliss fills you. Perhaps you feel a joy so deep, only sadness can

color your countenance. On an icy December night, in the majestic Oriental Theater, the one where restored friezes of Buddha muse from the walls above, I, alone, saw that movie

the one where Daddy, driven by a love without compassion, tortures his gifted boy. The boy dreams of playing Rachmaninoff more than he desires to stay sane.

And just as the piano hammers its strings, Daddy strikes the boy right out of his mind. When I was a boy, I did things that boys my age weren't supposed to do—

I had sex with grown men; other things were harder. A David to life's Goliaths, I tried to haul forty pounds of wood up a hill for a campfire.
I was twelve, maybe all of ninety pounds. Daddy looked on as I nearly

broke my back; he knew I'd taken seriously the platitude he often repeated, *If at first you don't succeed...*

I saw the movie once more with a frightened boy who thought himself a man. Perhaps I'll see it again with you.

I see many films more than once: classics, noirs, the one in my dreams where my lover and I open the earth together. The first season, we reap a full harvest; by next year's crop,

he's gone. The film plays again, same ending, no explanation.
Buddha cedes no solace.
But oh what beauty springs forth from the mire!

Even a rose blooms in dirt.

Perhaps it's cliché to say how easily we wallow in fear, paralyzed
at the foot of the hill,
though I might be mistaken.

Initiate me in the rituals of togetherness, so I might resolve the images that replay without resolution.

Play me Rachmaninoff!
I want music that grows
more aching with each arpeggio, more pensive with each pause,
more crucial with each crescendo.

If we are not eaten
alive by some
force—unseen,
unnamed—
we will prevail,
all the wiser,

to face each moment
with the newness
of a sunrise in spring.

Song 9

The Wedding Song.

WHEN the weather breaks, stand before the unquilted stretch of land and gaze directly across into your lover's eyes. Resist the half-second instinct to blink.

                Ready yourself
for designing earth too hard to chop. Remove the gloves of shame. Clip the nails of fear. Fall, in unison, to your knees. Fertilize the earth with
raw honesty.

                Weed out
dissension. Plot vegetables and flowers and talk about the colors that will bloom. Water often with fluid from
a red, red heart.

                Welcome
imperfection. When needed, rest in solitude near the tree-rooted corner. Surrender to the half-second instinct to blink. Pray. Pray.

                Pray. Refreshed,
Work steadfast till night's star-nailed, pewter close. Lie in your lover's arms. Gaze once more into his eyes. Anoint each other with moonlight.

                Sleep in the
embrace of rich harvests to come. Crack open fever-bright
eyes and awake to morning's
sun-forged opening.

                Begin again.

BOOK V
Songs 10 – 14

Song 10

Shoptalk

Of April.

OHONEYS, I loves me some Black Queens, you know what'm sayin? In this line of work, I'm down with'm all the time. Here at J's His and Hers Salon, I'm the weave specialist and, honey, I do me some fierce weaves. These fingers right here—certified. You sit in my chair, I'll hook you up. Like you aint never been hooked up before.

    Everybody seem to be wantin all kinda extra hair now: braids, folds, beehives, buns. We even weavin in dreads these days. Save folk all that beeswax, plaitin and twistin. Come outta here in five hours, you be ret to go back to Jamaica, you know what'm sayin?

    Yeah, I get me some of my best referrals from word of mouth. Talk of my talent has spread so fast, you'd think I was the only one in Boston weavin. Ooh, but let me stop complainin, you know what'm sayin?

    I'm just glad to be gettin all this work. In fact, this week is booked so solid, I aint had a chance to get my nails wrapped. Shit, last night I just started bitin'm off. But, *heeeey*. As long as the rough edges dont interfere with the weavin process, you know what'm sayin? —the *process*—everythang'll be all right, baby.

    My hair? Of course it's real; I just jazz it up a bit for sex appeal. I stole that shit from En Vogue. You know those sisters is too tough. I would love to work some of my magic up in all that hair. I mean, dont get me wrong, they always look good. Like did you check them out on the Grammy's a coupla years back, how they descended down in their silver lamé gowns, hit that stage and turned it out like they was the Dreamgirls themselves. I was like, *woooooork* me goddamnit. And their hair—too, too tough. Still, if I could just get one consultation with those Funky Divas, I know I could hook them up with a look that would turn they fans out for days on end, or my name aint April Marie Lynette Jones, and I aint standin in fronta you talkin right now.

Umph, umph, umph. I done got all off the subject. What was we poze to be talkin bout? Oh yeah—that's right—Black Queens.

Well, lemme say first, I know some folk dont like to be called that, but I say it like this, honey—if somebody wants to call you royalty, you better put on that crown and wear it well, honey.

We got this one brother work up next to me. Richie is his name. And, honey, he is too funny. Child, Richie can make me laugh just by throwin some shade my way. He do weaves almost as good as me, but if I ever catch him starin too close when I'm workin one of my secret techniques, you know, I have to twist around and throw some ass up his way. That'll usually throw him off right quick.

He fits into some of them stereotypes you hear about sometime. You know, he fine as hell, always dressed to the nines in some fierce black clothes, got more shoes than I got Fashion Fair eye pencils. See? I know you know what'm sayin. But it dont make no never mind to me.

But it do make some never mind to Miss Hattie Mae. Now Hattie Mae Holyfield come up in here always dressed for Sundaygomeetin, totin the scriptures, and preachin like she the one up on the mountaintop overlookin the Promised Land. Well, it used to be Richie was her one and only stylist. Then one day, while he was curlin her hair, she overheard him say somethin bout some new man he got. Honey, she jumped out that chair so fast, the curlin iron singed the back of her neck.

We didnt see bout her for a while. Then she come up in here and want me to curl her hair, talkin bout, "I dont wanna catch the Lord's scourge that He put upon those who went that way."

Humph. If she look in that mirror long enough, she'd realize she already caught somebody's scourge, as tore up as she was lookin.

I turned her down flat. I dont do curls, except for my special clientele—that she was not—and I know my weaves would not work peepin out from them big old tacky hats she be wearin. She need to peek out that Bible long enough to realize you aint liable to be catchin nothin from nobody's hairstylist, and you know she aint catchin nothin no other way.

I didnt care if we ever saw her up in here again, with her dresses two sizes too small, and her feet oozin out from them ugly shoes she be kickin. Well, it turned out Mabel started curlin her hair, so she tip up in here twice a week, walk right past Richie, roll her eyes to the heavens, and sit down and let Mabel get to goin on her head.

Humph. I wish I did have time. I'd sit that woman in my chair and pull every last strand of her righteous, nappy hair right outta her head, you know what'm sayin?

You know, it just don't seem that folk wanna respect folk for who they are and just let'm be, child, but I say it like this, honey, somebody don't wanna deal with Black Queens, they either jealous or crazy, that's right, I said jealous or *crazy*, cuz you can say you heard it like this before or not, but they be some of the best friends you ever wanna have, so put that up in your hair, and weave it!

Anyway, I got to get on back to work, children, I got this sistergirl comin up in here for my special African-crown headdress with much attitude. I'll talk to ya'll later.

Song 11

Field Trip

Serenely sauntering into the Worcester Art Museum to expose a predominantly white, suburban audience to the intricacies of inner-city poetry, toting a big black bag, inconspicuously clad in everyday attire, I nonetheless was singled out by the security officer, rapidly approaching from behind the safety of his desk, as if to interrupt some impending disaster on his desperate journey toward me.

"Hey you! What's the bag for?"

The air around me sputtered in search of retort, while my tongue lay hostage against a confused palate.

As the approaching crowd began to smell the progression of fear, to caution, to his Robin-Hood rush to save a museum in distress, a thick curious tension rushed in on a whirlwind, besieging the small crowd, now marveling at what might become an adventure Worcester hadn't seen in decades.

"I said, what's the bag for and what you got in it?"

Now, empowered by the women around me, I could stay silent no longer.

"It's my purse, just like hers, hers, and hers, and what's in it is none of your business!"

"Well, that's an awfully big purse!"

"And I'm an awfully big girl, now back off!"

What could his mind have conjured?

Perchance he thought I was gonna swipe some art museum treasure more priceless than a Van Gogh original, fold it up in, say, sixteen sections, secure it neatly in my bag, from which I'd just retrieved my compact Uzi, threaten to take out anyone who dared stop me (subsequently raping his wife and children) and rush out past the front desk into a welcoming black night.

Or perchance he thought my bag was loaded with several pounds of coke, a hundred vials of crack, and all kinda dope I was eager to deal to a museum crowd desperate for a fix.

Or perchance he thought I was just some loose cannon vandal, up to no good, armed with several cans of metallic mauve spray paint.

Or more likely, a big old watermelon, which I'd smash on the floor, scooping up large chunks to smear across the designs displayed on the walls of his big white castle on the hill, leaving behind my own art, my mark, a trail of little black seeds following me out the back door.

As I moved past this suspecting man, the strap of the bag biting my shoulder, its contents pulling me down a bit closer to the earth I walk on, I realized the bag I carry around daily

is weighted with memories, wishes
dreams, and stories yet untold;

is weighted with city streets, country
roads, highways, and rivers to places yet
unseen;

is weighted with groans, laughter, cries,
and screams yet unheard.

And deep down, somewhere near the
bottom of that big black bag, my purse,
there's a neighborhood, a city, a
country, a world where no person
carries the fear to dare ask what's inside
it.

Song 12

Mirror, Mirror

UNTIL I found them, the mirror
reflected only me to me.
The large intense eyes, those tiny ears
with no upper rim,
that protruding bottom lip, the square
jaw and pointed chin,
those eyebrows that arch without effort,
provoking envy in girls and women.
Who do I look like? I asked the mirror.

For 33 years, the mirror had no reply.
Now, it reveals the family's teensy ears,
my birth mother's slightly gapped teeth,
the curl of my uncle's hair,
my birth father's egg-shaped head, the
pug of my nephew's nose,
my brother's flared nostrils, the point of
my cousin's chin,
my grandmother's under bite, the
reddish hue in my sisters' skin.
I see the future there as well.
Still, some features belong to me
alone, but now they command
my focus no more.
For the first time in my life,
I see my people in me.

Song 13

Freedom Walk

A song for Rwanda.

MY LEFT foot falls on concrete,
My right, on brick.
Such is a walk
on Portland sidewalks,
mixing old and new,
near and far.
Free Street feels like
a Spanish Isle in the
Mediterranean, all
sun-splashed storefronts
and sand-colored facades.
A few blocks up and over,
State Street conjures
Victorian-era New England,
all majesty and order.

Present and past pour
out on every side of me,
whispering stories and tales and
anecdotes I can only imagine,
but never know.

So, too, I can never know
what it would have been like,
growing up, your big
brother. Our little sister
is now mysteriously sick.
I have my thoughts about why
this is, you have yours,
but either way we see it,
the fact remains, our little
sister is sick with mystery.

What can I do? How can it be
that you are concerned now with my
named identity? You say our sister,
weary in bed, had no idea who I was
when I called and said, "This is Craig."
I say she has no idea who I am since
she thinks of me as Joseph. I cannot
be something that I'm not,
and little baby Joseph turned into
little boy Craig in April 1969.

I allowed you the
fantasy of having a brother
named Joseph in 2001,
but the fantasy was based upon
stories and tales and anecdotes
we can only imagine but
never ever know.

Our sister is sick with mystery,
wounded by worry. Despite your
proclaimed faith in God,
who controls all things,
you, too, are too sick
with mystery, too
wounded by worry.
Our bodies house the
illnesses of our minds.

When you walk the streets,
notice what's in front of you.
Concrete is concrete,
brick is brick. Whatever
stories they might whisper
from the sidewalks or buildings,
see them only for what they are
and free yourself.
There is no mystery in the
sand-colored facades,
nothing to worry about
in the slate-covered rooftops.

Song 14

Little Black Girls

An anthem.

Honey child
girlfriend
double-dutch
hopscotch
patty-cake
jack-throwin
roller-skatin
hula-hoopin
eye-rollin
neck-wavin
gum-poppin
foot-stompin
finger-snappin
nappy-headed
divas!

In my reverie—

April and Lisa,
Sheila and Gina,
All my girlfriends!

Yall was jealous (yes you was)
Cuz I was better than you:
Jumpin rope
Playin jacks
Chalkin up 24th Street
For some fierce hopscotch.

Humph! Or simply throwin attitude.

—I pay tribute to thee.

BOY! Daddy thought
I'd always be
a sissy.

Fasten up that robe,
said Mama.
Girls let their robes
flare all behind them
like that, not boys.
What did I raise?

Guess they were afraid
I might lose my masculinity
that you girls were a bad influence.

They were wrong.

I am man (snap!)
I am fierce (two times!)
I am faggot (maxi-snap!)

But I will always
cherish
the little black girl
in me.

CRAIG HICKMAN poet, performance artist, and author of the bestseller *Rituals: Poetry & Prose*, is a graduate of Harvard University. He lives in Maine. *Fumbling Toward Divinity* is his first book in eleven years.